D1707622

Keepers of the Motherland is the first comprehensive study of German and Austrian Jewish women authors. Dagmar Lorenz begins with an examination of the Yiddish author Glikl Hamil, whose works date from the late seventeenth and early eighteenth centuries, and proceeds through such contemporary writers as Grete Weil, Katja Behrens, and Ruth Klüger. Along the way she examines an extraordinary range of distinguished authors, including Else Lasker-Schüler, Rosa Luxemburg, Nelly Sachs, and Gertrud Kolmar.

Although Lorenz highlights the authors' individualities, she unifies *Keepers of the Motherland* with sustained attention to the ways in which they all reflect upon their identities as Jews and women. In this spirit Lorenz argues that "the themes and characters as well as the environments evoked in the texts of Jewish women authors writing in German resist patriarchal structures. The term 'motherland,' defining the domain of the Jewish woman's native language, regardless of political or ethnic boundaries, is juxtaposed with the concept 'fatherland,' referring to the power structures of the nation or state in which she resides." Lorenz describes a vital, diverse, and largely dissident literary tradition—a brilliant countertradition, in effect, that has endured in spite of oppression and genocide. Combining careful research with inspired synthesis, Lorenz provides an indispensable work for students of German, Jewish, and women's writings.

Dagmar C. G. Lorenz is a professor of German at The Ohio State University. She is the coeditor of *Insiders and Outsiders: Jewish and Gentile Culture in Germany and Austria.*

KEEPERS OF THE MOTHERLAND

GERMAN TEXTS BY JEWISH WOMEN WRITERS

Dagmar C. G. Lorenz

University of Nebraska Press

Lincoln and London

⊗ The paper in this book meets the minimum
requirements of American National Standard for
Information Sciences—Permanence of Paper
for Printed Library Materials, ANSI Z39.48-1984.

Library of Congress
Cataloging-in-Publication Data

Lorenz, Dagmar C. G., 1948–
Keepers of the Motherland: German texts by
Jewish women writers / Dagmar C. G. Lorenz.
p.   cm. – (Texts and contexts)
Includes selections translated from German.
Includes bibliographical references and index.
ISBN 0-8032-2917-8 (cloth : alkaline paper)
1. Jewish women – Germany – Intellectual life.
2. German literature – Jewish authors –
History and criticism. 3. German literature –
Women authors – History and criticism.
4. Holocaust, Jewish (1939–1945) – Germany –
Influence. 5. German literature – Jewish
authors. 6. German literature –
Women authors. 7. Jews – Germany –
Intellectual life. I. Title. II. Series.
DS135.G33L59 1997
943'.00431 – dc21 96-30057
CIP

In memory of my father-in-law,
Sheikh Ahmed Abdou
(1911–1995)

Contents

Acknowledgments

My interest in German-speaking Jewish and Jewish-identified women writers began in 1974, in the course of writing my dissertation under the direction of Jerry Glenn, who steered my attention to the Jewish aspects in the works of Ilse Aichinger and those of other survivors of the Nazi regime. At that time, the connection of these authors' works to the Holocaust was not widely discussed in *Germanistik,* and the scholarly establishment, particularly in German-speaking countries, avoided examining the effects of the Shoah on postwar German and Austrian literature. During my years at the Ohio State University, my scholarly activities and publications increasingly included issues of marginality in German-language literature and Central European culture of the nineteenth and twentieth centuries, and I taught and developed courses on German-Jewish and women's literature and the representation of the Shoah in German-language literature and film.

For the study at hand, dealing with the textual tradition established by Jewish women writers, I have incurred debts of gratitude to numerous individuals and institutions, which I acknowledge with pleasure and appreciation. I am indebted to the Melton Center for Jewish Studies and its director, Tamar Rudavsky, for the ongoing support of this book through travel grants, grants-in-aid, and a small research grant (1994, 1995) and to the Department of Germanic Languages and Literatures and the College of Humanities at Ohio State for granting me special research assignments (1995, 1991) and a faculty leave (1992–93) to pursue the project. I am also grateful to the graduate students who served as my research associates, especially Jeni Cushman, Lisa Jenschke, Robert Fuhrmann for their assistance. My most heartfelt appreciation goes to my colleagues and professional friends at Ohio State and in the profession for their availability to discuss my research and for being supportive in important direct and indirect ways—Sander Gilman, Ruth Klüger, Jack Zipes, Ruth Beckermann, Nadja Seelich, Neil Jacobs, Gabriele

Weinberger, Bernd Fischer, Les Tannenbaum, Michael Berkowitz, and Alan Levenson. In addition, I thank Heinz Lunzer and the staff of the Vienna *Literaturhaus* and Rachel Salamander for their suggestions and assistance in locating materials and texts.

Finally, I would like to recognize the invaluable contributions that my family—my husband, Mohsin Abdou, and my mother, Charlotte Lorenz—have made to all my professional endeavors, including this book, by offering me their encouragement, generosity, tolerance, and wisdom.

Introduction

The volume and quality of German literature produced by Jewish women writers over the last two centuries are significant enough to warrant exploring it as a tradition all its own. The affinities between different authors and the mutual reception of their works have created a partly deliberate, partly spontaneous network. In addition to direct personal interaction, a common literary and cultural frame of reference informs the writing of German-speaking Jewish women. Many of the authors articulate their intellectual and emotional kinship with one another directly; in other cases, there is a similarity in perception and expression. Ever since the late eighteenth century, when Jewish women stepped into the public arena as authors and critics, they have written against the patriarchal structures of both Gentile and Jewish culture through the issues they raise as well as through their use of language and the characters they create.[1] Questioning, criticizing, or openly rejecting their two fatherlands' androcentric power structures, their works suggest as their anchoring point an elusive motherland where the Jewish woman's language and voice reign supreme, defying the political boundaries and institutions of her nation or community.

The memoirs of Glikl Hamil, written prior to the emancipation debates, are still unencumbered by the identity problems expressed by later authors. Situated at the center of her Ashkenazic motherland, Glikl's writing is set exclusively within this sphere, which more recent works reflect only indirectly. Nonetheless, the indifference to nationalistic concerns, the presence of an authoritative female voice, and the significance of maternal relationships in the works of the majority of Jewish and Jewish-identified authors are a common theme in Glikl and later authors. An example is Ilse Aichinger's poem "Common Principle":

And if one travels to Turkey,
My grandmother says,

And dies there,
One will be buried, of course,
In a Turkish graveyard (1974, 56).

Dominant female characters, matriarchal structures, and close female-female relationships evoke a feminine realm, an intercultural and multilingual motherland, in the works of authors as diverse as Else Lasker-Schüler, Gertrud Kolmar, Nelly Sachs, Rose Ausländer, and Katja Behrens. So do Jewish women's autobiographies that tend to highlight women's concerns. Ruth Klüger, for instance, in *weiter leben,* her recollections of pre-Shoah Vienna, perceives men as "marginal figures" who "ruled over us at the periphery" (1992, 229).

Whether German and Austrian Jewish women authors attribute positive or negative connotations to the figure of the mother and the realm associated with her, the mother figure represents an internal point of reference from which they derive energy and inspiration. An alternative feminine or feminist view of reality strengthens their creativity and provides them with norms against which to measure their androcentric everyday environment. The ability to envision such a realm surrounded by, but separate from, patriarchy produces a distinct narrative stance and timbre. Not only do characteristic themes occur in Glikl's memoirs, Dorothea Schlegel's Romantic novel *Florentin,* and in Fanny Lewald's novels and essays on the plight of Jewish mothers and daughters, but these texts are written from a similar point of view. Bertha Pappenheim's Isenburg, a refuge for Jewish women in need, represents a concrete manifestation of the motherland in the twentieth century, and Rosa Luxemburg's unfulfilled dreams about a safe haven outside the public sphere reveal the allure of this realm for Europe's foremost woman revolutionary.

Even before the full extent of the Nazi genocide had come to light, Nelly Sachs, in her mystery play *Eli,* commemorated the Ashkenazic motherland and the Yiddish mother tongue, the מאמע לשון (*mame-loshn*). Similarly, the memory of the destroyed European Jewish culture informs Ilse Aichinger's portrayal of Jews, women, and other marginalized groups and individuals. Generally speaking, post-Shoah Jewish women's literature features protagonists who embrace marginal positions to establish or confirm their sense of an outsider's identity. The all-female households portrayed by Esther Dischereit and Katja

Behrens, the symbiotic mother-child relationship in Barbara Honigmann's *Roman von einem Kinde,* and the community of women prisoners in Ronnith Neumann's *Nirs Stadt* represent reflections of the endangered motherland at the verge of destruction. Even Elfriede Jelinek's biting social satires with their unyielding indictment of male-identified mother figures, reminiscent of similar characters in works by Claire Goll and Cordelia Edvardson, presuppose a reality outside of patriarchy where nurturing relationships would be possible. Depending on the author, the motherland assumes different dimensions and qualities: it may be set in the past or transposed into utopia, or it may denote the whole of Ashkenaz, the territory and culture of European Jewry and the Yiddish language, or merely the Jewish nuclear family, occasionally configured only as mother and child. Frequently the concept *motherland* also carries spiritual connotations through which the author reclaims her Jewish heritage.

Throughout history, the positions associated with the terms *Jewish, Christian, German,* and *Austrian* have been variable and interdependent. The self-referential anti- or philo-Semitic Gentile discourses about Jews, incapable of reflecting Jewish reality, disclose the views and interests of non-Jews that dominated and contained the interaction between majority and minority. Jewish identity as perceived within the Jewish context was no factor in Gentile agendas. Yet, whereas non-Jewish concepts of Jewishness, shaped in specific social, political, and religious contexts, did not directly affect the way in which Jews defined themselves, they did determine the conditions under which Jews had to live.

Regulating and controlling the Jewish minority, too small to pose an economic or political threat, provided the Christian majority with a sense of boundaries. Whether they interpreted Jewishness as a religious, national, ethnic, or racial phenomenon, the Jew in an abstract sense was required as a unifying element to prevent the disintegration of the volatile political entities and identities of the nineteenth and twentieth centuries: just as the Jews had been a necessary construct to Christian identity, *the* Jew as Other was a prerequisite for shaping a German national identity. Jews, in turn, when adopting the German language, came to use the concept of the non-Jew as well as that of the unassimilated Jew for their own group cohesion. Shortly before World War I, authors such as Martin Buber and Max Brod, in their search for Jewish authenticity, began to hold up East European Jewish culture as an example to the

West European Jews, who they believed had lost their authentic Jewish identity (Baioni 1994, 14ff., 63).

German Jews defining themselves against the Gentile majority outside of the parameters of Yiddish could not help absorbing the stereotypes embedded in the German language. Neither could they break out of the vicious circle that linked German Jewish with German non-Jewish identity. The perpetual shift of paradigms—religious, social, educational, linguistic, national, cultural, and racial—resulted in a paradoxical situation: persons defined as Jewish according to Gentile standards might not be considered so by other Jews, and someone regarded as a Jew at one given period would not be at another. The Enlightenment produced secular Christians and Jews; nationalism produced German and Jewish nationalists. The Austrian multination state fostered cosmopolitan identity ideals among Jews and Gentiles. Linguistic paradigms differentiated between Yiddish- and German-speaking Jews, and European racism generated models of identity based on racial ideology. The German variant of fascism, National Socialism, forged a binary model of identity, Jewish and German, non-Aryan and Aryan. These were and still are reproduced in the binary concepts of victims and perpetrators, Jews and Germans, Jews and Nazis, and Nazis and non-Nazis formed by certain exile and post-Shoah authors. In fact, within the German and Austrian context, these discursive practices are meaningful in that they challenge patterns underlying much of German literature to this day. Because Jews were *the* perceived minority in Central Europe, they remain the most frequently problematized and stereotyped group in German literature.

Moses Mendelssohn's translation of the Bible into German, rather than Yiddish, in the late eighteenth century encouraged Jewish women and men to make German their language of choice. Mendelssohn's text was printed in the Jewish alphabet, as was his later translation of the Psalms, which included a glossary of difficult German words for his Yiddish-speaking readership. The processes set in motion by Enlightenment philosophy included the revolutions in America and France, and they affected the status of the Jews.[2] Among the champions of Jewish emancipation in the final phase of the Roman Empire of the German Nation, the most influential were Moses Mendelssohn, Gotthold Ephraim Lessing, Christian von Dohm with his treatise *Über die bürgerliche Verbesserung der Juden* (On the Improvement of the Social Status of the Jews), and Emperor Joseph II, the force behind the Toleration Edict. All of them endorsed a course of action aimed at curbing the distinct language and culture of the Jews for the sake of their integration. While being exposed to the same inimical forces as Jewish men—Gentile anti-Semitism and negative Jewish stereotypes internalized by German-speaking Jews—Jewish women also had to assert themselves against Jewish and Gentile misogyny. German-Jewish women's writing evolved at the boundaries between Jewish and Gentile language and culture and in conjunction with the emancipation movements of the bourgeoisie, Jews, women, and the workers' movement. The fact that German-Jewish literature evolved concurrently with social and political struggles against the established order placed Jewish writers into a problematic position from the start. In addition, Jewish women authors were uniquely affected by a double and triple marginalization, precisely because their condition was linked both with that of Jewish men and Gentile women. Marion Kaplan characterizes the situation as follows:

> Jewish women faced double jeopardy, as women and Jews. They had to adapt in both areas. Jewish women had to strive for the right to achieve their full human potential. When Jewish men were enfranchised, Jewish women still had to wait until their sex was enfranchised and they were granted rights that Jewish men enjoyed. Even after they had won limited rights as German women, they found themselves subject to antisemitic prejudices as well as traditional religious restrictions against their sex within Judaism. They struggled with anti-feminism and antisemitism. (1981, 202) [3]

Yet, it is precisely the tenuous position at the crossroads that proved to be a creative stimulus for many authors, as is evinced by their rich literary production. However, the discrimination, oppression, and anguish they faced are a high price to pay for achievements that were frequently underrated or unrecognized.

In the late eighteenth century, German-speaking Jewish women began to come to the fore as authors of literary and nonliterary works.[4] Although their writing shared the characteristics of the overall literary trends, they also addressed specific concerns of Jews and women in a way that set them apart from the production of male authors, Gentile and Jewish. Lois McNay's arguments against mainstream feminism's tendency to posit the experience of Caucasian women as the norm and generalize it "in the assumption of a universal and shared oppression between women" also apply to the situation of German Jewish women writers. Indeed, the background experiences and the conditions of production have differed markedly among Jewish and Gentile women, and as a result, so did their texts. A look at Simone de Beauvoir's pioneering feminist treatise *The Second Sex* confirms this assertion. Despite its professed universality, the work draws primarily on examples taken from Catholic culture. The priorities set by Jewish women and their views on gender roles would be different, and if they were to appropriate the Gentile paradigms at all, they would display a certain distance toward them.

In the study at hand, the term *German-Jewish* signifies a linguistic and cultural rather than a national and religious concept. By the twentieth century German had become the language, or target language, of a large segment of Central and Eastern European Jews. Among the conservative, educated middle class, German, being associated with high culture, progress, and tolerance, occupied a higher status than Yiddish or the Slavic languages. The Jews of Eastern Europe looked to Vienna and Berlin and, perhaps, to Paris and New York, for refinement and sophistication. The rejection of Yiddish to the point that it becomes the language that *frightens,* as Deleuze and Guattari observe (1986, 25), and the widespread adoption of German reflect attitudinal changes, including the espousal of a Gentile bourgeois lifestyle. Afraid of undermining the process of assimilation, the new Jewish bourgeoisie shied away from traditional Jewish culture. Among other things, these developments created a leisure class of privileged Jewish women analogous, but not identical, to that of Gentile *bourgeoises.*

In terms of education, the expectations for Jewish women had traditionally differed from those for men in that women did not customarily study Hebrew and Scripture. Since young middle-class women were not bogged down by domestic tasks, many of them received a secular education, such as Henriette Herz, Dorothea Mendelssohn, and Fanny Lewald. According to Jacob Katz, the daughters of the well-to-do families in the ghetto were the first to benefit from the new opportunities: they studied the surrounding Gentile languages and read world literature. They also acquired the social skills that enabled them to hold their own in a society not limited to Jews (Katz 1980a, 84). Later generations of Jewish daughters attended public or Christian, often Catholic, schools. As a result, the imagination and creativity of Jewish middle-class women were shaped by German culture and the German language to such an extent that many of them came to view Germany and Austria as their motherland.

Aided by the expansion of the book market and early feminism, the volume and scope of publications by Jewish women rose in the early twentieth century. Like their male colleagues, they benefited from the relative openness of European culture in transition, notwithstanding serious undercurrents of anti-Semitism. Joseph Roth observed that the children of Eastern European immigrants moved away from their parents' traditional occupations, banking and business, becoming instead lawyers, doctors, journalists, writers, and actors (Roth 1927, 65, 53f.). Indeed, the writing of German Jews of this era shows a stylistic and ideological diversity that places it into the context of German high culture and world literature. Yet, this body of literature also manifests certain thematic and stylistic idiosyncrasies and attitudes residual of the Jewish experience. Moreover, numerous authors discuss the impact of anti-Semitism and their struggle against a hostile environment directly dominated by Gentile men. Although terms such as *communality of fate* must be used with caution because of the danger of overgeneralization, the exposure to similar kinds of oppression does lead to similar ways of relating to reality, and the honing of specific survival strategies and the awareness of a constant latent threat from the outside is often reflected in a particular artistic and intellectual sensitivity.

Jewish women's writing occurred neither apart from nor entirely within the bounds of mainstream literature. Until the Nürnberg Laws officially deprived German Jews of their rights as citizens and individuals, women of Jewish background had positioned themselves in a multitude of ways within German-speaking culture—as feminists, as fighters for Jewish rights, as Jewish nationalists, German patriots, socialists, and communists—as political and cultural progressives and conservatives. A large number of the women defined as Jews by Nazi law had not even belonged to the Jewish community; some of them had been born to Christian parents or had converted. All of them were forced into otherness because of their Jewish descent. There are also numerous examples of women who reclaimed their Jewishness in extreme circumstances.[5]

It would be inaccurate to assume rigid divisions between former Jews who had been baptized or left the community as "freethinkers," and those who remained Jewish. For the most part, men and women seeking integration into German society did not abruptly step out of their old environment; they continued to interact with their Jewish friends and family, as well as with other new converts like themselves (Pass-Freidenreich 1991, 17–18). Their shared experience, family ties, and friendships were not annulled by their often pragmatically motivated decision.[6] The situation within the Jewish community itself was complex as well. Until 1933 the number of persons registered with the Austrian and German *Kultusgemeinden* (official Jewish communities) amounted to approximately 1 percent of the overall population. Apart from certain neighborhoods in metropolitan areas such as the *Scheunenviertel* in Berlin and the *Leopoldstadt* in Vienna, whose inhabitants consisted largely of newly arrived immigrants from Eastern Europe, even a modicum of cultural, let alone political, autonomy was impossible to achieve. The close proximity and the necessary interaction with non-Jews transformed German-Jewish culture; it, in turn, influenced Gentile society.

Within the German mainstream, as well as the Jewish, Jewish-identified, and formerly Jewish circles, women writers and intellectuals constituted a minority. In both contexts Jewish women in the public arena were exposed to pressures that prompted major lifestyle adjustments, leading in most cases to assimilation. Partly out of conviction, partly out of necessity, many of them converted and married non-Jews, only to learn that none of these steps would ultimately lead to their full integration. Others, alternately, found allies among individuals and groups that, for one reason or another, lived apart from mainstream culture as well. Thus the biographies of Jewish women writers since the Romantic period are the biographies of outsiders or bohemians. Their most prominent representatives traveled in nontraditional circles and were viewed as anomalies, most frequently in a negative light, for having left the sphere allocated to women in Jewish and Gentile cultures.[7] Hence they were differently and more immediately affected by the social and political developments in nineteenth- and twentieth-century Germany and Austria than Jewish and Gentile men and Gentile women authors.

Jewish women and men alike obtained no direct access to German culture without making major emotional and mental adjustments, and they were by definition excluded from anti-Semitic groups and Nazi society. Until 1933, the year of the Nazi takeover in Germany, and in Austria until the annexation in 1938, Jewish women had participated in shaping their native countries' culture. For obvious reasons, only a few adopted radical nationalist views, and even for those who did, supporting race- and gender-related double standards did not prove to be the proverbial entrance ticket into Gentile culture.[8] Educated women, women's rights activists, and women as public figures incurred the disapproval of the public at large. Jewish women were favorite targets of the male-dominated press, militaristic groups, and the ever-growing anti-Semitic movements. The German mainstream inscribed the bodies and minds of Gentile women as inferior because of their gender: Jewish women were relegated to an inferior status by the minority and the majority culture alike.[9]

One way for Jewish women intellectuals to align themselves with insider positions was by advocating humanist and cosmopolitan principles, by espousing leftist, often Marxist, views, or, as writers, by basing their identity solely on their intellectual prowess and the German language. The concept of the mother tongue (*Muttersprache*), used in juxtaposition to the term *Vaterland,* which signifies patriarchal institutions and practices, evokes the matrilineal tradition according to which the child of a Jewish mother is Jewish, regardless of the father. By positioning themselves as the daughters of matriarchs and as matriarchs in their own right, Jewish women have traditionally defied the power structures of Jewish and Gentile culture. Furthermore, they forged a position of centrality for themselves by deconstructing the mainstream and embracing marginality as the normal condition. The posture of the bohemian as well as that of the mother allowed Jewish women writers to choose and create their own conventions and subcultures.

Identity is produced from two vantage points: from the view an individual has of herself and from the perceptions of others. To a certain extent, the former is a matter of choice, while the latter is beyond the individual's control. However creatively an individual may construct her identity, her environment determines whether her identity choice succeeds or not. An identity that fails to conform with external standards and conventions is a cause of internal struggle and external disapproval. The disparity between self-definition and outside perception has been a problem for German Jews since the Age of Emancipation and thus deserves a closer look. David Sorkin asserts that around 1840, Jewish history in Germany and in the Habsburg monarchy, rather than leading to the desired integration, culminated in the formation of a distinct subculture. In spite of the fact that, at that time, it "did not yet encompass the majority of German Jews, it did represent the trend of the future" (Sorkin 1987, 173). The social and professional disenfranchisement of Jews persisted well into the twentieth century in spite of their efforts to conform to the German ideal of education (*Bildung*) and a middle-class lifestyle, and discriminatory government practices prevented Jews from entering the Gentile mainstream (130). The biographies of Sigmund Freud, Albert Einstein, and Gustav Mahler reveal the prejudices with which even the most prominent persons of Jewish ancestry had to contend, whether or not they converted to Christianity.

Sorkin's observations concerning the formation of subcultures apply to women as well. At the time when Jews sought entry into the German mainstream, the so-called Women's Question had evolved from earlier debates on the nature and proper place of women. Contrary to von Dohm's treatise on the status of Jews, Theodor Hippel's discussion of the status of women in *Über die bürgerliche Verbesserung der Weiber* was not even taken seriously. The feminist positions taken by women such as Olympe de Gouges and Mary Wollstonecraft were highly controversial, and the execution of de Gouges and her adherents shows the risks involved in fighting for gender equality. Like the Jewish minority, women considered education the major tool to gain access to Germany's and Austria's cultural establishment. They met with resistance on the part of both Gentile and Jewish men and faced prejudices regarding their status as human beings as well as their physical and intellectual abilities because of their biological characteristics and gender role. At least in theory, Christian culture allowed Jewish men full access through conversion, whereas the best that Jewish women could hope for was to move from one position of oppression into another. Yet, they made great strides in the social arena and established bridges between Jewish and Gentile society, perhaps because they were considered less threatening than Jewish men (Krobb 1993, 66). Sharing a common background, Jewish women and men were familiar with specific religious and social conventions and customs, and they faced religious and social prejudices and anti-Semitism. In their exclusion from certain formative experiences due to the differing gender role expectations, however, the plight of Jewish women also resembled that of Christian women. Professional Jewish and Christian women authors were generally viewed as overstepping their boundaries. Moreover, by writing in German, Jewish women challenged not only traditional gender roles but also the demarcation lines between Jewish and Gentile cultures.

Although the aspirations of Jewish women were the same as those of other authors publishing in German, their point of departure was distinct from that of male authors, Gentile and Jewish. Sorkin's thesis concerning the separateness of the experience and vantage point of male Jewish intellectuals applies to women to an even greater extent (Sorkin 1987, 122). In one sense Jewish women writers belonged to the Jewish subculture, in another they stood apart from it, for the majority of them achieved neither the status nor the security to join the ranks of the bourgeoisie on their own. Disenfranchised from the German-Jewish subculture as well as the German mainstream, they, in effect, formed a subculture within a subculture.

Jewish women brought their cultural, religious, and linguistic experience to German culture. Rahel Levin Varnhagen, for example, stepped out of the Yiddish language; she compensated for her background and her socialization, but she did not leave them behind. Rather, she added to them a secondary layer of identity, structured by the German language that she learned on her own through models of German literature.[10] In addition, self-taught and intuited patterns of communication enabled her to function in the company of privileged Gentiles, predominantly male. The style and form of expression achieved by her and others in her situation were uniquely their own. They enabled such women to leave their home base and make contact with Gentiles, but they did not effect assimilation. Having achieved a superb command of Gentile discourse and the reputation of being exceptional exotic creatures, these women nonetheless remained associated with their motherland, their Jewish origins.

Jewish women and men had different strategies at their disposal with which to struggle for access into Gentile society. Excluded from universities, women could not obtain academic credentials of any kind. Hence they tried to gain acceptance in the private sphere, through personal relationships, including marriage. They may have been spared the disappointment and humiliation in the academic world as experienced by Heinrich Heine, Theodor Herzl, or Arthur Schnitzler, but they were also more vulnerable, lacking the social tools to compensate for religious or racial rejection. Jewish women encountered discrimination close to home, and society required that they have male intermediaries in their professional and social dealings. The Gentile husbands of Dorothea Mendelssohn Veit Schlegel, Rahel Levin, and Fanny Lewald enabled their wives to participate in the cultural arena. In contrast to them, single and divorced Jewish women writers faced social and material hardships, a fate of which Else Lasker-Schüler is a prime example.

Arguing that the division of the sexes is "a biological fact, not an event in human history," Simone de Beauvoir dismisses the analogy proposed by Marxists between gender and class issues. She asserts that women, unlike the proletariat, cannot even dream of exterminating their (male) oppressors, as "the bond that unites her to them is not comparable to any other" (de Beauvoir 1957: xix). Hence "among the workers of the land the unmarried woman is a pariah; she remains a servant of her father, of her brother-in-law; she can hardly join the exodus to the cities, marriage enslaves her to a man" (430). While this characterization also does apply to the situation of Jewish women in Gentile society, the subculture of German-Jewish women writers is shaped by an additional dimension, derived from similar experiences and aspirations, including the obstacles facing Jews as a group and the predicament specific to Jewish women who write for a predominantly Gentile audience.

The seventeenth-century autobiographer Glikl Hamil writes within an exclusively Jewish world. Her work precedes the tradition of German-Jewish women's writing. Written in Yiddish before the opening of the ghettos, her memoirs were not intended for public consumption and made no allowances to accommodate a general readership. Rather, Glikl portrays an exclusively Jewish reality from which German-writing Jewish women distanced themselves, and which at the present many German-speaking Jewish women are trying to recapture. A look at Glikl Hamil's separate world is a necessary step in properly assessing the pioneering work of the first generation of German-speaking authors and the sense of loss experienced by later generations.

In contrast to Glikl's own perceived centrality, today's German-Jewish women writers are keenly aware of both their marginality and their history. As they explore and question cultural norms, they reconfigure the demarcation lines of center and periphery, constantly redefining the domain of the motherland.

KEEPERS OF THE MOTHERLAND

Writing the Motherland

Historical Perspectives

The imagination and literary approaches of German-speaking Jewish women have been shaped in a historical continuum that accounts for the affinity between a Yiddish-speaking preemancipation writer such as גליקל האמיל, Glikl Hamil, known in German as Glückel von Hameln, and contemporary authors.[1] Glikl wrote from a surprisingly modern, urban perspective, with social and personal interaction as her primary concern. External conflict and inner turmoil, resulting from the powerlessness of women and the precarious situation of the Jewish community in general, are central motifs in Glikl's זכרונות, or *Zikhroynes* (Hamelin 1977), her memoirs, and they continue to be prominent in the works of nineteenth- and twentieth-century authors.[2] Indeed, Viola Roggenkamp draws parallels between Glikl and one of her most prominent translators, Bertha Pappenheim (Roggenkamp 1994: vii).

Glikl began writing her seven books of memoirs in the year "5451 after the creation of the world," that is, in 1690–91 and completed them in 1719 (Hameln 1979, 11; Bilik 1992, 5). At that time, she was a widow, financially independent and maintaining her own living quarters with a maid at her disposal; in other words, she met the conditions that according to Virginia Woolf are the prerequisites to become a writer: autonomy and space. Glikl drew from her own experiences and Jewish tradition; she possessed a superior command of language. Her age and her status in her family and community afforded her a position of respect, which is reflected in her text.

Glikl's memoirs begin with her family's expulsion from Hamburg and end with a mysterious panic at the synagogue in Metz. The tangible event and the inexplicable rumblings during a service that caused part of the congregation to run to their death exemplify the dangers and the anxiety overshadowing Jewish existence. Glikl explores the strategies of

Jewish women in coping with these difficulties, such as focusing on the here and now, creatively transforming misfortune into an asset, and recasting reality, including one's own self, through language—in her case, two major Jewish languages. In contrast, Heinrich Heine's late Romantic novel fragment *Der Rabbi von Bacharach* shows German and Jewish discourses as inextricably intertwined. Indeed, Ashkenazic, non-Jewish German, and Slavic cultures developed in contact with one another. In the early Middle Ages, the interchange between the Germanic population in the process of being Christianized—often by force—and the Jews included peaceful neighborly interaction. The segregation of both groups and the persecution of the Jews began during the crusades and culminated in the building of ghettos.

The medieval ghettos served a twofold purpose: to keep Jews and Christians apart and to protect the Jews from Christian hostility; therefore, the Jewish communities were forced to pay for the construction and upkeep of ghettos. To prevent social, particularly sexual, contact between both groups, laws forcing Jews to wear special garments or markings were enacted. The size of the Jewish population was regulated through the restriction of the number of marriages, by granting protection to only a limited number of persons, and by imposing high taxes. To prevent the expansion of the ghettos, Jews were denied the right to acquire real estate and to relocate at will, and they were required to pay a body tax when crossing borders.

From the Middle Ages until the end of the eighteenth century, and in certain regions until the middle of the nineteenth century,[3] Jews and Christians formed distinct societies according to religion, culture, and language. The Jewish population was predominantly urban, as Jews could not exist in isolation for religious and pragmatic reasons. Their communities can best be compared to islands surrounded by alien territory. At times they were met with a certain degree of tolerance; at other times, with open hostility. Since the Jewish minority was minute in comparison to the Gentile population, negotiation was the only way Jews were able to influence the Gentile legislation that decided their fate. Internally, however, they were autonomous—provided that their presence was financially advantageous to their protectors, and that they did not incur the wrath of their neighbors. The so-called Court Jews— bankers and merchants—served as mediators between the ghettos and the Christian rulers. In their role as go-betweens, they stepped out of their environment, physically and culturally. Still, they were perceived as foreigners by the non-Jews. The familiarity with Gentile customs and languages on the part of the Jewish financiers exceeded the horizon of their average co-religionists, and some of them emulated Gentile court culture. Glikl Hamil and her peers, on the other hand, possessed only limited knowledge of Gentile society, and she does not analyze the way in which it defined the status of Jews. She seems to have been unaware of the Gentile origins of certain customs practiced in her community, such as the Dance of Death performed at a wedding or the wigs worn by Jews imitating French courtly fashions.

The Court Jews of the pre-Enlightenment era were at the mercy of their royal and princely patrons. At the same time, the fate of their communities was tied up with their personal successes or failures. Having no enforceable rights, they could be taken hostage, used as leverage for extortion, and killed to clear a burdensome credit balance. The same applied even more so to petty Jewish merchants and money lenders, who were welcome when they extended credit and unpopular when they demanded payment. Given their legal and cultural situation, it was impossible for Jews to break out of their confines short of apostasy. But as anti-Jewish folklore and the pronouncements of Christian leaders illustrate, not even baptism guaranteed acceptance.[4] From the Middle Ages into the nineteenth century, only a limited number of occupations were accessible to Jews. They were excluded from the guild system, which regulated the premodern economy, and were forbidden to work as craftsmen outside of the ghetto. Unable to buy or own land, they could not settle as farmers either, and as bona fide foreigners, they were prohibited from bearing arms. Disqualified from government and military positions, Jews could not improve their status. Commerce and usury were their best options to make a living, activities that enjoyed no respect in Christian society except when prominent Christian families such as the Fuggers engaged in them on a large scale.

Trade and money lending were identified as Jewish occupations, and they exposed Jews to widespread antagonism since Jew-hatred, eloquently preached by the apostle Paul, was condoned by the Christians, who held the Jews responsible for killing Christ. Traditionally, Jews, like women, were suspected of occult practices. Both Catholics and Protestants conducted witch-hunts and persecuted Jews, with only the former subsiding with increasing secularization. Into the twentieth century,

Jews have been tried for the ritual slaughter of Christian children and have been accused of conspiracy against the Christian world (Trachtenberg 1943). Since Jews were prevented from establishing permanent roots, Jewish refugees were a familiar sight in all parts of Europe, giving rise to the legend of the Wandering Jew, a demonic figure that preoccupied not only fifteenth- and sixteenth-century Europeans but also modern anti-Semites, including the Nazis.[5]

Jews lived collectively and individually under the constant threat of expulsion and annihilation. Following the recurring massacres and expatriations, Christian rulers tended to extend invitations to the survivors and exiles to return; thus even major communities such as Berlin and Vienna lacked continuity.[6] In order to cope with the instability in their lives, European Jews were forced to develop a high degree of mobility and resilience, which set them even further apart from feudal and early bourgeois Christian society. Beyond their local communities, they established a supranational network and tried through pan-European alliances to protect fugitives and to maintain family and business connections with other Jews. As the followers of a non-Christian faith who owned no visible property, conversant in several languages including Hebrew, whose letters the Christian world associated with magic, and engaged in unpopular trades, Jews aroused misgivings and, in turn, found good reason to distrust the Gentiles.

The familial and social structures of Ashkenazic Jewry formed in response to these difficulties. The frequent absences of Jewish fathers and husbands, the likelihood of losing family members, and the possibility of having to leave and regroup elsewhere required every family member's ability to fend for himself or herself. Even the women of privileged families led a less sheltered life, less removed from the business world, than their Gentile counterparts. Many Jewish women engaged in trade and commerce on their own (Carlebach 1981, 162). In addition to being wives, mothers, and homemakers, many Jewish women managed the family business as well.[7]

A Separate Reality: Glikl Hamil's זכרונות *(Zikhroynes)*

In her memoirs, Glikl Hamil (1646–1724), one of the six children of Loeb Pinkerle, the *Parnas* (president) of the Jewish community of Hamburg, the wife of Chayim Hamil, and a businesswoman in her own right, reveals the inner economy of the Jewish merchant families as being based on teamwork and shared tasks (Weiss-Rosmarin 1940, 77). Like all Jewish women, Glikl was fully integrated into the patriarchal structures of her community. Moreover, she occupied a place in the women's sphere that remained invisible both in the context of religious life and from the point of view of the Gentile world, hidden, as it were, by the partition of the women's section in the synagogue and the ghetto walls.[8] The representatives of the ghetto were men—businessmen and occasionally wise men and alchemists.[9] Although concealed from the public eye, Jewish women have preoccupied the imagination of Gentile authors from Shakespeare to Grillparzer. They were depicted as beautiful and alluring, having no greater desire than to follow a Christian suitor into his world or, in less overtly sexual terms, as pious converts or vulgar market women (Krobb 1993, 21–49).

The actual world of Jewish women has been examined less thoroughly; in cultural history the experience of women has been traditionally ignored. Since men have defined the cultural standard, the male condition is generally viewed as the norm. The Jewish women most carefully scrutinized were transitional figures between Jewish and Gentile culture, such as Rahel Levin Varnhagen and Fanny Lewald (Wallach-Faller 1985, 152–72). As exceptional personalities, they fascinated the Gentile public and frequently aroused the disapproval of Jewish critics who considered them renegades. In contrast, Glikl, firmly grounded in her community, portrayed the lives of average Jewish women. She herself led a traditional life without any desire to do otherwise. For this reason, her work provides unique insights into Jewish women's reality. It is an important source of information on the community and family life of the Jews in sixteenth- and seventeenth-century Western Europe (Weiss-Rosmarin 1940, 77). In personal terms, Glikl's memoirs chronicle the author's life.[10] According to Trude Weiss-Rosmarin, writing memoirs and autobiographies being rare in Jewish literature, it is "doubly interesting that a woman was the author of a book of memoirs that occupies a unique place in Jewish literature" (1940, 76f.). In addition, written in retrospect, Glikl's memoirs define different phases of a Jewish woman's life. As Dorothy Bilik observes: "Glikl's seven books correspond roughly to the decades of her life" (1992, 8).

From Glikl's point of view, that of a Jewish woman positioned at the center of her society, only the margins of the Christian world become discernible. Living in a state of disenfranchisement fostered an in-group morality isolating Jews from the outside world (Carlebach 1981, 164). From a Jewish point of view, the Gentile world appeared hostile and unjust. "What they had and enjoyed was either on sufferance or as a privilege," Carlebach writes. Glikl considered Christian culture as a reality to be coped with in practical terms; she never sought the company of Gentiles and was otherwise disinterested in the non-Jewish world. Unlike Jewish men and women of later generations, Glikl neither perceived Gentile culture as superior nor copied Gentile fashions and customs. She learned as much of the Christian languages as was necessary for business—some Dutch and some German.

Since Glikl's geography is that of a seventeenth-century Jew who considers the supranationality of the Ashkenazic sphere to be the norm, Glikl herself did not view the Jews as a minority. Her internal homeland stretched from Russia to the Netherlands, with Yiddish as its indigenous language. Within this domain, families and communities shared a common religion, lifestyle, and culture. For Glikl, the boundaries of Christian countries were mere trade and tax barriers. Her frame of reference consists of trade cities and Jewish communities such as Vienna, Prague, Berlin, Leipzig, and Braunschweig, as well as the Eastern European centers of commerce and learning (Hameln 1979, 185, 328).[11] Likewise, her notion of history is also exclusively Jewish. She takes notice of Gentile history and activities only as they affect Jewish life—pogroms and wars —but she does not even mention the Thirty Years' War, the most devastating Christian religious war, whose aftermath overshadowed Europe for many decades. Instead, she discusses the exodus of the Vilna Jews from Poland in 1648, the Cossack rebellions, and the settlement of a group of survivors in Hamburg (30).

Glikl meets Gentiles with the attitude of a foreigner: secure in her own identity but with caution, aware of her vulnerability as a Jewish woman. Each time an encounter with Christians ends without her or her family being mistreated, she is relieved. Topics such as intermarriage and integration are not even an issue. Glikl does not imagine herself to be German; nor does she want to be. She writes in the languages of Ashkenazic Jewry: Yiddish, with Hebrew prayers and benedictions interspersed, and she considers her language to be the linguistic standard rather than a deviation from German (Weinreich 1993, 103). This point of view prevailed among Jews well into the eighteenth century—

Yiddish-speaking German and Eastern European Jews called themselves Ashkenazim to differentiate themselves from the Spanish and Portuguese Sephardic Jews who spoke Ladino/Judesmo (4).

As the daughter of an influential family, Glikl attended Cheder and studied Hebrew, as did other women, among them Rebekka Tiktiner, the author of a book entitled *Meneketh Riwkih* (Weinreich 1993, 292). During most of her adult life, however, Glikl suspended her intellectual pursuits for the sake of her family and business—twice married and twice a widow, she was the mother of thirteen children.[12] Regarding her education and her career, Glikl's professional situation resembles that of Christian city women in medieval times who were less restricted than those of the Baroque era (Shahar 1983, 164–202). Perhaps this is the reason why the conflicts addressed in her memoirs do not include her identity as a Jew and as a woman, or perhaps she does not question convention for lack of an alternative. In that case, Glikl's text, reflecting the moral and religious concepts embedded in the Jewish languages, would confirm Wittgenstein's dictum that the limits of one's language define the limits of one's world.[13] The symmetry of Glikl's thought and language produces a cohesive discourse with only external sources of conflict.

Since Glikl accepts the precepts of Judaism, including traditional gender roles, and manipulates them skillfully, as Roggenkamp points out, her identity is at no point threatened (1994, vii). Even in her discussion of the financial mismanagement by her son Löb and the fiasco involving Hirz Levy, her second husband, who had concealed his near-bankruptcy from her, she criticizes the individual man rather than the institution of marriage or patriarchy.[14] Trying to get along within the patriarchal structures, Glikl seems unaware of the fact that the cards are stacked against her. Only indirectly does her story reveal the extent to which the traditional family structures work to her disadvantage: Neither protected by nor provided for by her husbands—her husbands' estates consist only of debts—she gains hardly any recognition for coming to the rescue of her family time and again. Nor does she earn respect for providing for herself and her children. Rather, her toil and labor are taken for granted.

Glikl describes each of her life's phases as having its own rules—childhood, engagement, marriage, motherhood, and widowhood. She plays her preordained role in each of these cycles, for the key to acceptance by her community is adherence to convention. In return, her community provides her with a predictable structure, including her rights as well as her obligations to her parents, to her husband and children, and to Jewish society at large. Over time, she develops a certain virtuosity in working within the limitations imposed upon her as a woman and the external restrictions imposed upon the Jewish community. Yet, her very act of writing, especially in Yiddish, constitutes a type of rebellion against societal norms that seems incongruent with the obedience with which she observes Halakhic law and secular Jewish customs.

Like all women, Glikl thanks God in her morning prayers for creating her according to his will as a woman, and she defers to the authority of men, namely her husbands and to an extent her older sons, despite her superior competence. Ironically, her sense of duty and her compliance expose to a certain extent the arbitrariness of Jewish gender roles to the readers. Like herself, many of the women she portrays are competent individuals, but their abilities are curtailed by patriarchal structures. It is not surprising that once widowed, women, among them Glikl's mother, are unwilling to remarry. Glikl herself justifies her mother's decision and follows her example later in life. She portrays widowhood as a time when a woman can devote herself to her own projects, including community service and writing.

Considering bearing and raising children the primary duties of a woman in her childbearing years, whatever emotional ties, or lack thereof, husband and wife may share, Glikl does not hesitate to marry off her children "joyfully in wealth and honor" (Hameln 1979, 149). She depicts marriage and motherhood in business terms without prudery, but also without romantic notions, as did her parents, whose deliberations to arrange for Glikl's engagement with Chayim Hamil were dominated by material concerns. Details regarding the contract and the ceremony are also emphasized when Glikl enters her second marriage as a woman in her fifties. In both instances, the criteria for selecting a husband include his family background, his financial standing, his prestige, and the reputation of his community.

In conjunction with the strict order of Halakhic law, the importance ascribed to these external factors makes it possible to contract viable unions across long distances, regardless of the individuals involved. Usually women and men were married at a young age, when they could be assumed to have the flexibility necessary to adjust to their new environment with ease. Not even as a first-time bride does Glikl seem to have been preoccupied with emotional or sexual matters, as is suggested by her interest in tangible issues and her matter-of-fact attitude toward sex. As is to be expected in a society that assigns different spheres to both sexes, female bonding is an important theme in Glikl's memoirs. Carlebach highlights it as a major structural element of Jewish culture, noting that women, not confined to the home, were involved in communal activities and formed work and friendship groups (1981, 164). The extraordinary strength with which Jewish women intellectuals of later generations confronted problems within and outside of their communities seems to have emanated, at least in part, from a culture that accorded them a space, albeit limited, of their own. Not surprisingly, Glikl portrays the relationships among women, particularly mothers and daughters, as nurturing and intimate, one of the strongest examples being her account of herself and her mother giving birth to daughters together on the same day. The latter episode represents a highlight in Glikl's life, uniting her with her mother in an almost sisterly union. The emotional ties between Glikl and her daughters were equally strong, reaching far beyond household and family concerns. Albeit with great misgivings and not until severe health problems forced her to give up her residence, Glikl turned to her married daughter for help in her old age, rather than to her sons (Hameln 1979, 290). The gradually evolving trust and affection between her and her son-in-law outweigh her attachment to her sons.

On the other hand, counter to familiar stereotypes of the close-knit nurturing Jewish family, Glikl's memoirs reveal that the bonds between the individual members of a family were relatively loose, as is made apparent by the fact that after her first husband's death, her relatives leave her to cope with his debts and open-ended business ventures on her own (180). Neither is the help Glikl extends to her closest relatives, including her sons, unconditional; she shows no inclination to sacrifice herself for her children. In her dealings with family members, she adheres to the conventions regulating business transactions in general.

Within Glikl's environment, mothers and daughters clearly form the inner circle. The larger circle is the extended family, whose members live scattered all across Europe. Glikl takes pride in the prominence of her relatives and in-laws, whose standing advances her and her children's status. Among them are Juda Berlin; Jost Liebmann, the court jeweler of the Prussian Elector; and Samson Wertheimer, the chief rabbi of

Vienna.[15] Nonetheless, Glikl is not blinded by authority and she exposes injustice and cruelty on the part of other Jews, including her closest relatives and dignitaries of the community (1979, 293–95). Knowing that the way women establish themselves in the community is through their male relatives, who had the task of networking, she tries to contract advantageous unions for herself and her children. Study, apprenticeships, business, and marriage were the major mechanisms through which to extend the ties between families throughout the Ashkenazic realm.

Particularly striking about Glikl's view of the world is the fact that she does not distinguish between objectively existing and subjectively experienced phenomena. Her accounts of empirically experienced events and the secondhand reports by others stand side by side with facts and figures, the display of emotions, empirical perceptions, fantasies, prayers, and benedictions. In her Yiddish narrative, she does not separate the profane from the sacred, but she does reserve Hebrew entirely for holy subjects — prayers and quotes from the Scriptures and frequent invocations, such as "God forbid" (256). Yet, Glikl's primary focus is on the here and now and the material world, depicted in the *mame-loshn*.

The directness of her expression and her colorful writing style make the lack of differentiation between material and spiritual phenomena, physical and imagined reality, all the more interesting. In certain ways, her integrated concept of reality reflects Jewish discourses, including that of the Bible, which, although concrete, is permeated by the belief in the ever-present spirit that can manifest itself at any place and at any time. Glikl is as far from being an enthusiast as she is from the scientific world view that was to emerge during the Enlightenment. She believes that the spiritual world and the physical realm are separated as if by a curtain that can be lifted at any time. Her description of the disaster at Metz is a case in point; if Glikl were not entirely literal, it would invite a symbolic or psychoanalytical interpretation. Her reaction to the disaster suggests instead that she feels she has caught a glimpse of the beyond. This is also the case when she emphasizes her connections to the realm of the dead. Not only Glikl but also those around her are convinced that apparitions can manifest themselves at any time of the day or night, and they consider such occurrences natural and normal. In some instances, Glikl interprets the apparitions as dreams, and in others as revelations. She asserts that spirits appear in order to inform the living of concealed crimes or to announce impending deaths. As is also true for Rahel Levin

Varnhagen, actual dreams occupy an important place in Glikl's psychology as well.

Glikl meets the uncanny with the same matter-of-factness as she does mundane phenomena. Her relationship to the supernatural is free of apprehension, an attitude that derives in part from her familiarity with and trust in folk medicine and faith healing. Neither her outlook on ghosts nor on healing involves the concept of sorcery (162). Only once, during her daughter Mate's illness, does she resort to a magic ritual: she and her husband pray in different corners of a room, hoping that by imitating Rebecca's and Isaac's prayers they will lend greater power to their plea (69).

To certain individuals Glikl ascribes mystical proclivities, and she admits that she herself was once impressed with Shabbatai Zewi, the false messiah, whose downfall disappointed her as it did many Jews in Hamburg.[16] Even in retrospect, she recalls vividly the hope for deliverance caused by the prophecies of Zewi (61–63), and she is not ashamed to write about her joy at his arrival and the celebrations in his honor. Some of her relatives even sold their homes and prepared for the Holy Land. To overcome her dismay about Zewi's capture and his conversion to Islam, Glikl consoles herself with the idea that God sent an impostor as a punishment.

One major difference between mysticism as discussed by Glikl and Christian writers is the role of eroticism. In spite of her eloquence, her language lacks the nuanced register to express feelings of passion. Approximately one hundred years later, Rahel developed the vocabulary of the heart and the senses, but she did so in German rather than in Yiddish. In contrast to Rahel, a master at evoking atmospheres and ambiances, Glikl writes action- and fact-oriented memoirs. This applies also to her unsentimental "second vision," which presupposes the presence of death within life and the divine within the world. A similarly integrated view of reality, physical and transcendental, is characteristic of later Jewish women writers including Else Lasker-Schüler, Nelly Sachs, Gertrud Kolmar, Ilse Aichinger, and Barbara Honigmann. Like Glikl, these authors encounter reality as a totality of spirit, mind, and body, without emotional excesses.

In a Baroque or early Enlightenment context, Glikl's memoirs stand out as an astonishing document. The sober attitude of her personal narrative shows her to be a realistic writer to whom exaggerated notions about any aspect of life are alien. Only in her didactic and religious digressions does Glikl display some of the exuberance characteristic of the seventeenth century. In addition, her memoirs lack the heroic characters of Baroque literature. Instead, her modest narrative voice of a god-fearing mother writing her memoirs brings to mind Grimmelshausen, the author of *Simplicius Simplicissimus*. The way in which Glikl must fend for herself during most of her adult life is reminiscent of the fate and fortunes of Grimmelshausen's *picaro*. Like Grimmelshausen, Glikl reviews a life of tribulation with the detachment of an aging person who has retired from worldly affairs. Closer yet is the affinity to Grimmelshausen's women characters whose hard work and perseverance ensured their society's future in chaotic times. Rather than being the exception, however, Jewish women had to live with chaos.

Glikl's memoirs show the condition of Jewish women to be fundamentally different from that of Christian women of the middle class. Because privileged Jewish women had the potential to reach financial and personal autonomy, their status in some ways resembled that of women of the aristocracy, but the disenfranchisement of their entire community prevented even the most privileged Jewish women from intermingling with the Gentile upper class or the bourgeoisie. Hence Glikl is unfamiliar with the evolving ideology of feminity and *Herzensbildung*, the education of the heart, propagated by Pietism and the Moral Weeklies. Void of the refinement and sensitivity promoted as desirable feminine attributes, Glikl's energetic narrative voice appears almost masculine in the Christian context.

Glikl squarely assumes responsibility for her own destiny, takes credit for her successes, and accepts the blame for her failures. As she does with her fellow human beings, she negotiates and converses with God directly and with self-assurance. Taking personal charge of the text, she has no need of a literary framework. Seen in this light, even her apologies, dictated by convention, are little more than polite gestures. Her claim to write mainly for the benefit of her children is undermined by her authoritative stance, and her ostensible reluctance to write must be taken with a grain of salt in view of the seven volumes she produced. Of course, she does not want to overstep her bounds and invokes the Jewish religion and customs as her sources of inspiration, but neither does she allow her gender to prevent her from expressing herself. Assuming the role of teacher vis-à-vis her male and female readers, Glikl does not hesitate to set herself up as an example.

Positioned at the center of her text as author and major informant, Glikl displays a self-confidence that is in part derived from her assumed rapport with her readership and her familiarity with religious and social practices, health issues, and education as they affect her family and community. As is the case with Baroque authors in general, Glikl presents a wealth of encyclopedic information alongside the main story line, her autobiography. Her narrative style may be influenced by the *muser*, Hebrew and Yiddish ethical and didactic literature, but going beyond these models, she does not hesitate to assert her own view against accepted authority (Bilik 1992, 6).

The contact with Gentile language and values and the desire for emancipation on the part of Jews of the following generations undermined the self-confidence underlying Glikl's text. In the process of expanding their horizons and gaining access to German culture, many Jews began to criticize Jewish life and thereby question their own identity. At the same time, they were unable to espouse their target culture at face value. The price they paid for their biculturalism was self-doubt, even despair, which was manifested in severe psychosomatic conditions. The lives and works of the German-Jewish salonnières reflect the struggle of exceptional women between two or more cultures. Before the beginning of the Jewish-Gentile dialogue there was no need to write against the Gentile mainstream. Later, the increasing interaction between Jews and Christians caused Jews to assume a dual perspective, which is manifest in texts that reflect certain aspects of the authors' culture of origin as well as characteristics of the surrounding dominant culture.

Writing in German indicated a Jew's desire to transcend Jewish culture. Such a text addressed either a Gentile readership or a Jewish audience willing to learn German and to step out of the confines of their community. On the part of women, this step entailed an even more radical reorientation. The attitudes engendered through the contact with German culture differed markedly from Glikl's Jewish exclusivity. It required them to transgress against traditional gender roles as well as Jewish tradition. Jewish women who excelled in the German-speaking environment at the end of the eighteenth century and the beginning of the nineteenth were more than unconventional; they were rebels.

From the Ghetto to the Salon (Fanny von Arnstein, Henriette Herz, and Dorothea Mendelssohn Veit Schlegel)

The change of language and discourse fostered by the Haskalah and the emancipation cleared the path toward conversion and assimilation. When German gained priority over Yiddish, the latter was relegated to use among family and friends and eventually abandoned. Persons with social aspirations were careful to avoid the Yiddish accent and vocabulary characteristic of the so-called *Jargon*, Jewish German. Jewish practices were adapted to resemble the dominant Christian ones. Moses Mendelssohn's Bible translation, written in German with Hebrew letters, ultimately became a medium to facilitate the shift from Yiddish to German.

Hand in hand with the linguistic adjustments went sweeping changes involving customs, fashions, and names (Bering 1987). Persons seeking integration into German society moved away from Halakhic law, and it became a matter of personal preference as to which aspects of the Jewish ritual were retained and which holidays celebrated—often Christian and Jewish festivals were observed as secular occasions. As a result of the fast-occurring scientific breakthroughs and the humanist ideology espoused by the educated bourgeoisie, secularization was a universal phenomenon, affecting all European religious groups. However, rather than producing a generic urban society, it had a different impact on Christians and Jews. Even in privileged, enlightened Gentile circles, converted Jews such as Rahel Levin Varnhagen and Heinrich Heine, remained pariahs, as Hannah Arendt elaborates (1978, 67ff.). Conversely, traditional Jews treated those who left the fold of the community as renegades. Secular Christian, German national, and modern Jewish identity had evolved over time, but the most noticeable changes in the traditional standoff between Jews and Germans occurred in the post-Enlightenment era. The disassociation from Judaism involved major adjustments to the collective and individual self. Rather than causing a loss of Jewish authenticity, these processes represent a complete transformation resulting in a new German-Jewish identity.

In his discussion of the incompatibility of the basic concepts structuring the Jewish world and Christian and secularized Europe, Sander Gilman argues that adopting a language such as German resulted in a tragic inner conflict for the Jewish speaker, since the languages of

Europe were shaped by the anti-Judaism entrenched in Christianity (1994, 15–28). Already in the Gospels, Jews represent the prototypical Other, whereas Jesus is removed from the Jewish context altogether. He is Christianized, so to speak, but the Jews are linguistically marked as aliens and the satanic antithesis to Christ and his flock (19–21). Following the Manichaeistic structure of Christian thought, every Christian language reproduced the concept of its own group as God's children and the Jews as anti-Christ (E. Schwarz 1994, 52). Julius Schoeps, quoting representatives of the Protestant Church in Germany (EKD), documents that such attitudes persisted in official circles after 1945, unaffected by recent events (28). Also, in painting, sculpture, and literature, Christ was depicted as a member of Christianity. He bore the physical features of each newly Christianized ethnic group and was represented as a native speaker of whatever language into which the Bible was translated. The portrayal of the Jew as a foreigner with a grotesque physiognomy had sustained the Judeophobia of the Middle Ages and continued to do so under a new, supposedly scientific racial nomenclature in the modern era (50).

Jewish authors who first adopted the languages of Christian nations did so in defiance of a hostile audience and the resistance of the respective language. There is no comparable conflict for Christians writing in their native language or any other Christian language, or for Jews in Jewish languages. Originally Gentile languages were not designed to communicate Jewish experiences. As difficult as it is for women to ignore the misogyny embedded in the grammar, idioms, and clichés of their native languages, it is equally difficult for Jewish speakers of German to extrapolate themselves from the all-pervasive anti-Judaism that sets them up as a target. Moreover, in its structural details, German differs from the Jewish languages, which makes it hard, if not impossible, to transfer specific concepts, views, and ideas. In contrast to Jewish women, though, Jewish men came from a linguistic universe that validated them as men. The fact that no such linguistic safe haven existed for women in either language may have facilitated their transition from speakers of Yiddish or Ladino to speakers of German.

The change from Yiddish into German moved Jewish men and, to a lesser extent, Jewish women from a position of centrality within their own culture to the marginal position of a minority. In order to convey their ideas, Jewish writers were forced to infuse the German language with new meaning. They shaped and fine-tuned their new medium in such a way that it could also accommodate the Jewish experience. Jewish women authors faced the daunting task of not only having to construct a vehicle to carry their voices as Jews but also to overcome their marginality as women and to position themselves as author and subject. Many did so with apparent ease, since they were less invested in their native language than men and were used to modifying androcentric codes to fit their needs. Many of the salonnières had been socialized in Yiddish, which continued to be the language of their relatives in the provinces, if not of their immediate family. They acquired German on the basis of their linguistic and cultural training as Jewish women, often overcompensating for perceived shortcomings and inadvertently setting themselves up for ridicule (Krobb 1993, 61; Arendt 1962).

Rather than acquiring a dual identity and becoming full participants in both cultures, German-speaking Jewish women moved between the fronts. Much like the Court Jews, the salonnières never quite crossed the boundaries into the Gentile world. Living among Gentiles, they attempted to deemphasize the traces of their origin. Only a few of them succeeded in synthesizing the disparate aspects of their existence — according to her husband, Rahel came to terms with her German-Jewish identity only on her deathbed: "I think of my origin and my entire life circumstances with sublime bliss. The most ancient memories of mankind are lined with the most recent events, the vastest stretches of time and space are connected. What I considered for such a significant part of my life my greatest stigma and the cruelest and most painful misfortune — having been born a Jewish woman — at no cost do I want to miss that now" (Varnhagen 1983, 1:43).

Proficiency in German and the mastery of Gentile customs were the minimal requirements for integration. To achieve both, Jewish women needed a certain degree of independence. Not surprisingly, the wives and daughters of prominent families, such as the Viennese banker's wife Fanny von Arnstein (1758–1818) and her sisters, spearheaded the process. Although they possessed the means and the necessary erudition to participate in intellectual life, they had to cope with anti-Jewish prejudices and the constraints of traditional gender roles. As Hannah Arendt pointed out, the prominence and the public acclaim enjoyed by a Jewish woman were not synonymous with respectability, and a woman's social visibility was in itself abnormal.

Fanny von Arnstein, the wife of a rich and tolerant husband, was an exception in that she reconciled her public life and her duties as wife and mother. For the most part, however, the patterns of Glikl Hamil's biography apply to those of the salonnières as well. They had to struggle for economic stability and personal autonomy before they were able to engage in social and literary activities. Most lived by themselves—unmarried women, widows, or divorcées. Henriette Herz (1764–1847) excelled in beauty and intelligence, but prior to her husband's death she did not write for the general public (Seibert 1989); Rahel Levin Varnhagen (1771–1833) established her salon after her father's death, long before she was married; and Dorothea Mendelssohn Veit Schlegel (1764–1839) wrote her novel *Florentin* after her separation from her first husband, Marcus Veit, and prior to her marriage to Friedrich Schlegel. The majority of the salonnières had the odium of notoriety attached to them, which haunted the *bohème* throughout the ages. In an exceptional era like the period between the French Revolution and the Napoleonic Wars, being an outsider was relatively unproblematic. The spirit of the revolution opened seemingly infinite possibilities, including the opportunity for a Jewish woman to leave her culture and enter into uncharted territory. It is in this era that German-Jewish literature is rooted.

Compared to Christian women of the bourgeoisie and lower nobility, the education of the Jewish salonnières was exceptional. Their rigorous secular education, which compensated for their lack of religious training, not only estranged them from Judaism but also prevented them from assuming traditional women's roles. The less than successful traditional marriages of Henriette Herz and Dorothea Mendelssohn Veit to Jewish professionals reflected the awkward situation of educated women. So did the tribulations overshadowing the lives of Rahel Levin Varnhagen and her friend Pauline Wiesel (1779–1848). Many of these women possessed equal or better qualifications and worldly experience than upper-class Christian men, but as women they were barred from entering professional careers.

The first generations of German-Jewish women writers acted as pioneers without a model or a tradition upon which to fall back. Without direct access to Gentile society, they established semipublic salons in their homes to create neutral spaces for cultural exchange (Krobb 1993, 67). In the salons, the usual segregation of social classes and religious groups was suspended, so that a dialogue between Jews and Gentiles, aristocrats, artists, philosophers, actors, poets, and men and women could take place. Yet, the hospitality of Jewish women was generally not reciprocated, and the salons remained a symptom of their founders' marginality; the salon was the only way for them to reach out. Moreover, they connected with artists, literati, and the most open-minded men of the aristocracy and the bourgeoisie rather than with the Gentile mainstream—salons were not family institutions (Weissberg 1987, 208). The literary coffeehouses of the nineteenth and twentieth centuries must be considered the continuation of the salon culture, since they fulfilled the same social function as a gathering place for intellectuals, socialites, artists, and their sponsors. The salons prospered during an era of liberalization, but they declined as a result of the nationalism that accompanied the Wars of Liberation. The ensuing enthusiasm for the Germanic world and Protestant northern Germany, which Hegel and Fichte had declared the apex of world history, also set an end to early Romantic feminism (Hegel 1955, 256f.). Parallel to the reawakened hatred of France and French customs went a fanatic anti-Judaism that all but eradicated the legacy of the Enlightenment.

The salon of Fanny (Vögele) von Arnstein in Vienna was one of the first major salons hosted by a Jewish woman, and it scandalized Viennese society, even after the Toleration Edict had been issued to promote the cause of Jewish acculturation (Spiel 1962).[17] To be sure, the effects of the edict were less dramatic than is often assumed. To illustrate social reality thereafter, Hilde Spiel examined a notorious spy intrigue. Here, as in the Dreyfus affair one century later, the authorities targeted the most vulnerable party, namely, a destitute Jewish woman, and the offender, a Gentile aristocrat, went free (117ff.).

In this general climate, it was not easy for women, even if they came from the best possible background, like Fanny von Arnstein and her sisters, to assume a public role. Von Arnstein was the daughter of the Prussian court banker Daniel Itzig, whose extended family included the Prussian court jeweler Jost Liebmann, a member of Glikl Hamil's circles.[18] The prestige of the Itzig family, the standing of von Arnstein's husband, and her own social skills made it possible for her to challenge convention (Krobb 1993, 63–64). Unlike the salonnières of the next generation, she remained rooted in her community, but her children followed the path of conversion and assimilation (Spiel 1962, 143).

Von Arnstein, an enlightened cosmopolitan and a proponent of emancipation and tolerance, was a brilliant conversationalist and letter writer, but not a literary author. Her salon attracted predominantly business-men, politicians, and intellectuals. She played a major role in creating an environment favorable to the advancement of Jewish women who, according to an eighteenth-century observer, had achieved "sophistica-tion of manners" and "refinement of language" by the 1780s—a diction free of residual Yiddish (Krobb 1993, 62). Interaction with—but by no means acceptance into—Gentile society came at the price of unilateral acculturation, the disadvantages of which are obvious from a compari-son of Glikl Hamil's position and that of eighteenth- and nineteenth-century Jewish women. With Jewish families assuming a place in the bourgeoisie, capable women were forced into the type of cultivated do-mesticity characteristic of this social stratum. This process increasingly estranged German-Jewish women from Ashkenazic culture at large.

This kind of assimilation was out of keeping with Mendelssohn's con-cept of tolerance, but it corresponded to von Dohm's program of curb-ing Jewish otherness (1973). Ultimately, it led to the creation of "Jews who are no Jews," as one of the characters in Gotthold Ephraim Less-ing's drama *Die Juden* puts it (1967, 166). Not only the von Arnstein children but also Mendelssohn's sons and daughters, as well as Rahel Levin and Henriette Herz, were baptized. Conversion was the prerequi-site to marry a Gentile, and Heinrich Heine termed it the "entrance ticket to European society." However, as was the case with Rahel and Heinrich Heine, conversion was often followed by regret and an inner reorientation toward Judaism. The experience of many apostates illus-trates furthermore that conversion afforded them only limited access to the mainstream while it entailed a painful separation from the Jewish community.

As mentioned earlier, the first German-Jewish women intellectuals were the daughters and wives of exceptional men. Their "masculine" or "haphazard" education enabled them to socialize with the intellec-tual elite of their time, and in turn, Gentile men appreciated culturally sophisticated women. Deborah Hertz characterizes the salon guests as coming from three groups: "the nobility, the *Bürgertum* and the Jew-ish community," specifying, however, that these groups were not repre-sented in the salon in equal proportions. According to her estimation, four times more Jewish women than men frequented salons, over half of the guests were members of the nobility, and one-third belonged to the upper middle class, while the lower middle class was not represented at all (Hertz 1978, 101–4).

Products of unusual circumstances, the biographies of most Jewish salonnières seem eccentric. They include scandals, divorces, and name changes that made it difficult for critics to decide how to refer to the authors—by their first name, their last name, and if so, which ones. Rahel Levin, for example, began calling herself Friederike Robert prior to her baptism and her marriage to Varnhagen von Ense, whose name was also her creation; Brenna Mendelssohn Veit adopted the name Dorothea after her divorce and was baptized Friederike prior to her marriage to Schlegel. Liliane Weissberg and Pauline Paucker illustrate the transformations of Jewish life in Germany by analyzing portraits, pointing out, for example, that Henriette Herz posed in a classical Greek costume, wearing her own hair (rather than a bonnet or *sheitl*). Later in life, however, she wore a turban, possibly to accommodate her guests' fantasies of an exotic Jewish woman (Herz 1984, 455; Paucker 1993, 29–46). Rahel, on the other hand, posed in a traditional bonnet.[19] The language proficiency of German-Jewish women writers reveals similarly divergent patterns.

Ashkenazic Jews constructed their German on the basis of Yiddish. Pauline Wiesel's sketchy, grammatically and structurally deficient letters and Rahel's ongoing quest for the correct word, phrase, and spelling show that language acquisition was an involved process, the results of which varied from individual to individual. Many famous letter writers never developed a literary language, and the predilection for autobiographical forms of writing suggests a need for self-expression reminiscent of Glikl Hamil.

Henriette Herz, the daughter of a Portuguese-Jewish doctor and his French-born wife, began by writing letters. Later, she became a chronicler and autobiographer. Her memoirs are significant as a historical and a personal document—they survey German society in transition from the perspective of an erudite, well-connected woman. The patterns structuring her youth, which ended at the age of twelve with her engagement to a man twice her age, are identical to the younger years of Glikl Hamil and Fanny von Arnstein. Unlike Glikl, however, Herz became a socially visible personality, praised for her beauty and intellect by Mirabeau, Laroche, the brothers Humboldt, Gentz, Schlegel, Schleiermacher, and Börne. She turned to writing after she became a widow,

and like Glikl, she lived on a limited income, but without family obligations, in an apartment, engaged in writing and charitable work. Among
Herz's numerous visitors were Ludwig Börne and Fanny Lewald.
Similar to Glikl, Herz portrays her life according to phases, the first
one being as a law-abiding Jewish daughter and child-wife, followed by
the phase of an adult woman and widow on a path toward inner emancipation, externally expressed by becoming baptized after her husband's
death. As is the case in Heine's *Der Rabbi von Bacharach,* the epic flow
of Herz's prose is suddenly disrupted, perhaps because the author was
unable to sustain her narrative. Although Herz's autobiography disintegrates into prose vignettes, it represents a significant step in German-
Jewish prose. Aside from the difference in language, these memoirs are
distinct from Glikl's in that Herz is at home in Jewish *and* Gentile culture. She knows that the latter does not accept her as an equal, but she
comes to terms with her marginality. Rather than blaming anti-Judaism,
she suggests as the reason for her isolation later in life the absence of an
intellectual Christian middle-class culture (Herz 1984, 64–65).

From a structural point of view, Herz's memoirs are indebted to the
German educational novel. Like Goethe's *Wilhelm Meister,* they open
with the family background of the central character, herself. She informs
her readers about her great-grandfather's adventures—he fled from Portugal during the Inquisition—and her own childhood, overshadowed
by her dislike of her mother. For her father she professes love and admiration throughout (14–15). In the discussion of her family background,
Herz refers to culture-specific phenomena. She does so by using German
terms—for example, *Sonnabend* (Saturday) stands for *Shabbath, Laub-
hütte* for *Sukka.* This nomenclature supports Herz's frequently made assertion that women grew up estranged from Judaism and Jewish culture.
For her, this alienation presents a serious predicament. She laments the
fact that girls received only a superficial introduction to Jewish customs
and traditions and were left entirely ignorant in spiritual matters (11).
Rather than considering women's lack of traditional learning unique to
Jewish culture, Herz views it as symptomatic of the progressive secularization of Europe that causes enlightened parents to deny their children
a religious education.

Herz's difficulties regarding her identity manifest themselves in a
variety of ways, including her frailty and ill health, which signal a deep-
seated anxiety. Moreover, her physical beauty causes her considerable

distress. Being the object of popular admiration already as a child, Herz felt awkward and intimidated. Her sense of being abnormal was heightened by her parents' concern for her safety, causing them to disenroll her from public school and have her educated by private tutors. These factors may have contributed to her unquestioning, even joyful, acceptance of her betrothal to Marcus Herz, which stands in conflict with her earlier rebellion against convention (21). She may have hoped to escape from eccentricity into normalcy by becoming a bride in accordance with her parents' wishes. Like Glikl, Herz seems to have been disinterested in her future husband's age and physical appearance. Her father's haggling over her dowry, however, disappoints her, since her father is, as she emphasizes, the only man that matters to her. The wedding is mentioned in passing, but the anguish with which Herz takes leave of her father is elaborated in detail. The detached third-person narrative about "the young couple" and the "fifteen year old wife" intensifies the impression of alienation (25–26).

As in Glikl's *Zikhroynes*, married life is conceived of as a phase of individuation. Herz becomes increasingly critical of her husband and less willing to comply with Jewish customs. She begins by shirking the dress code (35). She also liberates herself from emotional constraints by giving up trying to fall in love with her husband; she does not consider him attractive and detests his irony (27). Resigning herself to life without romance, she comes to appreciate Herz's social skills and turns to his young friends for inspiration. Supported by him, she decides to host a salon.

Having established her narrative identity, Herz proceeds to describe her salon, at which point her text splits up into a collection of articles about prominent personalities in which Dorothea Veit Schlegel occupies the most prominent position (53ff.). As an old friend of the Mendelssohns, Herz is in a position to provide a comprehensive portrait of her friend and comment on Dorothea's divorce. In conjunction with this event, Herz expresses her complete support for her friend, condemning the laws that restrict a woman's right to decide the course of her own life, with no less determination than was later displayed by Fanny Lewald. Yet, Herz is far less outspoken when it comes to her own private affairs; she discloses neither her feelings nor her friendships with men. Be it that she lacks the language of passion, she shies away from intimate revelations and focuses on the social and political arena

as her topic.[20] Although she claims that women are uniquely qualified
to observe nuances and feelings, her salon was a forum for political debate (158). Indeed, her observations about the American and the French
Revolutions as well as her discussion of the rebellion against the Enlightenment and French influences during the Napoleonic Wars show
her to be a competent political and social critic (185, 156–57). It is therefore surprising that she fails to comprehend the political implications
of the enthusiasm for rediscovered Germanic literature—courtly songs
and medieval epics—in light of German nationalism. Just as naively as
she observes the new nationalist fervor does she welcome the activities
of the German freedom fighters, and she hardly mentions the dangers
of anti-Judaism and the "Hep-Hep" riots, the pogroms of 1819.[21]

At the age of thirty-four, Brenna Mendelssohn Veit became the center of public attention as the result of her affair with Friedrich Schlegel,
whom she had met at Herz's salon. The relationship of a Jewish wife and
mother with a poet nine years her junior was compromising in legal and
social terms. To fend off financial ruin, Moses Mendelssohn's daughter
had to work as a translator and critic in the circle of August Wilhelm
and Caroline Schlegel, and she collaborated with Schlegel on numerous
projects.[22] Supposedly to support herself and her lover, but probably
just as much to display her linguistic and literary competence, she wrote
a Romantic novel, a fragment, entitled *Florentin*.[23] Although the work
appeared under Friedrich Schlegel's name, Dorothea Veit's authorship
was a generally known fact. Her baptism and her remarriage immediately thereafter in 1804 mark her retreat into the private sphere as a devout Catholic.[24]

Although limited in scope, Veit's novel, with its subtle timbre, represents a milestone in the history of German-Jewish women's literature.[25]
Following Schlegel's theory of Romantic literature as progressive universal poetry, *Florentin* blends prose and poetry, seemingly in an attempt
to create the aphysical, ahistorical panorama that characterizes the prose
works of Novalis, Tieck, and Brentano. However, her work lacks the
transcendental dimensions, the yearning for death and eternity of the
earlier Romantics, and the sentimentality of the later Romantics. *Florentin* disappointed particularly those readers who had expected the work
to be a feminine counterpart to and perhaps a continuation of Schlegel's
Lucinde, revealing a woman Romantic's experience of love, marriage,
and poetry. While both novels focus on gender roles, androgyny, and

romance in a world of artists and beautiful women, *Florentin* reads almost like a rebuttal of *Lucinde,* steering clear of the titillating discourse on physical love that caused the latter's notoriety.

The intrigues, duels, and costumes of *Florentin* suggest a Renaissance, rather than a medieval, setting (Weissberg 1987, 231). The departure from the Romantic myth of the alluring Middle Ages in conjunction with the motif of transience is part of a hidden Jewish subtext. Leaving his Mediterranean country in search of a new life in America, Florentin, a young man of obscure origins, recalls Christopher Columbus, who, according to some sources, was of Jewish background. On that level, the figure of Florentin functions as a cipher for the expelled Jews in search of a new life in America, a more auspicious place than their European home countries. Contrary to the Romantic quest for the legendary *Blaue Blume,* Florentin's travels must be understood in concrete terms; they presumably take Veit's protagonist to a new continent, but not necessarily to a higher spiritual plane. Without a trace of Friedrich Schlegel's transcendental sensualism and his esoteric speculations about the nature of love and poetry, Veit does create a rarified atmosphere by borrowing freely, if not carelessly, from Classical and Romantic literature.[26] Elaborate panoramas and interiors, alluring female bodies, and male chivalry evoke a golden era with human interaction evolving unencumbered by the material cares of middle-class life with which the author, herself an outsider to the world of glamour, was only too familiar.

The trappings reminiscent of the picaresque, gothic, and educational novel serve to test the characters' progress as if in a laboratory; thus Veit's plot develops somewhat predictably: encounters are staged to teach individuals necessary lessons or to unite couples destined for one another. Indeed, those who belong to the privileged Gentile society move seemingly effortlessly from one rarified idyll to the next, but like the author herself, Florentin is foiled by external and psychological factors from attaining emotional and social stability. His goal, achieving integration, is so far out of reach from a Jewish and a woman's point of view, it cannot even be visualized. Florentin's never-ending search encodes both the Jewish fate and the situation of women under patriarchy.

Devices to help the spiraling plot along include the discovery of letters, a reflection of the letter culture in which Veit participated. These elements are employed with considerable virtuosity, but they do not emulate the teleology of the *bildungsroman*—in part, *Florentin,* with its conflicting discourses, reads like a satire on Goethe's *Wilhelm Meister.* It is difficult to determine whether Veit intended to write a fashionable Romantic fragment or if she was unable to complete her novel in the absence of a German-Jewish narrative tradition, as seems to have been the case with Heine's *Rabbi von Bacharach* (D. C. G. Lorenz 1992b, 16). In either case, the conventional "happy" ending, the protagonist's marriage and his integration into society, does not occur.

For German-Jewish authors, the repressed Jewish reality is of equal importance as the Gentile world portrayed. The Jewish subtext with its silences and hidden meaning is an integral part of their works—since the beginning of German-Jewish discourse, Jewish authors have made use of silence. In the post-Holocaust era, the impossibility of articulating the unspeakable has taken on special urgency. The tension in works by Jewish authors is often caused by the antithetical relationship between the author's language and the language of the general public, the private and the official medium of social interaction. Except in the most elusive way, Veit avoids Jewish topics. Instead of revealing the world of which she had firsthand knowledge, she turns to Gentile discursive models to construct an imaginary literary universe seemingly detached from the reality that she wants to elude. By virtue of its overcompensation, *Florentin,* rather than being proof of Veit's integration into the Gentile world, is evidence of the opposite. Having transcended the stages of letter writing, criticism, and translation, Veit demonstrates that she can "pass" as a German poet, as a novelist, and even as a male author. In other words, this novel by a Jewish woman trying to assimilate herself must be read as a literary and cultural apprenticeship work, hence the adherence to traditional patterns and the lack of originality. But in spite of the less-than-fascinating plot, the little novel holds its own in the author's target language, and it surpasses by far the literary attempts of the majority of Veit's Gentile contemporaries.

The need to create a reality antithetical to the author's own experience, such as the one represented in *Florentin,* reveals the degree of repression required of Jews wishing to successfully assimilate themselves. The latent anxiety that permeates Veit's seemingly harmonious text is more intense than the artfully created suspense in Schlegel's *Lucinde* because it stems from actual inner contradictions. Set in a Gentile environment and constructed exclusively from components of Gentile discourses, the journey of Veit's Florentin through a Christian never-never land is pure fantasy.[27]

The conversations of Veit's characters are removed from ordinary discourse and no less contrived than Adalbert Stifter's prose. Their manners and behavior are concocted from literary conventions alone.[28] Veit, the Jewish woman seeking integration into her lover's society, and Stifter, the teacher from Bohemia who wanted to educate Austria (1962, 239), composed an overly perfect language removed from colloquial and literary German. It is precisely this language that introduces a utopian perspective into Veit's novel, which otherwise displays no utopian elements. Heinrich Heine faced a similar dilemma as Veit when he wrote *Der Rabbi von Bacharach* in 1824–25, a novel intended to enlighten the public about Jewish culture. Twenty years after the publication of *Florentin,* there was still no language available in which to communicate the Jewish experience: its oppression by Christian culture and the hope for liberation from the diaspora existence. Also, for his purpose the educational novel was an unsuitable vehicle. Even when a German-Jewish epic tradition formed at the time of Philippson's 1837 work *Marannen* and Riespart's 1841 work *Die Juden und die Kreuzfahrer,* the tension between the content and the form of Jewish fiction remained.

Whereas Heine in his novel fragment raised doubt about the future of Jews in a hostile European environment, Veit leaves no room for such speculation in her literary universe. Rather, she suggests that among enlightened, educated people mutual understanding is possible—if not in Europe, then in America, thereby deemphasizing the categories that make her most vulnerable, nationality and religion. Heine's fragment, on the other hand, reveals that a closer examination cannot avoid exposing the rift between Jews and Gentiles. For a woman about to take the ultimate step toward integration, these facts would have been too distressing to articulate.

The Creation of Space and the Invention of Language
(Rahel Levin Varnhagen)

Although Rahel Levin Varnhagen's work consists primarily of notes and letters, it has attracted more attention than Henriette Herz's autobiography and Dorothea Mendelssohn Veit Schlegel's novel. Like Herz, Rahel was a chronicler of her time, but her works, overwhelming by their sheer volume, explore the author/protagonist's subjective sphere. She delineates her activities and perceptions in such detail that critics have referred to Rahel's production as a life as text.[29] According to Barbara Hahn, Rahel's work documents an entire communicative network through which the most diverse persons were connected (1993, 386). Rahel's writings illuminate the gentrification process of women on the margins in unparalleled detail by presenting herself as the producer, the material, and the topic of her texts to the reading public.

Because of its apparent authenticity, Rahel's work appeals to a wide variety of audiences—Her notes and correspondences can be interpreted alternately as a Jewish woman's path to assimilation, as the making of a poet, and as a woman's personal confessions. They are also an excellent source of information on the Romantic circle of poets and Romantic literature, to which another Jewish author, Heine, devoted a sizeable treatise, *Die romantische Schule* (1979, 121–244). Rahel's work, furthermore, is a significant document of the salon era, the Wars of Liberation, and, following those, the Young German and Biedermeier periods. Her apparent candor also appeals to male readers seeking insight into the female psyche, a favorite topic of eighteenth- and nineteenth-century expert and dilettante studies.

Precisely because she took risks, Rahel became the most exposed Jewish salonnière. As a result of her visibility, she experienced the reaction against Jewish emancipation and early feminism after 1807 more immediately than other women, but her fame did not fade before the 1840s, with their hostility toward women intellectuals (Schweikert 1983, 24).[30] In fact, the recurring elimination of Jewish and women authors from the annals of literary history confirms Hannah Arendt's opinion that individuals like Rahel remained outsiders rather than making inroads into the mainstream, advancing from the status of a pariah to the equally precarious one of a parvenu (Arendt 1962, 162; Susman 1929, 97).

Like Henriette Herz, Rahel also suffered from lifelong anxiety as a result of her existential insecurity. It is impossible to separate her frailty (in her letters she mentions infections, rheumatism, and nervous disorders) and her physical disability (like Rosa Luxemburg and Veza Canetti, Rahel suffered from a hip deformity) from her situation as a Jewish woman and a bohemian; at least, such is the way in which an established Prussian author, Theodor Fontane, viewed Rahel and her circles. Contrary to Herz, who problematizes her beauty, Rahel laments

her ugliness and expresses self-loathing on numerous occasions (1983, 9:
97). As Margarete Susman observed, Rahel projected an air of serenity
and malleability that concealed her unresolved conflicts, but the energy
she expanded in order to appear in control seems to have prevented her
from developing her full potential as a writer (1929, 97).

The name Rahel connotes the synthetic public persona constructed
from Rahel Levin Varnhagen's activities as a salon hostess, letter writer,
and conversationalist, as well as the response to her works and her public image. Best known by her biblical first name with all of its connotations, Rahel was iconized as a Jew and a woman, regardless of the
fact that she rarely debated Jewish topics, as Gabriel Riesser noted with
some misgiving. Gentile critics such as Wolfgang Menzel, on the other
hand, considered her the epitome of Jewishness and reproached her for
her lack of German patriotism (1983, 10:143–46). Rahel's name changes
and her conversion to Christianity may have added to her inner turmoil, as Hannah Arendt argues, but she continued to be perceived as a
Jew. According to Konrad Feilchenfeldt, Rahel's baptism did not oblit-
erate her Jewish upbringing, a view confirmed by the recurring motif of
Arendt's biography of Rahel, "One does not escape Jewishness" (1983,
154–55). This assertion applies to the dilemma of the critic confronting
National Socialism as well as to that of Arendt's subject, Rahel, facing
German nationalism and nineteenth-century anti-Semitism (176ff.).

Much of Rahel's efforts were devoted to defining and positioning
herself in order to create a situation that would allow her to pursue
her social and literary goals. Patsch correctly terms baptism a step on
the way toward emancipation, and he quotes Rahel's statement in a
letter to Theodor Robert: "People like us cannot afford to be Jewish"
(1991, 160). To achieve this purpose, she needed both the criticism and
the approval of other individuals who would encourage her to explore
situations other than her own, hence the "dialogue character" of her
correspondence.[31] At one point, when her attempt to reach out to the
world seemed at an impasse, Rahel appears to have wanted to end her
flight from self and to take refuge in a Gentile identity, but neither
her circumstances nor her character allowed her to do so. Contrary to
Dorothea Schlegel, Rahel remained in the limelight because she lacked
her friend's adaptability and because her mate did not possess the prominence of Friedrich Schlegel. Rahel's half-hearted attempts to conform
to August Varnhagen's expectations of her added to the incongruities

in her life, but in contrast to Dorothea Schlegel, she continued to write (Schweikert 1983, 24).

The eldest daughter of Markus Levin, a Berlin merchant, Rahel was an autodidact. A ravenous reader and a compulsive writer, she acquired an astounding virtuosity in German and an excellent command of other European languages.[32] Already her early letters reveal her estrangement from Jewish culture and her family, particularly from her father, whom Henriette Herz described as a brilliant despot (1984, 42). Propelled by her alienation, Rahel engaged in extensive correspondences that helped her to overcome her isolation. Language was her primary tool to explore reality and create her own identity. A half-orphan at nineteen, Rahel established a salon at her parents' house that attracted Romantic poets, philosophers, political figures, and socialites, among them Pauline Wiesel, an adventuress famed for her beauty, and her lover, the notorious Prussian prince, Louis Ferdinand. Although Gentile upper-class men, including the prince and the conservative Viennese diplomat Friedrich Gentz, admired Rahel, her hopes to marry a Gentile man came to naught several times—her unhappy affairs with the Prussian aristocrat Karl von Finkenstein and the secretary to the Spanish ambassador, Raphael D'Urquijo, both of whom gave in to family and peer pressures to leave Rahel, just to mention two.

Rahel's Jewishness, her fame, and her intellectual superiority prevented her from entering into a union with any of these attractive, conservative, and anything but brilliant men. This factor is overlooked by critics who question Rahel's motives for marrying August Varnhagen in 1814, immediately after she was christened Friederike Antonie Robert-Tornow, a name she had already used before her baptism (Patsch 1991, 156). Since Varnhagen's talents were less stellar, critics have ascribed purely pragmatic motives to Rahel. Considering that despite some scandalous (at the time) exceptions, marriages of convenience were still the rule, this would in no way diminish Rahel's stature. The predilection for romance on the part of Rahel's contemporaries found its outlet most commonly in literature, but not in life. Especially in light of Jewish convention, it would hardly be shocking if Rahel had married out of practical considerations. A closer examination, however, reveals that Varnhagen, a man thirteen years Rahel's junior, was precisely the kind of partner Rahel preferred, discounting perhaps his somewhat obscure background. Indeed, there is a pattern of involvement with younger men on the part of Jewish women intellectuals; for example, Dorothea Schlegel, Henriette Herz, and Else Lasker-Schüler, to name only a few. Rahel's love letters to Varnhagen reveal the affection of an experienced woman for a younger man, not unlike Else Lasker-Schüler's attachment to Herwath Walden. In both instances, the women forged their husbands' careers and public identities, while the men acted as their wives' managers and promoters.[33]

Varnhagen appreciated Rahel's creativity. Most importantly, however, he was not an anti-Semite. During the years of the Napoleonic occupation, political clubs called *Christlich-Deutsche Tischgesellschaft* (Christian German Dinner Society), which catered exclusively to Gentile men, replaced the salons. Faced with the demise of her salon and the culture in which it had prospered, Rahel attached herself to Varnhagen with greater determination than to her previous lovers. Her career, threatened by the fanatic nationalism, with the French and Jews as its prime targets, was endorsed by prominent personalities such as Achim von Arnim and Heinrich von Kleist. Without her salon, Rahel, who was thirty-five years old at the time, faced an uncertain future (Gerhardt 1983, 25). Clearly, her existence was stabilized as a result of her union with August Varnhagen von Ense, but her conversion and her new status as a man's appendage disturbed her. Eventually she established a second salon in Berlin. It was successful but lacked the aura of the first. When Heine visited Rahel in 1821, he bestowed the highest praise upon her, calling her salon his *Vaterland* and proclaiming, "*j'appartiens à Madame Varnhagen*." Nonetheless, he was a rare guest (Gerhardt 1983, 29). Like von Arnstein and Herz, Rahel became a living monument and her salon an institution, acclaimed by many, but no longer a factor in the current debates.

Rather than Rahel's best-known correspondences, her letters to other Jews, including her family, written in Yiddish or Jewish German, reveal the author's private thoughts and show the far-reaching linguistic and conceptual territory Rahel had to cover in order to accommodate her Gentile readers. Most of her letters addressed to non-Jews are carefully composed for public consumption, although they project an ostentatious spontaneity.[34] Some may seem passionate and even mystical at times, but they are as public as Rahel's salon. Rahel's most intimate letters are addressed to her siblings and Jewish friends—for example, her affectionate, but intellectually insignificant, notes to her sister Rose.[35]

With David Veit, a friend from her youth, she shares her thoughts about the plight of women, Jews, and converts—issues that Rahel generally does not discuss with Gentiles.[36] Overall, these parts of Rahel's correspondence confirm Schweikert's assertion that in the nineteenth century, no one could "resign from Judaism as one might accept baptism and forget it again" (1983, 26–27).

Before Rahel addresses the plight of Jews in Germany, she examines her predicament as a woman. At age twenty-two, in a letter to Veit, she voices bitter protest against her seclusion as a woman:

Is it a woman's fault that she is *also* a human being? If my mother had been good-hearted and tough enough and had sensed of how I would turn out, she should have suffocated me here in the dust upon my first cry. A *powerless* being who supposedly *does not mind* staying home *like this,* and who would be opposed by heaven, earth, humans and cattle if she wanted to get out (and has thoughts like any other human being), but is forced to stay home, and who has to swallow all sorts of reproaches under the pretext of *reason,* when she moves about and is noticed. (Varnhagen 1979, 2:19, 2 April 1793)

Rahel often complains about the self-control demanded of women and compares their dependence on men to a prison term (Gerhardt 1983, 9–10). In her opinion, the gender segregation creates two coterritorial nations living under a different legislature, and she declares marriage synonymous to the "trade with black slaves" and war. In Rahel's view, women are undereducated second-class human beings who must be constantly on their guard and who are driven to dishonesty unless they dull their senses and intellect (1983, 1:259, 312; Isselstein 1993, 93–94). She also exposes the unrealistic images of women in literature, characterizing the unconventional women characters of Goethe as products of male imagination (1983, 1:316, 359).

According to Rahel, matriarchy is the only solution to the existing impasse; families ought to be headed by mothers, and children should be named after their female ancestors. Rather than by the fashionable use of Amazon myths in the literature of Schiller and Kleist, Rahel's antipatriarchal sentiments are inspired by personal experience and by the Jewish tradition of matrilineage. In her tongue-in-cheek interpretation of Christianity, for example, Rahel applies Jewish concepts to the Gospel. She characterizes Jesus, who "only has a mother," as the descendent of a matriarchal family, and she quips that matriarchy, rather than Christian patriarchy, has the capacity to cope with extramarital pregnancy (1983, 1: 19). The latter remarks, written in 1820, six years after her baptism, show that Rahel remained aloof to the dogma of Christ's divinity, but that she did relate on a personal level to the situations portrayed in the New Testament, reshaping them according to her own experience (1:43).

In her letter of 2 November 1793, Rahel outlines a strategy to overcome her plight as a woman. She decides to study, if only "a little bit," confident that knowledge will provide freedom (1979, 2:22). Her frequently voiced despondency of the following years suggests that she had to overcome considerable obstacles before her triumph over her anti-intellectual home environment: "I hardly ever go out any more; because no air is good enough for me, any society where *I* can go, *hateful,* the comedy is disgusting, so is the concert" (53, 22 March 1795). Eventually, Rahel's struggle leads to her partial acceptance of her gender role, but she remains critical of patriarchal structures. With growing experience, Rahel comes to consider women superior to men; according to her, they are closer to realizing humanity's full potential than males (204). Strangely oblivious to the sexism inherent in his views, she later becomes an admirer of Saint-Simon, the guru of the Young German movement, who proclaimed sexual liberation and the "emancipation of the flesh" without offering solutions to the exploitation of women for cheap labor and prostitution.

While wrestling with the problem of gender, Rahel discovered that her bond with Veit as a Jew outweighed their gender differences, as the following statement made in 1798 expresses: "Only the galley-slaves know one another" (57). Subsequently, Rahel's letters display an increasing awareness of attacks on other Jews and of the fact that anti-Semitism is the reason for many of the setbacks she encountered.[37] Yet, her passionate struggle with her own identity reveals that she considered her Jewish background as a "private misfortune," and she remained indifferent to the class issues involved in assimilation (Arendt 1962, 144–45). Like Heine, she spurns excessive patriotism and the concept of a national character and dismisses the word *Vaterland* as an empty phrase, hoping that the nations of Europe will recognize the barbarism inherent in chauvinism (1983, 3:77, November 1822; also 2:599). In an era of nationalism, Rahel's individualistic pacifist ideals and her cosmopolitanism prove increasingly inopportune as they deepen her outsider status at a time of virulent nationalism.

The full extent of Rahel's marginality, as well as her loyalty for others in situations similar to hers, is revealed in her correspondence with another Jewish woman, the banker's daughter Pauline Wiesel, née César.[38] The two women began to exchange letters in 1808, and their friendship lasted until one year before Rahel's death. Rahel entrusted Wiesel, who was neither an intellectual nor a poet, with her best-kept secrets.[39] Already at an early age, Wiesel was known as the "Fair Helen" of Berlin and a "femme fatale," whom Fanny Lewald, not without malice, described later as a pixie, boundlessly energetic and involved in countless affairs. Indeed, Wiesel was a scandalous figure because of her involvement with Gentile men who desired her physically but who had no intention of marrying her (Varnhagen and Wiesel 1978, 90). While still a married woman, but already the mistress of Friedrich von Gentz, Wiesel took up with Prince Louis Ferdinand, a musician, warrior, and ladies' man. After his death, she embarked on a life of travel since her notoriety made it impossible for her to live in Berlin.[40]

Against her husband's wishes—he claimed, among other things, that Wiesel had tried to seduce him—Rahel remained loyal to Wiesel until a misunderstanding ended their relationship late in her life (Arendt 1962, 169).[41] There are several other incidents to show that Rahel valued her relationships with women at least as highly as her friendships with men, but the playful tone of her correspondence with Wiesel (both women use extravagant and funny terms of endearment such as *Ralle* and *Pölle*) implies a deep mutual trust. In their discussion of serious problems, sobriety and directness prevail. Only in her letters to her sister Rose does Rahel exhibit a similar affection: She addresses Wiesel as a comrade, almost as an accomplice. Always quick to defend her friend against gossip, Rahel objects to Wiesel's being vilified or treated as a cult object (Varnhagen and Wiesel 1978, 103).

Wiesel's and Rahel's letters also reveal why the two women were drawn to each other: both were adherents of rationalism—Wiesel, for example, adores Voltaire and interprets her own life with a wit and an irony that is modeled after his (16, 107ff.). In addition, the dashing extrovert Wiesel seems to have found her natural counterpart in the introverted, sensitive Rahel. Contrary to her famous friend, Wiesel was caught up in external phenomena, fascinated by people, parties, and fashions, while Rahel makes only occasional references to her environment, not even when she finds herself in spectacular cities such as Vienna or Prague. Rahel processes her experiences through her moods and her physical sensations, whereas Wiesel relies on her eyes, through which she connects with the material world (Laschke 1988, 3). Rahel writes in order to overcome the distance between her correspondents and herself, but Wiesel lives in the here and now. Hence her approach is descriptive and whimsical.

There could be no greater contrast than between Wiesel's fast-changing moods and topics and Rahel's intensity. Rahel admires Wiesel's worldly experience and her courage to act out her fantasies, whereas Rahel, in turn, confines herself to imaginary feats. Conversely, Wiesel is in awe of Rahel's analytic abilities (Varnhagen and Wiesel 1978, 12–13). Yet, both kinds of activity, Rahel's intellectual pursuits and Wiesel's restless wandering, must be understood as the symptoms of a profound alienation, as is evident from both women's fantasies. Wiesel, claiming that it is only her desire to love and be loved that prevents her from following her domestic calling, asserts that she would rather be a housewife and mother than a courtesan: "Everyone made me into his woman the way he loved and desired her, and I allowed myself to be made without having the strength to stand up for myself and act; I was already corrupted in my cradle and the little goodness I possess they could not take from me—I was born with it" (53). Rahel voices similar longings, frequently expressing frustration about the lack of stability in her life. This missing element is intimately connected to her predicament as a Jewish woman intellectual, which she reveals in conjunction with specifically Jewish topics only to other Jews. For example, her harsh criticism of an acquaintance, Rebecca Friedländer, who changed her name to Regina Frohberg, and her disapproval of Friedländer's ostentatious behavior, expressed in a letter to Wiesel, suggest that Rahel herself must have had misgivings about her own name changes and position (Arendt 1962, 86–87).

Common experience and family ties pervade Rahel's correspondence with her brother Ludwig Robert, who shares her qualms about apostasy, including his own, after which he continues to be profoundly affected by Jewish concerns. The critical events that caused brother and sister to redefine their position concerning Judaism and their relationship to Gentile culture were the "Hep-Hep" riots. In his letter of August 1819, among other documents, Ludwig Robert articulates his outrage about the violent anti-Semitic unrests (1979, 4:388; also 495ff., 4 April 1819; 500ff., 22 August 1819). Stirred by her brother's compelling analysis of the mob activities he witnessed, Rahel reveals her own anxieties.

Rahel's reactions differ markedly from those of Henriette Herz insofar as she has no illusions about the Jew-hatred of the German public, including intellectuals and academics. She knows that, notwithstanding Germany's reputation as a civilized nation, there is an atavistic side to the country of Lessing and Goethe. Rather than comparing the pogroms to an epidemic, as does Ludwig Robert, likening them to the St. Vitus's dance,[42] she is aware of the historical specificity of the events and regards them as a direct reflection of her time. On 29 August 1819, she writes about her "infinite" sadness "because of the Jews." Her choice of words indicates a distance from the Jewish community, revealing the double bind caused by her baptism and her marriage, both of which link her to the party of the perpetrators. Yet, the tone of her letters reveals that she feels a close affinity to those who were hurt, humiliated, and rendered homeless.

Rahel's personal dilemma deepened over time. Her declaration that she felt safest in Berlin, where most of the local Jews were baptized, married to non-Jews, or were members of the military, indicates that she considered assimilation the only way to overcome anti-Judaism. At the same time, her differentiation between the local Jews and the unassimilated recent immigrants shows her awareness of the complexity of the situation. Moreover, her reference to converts as Jews draws into question the possibility of assimilation altogether. Her summary of the crimes perpetrated by the German public reads like a synopsis of the history of "Toleration" and an announcement of its failure:

They want to *keep* them, but in order to torment and despise them, in order to insult them as "Judenmauschel"; in order to make small, measly bargains, to kick them and throw them downstairs. This vicious, mean, poisonous, through and through morbid mentality is what hurts me so deeply, down to the terror which makes the heart cold. *I* know my country! *Unfortunately.* A lamentable Cassandra! I have said for *three* years: the Jews will be attacked; I have witnesses. *This* is the German revolutionary spirit. And why? Because they are the most well-behaved, well-meaning, peace-loving people in awe of their authorities. They do not *know* what to demand. (1979, 4:504, Rahel's letter to Ludwig Robert, 29 August 1819)

Although Rahel blames attacks against the Jews on the Catholic *renouveau,* she senses that hatred of this magnitude cannot be inspired by religion alone; she admits that the perpetrators are hardly religious people. Neither are they primitive and uneducated. Rahel has great difficulty coming to terms with the fact that the very people who advocate anti-Semitism were formerly her guests, including the poets Achim von Arnim and Clemens Brentano. Her letter about the 1819 pogroms is one of the few instances in which she resorts to religious rhetoric, expressing a sense of powerlessness too profound to bear without miracles or an escape from reality. Confronted with the news about the destruction of the Jewish communities, she invokes God as her last resort and chooses hope as the only viable principle *in extremis* (1979, 4:504ff., letter of 29 August 1819).

By documenting her successes and failures, and by exploring her own and her contemporaries' thoughts and feelings, Rahel was able to create a Jewish woman's voice with which to speak to her friends and to the public. By doing so, she laid the foundation for a Jewish discourse in German. Her vocabulary and diction by far exceeded the capacities of her native Yiddish to express a position of biculturalism, and they expanded the parameters of the German language to include Jewish concerns. Without her pioneering effort, German-Jewish literature such as Heine's *Rabbi von Bacharach* and Lewald's *Jenny* are inconceivable. Rahel's salon was the motherland of the following generation of Jewish authors. She set the pattern for a new kind of Jewish existence in the postemancipation era, that of the autonomous middle-class author, the *freie Schriftstellerin,* and she became the role model for countless women writers. Encouraged by her example, they emancipated themselves from their families or husbands. In this way, Rahel made the achievements of later authors such as Fanny Lewald possible.

2

At the Crossroads

Emancipation, Feminism, and Revolution

Rahel Levin Varnhagen died in 1833, one year after Johann Wolfgang Goethe. With her death, the formative era in the development of German-Jewish writing came to a close. When Fanny Lewald (1811–89) published her first novel, *Clementine,* in 1842, the linguistic and conceptual foundations with which to explore and criticize her position within Gentile society had been established, and authors of the second and third generation of acculturated Jews were active participants in the political and cultural debates of their time. They no longer relied on the relative protection of elitist circles and salons but addressed an anonymous mass audience. Their topics and style place them in the vanguard, while their points of view as Jewish authors distinguish them from the mainstream of the late Romantics, the Young Germans and realists.[1]

The novelist, essayist, and autobiographer Fanny Lewald was the highest-paid and best-selling German woman writer of her time—she may well be *the* German-Jewish author who conquered the public space from which Jewish women could speak to Jews and Gentiles alike. Her protagonists' problems caught the interest of a diverse readership, particularly since her prose texts lacked the exclusivity of earlier Jewish women's writing, such as Rahel's soul-searching correspondences, Henriette Herz's examination of intellectual elite, and Dorothea Veit Schlegel's immersion into Romantic aesthetics, all of which required specialized audiences. Lewald utilized accessible prose genres—the novel, the travelogue, and autobiography. The extent to which she is part of the mainstreaming process of German-Jewish prose is evident from the fact that unlike Heinrich Heine and her female predecessors, Lewald succeeded in writing complete novels about male and female Jewish protagonists in Germany. Her characters reflect a Jewish woman writer's effective appropriation of the German cultural discourse.

37

Influenced by the educational novel, Lewald modified the established conventions according to her own experience and transformed the patterns of dominant literature to reflect the double marginalization of Jewish women. In the mid–nineteenth century Lewald was already a key figure in the construction of what Deleuze and Guattari termed a "minor literature" with reference to Franz Kafka (1986, 17). To familiarize the general public with the plight of Jews and women, Lewald portrayed the situation of German-Jews in the objective arena of the auctorial novel. Her straightforward prose style is free of eccentric mannerisms, and in her plots she refrains from flights of imagination. Holding democratic views and addressing the general public, Lewald has the appearance of being more modern than Rahel, but ultimately both authors struggled with the same issues: Jewish and female identity. Lewald confronted her Gentile readership with the issues of anti-Semitism and misogyny directly, whereas Rahel excluded them from her more public texts.

Lewald witnessed the political developments leading up to the revolution of 1848 without any illusions that the issues of women's rights and Jewish citizenship would be resolved with any speed.[2] She knew that, like the French Revolution, the unsuccessful revolution of 1848 was a bourgeois revolution against the privileges of the aristocracy. The *Communist Manifesto,* which introduced the exploitation of the proletariat as a revolutionary issue, was an isolated instance and had no immediate impact. Later, the Social Democratic Party was the only political organization to support the cause of women and to reject anti-Semitism. Yet, following Marx's views, it considered these problems to be secondary, mere *Nebenfragen.* To complicate matters further, even within the feminist movements of Lewald's era there was no room for the concerns of Jewish women.

Lewald's works also display revolutionary tendencies that are, however, distinct from the activities of middle-class and aristocratic liberals, whose misogyny, nationalism, and anti-Semitism she exposes. Contrary to Rahel, Lewald did not consider being a Jew and a woman a personal misfortune; rather, she held the national community responsible for the suffering it inflicted upon certain individuals and groups. Aware of the wider ideological ramifications of antifeminism and anti-Semitism, she regarded them as political problems and class issues. Her central ideas evolved from her firsthand experience of the widespread prejudices against Jews and women on the part of the Gentile majority. She passionately endorsed the bourgeois ideal of individual freedom, which, for her, included equal rights for women and men, as well as for Jews and Gentiles.

Lewald's style, often criticized as unfeminine and journalistic (Rogols-Siegel [1988, 20] calls it "direct, didactic, and hard-hitting"), but not necessarily her intellectual positions, was inspired by the controversial Young German movement. In opposition to mainstream liberalism, with representatives such as Heinrich Laube and Karl Gutzkow, Lewald rejected pan-Germanism. Convinced that the oppression of women and Jews was in the interests of the aristocracy and the religious establishment, she was critical of organized Christianity. A confirmed rationalist, Lewald did not believe in a personal God, and she does not tire at exposing the self-serving character of conventional morality, the concept of the immortality of the soul, and life after death. She portrays religion as standing in the way of her protagonists' development, as, for example, in *Jenny.* On the basis of her own experiences, Lewald characterizes Jewish apostasy as an act of convenience. After her baptism, she continued to feel connected to other Jews for social and historical reasons. Considering religion a private matter, she defended the right of Judaism to exist alongside Christianity as an issue of personal and religious freedom.

Feminism and Jewish Emancipation (Fanny Lewald)

The personal development of Fanny Lewald resembled that of earlier Jewish women writers; she was educated by her father, David Marcus, a man leery of traditional training for girls because of its emphasis on housework and needlework and its superficial exposure to languages, literature, and music. He provided his daughter with a first-rate scientific and philosophical education but otherwise expected her to accept the established gender roles (Lewis 1992). Königsberg, Lewald's native city, was known as a center of Enlightenment, but the popular superstitions of the Middle Ages were anything but conquered when Fanny Lewald was born in 1811.[3]

Fanny Lewald had attended public school, but her father disenrolled her at the age of fourteen because, as a Jew, she had been terrorized and excluded from social activities. When in 1831 the Jews of Königsberg were accused of causing an epidemic, the Marcus family, afraid of popular wrath, assumed the less Jewish-sounding surname Lewald, which other relatives had adopted earlier under similar circumstances (Rogols-Siegel 1988, 17).[4] Living at home, Fanny suffered from isolation and alienation. Her mother, intimidated by the anti-Jewish activities around her, minimized her Jewishness wherever possible. Although Lewald's brothers received permission to convert after the pogroms of 1819, Fanny was prevented from doing so by her father because he believed that a woman's religion should be determined by her husband. Lewald, on the other hand, was attracted to Protestantism. Influenced by the views of Hegel and Fichte, she considered it the most progressive religion in world historical terms. In addition, the influence of German Idealism is also apparent from her admiration of Prussian militarism and the heroes of the Napoleonic Wars in her earlier years.

The tensions between the disparate discursive patterns informing Lewald's early works are reflected in a textual openness that shapes her texts of the prerevolutionary era. After 1848 her outlook changed considerably. Lewald acknowledged the reactionary role played by the Protestant clergy, and her travels opened her eyes to the backwardness of Northern Germany as compared to France, Italy, and Austria (1850, 87–104). As a result, she adopted a pacifist and, later, an anticolonial philosophy that led her to criticize Bismarck's power politics and to oppose Prussia's wars against Denmark and Austria.

Although it is true that Henriette Herz and Rahel Varnhagen's generation had laid the foundations for the advancement of future generations of Jewish women writers, women intellectuals continued to face severe problems, particularly concerning their private lives. Lewald also had to liberate herself from her family—a domineering father who demanded excellence and a simpleminded, conservative mother who undermined her daughter's literary pursuits. The double bind caused by her parents' divergent expectations is a leitmotif not only in Lewald's work. At the age of sixteen, Fanny Lewald underwent a painful but ultimately liberating experience: she fell in love with the theology student Leopold Bock. This relationship ended because of the objections of the young people's parents, and as a result, Lewald plunged into a life-threatening depression (Rogols-Siegel 1988, 13). After Bock's premature death the following year, in 1828, Lewald obtained permission from her father to convert. It appears that the taking of this official step inspired in Lewald an awareness of her ethnic and cultural heritage: "I was very conscious of the fact that I had carried out a decision, originally made with good faith, love and confidence, with a hypocrisy foreign to me, but I lacked the courage to admit to a mistake and to place myself in direct opposition to those I loved most. I had trespassed against myself out of fear of others and love" (1988, 1:217).

Lewald's work revolves around three major emancipation movements of the nineteenth century, those of Jews, women, and the middle class. Her privileged position as an educated assimilated woman and a professional writer allowed her to introduce the debate on emancipation and women's rights into literature. For the sake of progress and the emancipation of the individual, she called for the abolition of the established moral code and institutions such as marriage and the nuclear family.

With Herz, Rahel, and Heine as her models—she had learned from Herz's realistic approach and from Rahel's introspection and psychological method—Lewald forged her own ideals. In her account of her trip to Paris during the revolution of 1848, she portrays three personalities as emblems of social progress: Heinrich Heine, the German-Jewish author in exile; the feminist George Sand; and the Jewish actress Rachel, a child of the proletariat, whom Lewald describes as "the human form of the Marseillaise, the concept of the fight for freedom turned flesh" (Lewald 1850, 97, 195). Heine, incidentally, shared Lewald's enthusiasm for Rachel.

In addition to the feminist and liberal agenda, there is an unmistakably Jewish aspect to Lewald's choice of heroes. Heine had remained attached to Judaism after his conversion. As Lewald relates, he mentioned to her his daily conversations with "our old Jehova" (110), obviously cognizant of the fact that Christianity and Gentile culture had not become Lewald's home either. Similar to Rahel and her brother Ludwig Robert, Lewald and Heine were both proud and ashamed about diaspora Jewry, as is obvious from the fascination and revulsion they express toward one of Germany's major Jewish centers, Frankfurt. Heine immortalized the ghetto in the partly satirical, partly affectionate second chapter of his novel *Der Rabbi von Bacharach,* and Lewald wrote, deeply touched by the *genius loci* of the same site:

And finally the ghetto!—and if all the rulers in the world had been thrown into misery and sorrow, their tears would not outweigh the tears of sorrow which this unfortunate people shed during two thousand years of servitude and shameful oppression. When

41

we walked through the long, narrow ghetto, when I looked into the yards of these houses tall as towers, glued together like a bee hive, and when I thought Börne passed his youth here, here he was locked up every night like a criminal, and here they refused to open the gate, even during fire emergencies, I shuddered at the inhumanity of the so-called good old days! (1850, 297)

Lewald's emotional commitment and identification, no less than Heine's embarrassed irony, make for different reading than the descriptions of ghetto life by Gentile authors. Bettina von Arnim, for example, approaches the Jewish Lane in Frankfurt from the point of view of a would-be benefactor and a defender of the oppressed, casting herself in the role of the ruler of the Jews (von Arnim 1959, 3:268ff.). Lewald, in contrast, is filled with outrage when she compares the conditions under which Johann Wolfgang Goethe and Ludwig Börne—she knew and admired the latter since childhood—had lived and worked. Familiar with the dismal circumstances of Börne's formative years, she praises his perseverance against almost insurmountable odds and explains his failure to rise to Goethe's lofty heights by the hardship he endured in the ghetto and in exile. In view of the repression of Jewish genius and the century-old Jew-hatred, Lewald has nothing but scorn for the anti-Semitic attacks launched by established German conservatives and liberals against Jewish journalists who, justly dissatisfied with their circumstances, fought in the forefront of the revolution: "And not one of these accusers senses what honor he does the Jews with these words. Yes! Börne and Heine called out to the Germans since the July revolution and earlier: 'We are oppressed like yourselves!'" (Lewald 1850, 298).

Lewald mustered a similar perseverance: she prevailed against patriarchal structures and established herself as a successful author, an intellectual, and a businesswoman; she married the man of her choice and publicized her struggle for personal happiness in her memoirs. Having foiled her father's marriage plans for her, she embarked on a literary campaign against the bourgeois marriages of convenience, partly because of her own experience, partly as a witness to her aunt's dismal marriage.[5] Romantic thinkers such as Schleiermacher, who advocated a woman's right to follow her heart against tradition, women like Caroline Schlegel, who practiced free love, and contemporary utopian social projects were important sources of inspiration for Lewald. Her insistance on a woman's free choice in matters of the heart—she maintains that love is the only admissible basis for marriage—represents not only an endorsement of Romantic and liberal views but also a rebellion against Jewish convention, which had governed the lives of Glikl Hamil and Henriette Herz. Lewald never tired of protesting against the use of women as chattel in business deals negotiated by men.

Lewald became a professional writer in 1839. With the help of one of her relatives, August Lewald, she published short texts and her first novel, *Clementine,* under a pseudonym. In 1843, she ventured to Berlin, where she was introduced to Henriette Herz, the Mendelssohns, and the novelist Therese Bacheracht, Karl Gutzkow's lover. Encouraged by her contacts with women and men of letters and by her own research on the salon era—on Rahel, Dorothea Mendelssohn, Prince Louis Ferdinand, and Friedrich Schlegel—Lewald relinquished her anonymity. In contrast to the novelist Ida Hahn-Hahn, who wrote about the situation of aristocratic women, Lewald argued on the basis of bourgeois values and proposed a liberal program to solve the so-called Women's Question. Having had major obstacles to contend with on her own arduous road to independence, Lewald considered financial independence to be the cornerstone of women's emancipation, and she advocated vocational and professional training for women. To free wives and mothers from housework, which she regarded a form of slavery, she proposed communal kitchens and free child care (Frederiksen 1982).

In *Clementine* Lewald reviews her unhappy entanglement with Leopold Bock and a later disappointment that also involved a Gentile man. Her following novel, *Jenny* (1843), deals with the same topic, but with greater detachment and in a more complex setting.[6] *Jenny* explores personal and social issues in a fictional framework with a considerable number of diverse characters. Already in these two novels, as well as in her diaries, Lewald shows a predilection for documentary writing that she indulges even more in her historical novel *Prinz Louis Ferdinand* (1849), a portrait of Berlin at the time of Rahel's first salon.[7] Here, Lewald pays homage to her forerunners and pursues her sociological and psychological interests. In a penetrating analysis of the relationship between Rahel Varnhagen and Pauline Wiesel, Lewald, not without an occasional hint of envy, expresses her admiration for the Jewish salonnières. Herself uncomfortably situated between two patriarchal societies, Lewald possessed the necessary understanding to depict the mentality of the salonnières and the conflicts they faced. She seems to consider the opportunities created during the social and intellectual fermentation at the beginning of the nineteenth century as superior to those available in her own era.

Lewald's move into a modest apartment in Berlin in 1845 was an important step toward her independence (Rogols-Siegel 1988, 39). So was her journey to Italy soon thereafter, although, upon her father's insistence, she traveled with a chaperone. In Rome Lewald was introduced to the salons of Adele Schopenhauer and Ottilie von Goethe, where she met Adolf Stahr, a professor, a writer, and the headmaster of a school in Oldenburg; he was a married man and the father of five children. Lewald lived with him, although his wife refused to grant him a divorce, until, finally, in 1855 he was free to marry her. This relationship is chronicled in "Das Buch Adolf," the second part of Lewald's *Meine Lebensgeschichte* ([1866] 1988). There are some striking similarities between Rahel Varnhagen's and Fanny Lewald's biographies and their literary production, most notably their relationships with their husbands. Adolf Stahr, like August Varnhagen, was less gifted than his lover and later wife; he also became the adviser and manager for Lewald, whose work comprises countless works of fiction, essays, letters, and autobiographical writing. It is in her account about her journey to France, *Erinnerungen aus dem Jahre 1848,* that Lewald discovered her autobiographical voice, which made her memoirs, *Meine Lebensgeschichte* ([1866] 1988) one of the foremost of nineteenth-century women's autobiographies.

Lewald's primary topic was the oppression of women and Jews. In *Jenny* she explores the experience of growing up Jewish in early nineteenth-century Germany. The tragic consequences of the relationships between young Jewish and Gentile men and women, torn between their desires and the expectations of their elders, are the problem at hand. The fictional framework enables Lewald to discuss these issues without exposing herself directly, and the autobiographical elements ensure the impression of authenticity for situations and characters as well as the larger social setting. The presence of several different plots not only allows subjective and objective concerns to intersect but also allows her to codify the central episodes according to gender and culture specifically. The main narrative, one Jewish woman's tragic struggle for self-realization, is juxtaposed to her brother's plight as he falls in love with a Christian girl—the character of Eduard is, incidentally, modeled after Lewald's friend, the liberal politician Johann Jacoby. The less intricate love story of Jenny's Christian friend Clara, ending in a happy marriage between Clara and a Gentile man, and that of her Protestant fiancé's attachment to a Christian girl provide depth and perspective.

Jenny's and Eduard's parallel dual biography enables Lewald to discuss the Jewish condition in gender-specific terms. She differentiates between the problems facing men and women and comments on gender role expectations, while relating individual fates to historical, religious, and cultural issues. The oppression of women, religious differences, class issues, and anti-Judaism are portrayed as impediments to emancipation on a variety of levels. Rather than representing a mirror image of the author, the romantic and yet audacious Jenny, the daughter of a well-to-do banker, can be construed to represent Lewald's alter ego, who suffers, like Goethe's protagonists, a tragic fate, which the author avoids. In contrast to Lewald, Jenny becomes a victim of misogyny and anti-Judaism. She dies of a broken heart when her second fiancé, a nobleman, is killed in a duel fought to vindicate both his bride's honor and the Jewish people.

Among the most obvious parallels between Lewald and her protagonist are Jenny's school years ([1866] 1988, 1:182). Jenny is harassed and suffers a nervous breakdown as a result of the ridicule to which she is subjected. She has to leave school and finds herself in complete isolation: not even her best friend is allowed to see her. In addition, Jenny is infatuated with the theology candidate Reinhard, an intolerant and narrow-minded taskmaster, who is cast in a role not unlike the one Heinrich von Kleist assumed vis-à-vis his fiancée Wilhelmine von Zenge. This relationship mirrors Lewald's first love, including her conversion followed by remorse. But there are also differences; for example, Jenny's inability to conform with what Lois McNay describes as "Christian asceticism . . . based on a feminine model of virginity and a notion of absolute renunciation" (1993: 65). Lewald, in contrast, learned to manipulate conventions well and to her advantage. Unlike Lewald, Jenny is relegated to the feminine realm of private relationships and love; being a woman and an apostate, she fails to gain a firm foothold. The failure of her two engagements results in public embarrassment, suggesting a serious lack of stability.

Eduard represents the male countermodel to Jenny's story; surprisingly, his life resembles Lewald's fate more closely. Unlike Jenny, he survives his unhappy love for a Gentile woman because he has his work and his political mission in which to take comfort—both offer him gratification and recognition. A comparison between the life of the Jewish man and that of the Jewish woman suggests that Jenny's broken heart, rather than signifying love, is symbolic of the impasse facing a baptized woman of Jewish origin. Likewise, the romantic relationships function as a mechanism to explore social paradigms. The rationalist Jenny is the very embodiment of the qualities that the Gentile middle class, represented by Reinhard and his pious mother, considered unfeminine. At best, she can adjust to her fiancé's environment, but she can neither accept his values nor adjust to his frugal lifestyle in the long run. Lewald reveals that the particular brand of sentimental love and piety portrayed by Christian authors such as Gustav Freytag and the Pietist Marie Nathusius (1817–67) as the ideal basis for bourgeois family life, coupled with prudence and Protestant work ethics, is the domain of Gentile women.

Lewald emphasizes the differences between Gentile middle-class standards and Jenny's background, which puts her more on par with the aristocracy. Yet, the Prussian nobles also consider the "beautiful Meier" inferior—she is, after all, a commoner, and baptism cannot erase her Jewishness; Jenny and her future husband are not welcome in their midst. Quite in contrast to the popular concept of romantic love central to most nineteenth-century novels, Jenny does survive her first love and is capable of loving more than one man. Her tragic death results from the fact that her capacity for love and life exceeds her limited options, rather than from her failure in love. Unlike Jenny, Lewald left the traditional women's sphere after her first great disappointments. Much to the dismay of her father, who feared that she would end up unmarried, she wrote and championed the causes in which she believed. In order to do so, she entered one of the few avenues that her society had not closed to ambitious women intellectuals: she became a writer.

In her works, Lewald reverses the point of view from which Jews and Jewish society are traditionally portrayed in German literature. Rather than viewing the Jews as outsiders, she writes from the perspective of an insider to Jewish life who is at the same time privy to the workings of Gentile society. This perspective and her critical portrayal of her society's androcentric structures from a woman's perspective make her a true iconoclast who reevaluates established views and practices, including the aristocratic ritual of the duel, the notion that a man is a woman's spiritual leader, and the stylization of men and women as opposites. Christians of both genders as well as men, Gentile and Jewish, are depicted with a sharp critical eye in *Jenny* and *Prinz Louis Ferdinand*.

Lewald's nonconformism foreshadows trends that surface more fully developed in works of following generations. Her distinctly Jewish, albeit secular, perspective and her fascination for the Berlin *bohème* link her to Else Lasker-Schüler; her at times tragic view of the condition of Jewish women and Jewish fate in general connects her with Gertrud Kolmar and Nelly Sachs; her feminist social criticism and her attention to detail, coupled with occasional sensationalism and love for urban culture, correspond to similar attitudes in the works of Claire Goll. In addition, there are distinct affinities between her and the social reformers, politicians, and utopians Bertha Pappenheim and Rosa Luxemburg. With a spontaneous and yet firm approach, Lewald blends informative and entertaining elements in texts that bear a stylistic resemblance to the feuilletons of such later Jewish women journalists as Bertha Zuckerkandl and Claire Goll and the popular novelist Vicki Baum.

Because of their unique combination of feminist and Jewish concerns, including early Jewish nationalism, Lewald's works constitute an important link between the women authors of the emancipation era and the writers of the early to mid-twentieth century. Lewald's narrative strategies as an author of documentary and autobiographical materials and her choice of genre represent a milestone on the path toward the social-critical and theoretical texts of contemporary Jewish women authors.

Jewish Women in the Public Arena (Bertha Pappenheim and Rosa Luxemburg)

In her essays and fiction, Fanny Lewald defined and illustrated the major problems confronting nineteenth-century Jewish women: their status in the family, emancipation, anti-Semitism, education, their lack of professional opportunities, and the interaction between Jews and Gentiles in general. Yet, like the salonnières, Lewald was not a political activist. Notwithstanding her beliefs, she aspired toward a bourgeois life, entering upon the path of assimilation and conversion, marrying a Gentile professor, and befriending members of the aristocracy and the *haute bourgeoisie*. While she advocated reform programs and was committed to raising the status of women and Jews, she herself would hardly have made use of the communal kitchens and the child-care services that she proposed for the benefit of the disadvantaged.

Nonetheless, it was precisely Lewald's social and economic class that produced the women who most actively promoted social reform and even revolution. Unlike proletarian women, the women of the bourgeoisie had access to education, and some of them possessed the means to publicly voice their protest against the oppression of women, with which they themselves wrestled on a daily basis. They also had the necessary time to devote to these issues. Jewish women, moreover, had to contend with anti-Semitism, which was becoming a part of academic curricula and penetrated into every segment of society. Sensitized to intolerance and prejudice, many educated Jewish women realized that other oppressed groups were confronted with similar problems; they became interested in socialism, communism, or feminism, oftentimes ignoring the fact that misogyny and anti-Semitism also existed among socialists, communists, and feminists. Figures like Bertha von Suttner, the founder of the *Verein zur Bekämpfung des Antisemitismus* (the Association for the Struggle against Anti-Semitism) and the most prominent spokeswoman of the international peace movement, were exceptions indeed.

In order to function in the public sphere, women needed to adjust to the standards set by men. Without overstepping societal boundaries, many of them did so by casting themselves in traditionally male roles, thereby deemphasizing their female identity. Others even wrote under male pseudonyms and wore, if not specifically male clothes, as did George Sand, then costumes that emulated the professional male attire. Jewish women felt pressured to conceal their Jewishness as well; if they did not, they limited the range of their activities and their effectiveness. The result was a twofold alienation, as women and as Jews. For many Jewish women, the internalization of Gentile and male norms, which, try as they may, they were unable to realize, became a source of self-loathing.

Among the Jewish pioneers in the struggle for social and political justice, Bertha Pappenheim and Rosa Luxemburg stand out. Their respective careers are paradigmatic of two different paths that presented themselves to Jewish women dissatisfied with the social order of turn-of-the-century Central Europe. The lives and careers of both women, including their fame, their successes, and their ultimate defeat by right-wing militancy, reflect both their individual situations and the spirit of their times. Pappenheim, a conservative, a feminist (who, Marion Kaplan asserts, demanded complete equality for women), and a proponent of Jewish orthodoxy, worked outside the larger women's movement and the Jewish establishment (Kaplan 1978, 109). Rosa Luxemburg, on the other hand, situated herself within the Marxist context, but even there, her outsider position became increasingly evident during World War I. Nonetheless, her influence extended well beyond her death in 1919 into the early years of the German Democratic Republic (Mayer 1991, 40).

Although Pappenheim's and Luxemburg's convictions differ fundamentally, there are striking similarities in their development. Both women came from a secularized upper-middle-class background; both were afflicted with disabilities—Pappenheim struggled with a much-publicized psychological condition (Rosenbaum and Muroff 1984); Luxemburg, born with a deformed hip, was misdiagnosed with tuberculosis at a young age. Throughout their lives, they were torn between the desire for a traditional woman's existence and their social and political mission, and the discrepancy between their official personae and their private selves was extraordinary. They were spellbinding public speakers and negotiators, as well as devoted, affectionate friends, as documented in their intensely emotional correspondences and notes.

The psychological fragmentation experienced by Pappenheim and Luxemburg, beyond being indicative of their complex composite personalities, reflects the excessive demands placed on women in public positions. German society did not accommodate professionally active women and gave them even less of an opportunity to pursue a career and a family life simultaneously. Women intellectuals were faced with the alternative of becoming matrons or bluestockings, and many of them, even those in the highest places, were destroyed by being forced to make this choice. Luxemburg's and Pappenheim's mutually exclusive propensities for public activity and dreams of fulfillment as mothers and wives demonstrate that they themselves could imagine only two paradigms to emulate, the traditionally male or the traditionally female. In practical terms the former won out, as is obvious from the pragmatism with which they tackled their political and professional projects, but the traditionally female paradigm continued to be a frequent source of frustration—already Rahel Varnhagen, Pauline Wiesel, and Fanny Lewald had suffered from the very same discrepancy between ideological tenets and personal aspirations.

Fanny Lewald approached, but never crossed, the threshold to political activism outside of her writing. As a novelist and essayist she was, however, able to integrate her creativity and her private life, albeit late in life and with considerable difficulty. Yet, the discourse that developed in her works contributed to creating an environment in which Pappenheim's and Luxemburg's activism was possible—in effect, the efforts of the younger generation of activists put her ideas to the test. Pappenheim's polemics against prostitution, for example, are modeled after Lewald's analysis of the status of women in *Für und wider die Frauen* (1869). Like Lewald, Pappenheim argues that education leading to economic independence is the key to improving the status of women and women's autonomy.

In addition to being a social-critical writer, Pappenheim struggled as a feminist social worker against the opposition of the Gentile public and the Jewish establishment. She initiated programs providing vocational training to single Jewish mothers and former prostitutes as a stepping-stone toward their social reintegration. The communal principles according to which Pappenheim's home for Jewish girls and women at Isenburg was organized are analogous to the measures proposed by Lewald in her program for working women. Like Lewald, Pappenheim was acquainted with Marxist ideology, and she also remained critical of communism. Pappenheim distanced herself not only from socialism but also from Zionism, doubting that Marxist and Zionist men would accept women as equals. As Kaplan notes, allegiance to the *JFB*, the Jewish Association of Women, founded by Pappenheim in 1904, was a "product of class, age, ethnic and religious affiliations." The members of Pappenheim's organization typically came from middle-class Jewish families, and although they had received some Jewish religious instruction, their values came from their education in secular or Christian schools for privileged daughters (Kaplan 1978, 111; 1979, 71ff.).

Contrary to Luxemburg, Pappenheim worked exclusively for the benefit of Jewish women, aware of the widespread anti-Semitism in women's organizations and the two-pronged threat to Jewish women both as women and as Jews. She believed that the interests of average Jewish women would be best served within Jewish family structures, provided these structures were modified to accommodate emancipated women. By preparing the majority of their students for future careers as homemakers, mothers, teachers, and social workers, Pappenheim's schools guided women back into the Jewish mainstream.

Rosa Luxemburg, on the other hand, embraced Marxist ideology. She became engaged in the struggle for the creation of an egalitarian community of women and men, Jews and Gentiles. From a Marxist perspective, the discrimination against women and Jews was not a primary issue. Luxemburg subscribed to Marx's precept that in a classless society —the ultimate objective of communism—the problems of gender and Jewish identity would be eliminated. Convinced that religion and ethnocentrism obstructed progress, she distanced herself from Judaism in religious and cultural terms. Instead, she emphasized economic issues, which, in her opinion, determined ideological and social structures.

Propelled into the public arena by their special circumstances and extraordinary ambition, Luxemburg and Pappenheim overcame political, psychological, and physical barriers at a time when the bourgeois parties had answered the *Frauenfrage* (Women's Question) in the negative, and when anti-Semitism had become an issue of unprecedented magnitude. They paid a high price for their nonconformity: Pappenheim was a single Jewish woman, and Luxemburg, who had entered into a marriage of convenience for the sake of a visa, was otherwise known as a fanatic revolutionary and a Jew. Excluded from conventional family structures and the established social order, both women were exposed to misogyny, racism, slander, and violence.

In the Danube Monarchy and the German Empire, women's suffrage, even women's political clubs, remained outlawed. Women, having no voice, could rely only on male agents to represent them in their official transactions. As Pappenheim notes in "The Jewish Woman," women of all civilized nations occupied the legal status of children and mentally disabled persons, and she deplores the fact that Jewish women, regardless of their age or accomplishment, count less than a thirteen-year-old boy after the bar-mitzvah. "Before Jewish law women are not individual persons, they are valued and judged exclusively as wives and mothers" (Edinger 1968, 20).

The foundation of the *Allgemeiner deutscher Frauenverein* (ADFV) (General German Women's Association), spearheaded by Luise Otto-Peters in 1867, marked the beginning of the first organized women's movement in Germany. Moreover, despite the discrepancy between the tenets and the practice among Marxists, the publication of Friedrich Engels's essay *On the Origins of the Family, Private Property and the State* and August Bebel's *Woman under Socialism* represents major stepping-stones in the struggle for women's rights. The feminist movement came immediately under fire by an increasingly hostile legislature; in addition to its oppressive antifeminism and anti-Semitism, the German legislature also outlawed the Social Democratic Party.

Bertha Pappenheim, who counts Glikl Hamil and Heinrich Heine among her ancestors, was born in 1859 in Vienna, which was, paradoxically, not only a hotbed of anti-Semitism but also the cradle of Zionism (Kaplan 1979, 47). In spite of her own remarkable achievements, Pappenheim is to this day best known for being Sigmund Freud's Anna O., the object of Josef Breuer's and Freud's scientific studies. Her father, a staunch supporter of the orthodox Jewish community according to Edinger, followed the custom of his times and sent his daughter to Catholic school (1968, 13ff., 42). Neither Pappenheim's education nor her psychotherapy is discussed in her own writings, but her disapproval of both is implied by her refusal to send women under her care into psychiatric treatment and by her warnings not to allow Jewish orphans to become the "victims of Christian missions" (15, 41). In 1888, seven years after her father's death, Pappenheim moved to Frankfurt, where, inspired by Helene Lange's feminist journal *Die Frau,* she established a Jewish nursery school (16). In the following decades, her name became almost synonymous with the *Jüdischer Frauenbund* (Jewish Women's Association).

In her essay "The Jewish Woman," Pappenheim calls for a reconciliation of traditional and contemporary women's roles under the leadership of the *Jüdischer Frauenbund* (Edinger 1968, 80). Citing historical and cultural evidence, she argues that the status of Jewish women since biblical times had been progressively reduced. She recommends that special studies be undertaken "to show in the Diaspora Jewish women who were of importance for more than a small circle." Characterizing Glikl Hamil as such a woman (77ff.), Pappenheim proposes that women's role models be extracted from Jewish women's history and attempts of the Jewish leadership aimed at keeping women in their place be foiled. She challenges obsolete structures within Judaism because, according to her, they are the major reason why women reject their Jewishness, even if they realize that they will not be able to elude the stigma of their origin.[8] As her case in point, she mentions the women of the early nine-teenth century whose accomplishments did not benefit German-Jewish womanhood, and who remained emotionally and intellectually disen-franchised from the Gentile world (80).

"The Jewish Woman" calls for a radical improvement of the status of Jewish women with the goal of reintegrating estranged women into the fold of their community. The historical segments of the essay are devoted to the potential for women's spirituality within Judaism. In this context Pappenheim examines the Yiddish language as well as tra-ditional women's texts—*Zeenah u-Reenah,* the "women's bible," and *Maàsse.* Yiddish is characterized as the Jewish women's language and a "bridge to a world which slowly opened to Jewish women" German cul-ture (Edinger 1968, 78).[9] Without their exposure to this sphere, Pappen-heim argues, Jewish women would not have progressed as far as they did. Although she takes pride in the strides made by Jewish women— their multilingualism, their social and national consciousness, and their "definitely German interest in education"—she deplores that their igno-rance in religious matters has prevented them from cultivating a Jewish spirituality (79).

In the essay "The Jewish Girl" (Edinger 1968, 84ff.), Pappenheim's views on the status of Jewish women have become more radical. She maintains that the Torah accords to women and female children an in-ferior status by reducing them to chattel and determining their value on the basis of their physical attributes. Pappenheim considers this to be particularly true in East European Jewish culture. Her observations about the beauty of unmarried girls and the physical deterioration of wives and mothers lead her to the conclusion that women, indeed, represent a commercial commodity and that having a woman's body is a liability. This point is pursued in detail in Pappenheim's description of cultural practices such as a woman's preparations for marriage, the cutting of the bride's hair, and the wearing of a *sheitl* or bonnet (86). These rituals of inscribing an individual with a female identity, Pappen-heim argues, are the major reason why Russian or Polish Jewish girls join secular revolutionary movements, while the absence of such prac-tices and the improved status of women, resulting from more stable economic conditions and secular education, would reduce the defection of Jewish women (88). Yet, she has nothing but the most ambivalent praise for Westernized Jewish women, calling them "a chrysanthemum born unique and without a future," a characterization that has unmistakably autobiographical overtones: "The unmarried, mature, independent woman welcome in all cultural circles, who in her entire being can be, and is fully responsible for shaping her life, shaping her fate, in a sexual way fully responsible only to her self and completely free in the world, emerged" (88).

Pappenheim's publications in general highlight feminist and Jewish concerns—her German edition of Mary Wollstonecraft's *Vindication of the Rights of Women,* for example, as well as her literary works, essays, travelogues, and autobiographical texts, some of them published under the pseudonym Paul Berthold (Dick 1993a, 206). To make core text from the Jewish tradition accessible to German women, Pappenheim translated Glikl Hamil's *Memoirs,* the *Maàsse* Book, and *Zeenah u-Reenah,* as well as prayers, into German.[10] In Pappenheim's writings, Jewish and feminist views and conservative and progressive views intersect on multiple levels. Deeply committed to Jewish spirituality, Pappenheim blamed the secular feminist movement for neglecting women's spiritual concerns. Out of a passionate respect for life she took exception to the position of most feminists on abortion and birth control (Edinger 1968, 80, 93).[11]

In her letters to her women friends, Pappenheim expressed her subjectivity. She mentored and advised her confidante and co-worker Hannah Karminski (1897–1942), who was the executive secretary of the national organization of the Jewish Women's Association, as well as her associate, Sophie Mamelok.[12] Pappenheim's effervescent and flirtatious messages to them strike a similar note to the correspondence between Rahel and Pauline Wiesel. Much like the salonnières, Pappenheim assumes a masculine voice when she comments on female beauty, but in contrast to the male authors of her time, she exhibits respect for the intellectual, spiritual, and physical attributes of women, regardless of their status (Edinger 1968, 38; Pappenheim 1924, 40).[13]

Pappenheim's letters read like a diary that subtly accommodates its imagined readers. For the most part, the letters address professional concerns and, occasionally, art and literature. There are also a few introspective texts that appear to have been intended as a legacy to the women at Isenburg, a refuge for Jewish women; for example, there is a letter written in 1931 in which she calls for a balanced life, as too much work makes "caricatures of women" (Edinger 1968, 63). In another text Pappenheim scrutinizes her own motives for helping women to leave their homes. The majority of her letters, however, display self-confidence and single-ness of purpose. With a clear bias toward German culture, she criticizes the Jewish culture in Palestine, particularly the general lack of educa-tion and the commercialization of Jerusalem's holy sites. Overall, she experiences the Middle East as a realm torn by bigotry and ethnic strife, and she takes umbrage at the presence of German anti-Semites in Jeru-salem. The latter incidents only intensify her aversion to the Holy Land (43): "If Frankfurt is the German Jerusalem, then Jerusalem is the Ori-ental Frankfurt" (41). Above all, she condemns what she perceives as hypocrisy on the part of the Zionist elite, who avail themselves of the advantages of modern education and relegate those less fortunate to the status of second-class citizens (Pappenheim 1924, 120).

Pappenheim portrays the polarization of men and women—which is, according to her, a result of the discrimination against female chil-dren—as the root cause of most social ills in Jewish and Gentile culture at home and abroad. In her opinion, the preferential treatment of male children makes it impossible for men and women to become equal part-ners (Edinger 1968, 93). Hence Pappenheim denounced the exploitation of women as low-cost labor, as volunteers for charitable causes, and as social workers, and she condemned gender segregation and the legal-ized oppression of women wherever she encountered them.

To properly assess Pappenheim's vision, it is important to consider that women were not admitted to German universities as regular stu-dents as late as 1904, and that they did not achieve suffrage before the end of World War I. At that very time, Pappenheim demanded that women become doctors, lawyers, educators, and scholars, rather than nurses, secretaries, maids, and nannies (82). Moreover, Pappenheim worked on a global basis, but she nonetheless disagreed with the con-cept of the international proletariat. Rather, she differentiated between the status of men, women, and children, and asserted that everywhere, even among the proletariat, the latter two groups faced the most severe problems. Oppressed by the oppressed, women and children, because of their vulnerability in social and physical terms, were exposed to the most extreme poverty and exploitation (47–51).

The treatise *Zur Lage der jüdischen Bevölkerung in Galizien: Reise-Eindrücke und Vorschläge zur Besserung der Verhältnisse* (1904), based on Pappenheim's diaries, discusses Galicia's crisis state of impoverishment in its historical context. The plight of the population is examined in conjunction with the oppression of the Jews (1904, 21). As in her essays about the discrimination against women, Pappenheim argues that the exploitation of one segment of the population necessarily has a negative impact on society as a whole. As a first step to remedying the situation, Pappenheim calls for job training for women, including married women, and for an end to anti-Semitic practices. She holds that a reform of Jewish society is necessary as well since the major Jewish factions in Galicia, Zionists and Hasidics, oppose the women's movement (44). Pappenheim polemicizes not only against the degradation of women in Hasidic culture but also against the Zionists' failure to put their liberal theories into practice.

In 1905, Pappenheim took child survivors of the Russian pogroms to Frankfurt and established a refuge for troubled and delinquent Jewish girls and single Jewish mothers. Undaunted by public opposition and a defamation campaign in reaction to her initiative, she proceeded to investigate the status of Jewish women in Eastern Europe, the United States, Palestine, and Egypt and to rally support for her attempts to deliver Jewish prostitutes from brothels all over the world.[14] Having learned that 90 percent of the women kept as white slaves in the Middle East were Jewish, Pappenheim intervened with the respective governments on their behalf (1904, 39). Frequently made allegations about the involvement of Jews in prostitution and white slavery prompted Pappenheim to undertake a similar investigation in Eastern Europe, which revealed that the stereotype of Jewish men as the most notorious white slave traders turned out to be an anti-Semitic fantasy (Edinger 1968, 18, 45–48).[15]

Pappenheim was one of numerous Western travelers to explore Galicia between the turn of the century and World War I; Arnold Zweig returned in awe of Hasidic culture and the Yiddish language, and Martin Buber published his *Hasidic Tales* (Zweig 1920). Pappenheim's position, however, was ambivalent. She felt genuine admiration for Eastern Europe's cultural treasures, but it was surpassed by her horror at the oppression of Jewish women in Russia and Poland, a moot issue in the works of male authors. Yet, she has praise for the extraordinary wisdom and initiative of the sister of one miracle rabbi and concedes that it is not uncommon for the rabbis' wives to surpass their husband in intelligence (Pappenheim 1924, 42, 206). Her nostalgic image of the traditional Jewish family of Glikl's times, of which she takes Eastern European *shtetl* life to be a reflection, suggests that Pappenheim, notwithstanding her often-expressed preference for German culture, felt a deep affinity for the lost motherland.

Pappenheim's model for the broad-based *Jüdischer Frauenbund*—its membership amounted to 50,000 women, approximately 20 percent of Jewish women over age thirty—was Christian women's federations (Kaplan 1994b, 95). There was not a single rabbi to endorse Pappenheim's projects, which included the integration of women into the Jewish congregations as full-fledged members, assistance to East European immigrants, and the development of curricula for women, regardless of their status (Edinger 1968, 89).[16] Neither was there support for her pioneering efforts to solve the problems of unwed mothers, prostitutes, illegitimate children, and abandoned Jewish wives whose right to remarry depended on a divorce decree issued by their husbands or by a rabbi. These issues were taboos, and by touching on them, Pappenheim became a highly controversial figure (17).

Although in her life Pappenheim did not conform to the requirements of orthodox Judaism for women (i.e., marriage, procreation, and the support of male religious study), she never abandoned orthodox Judaism despite her critical attitude toward the Bible as a text written by and for men (Jensen 1984, 184). Neither did she consider Zionism a viable alternative. She did acknowledge the fact that the Zionists promised women greater freedom, but she was appalled by their disregard for traditional values and their "illiterate, uncivilized arguments, and impiety in all situations" (Edinger 1968, 81, 86).[17] Pappenheim felt that the strategies employed by Zionist organizations in order to attract women members were sheer demagoguery, and she argued that, by condoning prostitution as a "necessary evil" and denying the existence of white slavery altogether, the movement demonstrated an intolerable insensitivity to women's issues. After the Nazi takeover—which Pappenheim experienced as a terrible personal blow when the pornographic Nazi propaganda paper *Der Stürmer* took excerpts from her studies on white slavery out of context and reprinted them as examples of "Jewish corruption" (19–21)—and even after the enactment of the Nürnberg Laws, Pappenheim opposed the efforts of American Zionists to evacuate Jewish teenagers from Germany. She died in 1936, apparently unaware of the catastrophe awaiting the Jews under Nazi rule.

Along with the 1899 drama *Frauenrecht,* the three-act play *Tragische Momente: Drei Lebensbilder* (1913) is one of Bertha Pappenheim's major literary works. The latter play illustrates Jewish suffering in Galicia, Germany, and Palestine. The protagonists, Uri Gurewitsch and his lover, and later wife, Fella, escape a Russian pogrom in 1904, only to find themselves four years later in abject poverty in Frankfurt, subsisting on the verge of starvation and criminality. They are discriminated against as aliens, as Russians and Jews, and Fella bears the additional burden of being a student, a wife, and a mother.[18] In the third act, she succumbs to the hardships of pioneer life in Palestine, a life bearing no resemblance to the Middle Eastern idyll that Theodor Herzl had painted in his utopian novel *Altneuland.* In the country torn by conflicts between Jews and Arabs and the rich and the poor, Uri loses his son, Schiri, to an anti-Zionist way of life. The young man abandons his Hebrew name for the European-sounding "Jerome" and leaves Eretz Israel with his fiancée, convinced that it is impossible to lead a religious life in a Zionist state.

Pappenheim's play portrays Zionism as an ineffective social movement and a profoundly anti-Jewish movement that exploits the poor and destroys their spiritual basis. Nowhere in the world does there appear to exist a preordained place for Jews—least of all in Palestine. *Tragische Momente* characterizes the Zionist ideal as a delusion, demonstrating that modern Jews are Europeans of German language. Moreover, in contrast to Herzl, Pappenheim considers Arab resistance a serious threat to Jewish settlement. She argues that in an already densely populated country such as Eretz Israel, the Jews will constitute a minority no less than they do in Europe.

Tragische Momente begins with a stirring portrait of ghetto life as observed firsthand by the author in Galicia. Throughout the play, Pappenheim steers clear of stereotypes; for example, the use of Yiddish language patterns that anti-Semitic German authors have traditionally used to defame Jews and Jewish culture. Rather, women's issues, female bonding, and solidarity among women of the same class are highlighted. In contrast to lack of solidarity among men of all backgrounds, the support extended to Fella by a lower middle-class Bavarian woman in Frankfurt implies the possibility of German-Jewish sisterhood. Similar examples of mutual understanding between Poles and Jews are not shown.

Tragische Momente is intended for Jews and Gentiles as a plea to improve the lot of East European refugees in Germany. The somewhat melodramatic portrayal of a young mother's plight is appropriate to alert a general public to the misery afflicting innocent people in that it brings home to the viewers the disastrous effects of the erosion of family life by depravity and crime. Thus, the drama supports Pappenheim's objectives, including the strengthening of Jewish institutions. *Tragische Momente* implies, furthermore, that Jewish culture and German culture are fundamentally compatible, although support against anti-Semitism is elicited by portraying sympathetic Jewish characters who become the victims of an irrational Jew-hatred. There is a strong suggestion that it is in the interest of all righteous Gentiles to support their Jewish neighbors, and for Jews to acknowledge their diaspora culture in Germany, rather than fighting a lost battle in Palestine.

The first act of *Tragische Momente* and the essay "The Jewish Girl" portray Rosa Luxemburg's cultural home environment. Luxemburg was born in 1870 in Zamosc, a Polish center of Haskalah. A merchant's daughter, she grew up in a secular environment that had a strong affinity for German culture. Throughout her life, Luxemburg used Christian holidays as points of reference, and German literature occupied a central place in her imagination.[19] Her cosmopolitan views conditioned her for the philosophy of the secret antinationalist *Sozialistisch-Revolutionäre Partei Proletariat,* with which she affiliated herself while a student at the progressive Warsaw Women's Gymnasium (Wimmer 1990, 35–36). Already then, she viewed politics from a global perspective, interpreting, for instance, the Polish insurrection against czarist Russia from within the context of the international class struggle rather than as a matter of national interest.

During her student years at the University of Zürich, a center for East European revolutionaries at the time, Luxemburg joined the Polish revolutionary movement. Her personal, professional, and political interests became inextricably intertwined—her friends were also her political associates. Particularly during her imprisonment, her career dominated her private life to such an extent that the latter became almost nonexistent.

While writing her dissertation on the industrial development of Poland, *Die industrielle Entwickelung Polens* (1898), Luxemburg and her lover, Leo Jogiches, founded the journal *Sprawa Robotnicza* (The Workers' Cause). Later, Luxemburg moved to Berlin, convinced of the key role of the German workers' movement. Already Luxemburg's early political essays and speeches combine communism and radical pacifism. They condemn Central Europe's class hierarchy, the very foundation of imperial Germany and Austria; they expose capitalist expansionism, which was, according to her, the cause of Third World poverty; and they condemn militarism and warfare.[20] As a result, Luxemburg became the target of nationalist attacks on the eve of and during World War I. Pacifists such as herself, Bertha von Suttner, and Auguste Stöcker were regarded as traitors by the majority. In the crucial debate on German Social Democracy, Luxemburg upheld traditional Marxist principles: internationalism and global class struggle. She opposed the revision of the SPD's Marxist program and the rapprochement between liberal middle-class movements and Social Democracy, which involved supporting the war effort.[21] She also disagreed with the changes envisioned by the Communist Party; namely, Lenin's plans to establish a core of professional revolutionaries, which she considered detrimental to independent thought. While she welcomed the 1917 revolution in Russia, she was wary of party dictatorship. Hence she and her associates left the German SPD and distanced themselves from the Communist Party by founding the *Spartakusbund* and the KPD (Communist Party of Germany).

There are striking parallels between the biography of Rosa Luxemburg and another increasingly marginalized revolutionary of Jewish background, Leon Trotsky, a contributor to her journal and a supporter of her theses on party unity.[22] Luxemburg was murdered by right-wing extremists during the uprisings in Berlin in January of 1919;[23] Trotsky was assassinated in Mexico in 1940 by an agent of Stalin's GPU.

As a political agitator, Luxemburg faced even greater obstacles than Pappenheim did as a social worker. A foreigner from Eastern Europe, a Jew, and a disabled woman, Luxemburg was socially and politically a nonperson. Since the German *Sozialistengesetz* suppressed the expression of leftist views and revolutionary activities, her activities were considered criminal. She engaged in her speaking and publication activities at a considerable personal risk; like other dissenters, Luxemburg was subject to frequent arrests and prison terms.[24] Luxemburg's attempts to distance herself from Jewish and feminist issues proved ineffective; in addition to being denounced as a radical and referred to as "Red Rosa," she was stigmatized as a Jewish woman.[25]

By mentoring other women, Luxemburg contributed to the struggle for women's rights, albeit indirectly.[26] She argued that "Social Democracy always took the side of those who struggle for freedom" (1972, 1, part 1:63), which did not mean that she closed her eyes to reality. She was critical of the fact that capitalist systems turn women into commodities and force them into the working world without granting them any security (1972, 1, part 2:291). All in all, however, her sporadic remarks fall in line with marxist doctrine, such as when she characterizes middle-class women as parasites but praises the class struggle of working-class women.[27] This same perspective prevails in her criticism of Wilhelminian children's legislation. Luxemburg contrasts the laws protecting privileged children to the legalized exploitation of proletarian children, but she avoids contextualizing these as an integral aspect of patriarchal structures.[28] In "Frauenwahlrecht und Klassenkampf" (1912) and "Die Proletarierin" (1914), she predicts that the victory of the proletariat will render problems of gender, ethnicity, and religion obsolete.

Luxemburg's conspicuous neutrality toward feminist and Jewish issues points to the most problematic areas in her philosophy. Many of her works focus on geographic areas with a significant Jewish population; for example, her dissertation, "Aus Posen," and "Ausnahmezustand über österreichisch-Galizien" (1972, 1, part 1:222–25, 226–27). The careful avoidance of Jewish issues conveys an impression of the intensity of these issues for Rosa Luxemburg,[29] who, like other Jewish intellectuals—Herzl, Freud, and Trotsky—was trapped in a double bind: if she debated Jewish concerns, she ran the risk of being dismissed by Gentile readers, including her non-Jewish fellow communists, as rallying for Jewish special interests. Remaining silent, however, was no solution either, since attacks on the Jewish intellectual elite were an everyday occurrence. Distancing herself from the so-called Jewish Question entailed the denial and even the repression of a significant part of a Jewish author's experience, and it did not safeguard her from anti-Semitic invectives or, ultimately, assassination.

Not surprisingly, this predicament produced an almost allergic reaction to the residue of Jewishness with which authors such as Luxemburg attempted to come to terms. Marxism offered no solution to this problem; neither did Luxemburg herself, as is apparent from her unusually harsh and irrational advice to her Jewish mentee Mathilde Wurm—namely, to steer clear of accounts about Jewish suffering. In this correspondence Luxemburg declares the plight of Jews as irrelevant to the struggle of the proletariat, and hence a nonissue, despite the fact that she knew firsthand of the persecution of Eastern European Jewish women and men in all parts of Europe. Her adherence to an ideology that promised to vindicate the oppressed regardless of nationality, gender, and race was Luxemburg's way of dealing with the Jewish Question (1982, 48). In her 1898 essay "Die Krise in Frankreich" (1972, 1, part 2:264–69), Luxemburg comes closer than anywhere else to confronting a Jewish issue, the Dreyfus affair, which kindled passionate responses all across Europe. Not surprisingly, her article does not indicate any personal involvement; rather, it presents the facts as if in an abstract, historical, textbook case.

Luxemburg's brilliant scholarly treatises and her essays differ greatly in tone and style from her intensely emotional personal letters, which display a sense of humor and a capacity for affection, demonstrated by her use of terms of endearment (1982, 126). The synthesis of Luxemburg's varied forms of expression is achieved outside the texts through the author's relationships with the recipients of her letters—Leon Jogiches, for instance, was her mentor, her lover, the man she wished to marry, her financier, and her lifelong comrade; Clara Zetkin, the mother of her lover Kostja, was her friend, her confidante, and, until their ideological fallout, her political ally. Even Luxemburg's official letters, showing her as an effective, strong-willed political leader, retain a personal element; usually they are signed "Rosa." Nowhere but in a few letters to government offices does she use her full name and title, Doktor Rosalie Lübeck-Luxemburg. Like Pappenheim, Luxemburg tailored her letters to suit a diverse group of recipients: her comrades and their wives, and people who worked for her. The level of intimacy between Luxemburg and certain individuals was such that it allowed her to confide her secrets to them, including weaknesses that she condemned in others; her bouts of depression—particularly in jail—and, as she writes in her letter of 6 July 1917, a low tolerance for the "devils within."

Luxemburg's struggle with gender role expectations comes to the fore in her early correspondence with Jogiches, which in certain ways resembles the already mentioned correspondence between Heinrich von Kleist and his fiancée. Like Kleist, Jogiches places himself in a leadership role, posing as his lover's teacher. She, on the other hand, pleads for understanding and love from this model revolutionary and composes idyllic visions of their future together: "A little apartment for the two of us, our own furniture, our library; peace and quiet and regular work hours, walks together, from time to time a visit to the opera, a small, a very small circle of acquaintances whom we invite for dinner occasionally, going to the country one summer evening, entirely free of work! . . . (and perhaps such a small, tiny little baby? Will that never be allowed to happen?)" (Luxemburg 1980, 53). These conventional dreams are antithetical to Luxemburg's crisis-filled life on the fringes and to her political beliefs. In light of her actual decisions, these escapist reveries are hardly believable as her true intentions. They are, nonetheless, indicative of the degree of repression and self-discipline that the woman who harbored them required of herself in order to collaborate on a professional level with a man who evoked, and at the same time frustrated, her desires. Her letters to Jogiches exhibit a surprising tolerance for male authority, if not a yearning to be dominated and cared for, on the part of a woman who in the political arena was virulently opposed to traditional structures, domineering men, and unbending party discipline.

Furthermore, Luxemburg's correspondence attests to her extraordinary talent for overcoming setbacks. Faced with adversity on a multitude of levels, she was forced to develop an almost unshakable stoicism and an iron will. Regina Kecht notes that these skills were acquired at a high price: Luxemburg suffered frequently from nervous and psychosomatic disorders. The self-irony with which she makes light of her suffering in jail and her letters written under dire circumstances (1982, 44–46) attest to her heroic disposition. Even in moments of despair, she avoids burdening others with her misery. At the same time, her trust in the Marxist philosophy of history takes on a religious intensity under duress, such as when she uses it to dispel her own and a friend's disenchantment with the easily influenced masses. She recommends that he disregard his personal disappointments and place his faith in the "iron law" of history (47).

This and other similar instances show that when interpreting Luxemburg it is important to heed Ossip Flechtheim's warning not to forget about "Bloody Rosa," the dread of Philistines and party agents (1985; 1975, 34). Recent criticism and Margarete von Trotta's feature film dwell on Luxemburg's private life, turning her into a sentimental heroine, but her steadfastness and determination were as integral to her character as her kindness. She herself was aware of these traits when she compared herself to the tenderest and at the same time most ferocious character of German literature, Kleist's queen of the Amazons, Penthesilea (1982, 82).[30]

Apart from the marked differences in Luxemburg's and Pappenheim's political convictions, there are parallels between their lives and their works. Their predilection for German literature and their conservative aesthetics suggest a more than superficial affinity; indeed, their strategies in organizing their lives and coping with difficulties are quite similar. Their acknowledged brilliance enabled them to transcend the constraints of patriarchal society, and it was precisely their position as social and political outsiders through which they were able to expand their sphere of influence far beyond that of other women. Both women benefited as well as suffered from the abnormality of their situation.

Luxemburg and Pappenheim promoted their causes with an assertiveness that shocked their contemporaries, but in private they adhered to the ideals of the Jewish middle class. Luxemburg, incapable of integrating the divergent expectations of her gender and class, divorced herself intellectually from Jewish culture by following a path prepared by an earlier revolutionary of Jewish background, Karl Marx. Pappenheim, on the other hand, rejected Marxist ideology, secular feminism, and Zionism, which left her in an extremely marginal position in the context of Jewish orthodoxy, to which she adhered. To add insult to injury, the Nazis subverted her work to their own ends.

Pappenheim and Luxemburg worked effectively with like-minded female comrades—many of Luxemburg's and all of Pappenheim's fellow workers were women. While they remained childless and unmarried, they did establish surrogate families consisting of their friends and associates. Luxemburg's synthetic family includes mother, father, son, brother, and sister figures. In Pappenheim's matriarchal setting, the male element, although conspicuously absent, is replaced by female authority figures. Luxemburg, who compares herself to Penthesilea, a renegade from a matriarchal universe, would not have been a stranger in this world. For everyone but the founding mother, Pappenheim's Isenburg was a transitional safe haven for women from which they could enter heterosexual society.

Pappenheim and Luxemburg drew gratification from their service to others in compensation for having sacrificed their private lives, and like the men of their generation, they sustained their public roles with the support of loyal housekeepers, secretaries, and co-workers. However, their public and professional male roles were complemented by some of the accoutrements of traditional womanhood: intimate friendships and devotion to the point of self-sacrifice. To reach a proper assessment of Luxemburg and Pappenheim, it is necessary to remember that romantic love played an insignificant role in the lives of prebourgeois Jewish women and that extended family and marriages of convenience were the norm for most Jewish women, even in the post-Enlightenment era. So was the concept of mutual support across geographic and political boundaries for one's allies, coupled with a certain disdain for the affairs of individual Gentile nations as part and parcel of Luxemburg's and Pappenheim's traditional legacy.

Some of the presumable inconsistencies in Luxemburg observed by critics are already displayed in Glikl's memoirs. For example, Glikl's energy and independence do not preclude her acceptance of conventional family structures; neither does her practical sense rule out idealism, spirituality, and the need to belong to a community. Glikl's example shows that Jewish women were accustomed to playing multiple roles as wives, mothers, businesswomen, and autonomous individuals. What distinguishes earlier Jewish women from Luxemburg and Pappenheim is the fact that the latter two broke out of the women's domain and assumed public roles in male-dominated spheres. Playing a man's game in the larger context of secular Christian societies, without actually being men, these women relinquished their access to the status of mothers and wives in a way unthinkable in the segregated Jewish world, to which a monastic way of life was fundamentally foreign. Luxemburg and Pappenheim were familiar with patriarchy, but it is unlikely that they comprehended the specifically German turn that patriarchy took early in the twentieth century. In all likelihood, neither Luxemburg, who was murdered in the forefront of a failing revolution, nor Pappenheim, who was saved from the Holocaust by her death, realized the full extent of their sacrifices or the ultimate futility of them.

Inventing Identity, Creating Reality (Else Lasker-Schüler)

By the end of the nineteenth century, Jews in Germany were sufficiently assimilated for some critics to speak of a German-Jewish symbiosis—as late as 1944, Sol Liptzin likened German Gentiles and Jews to the two antithetical souls existing alongside each other in the psyche of Goethe's

Faust (1944, 1–3). Not all observers assessed this rapprochement as positive; Theodor Lessing, for example, observed a widespread malaise among German Jews, which he termed "Jewish Self-Hatred." According to him, the alienation that Jewish men and women experienced as a result of having lost touch with their heritage caused them to devalue their own qualities and to engage in a futile endeavor to merge into the German and Austrian mainstream. A Jewish student named Otto Weininger, who committed suicide after completing his doctoral dissertation, entitled "Sex and Character," at the University of Vienna, figured as the prototype of Lessing's thesis. Weininger asserted the superiority of qualities that racial ideologues ascribed to the Gentile, Christian, and "Aryan" world, and he denounced the psychological and physical traits that were commonly defined as feminine and Jewish (T. Lessing 1930, 30, 71). Leading Nazi figures, among others, hailed Weininger's work as an authentic analysis of Jews and women; others rejected it as the work of an anti-Semitic Jew, a misogynist, and a crank. What is most distressing about Weininger's work is that a comparison with other authors of the same era—health professionals such as Freud, philosophers such as Nietzsche, art and literary critics such as Wagner—illustrates that radical though it seems, Weininger's view of women and Jews, including the analogy he establishes between them (he characterized the Jewish people as feminine and the "Aryans" as masculine), was anything but extraordinary at the time.

The status of equality for German Jews was undermined by the bourgeoisie and the lower nobility as soon as it had been established because these two groups were particularly vulnerable to the social displacement effected by industrialization, the ongoing social changes, and economic disasters such as the collapse of the stock exchange in 1873. Supported by nationalists, students, and professors, both groups expressed their anxiety by calling for the elimination of their Jewish competitors. All across Germany and Austria, anti-Semitic clubs sprang up, cultivating the legend of a Jewish world conspiracy. By the early 1880s most academic fraternities had introduced so-called Aryan clauses that denied membership to Jewish students and declared them dishonorable and unfit to participate in duels (Schnitzler 1968; E. Schwarz 1994, 54–55).

The way in which the pan-German movement combined Christianity, anti-Semitism, and misogyny appealed to Austrian and Southern German Catholics no less than to the Northern German Protestants.

Vienna, Munich, and Berlin became centers of anti-Semitism; in Berlin, Nietzsche's brother-in-law Förster (Nietzsche's sister Elisabeth Förster-Nietzsche admired Hitler and proclaimed him her brother's successor), the university professors Heinrici, Sonnenberg, and Treitschke, as well as the emperor himself, were spreading anti-Semitic propaganda (Katz 1980a, 1). Otto von Bismarck, the chancellor of the newly founded German empire, manipulated popular anti-Semitism as a political tool to create a distinct enemy image of "the Jew" in order to discredit liberal forces. In Vienna, Karl Lueger, a leading member of the anti-Semitic Christian-Social Association and the author of a manifesto calling for the exclusion of Jews from the professions and a ban on immigration, won the Viennese mayoral elections in 1895. Adolf Hitler encountered Austrian anti-Semitism in Linz, where the radical right-wing politician Schoenerer demanded the removal of all Jews from the public sphere, and then in Vienna. In addition, the pedophile racist fantasies of Nordic youths, promulgated in Lanz von Liebenfels's journal *Ostara,* the esoteric séances and publications of the Ludendorff circle, the occult doctrines of several Germanophile societies, as well as the racial spiritualism of Artur Dinter, among others, inspired Hitler and his cohorts (Oxaal 1987, 11). The publication history of Jewish authors, artists, and intellectuals and their biographies illustrate the fragility of assimilation: they experienced exclusion from public office, were denied promotions, and suffered ad hominem attacks and the censorship of their works. Notwithstanding this, the metropolitan Jewish population in Germany and Austria played an important part in shaping the national culture; beyond the Holocaust, their legacy lives on in the works of contemporary Jewish and Gentile authors.

Theodor Herzl's *The Jewish State,* published in 1897, and the first Zionist Congress, held in Basel, promoted a new self-awareness among German and Austrian Jews. In response to the European nationalist movements and the threat of global anti-Semitism, Herzl urged the Jews of all nationalities to relinquish their attempts at assimilation and to establish a state in Palestine or elsewhere so that Jews would no longer have to live as a minority (Carmely 1981, 19). Zionism, the fascination with Eastern European Jewish culture in the wake of the late Russian pogroms, the assimilation debate, and the threat emanating from the intensifying religious, economic, political, and racial anti-Semitic movements, account for the preoccupation with Jewish concerns at the end of the nineteenth century. There was an increasing demand for information on Eastern European culture, and after World War I, the works of Joseph Roth, Lion Feuchtwanger, and Alfred Döblin established connections between German and Yiddish literature in aesthetic and thematic terms. The dual perspective of the outsider who possesses an insider's knowledge is characteristic of the social-critical Jewish authors of the first part of the twentieth century, including Else Lasker-Schüler, Claire Goll, Veza Canetti, and Gertrud Kolmar. Like Franz Kafka, but with different literary tools, Lasker-Schüler transformed marginalization into art. She created her own synthetic identity from elements of her family history and her biography, and a Jewish motherland in the German language, constructed from history, fairy tales, and folk legends. With her fanciful utopian visions of a faraway spiritual homeland and of an entourage of noble friends, Lasker-Schüler became the icon of German-Jewish women's poetry at a time when invention and mythmaking were necessary for women to define their Jewish identity.

Born in 1869 in Elberfeld, a suburb of Wuppertal, as the daughter of a banker-merchant, Lasker-Schüler, like Bertha Pappenheim, was enrolled in a Catholic school and was socialized in an almost completely assimilated environment. Only the severe public reaction to the legislation finalizing Jewish emancipation in 1869 prevented her and the women of the next generation from blending into the German mainstream. Lasker-Schüler's accomplishments must be appraised in view of the fact that her Jewishness confronted her primarily negatively. In *Der Name als Stigma,* Dietz Bering maintains that hand in hand with the abolition of the actual ghettos went the erection of a symbolic ghetto; Jewish-sounding names were stigmatized; so were persons physically resembling the Jewish stereotypes, as did Lasker-Schüler.

In contrast to the women of earlier generations, however, Lasker-Schüler did not reject her public image as a Jew; rather, she made the most of it (Benn 1968, 4:1101–2; Ben Chorin 1989, 339–40; Bauschinger 1985). She displayed her Jewishness in such a way as to denounce assimilation, the failure of which she had learned from her own experiences. Lasker-Schüler's decision to become a poet allowed her to blossom as an eccentric. Black-haired, dark-eyed, and vivacious, she came to be known to critics and friends as the "Black Swan of Israel" (Bänsch 1970, 52ff.). Through her ostentatious apparel and garish jewelry, she underscored her Mediterranean appearance; in her texts, artwork, and performances,

68

including staging herself in Jerusalem, she claimed a place for herself in the context of Middle Eastern and Jewish history (Schuller 1993).[31] Considering that within the Jewish community, particularly in Berlin, an active redefinition of gender roles also took place, resulting in 1931 in the ordination of the first woman rabbi, Regina Jonas, Lasker-Schüler is obviously a part of larger societal trends (Kellenbach 1993).

Traumatized by the Jew-baiting in her school, Lasker-Schüler had to be tutored at home. The pressure to which she had been exposed seems to have resulted in a condition similar to chorea minor, St. Vitus's dance, which is portrayed in her 1932 work *Arthur Aronymus*. Clearly, Lasker-Schüler did not experience her epoch as a harmonious one, let alone as the golden age of the German-Jewish symbiosis.[32] Rather, she portrayed her father's generation as such a golden age. According to the novella and the play *Arthur Aronymus,* it was during his lifetime that a respite occurred as far as the oppression of the Jews was concerned. However, since *Arthur Aronymus* was written immediately before the Nazi take-over, these works must be taken with a grain of salt — as fantasy, irony, or both. History itself disproved the idyllic ambiance of *Arthur Aronymus* and the presumed end of anti-Judaism.

Lasker-Schüler was a lyric poet, a prose writer, a dramatist, a polemicist, and a writer of letters. Her work represents the zenith of early twentieth-century women's writing, and it marks the final phase of pre-Shoah literature. Her distinctive style, her choice of topics, her boundless creativity, and her flamboyance made Lasker-Schüler the key figure in modern German-Jewish women's literature — she was one of the most striking personalities of the Berlin *bohème*. Having abandoned her bourgeois origins, she styled herself as the archetypal stranger, as the embodiment of the Jewish woman in the German *Galut* — an enigmatic creature fit for the company of the princes and princesses of the *Arabian Nights*. Although she wrote in German, Lasker-Schüler maintained that Hebrew was the language of her soul.

The atmosphere of late Wilhelminian Germany and Franz Josephinian Austria was repressive and exuberant at the same time. Whereas the term *Gay Apocalypse* has been aptly used to characterize prewar Vienna, the Berlin *bohème* indulged in a less ornate kind of anarchy, and Munich with its sensuous and rebellious art scene represented an intermediary position between the German and the Austrian metropolis, accommodating the satirist Frank Wedekind as well as Frieda von Richthofen,

D. H. Lawrence's wife. Significantly, these three centers of modernism, where anarchy, reform, and revolutionary movements intersected, later became key positions for the Nazi movement.

The annihilation of traditional structures advocated by bohemian anarchists such as Peter Hille, Lasker-Schüler's first mentor, and vagabond poets such as Hugo Sonnenschein and Waldemar Bonsels appealed to those who wished to escape from traditional structures and gender roles. As a Jew and a woman, Lasker-Schüler had little to gain from patriarchal structures, but she still had to pay a high price for her rebellion against them.[33] Being divorced and, later, the wife of a not yet established intellectual considerably younger than herself, she had to fend for herself and her son, Paul. Her works articulate both the exhilarating feeling of being free and the agony of isolation and poverty. From her position of marginality, Lasker-Schüler constructed alluring imaginary realms of pain and pleasure, inviting women in particular to experience eroticism and ecstasy. Yet, her radical departure from the lifestyle of her youth did not include abandoning the Jewish sphere; on the contrary, her Jewishness became her primary identifier. Her understanding of Judaism was, however, anything but orthodox, and she picked and chose among customs and traditions as she saw fit. She blended Jewish elements with motifs and ideas from a number of different civilizations, thereby creating a mythology that invited her readers to play with different identities.

A major characteristic of Lasker-Schüler's texts is the integration of Jewish and Gentile German culture. Lasker-Schüler was conversant with the discourses and customs of both groups but did not completely identify with either one. Her desire for greater gratification than either one offered to women compelled her to deconstruct the Jewish and the Christian heritages and to reassemble the elements that pleased her in new constellations—she was a virtuoso at creating intercultural texts. From her disregard for patriarchal law sprang her poetic voice, the voice of a German-Jewish woman set free.

Lasker-Schüler embarked on her radically individualistic course at a time that promised unparalleled progress for Jews, women, and the working class, but the era's nationalism and militarism prevailed and ultimately led to World War I. She became the beneficiary of the earlier advocates of emancipation in that she had a basis from which to expand the range of options available to women, and her work continues to be a source of inspiration for authors and filmmakers. When Lasker-Schüler ventured out of her protected middle-class life, feminist associations and Zionism had already emerged, inspiring Jewish authors, Zionist or not, to develop new perspectives and to reconsider their Jewishness. The late nineteenth-century debates about Germans and Jews, nation, race, and *Vaterland* motivated many of them, including Lasker-Schüler, to represent the Jewish people and Jewish history according to these new paradigms. Her texts reflect upon central issues of German-Jewish discourse since its inception, but her relentless attacks against the status quo undermine the categories of ethnicity, religion, gender, and sexuality. Her visions are no less iconoclastic than those of Nietzsche, as was immediately obvious from her first volume of poetry, published in 1899 (Bauschinger 1980, 32; Hessing 1985, 62).

Lasker-Schüler stood at the forefront of the avant-garde; her friends included Franz Marc, Karl Kraus, Georg Trakl, Gottfried Benn, Martin Buber, Gershom Scholem, and Walter Benjamin. Because of her visibility, she was a target of anti-Semitic attacks even before the Nazi takeover. In 1933, she was physically assaulted and escaped to Switzerland, her country of exile until 1939. Her first journey to Jerusalem in 1934 inspired her exuberant account *Das Hebräerland,* documenting her impressions of the Middle East. During her third stay in Jerusalem in 1939, she was denied reentry by the Swiss authorities. The separation from Germany, especially her beloved Berlin, caused the aging poet severe distress, and being cut off from her mother tongue was an altogether unexpected turn of events (Bauschinger 1980, 266).

Losing contact with the German-speaking public crushed Lasker-Schüler's hopes for a wider reception of her works, particularly her plays. Her attempts to reconvene her friends in Jerusalem in a loosely knit literary circle, the *Kraal,* were not unsuccessful, but Jerusalem, torn by war and unrest, bore no resemblance to Berlin as she had known it in the 1920s. Moreover, the poet had changed; uprooted, sick, and disillusioned, she was highly critical of Palestine and denounced both the oppression of the poor and the animal abuse in Palestine.[34] Lasker-Schüler's later poems reveal her estrangement from the here and now and her longing for the past, often phrased as a desire to return to the womb or to childhood, envisioned as a lost paradise. Many of her friends dismissed her fear and pessimism as paranoia, yet history proved her right: she did live in a hostile world that persecuted her beyond her death in 1945. Her tomb at the Jewish cemetery on the Mount of Olives was vandalized and rediscovered only in 1967.

Lasker-Schüler's poetic vision evolved from her life on the fringes of German, Swiss, and Jewish society. The role of a *troubadoura,* into which she cast herself, enabled her to cope with poverty, the destiny of women under patriarchy. Lasker-Schüler faced material hardship as a twice-divorced bohemian who, although she had no regular income, went to any length to meet her ailing son's special needs. In her 1925 pamphlet *Ich räume auf! Meine Anklage gegen meine Verleger,* she articulated her outrage about being exploited by her publishers, but her poetry remained unaffected by her bitterness—her appreciation for luxury was untainted by greed, and her love was free of selfishness. She bore few grudges, even toward her former husbands, treating her relationships as if they were cosmic processes (Schuller 1993, 245). Consumed with a passion for humankind, Lasker-Schüler, however, was unforgiving of fanatics, anti-Semites, militarists, racists, misogynists, and animal abusers. Although her situation in Switzerland was somewhat better than that of other exiles who were forbidden to earn money, she found herself in dire circumstances and, as a Jew, was considered an unwelcome alien. Although in Jerusalem her economic situation improved somewhat, the daily exposure to life in the Middle East brought about the destruction of the poet's imaginary motherland.[35] She coined the sarcastic term "Misrael" to express her frustration and pined for Germany, which she was never to see again (Lasker-Schüler 1969b, 2:197).

When Lasker-Schüler first moved to Berlin, she lived the exuberant anarchism of the pre–World War I era to the fullest. This formative experience distinguished her from Gertrud Kolmar and Nelly Sachs, with whom she is frequently compared. Her work was rooted in the multicultural atmosphere of the German capital, which had proven a fertile ground for the intellectual development of many Jewish women.[36] At the cutting edge of modernity, Lasker-Schüler used to her advantage the fluidity of gender roles brought about by the industrial revolution. She assumed imaginary guises, referring to herself as Princess Tino of Baghdad and Prince Jussuf of Thebes, and made the literary transformation of her biography a central aspect of her aesthetics. A passionate moviegoer, she applied the make-believe of cinema to her own life. She changed her birth date, invented a grandiose family background, and bestowed fanciful names and titles upon herself and her friends to poeticize her world. These efforts represent the literary equivalent to the programs of turn-of-the-century painters and designers such as Gustav Klimt and Otto Wagner to adorn everyday life. The stylized nature imagery and the exotic figures of Lasker-Schüler's early poetry and sketches in *Styx* (1902) and *Der siebte Tag* (1905) evoke rarified Jugendstil atmospheres. Likewise, the intense prose of *Das Peter Hille-Buch* (1906) and *Die Nächte Tino von Bagdads* (1907) reveals a predilection for exquisite moods.

In the anonymity of the metropolis, Lasker-Schüler tested her limits outside of bourgeois norms. She lodged in inexpensive hotels and used coffeehouses as her salon and study. In this milieu, where the intellectual establishment and the avant garde, Gentiles and Jews, met, she held court, being the friend of a host of intellectuals and artists. Her emphatic statement to Ludwig von Ficker, "Thank God I'm a Jew," using the masculine rather than the feminine, expresses her iconoclastic proclivities in a nutshell (Lasker-Schüler 1969a, 1:112). Lasker-Schüler lacked the protection traditionally enjoyed by women of her background. Unlike Rahel Varnhagen and Fanny Lewald, she managed her affairs without a home base and male support, and she stood out as a target for hoodlums. Not surprisingly, she tried to retreat into her imaginary antiworlds as a refuge from her increasingly fascist and technocratic environment, as well as from her anguish over the untimely death of her son. After her escape to Switzerland, her works were still accessible in Germany to the Jewish *Kultusgemeinde,* but its activities were terminated by the Nazis after the *Kristallnacht* simultaneously with the dissolution of most Jewish institutions, including Bertha Pappenheim's Jewish Women's Association (Kaplan 1994b, 108). Then Lasker-Schüler's works were outlawed—forgotten and only slowly rediscovered in postwar Germany.

Early in her career, Lasker-Schüler problematized social norms, gender, and Jewish identity but rarely individual rights and nationality. The radicalization of the public sphere at the end of the Weimar Republic led her to a heightened appreciation of her individualism and her native language and country, although it made her particularly vulnerable. Unlike the polyglot Claire Goll, Lasker-Schüler wrote exclusively in German. Her affinity for Judaism in religious, spiritual, and national terms was not strong enough to counterbalance the loss of her German existence.

The collective experience of persecution was the cornerstone of Lasker-Schüler's Jewish identity. The poet's attachment to the Jewish people and the Hebrew language was intuitive, based on her ancestry and an affection for Judaism that corresponded in certain ways with the racial concepts of the time; Lasker-Schüler characterized Jewishness as an innate set of characteristics and a collective fate. In fact, Jakob Hessing surmises that her appreciation for German literature, particularly the classical and Romantic authors, was a more significant factor in her writing than her Jewish heritage (1985, 28). Indeed, Lasker-Schüler was quite unfamiliar with the Jewish tradition and Halakhic law, as her erroneous accounts of Jewish customs and her romanticized notions of Jewish spirituality in her 1920 work *Hebräische Balladen* reveal. Yet, it would be incorrect to consider these deficiencies exclusively a result of assimilation, as Rahel Varnhagen's, Fanny Lewald's, and Bertha Pappenheim's complaints about the ignorance of Jewish women in religious matters suggest. Lasker-Schüler's stirring 1905 poem "Mein Volk" (1959, 1:137, 292) and *Hebräische Balladen* (1959, 1:291–311), which struck a cord with numerous Jewish women writers, construct Jewish identity from an ethnic, historical, and mythical perspective, rather than from a religious point of view.

Even texts that do not address Jewish topics draw on the above-mentioned sources. In the 1906 play *Die Wupper,* set in the landscape of Lasker-Schüler's childhood, the dominant perspective is that of an outsider looking in as Germany's western industrial region is transformed into a magical but cruel "soul scape." The self-portrait of the poet on the book cover as the Prince of Thebes, a Mediterranean-looking woman's head with short black hair, represents the poet in the *Galut,* while the rural working-class environment is reminiscent of Georg Büchner's *Woyzek.* The regional dialect, the fairy-tale motifs, and the characters— a lecherous grandfather; a witchlike matron, an interloper between the oppressed and the privileged, who symbolizes the role traditionally played by Jews; a precocious girl; and her bourgeois seducer by the name of Heinrich, like Goethe's Faust—associate *Die Wupper* with the popular drama that has traditionally empowered the oppressed. Since the drama addresses social issues, it was occasionally produced in an unadorned Bauhaus style, but the charismatic aspects also occasioned expressionist-style performances.

Having at times lived on the verge of homelessness, Lasker-Schüler was uniquely qualified to portray the misery, as well as the grandeur, of vagrant life. The three transients in *Die Wupper,* equally pathetic and poetic men, are endowed with the demonic qualities of witches and the magic of Hasidic miracle rabbis. Rather than functioning as agents of social criticism, they are portrayed without moralizing. Pendelfrederech's exhibitionism, Lange Anna's transsexuality, and Gläserner Amadeus's pathology represent different paths to glory. Likewise, the senile grandfather is assigned wisdom and dignity; his nonsense words *Tum Tingeling* are a magic formula in the midst of chaos (1969b, 2:980, 989). Familiar with socialist literature, Lasker-Schüler confronts class-related issues without endorsing the revolutionary cause. Instead, *Die Wupper* reveals that, independent of money and status, the oppressed wield a power derived from the sexual and emotional needs common to all classes. All characters are dominated by the same instincts, and there are no outsiders to the human condition, not even the exponents of modern bureaucracy, represented by the gentlemen wearing top hats.

The ultimate power resides with the card reader, faith healer, and procuress Grandmother Pius, a multivalent figure like Elias Canetti's Therese (*Die Blendung*) or Broch's Mother Gisson (*Bergroman*), partly a witch, partly a "Great Mother" figure. None of the moderns are a match for this archetypal character, who manipulates their desires. As the surface structures of patriarchy and capitalism are gradually exposed, various illicit sexual relationships come to light. Among them, the seduction of a young girl by an older man is the most conventional, but, ironically, it causes a scandal, while other transgressions, less accessible to public discourse, do not. *Die Wupper* is epic theater, but in contrast to Bertolt Brecht, Else Lasker-Schüler avoids didacticism. Her play's aloofness reflects the poet's own situation: not only was she, as a Jewish woman, more immediately affected by the conditions she portrayed, but she was also more marginal to the system than proletarian men; hence her detachment.

Jewish authors, including Lasker-Schüler, were prevented by their marginal position from being emotionally invested in the concerns of the dominant culture. Not coincidentally, the most "German" of German dramas, *Faust,* has often been the target of their satire. As does *Faust* (part 1), *Die Wupper* revolves around the sexual encounter between an underage girl and a privileged man, but while Goethe's Gretchen is later elevated to embody the "Eternal Feminine," Lasker-Schüler's Lieschen remains a nobody who is sent to a reform school because her provocative sexuality is a threat to the repressive social system. What was once the material of a lofty romance is reduced to a deadly farce that involves the death of the seducer, an officer, thereby reversing the order of events in traditional German drama.[37] By ascribing overt sexual desires to her female and child characters, Lasker-Schüler questions the established moral code as well as the official discourse on sexuality. Indeed, she exalts the openness and spontaneity of children and poets because they pose a threat to the established order. In her erotic poetry, for example, Lasker-Schüler often assumes the role of a minstrel, showering her beloved with adulation and—imaginary—gifts.

Long before National Socialism, Lasker-Schüler explored alternatives to an exclusively German identity by reconstructing Jewish identity, an undertaking that required considerable resourcefulness on the part of an assimilated woman. Despite her general dislike of East European Jewish culture, she was fascinated with its mysticism and oral tradition as transmitted by Martin Buber. She also looked to Egypt, Iraq, and Palestine for inspiration. Her ideal was a Jewish-Christian synthesis to keep both religions intact and to end the Jewish Question. As the situation in Germany worsened and matters of content became the first priority for Lasker-Schüler, she turned to drama and prose as her major genres. The authorial voice in *Konzert,* in the 1932 play *Arthur Aronymus,* and in the 1937 eclectic journal of her Middle Eastern travels, *Das Hebräerland,* vacillates between hope and despondency. Yet, these works project greater optimism than the texts she wrote during her last years in Jerusalem.

In *Arthur Aronymus* Lasker-Schüler explores the foundations and the status of German-Jewish coexistence, using her own idealized family background as her example. The work's superficial harmony is foiled by an undercurrent of hatred and brutality. The incongruities in content and style contradict the conciliatory surface message established in the plot about Jewish-Christian spirituality. On the eve of the Nazi victory, Lasker-Schüler, herself a victim of the collapse of the tenuous German-Jewish symbiosis, acknowledges that after the Dreyfus affair and the Russian pogroms there was little hope for a coexistence between Jews and Gentiles.

The adult characters of *Arthur Aronymus* make an effort to lay to rest Christian anti-Judaism and the memory of the pogrom of Gesecke (1848–49), unaware that the minds of the children are already poisoned with hatred. A sense of impending doom overshadows the conciliatory laughter of the Jews and Christians who join as one family. Similar to Heine's *Rabbi von Bacharach,* the fairy-tale-like tone of *Arthur Aronymus*

76

softens the impact of the account of past atrocities—it is stated, for instance, that on Christmas Eve Jewish children were hanged "like candy" in the great hall of the school (1962, 2:560). The figure of Dorchen is a reflection of the poet's own experience of persecution, transformed into the story of a girl accused of witchcraft. Ironically, Arthur, the protagonist, formulates his religion of reconciliation during these troubled times. The happy ending, suggested in conjunction with a marriage between a Jew and a Christian, culminating in a feast during which both Easter and Passover food is served, seems to prove him right.

The union of the bishop's and Rabbi Schüler's families, Jews and Catholics, expresses the poet's yearning for harmony, but it does not neutralize the earlier tensions. Quite the contrary, as the actions of the children show; while the adults celebrate their newly established understanding, the children are playing witch-hunt. Under the leadership of the bishop's nephew, they proceed to burn Arthur, the most peace-loving Jew, dressed in his sister's garments. His jump across the fence prefigures Lasker-Schüler's escape to Switzerland. Arthur's costume suggests an analogy between anti-Semitism and misogyny, pogroms and witch-hunts; the children revel in the same sadistic pleasure that propelled the Nazi *Aktionen* and, centuries earlier, the burning of women. Lasker-Schüler's image of a Jewish boy in girl's clothes, being led to the stake by a cheering mob, is a foreboding as well as a fitting image.

Lasker-Schüler's name did not appear in the list of persons whose German citizenship was revoked prior to September of 1938. According to Bauschinger, this official act brought home to the poet the loss of her Berlin, with the *Romanisches Café* as her main reference point (Bauschinger 1980, 264–65). Before traveling to Asia, Lasker-Schüler had asserted that Palestine was her true home. After settling in Jerusalem, she was forced to confront the city of her dreams and her German-Jewish identity without disguises and role-playing. In Palestine, Lasker-Schüler was defined by her gender, her age, her German origins, her status as refugee and, most importantly, her poverty. Carl Stern, who recalls a "beautiful" poetry reading in Haifa, also remembers her "musty little room" and her "incredible indigence" (1989, 294). It seems a strange coincidence that he characterizes Lasker-Schüler by an image that occurs in Gertrud Kolmar's poem "Die Kröte" (Kolmar 1960, 159–60): Lasker-Schüler, wearing a gray fur hat with a turquoise-like stone, reminds him of "the tale of the toad and her jewel" (296–97).

The destruction of Germany as Lasker-Schüler knew it precipitated the breakdown of her inner reality. Jerusalem offered her no substitute for Germany, the motherland she had lost, and she encountered communication barriers that undermined her self-confidence. During her exile years it became obvious that German was her mother tongue and her medium; she never became fluent in Ivrit, although she loved it as the language of the liberated Jewish nation. Her despair was the same as that of other German-Jewish exile authors who had saved their lives but could not escape the odium of their native culture—in Palestine the German language was associated with anti-Semitism and the Nazi state. In the 1940s, German became identified with the Holocaust, and not only Zionists discouraged its use altogether. During this era, Lasker-Schüler's almost cosmic concept of herself and the world met with indifference or rejection. She embraced the internal and external Other: her female and her male self; her male and female friends; Jews and Christians; Jews and Arabs; rich and poor; but her contemporaries drew ever narrower racial, national, and cultural boundaries. Having escaped European anti-Semitism, she now became a witness to the Jewish-Arab conflict in Palestine, which proved that her lifelong struggle for deliverance and peace had come to naught.

In the 1943 poetry anthology *Mein blaues Klavier,* the major publication of Lasker-Schüler's Jerusalem years, austere forms and emotional detachment, almost numbness, prevail, suggesting a broken relationship to reality. In contrast to her earlier poetry, epithets are used sparingly so as not to interfere with the poet's search for universal values and her mourning for the times and places of her youth and her dead, particularly her son, Paul, and her mother. Lasker-Schüler, the great lover, is transformed into a mourner, yearning for an end to her suffering in a world that she experiences as diaspora. She yearns for the naïveté of youth in some other world, as the poem "Mein blaues Klavier" suggests (1959, 1:337). Clearly, Lasker-Schüler's proven methods of transforming reality—mythmaking, eroticism, and poetic subjectivity—prove futile against the terror spread by Nazi Germany's invasion of every country for which the poet had an affinity.

In the context of *Mein blaues Klavier,* even previously published poems assume a somber meaning: "An meine Freunde" (1959, 1:331–32) now reads like a declaration of loyalty with the Nazi victims, while others such as "Ich liege am Wegrand" (346) and "Die Verscheuchte"

(347) seem to lament the refugee's and survivor's dilemma. There seems to be no escape from devastation, neither by remembrance as in "Meine Mutter" (333) and prayer as in "Gebet" (338), nor by love and sensuality as in "Über glitzernden Kies" (339). As the imagery of the latter poem unfolds, it evokes the terror of the *Kristallnacht*, which the exiled poet can only imagine. Overall, the anthology conveys the suffering of a refugee unable to shake off the trauma of persecution and survivor's guilt. Only in a few poems a triumphant androgynous voice emerges, sustained by faith and acceptance. With this new spiritual posture, Lasker-Schüler confronted Jerusalem, the temporal and holy city.

In her last drama, *Ich und Ich* (1980), a vision of the concentration camp universe, Lasker-Schüler combines political satire with the language of classical German literature (1961, 3:85–103). The inclusion of English and Hebrew vocabulary intimates that the inferno created by Germany caused a global Babylonian confusion. Assuming a satirical stance, Lasker-Schüler associates her work with the anti-fascist *littérature engagé* of authors such as Heinrich Mann (e.g., his satire *Lidice*, [1943]). *Ich und Ich* is *Welttheater*, universal theater, set in Jerusalem's Hinnon Valley and in a garden close to the old city wall at a site representing heaven and hell. First and foremost, however, it is a German drama, replete with allusions to *Faust*, part 2. Imitating Goethe's storm-and-stress dramaturgy, Lasker-Schüler blends multiple time frames and levels of reality, which allow her to introduce literary and historical figures such as Faust, Mephisto, Nazi leaders, herself, and her friends.

The purposeful confusion of aesthetic and ethical values within the play calls for an examination of prefascist and antifascist discourses by authors such as Karl Kraus and Klaus Mann, of whom Lasker-Schüler is obviously critical because they ridiculed the fascists' bad taste, whereas the issue at hand was the Nazis' criminal intent. Rather than endorsing any specific resistance movement, Lasker-Schüler's work implies that Nazi Germany eludes the tools of a literary author. In the dialogue between Faust and Goebbels, for example, Faust expresses his shock at the brutality with which Herschel Grynszpan is treated by the Nazis. The young man whose attack on the secretary of the German embassy in Paris was used as a justification for *Kristallnacht* pogrom is abused and humiliated. Faust, who destroyed Gretchen and many other innocent people because he ruthlessly pursued his sexual desires and his lust for power, still subscribes to traditional values. Compared to their barbarism, expressed by drunkenness and offensive language on the part of even the most pretentious Nazi characters, Mephisto's and Faust's transgressions appear almost civilized. Resuming the witch motif from *Arthur Aronymus,* Lasker-Schüler exposes the perversion of justice in Nazi Germany; not the accused, but their accusers, are the villains.

Cognizant of the fact that no dramaturgy can convey the reality of World War II, Lasker-Schüler resigns herself to representing the shards of the civilization in which she had once placed her trust. Her approach is appropriate to illustrating the breakdown of Western civilization. If the existence of men such as Hitler, Goebbels, and Himmler proved German culture invalid, as many observers and critics maintained, then Lasker-Schüler was confronted with the fact that her life's work had become obsolete. This realization, in fact, pervades *Ich und Ich.* Lasker-Schüler demolishes the discourse of the educated German middle class and condemns an intellectual tradition that was so easily coopted by totalitarianism and an intellectual caste that so willingly followed the Nazis.

Ich und Ich traces the breakdown of language and symbols in the face of the unprecedented global catastrophe but does not offer any solution beyond the verdict that civilization as the author knew it had collapsed. All that was left for Lasker-Schüler, neither a Zionist nor a religious woman, to do was to commemorate her lost motherland and to mourn over the broken promise of reconciliation. In her last years, she acted as a guardian of Germany's legitimate literary tradition, but in the end she became a messenger of its demise. Lacking the energy to explore new directions, she revealed the plight of German Jews in exile and the end of the humanist tradition. Significantly, her drama ends with Goethe's famous *Gretchenfrage,* Gretchen's question to Faust: "Do you believe in God?" The figure of the poet, who, by being asked this question, is cast in the role of Faust, replies, "I am so content: God is 'here' " (1961, 3: 103). This ending transposes the solution to the crisis of European culture into the realm of religion and poetry.

Lasker-Schüler died in the year of the Allied victory over Germany, leaving behind *Ich und Ich* as her requiem to German-Jewish culture. She was spared the complete knowledge of the Shoah, and she did not live to see the State of Israel, of which she was skeptical even before its foundation.

❧ 3 ❧

The Troubled Metropolis

Jewish Women Writers and Modernity

The effects of the industrial revolution as characterized in Marx and Engels's *Communist Manifesto* (1848) were first portrayed by British and French authors such as Charles Dickens and Emile Zola. Their works on the plight of the urban proletariat in Paris and London also set the tone for German-speaking social-critical literature. Prior to the Revolution of 1848, only a few individual authors such as Georg Büchner had focused on the oppression of the working class and the need for revolutionary change; for the majority of Germany's and Austria's social critics, bourgeois interests, that is to say, the interests of their own class, had been the primary concern. With little regard to the situation of the lower social strata, they demanded the abolition of aristocratic privileges and the institution of a constitutional monarchy. Safeguarding middle-class privileges and defending them against the claims of women, Jews, and the poor was the agenda that fueled much of the literature by bourgeois male authors, who were afraid of losing their status to groups and persons whom they considered inferior. The phobia of social decline went along with an increasingly virulent nationalism, bolstered by racist and ethnocentric science and anthropology. Turn-of-the-century colonialism, anti-Semitism, antifeminism, and antisocialism were essential components of the very same anxieties and resentments. They produced a wide variety of literary stereotypes: the Jew as the ostentatious nouveau riche or scheming alien; workers and the working classes as an animalistic, destructive mob; emancipated women as militant bluestockings and lesbians; and non-German nations and non-European cultures as less than human.

Considering the repressive conservatism of both the German and the Austrian empires, statements such as Johanna Woltmann's—to the effect that "a young, aspiring Jew could ignore anti-Semitism completely, because society was relatively open, rewarded individual success, and even took up arms against the extreme and open Jew-hatred that manifested itself in France during the Dreyfus affair"—read almost like an apology and are plausible only in comparison with the abuses of the Nazi regime (1995, 22).[1]

Yet, in this precarious, if not chaotic, transitional period, increasing numbers of Jewish women became active as writers, critics, journalists, and scholars. It was precisely the turmoil of late nineteenth-century German and Austrian urban culture that eroded traditional family and class structures and provided for greater social mobility. As is evident from the example of Lasker-Schüler, metropolitan culture offered intellectual women no safe haven; as a result, many continued to rely on patriarchal institutions into which they fitted more or less successfully their literary and intellectual pursuits. Some, however, took advantage of the general confusion and embarked on an experimental course.

The predicament of women authors torn between a traditional private existence and modern lifestyles involving increased public visibility is expressed in texts problematizing urban culture from a social, feminist, ethical, and religious point of view. Around 1900, Jewish women poets, critics, journalists, and scholars had become too numerous to be considered exceptions, as had been the case with Rahel Levin Varnhagen and Fanny Lewald. But there was no safety in numbers; the escalation of hostile forces during and after World War I, anti-Semitism, an ethos of heroism and masculinity, and white supremacism threatened their existence in public and private. Undermined and jeopardized in so many different ways, they developed a keen sensitivity to societal conflicts and oppression, their own and that of other marginalized groups. The unprecedented caution they began to display toward the sphere that once had been their most natural environment, the city, is indicative of the changes that were taking place in urban Germany and Austria.

Before the Nazi takeover, a rich panorama of Jewish women's literature had evolved, including feminist authors such as Elsa Bernstein, better known under her pseudonym Ernst Rosmer, whose dramas scrutinize the underpinnings of Western civilization and recast mythological and religious women figures. Bernstein's approach resembles that of other authors, such as Alma Johanna König, a Holocaust victim, whose novel fragment *Der junge Nero* examines the psychological development of ancient Rome's paranoid leader in analogy to Hitler.[2] Such attempts at contextualizing in order to come to grips with the seemingly incomprehensible barbarism in Central Europe during World War I were an undertaking common to a number of Jewish authors, male and female, such as Gertrud Kolmar's *Robespierre,* Elias Canetti's *Auto-da-Fé,* and Hermann Broch's *Bergroman.* In addition, the latter two authors developed theories of mass psychology to examine the phenomena of mass psychosis, totalitarianism, and dictatorship, topics to which Hannah Arendt, Wilhelm Reich, Theodor Adorno, and Karl Kraus made significant contributions as well.

The centers of modernity—Vienna, Berlin, and Munich, and beyond them, Paris, London, and New York—attracted Jewish authors and artists, among them Claire Goll, Alice Schalek, and Bertha Zuckerkandl Szeps. The topics addressed by these authors, contributors to major publishers, include the arts, literature, architecture, and international affairs, as well as fashion and gossip. As was the case with most Jewish women authors, even those who had gained an international reputation during the interwar period, their activities remained by and large forgotten after World War II. After the Nazis had dismantled the political Left, journalists and authors with socialist leanings such as Käthe Leichter and Else Feldmann, both of whom wrote for the Viennese *Arbeiter-Zeitung,* disappeared from the public eye (I. Pollak 1993; Feldmann 1993a, 1993b). Feldmann, the cofounder of the *Vereinigung sozialistischer Schriftsteller* (established in Vienna in 1933), had been an advocate for destitute mothers and children. Her childhood autobiography, *Löwenzahn* (1993b), and her 1924 social novel, *Der Leib der Mutter* (1993a), portray the despondency and corruption of the Viennese proletariat with the same intensity that characterizes Elfriede Jelinek's *Die Liebhaberinnen* (1975) (see I. Pollak 1993, 106).

Only a fraction of the authors who were murdered in the Holocaust, Feldmann among them, or who were forced into exile were reintroduced into the literary debate. The same applies to women who, like Anna Freud and Yolanda Jacobi, had made their way into the forefront of psychology. After the gender barriers at the universities had fallen, and the status of women, including their suffrage, had improved following the demise of the empires, a considerable number of Jewish women made a name for themselves in philosophy and the humanities. Anna Seghers's dissertation "Jude und Judentum im Werke Rembrandts," Leonie Spitzer's dissertation on Rilke, Margarete Susman's study *Frauen der Romantik* (1929), and Hannah Arendt's dissertation on the concept of love in Augustine are but a few examples.[3] Frequently utilized by scholars, but rarely mentioned in the credits, these achievements are denied their due recognition to this day.

Although the works of Jewish women authors received little attention in postwar Germany and Austria, there is a continuity, albeit tenuous, between the prewar and postwar generations of German-Jewish women writers. In the most direct fashion, this continuity was maintained by authors who had begun their careers before 1933 and who, having survived the Nazi era, continued to write in their native language. Thus they imparted their legacy to the new German-speaking states. More indirectly, women authors of the pre-Nazi era inspired members of the following generation to write, even in the face of death and destruction. The works of Else Lasker-Schüler, Nelly Sachs, and Gertrud Kolmar, among others, were an integral part of the cultural life in the Nazi ghettos and concentration camps in Central and Eastern Europe and the exile communities in Switzerland and Palestine. In addition, writers such as Elsa Bernstein became inspirations to ghetto prisoners. Gerty Spies was one of the poets in Theresienstadt whom Bernstein mentored.

The Nazis crushed feminism along with socialism, banned the works of Jewish and feminist authors, and destroyed their reputations. Writers who engaged in feminist discourse and attempted to develop a language appropriate to the expression of women's sexuality undermined the phallocentric discourse of the conservatives and National Socialists—to name just a few examples, Paula Ludwig's sensitive examination of motherhood, love, and parenting, themes also addressed by Gertrud Kolmar and Veza Canetti, and Mela Hartwig's explicit portrayal of female sensuality in her novella *Ekstasen,* an attempt to refute androcentric psychoanalytical concepts, particularly the assumption that women were determined solely by their biological role. Hartwig opposed all biological determinism, including racism; in *Das Wunder von Ulm* she rallied against the persecution of the Jews and exposed the analogy between misogyny and anti-Semitism.

Claire Goll (pseudonym for Lang), née Klara Aischmann, Gertrud Käthe Chodziesner, whose pen name was Gertrud Kolmar, and Veza Canetti, née Venetiana Taubner-Calderon, who published under the pseudonyms Veza Magd, Martha Murner, and Veronika Knecht, are among the most significant authors of the interwar period. All three belong to the 1890s generation. They grew up in metropolitan areas and were concerned with similar issues. Goll, born in Nürnberg in 1894, grew up in Munich and moved via Switzerland to Paris. The Nazi invasion of France forced her and her husband, Yvan, into exile, and they lived in New York until 1947. She wrote and published in German, French, and English.[4] In 1977, she died an American citizen in Paris.

Except for her studies in France and a brief interlude in Hamburg, Gertrud Kolmar, the daughter of a prominent lawyer, lived in Berlin.[5] In 1943, she was deported to Auschwitz and murdered.[6] Canetti resided in Vienna, where the Second District, a center for East European Jewish immigration, had captured her imagination. In 1938, she and her husband, Elias, were forced into exile. They went to London, where she died in 1963. None of her works written after 1934 were published or performed until recently.

Like Kolmar and Canetti, Goll was born into a Jewish middle-class family with aspirations. Her father was an entrepreneur and diplomat. Her extended family included intellectuals such as Max Scheler and afforded her an exceptional exposure to cultural life. At the same time, it was a tense and trying environment. Highly critical of her background, Goll describes in her early 1940s autobiographical novel *Der gestohlene Himmel* (1990) the torment to which her overly ambitious and sadistic mother subjected her and her brother, supposedly driving him to suicide. Being socialized in the sophisticated but neurotic Jewish upper-middle-class circles (Klüger 1992, 7–68) provided Goll with access to European intellectual elite. Her first husband, Heinrich Studer, made a name for himself as a publisher, and her second husband, Isaac Lang (pseudonym: Yvan Goll), as a poet. Claire Goll herself entered the avant-garde as a poet, novelist, and socialite. She was affiliated with world-renowned personalities such as Joyce, Malraux, Einstein, Henry Miller, Picasso, Chagall, Rilke, Cocteau, Dali, and Jung, to name just a few.

Gertrud Kolmar's family, like those of many other Jews in Berlin, had its roots in Courland, an area in present-day Latvia.[7] Her father was a Berlin defense lawyer and a German patriot with a strong allegiance to the emperor,[8] and among her extended family were Walter Benjamin, her favorite cousin, and Hilde Benjamin, later the GDR Secretary of Justice.[9] Kolmar took care of her aging father until his deportation to Theresienstadt, although she experienced family conflicts no less severe than Goll. An introvert, she never discussed an abortion that she seems to have undergone as a young woman at her mother's request. This event, as well as her intimate relationships, remains a mystery to this day.

Like many Viennese Jews, Veza Canetti's parents had come to the Austrian capital from the outposts of the empire—her father was a Sephardic merchant of Hungarian descent, and her mother an heiress of Bosnian descent. In his autobiography Elias Canetti describes Veza Taubner-Calderon as a greatly admired, but withdrawn, personality in Karl Kraus's circles, an intellectual woman from a privileged but deeply troubled family, who devoted much of her time to service and charity. In temperament, because of her flamboyance and openly displayed eccentricity, Claire Goll resembles Else Lasker-Schüler, whereas introspection, introversion, and a certain reticence, perhaps part of the generational experience of Jewish women writers in German-speaking countries during the interwar period, establish an affinity between Gertrud Kolmar, Veza Canetti, and Nelly Sachs.

Kolmar was a certified translator of French, English, and Russian and a teacher for disabled children (Eichmann-Leutenegger 1993, 12); she served as a censor of the correspondence of prisoners-of-war at approximately the same time when Goll published flaming pacifist articles in which she denounced women's self-imposed passivity and submission to male authority.[10] A graduate of a public *Gymnasium,* Veza Canetti had completed the prerequisites for university study, but being independently wealthy, she pursued intellectual interests in private. She visited England frequently, and when in Vienna, she gave English lessons and tutored needy individuals. She was connected with members of the avant-garde, such as Wieland Herzfelde, which made her a part of other networks, including that of Anna Seghers. Canetti advocated socialism, feminism, and pacifism (E. Canetti 1980a: 77–87).

Canetti's genres of choice were prose and drama; Goll wrote essays and poetry; Kolmar's first love was poetry, and she turned to prose later. In the works of all three authors psychological and physical violence against women and children is a central concern. They used satire to raise social concerns, especially their criticism of the savage exploitation of women and the poor as sanctioned by capitalism and patriarchy. Canetti, Kolmar, and Goll exposed the problems of wife and child battery, rape, molestation, and prostitution in graphic detail. Their decision to confront brutality without apology forms the basis of their intense literary discourse on cruelty and oppression.

Aware of the problems inherent in the view of humanity in German classicism and idealism, and in opposition to cultural and ethnic biases, Canetti, Goll, and Kolmar developed strategies to expose the attacks on the Jewish and female body and psyche and to undertake a reexamination of the phenomenological world from the point of view of the underprivileged. Since the experience of World War I and the rise of National Socialism foiled any illusions they may have had about German culture, they also distanced themselves from the enthusiasm of expressionism: as women they could not identify with the call for the New Man; as Jews they were excluded from the national rebirth, and the Aryan supremacy proclaimed by the Nazis and other nationalist groups was designed to marginalize Jews and emancipated women. In addition, as the biting literary analysis of the New Woman by Irmgard Keun and Marieluise Fleißer suggests, which is confirmed by Klaus Theweleit's case studies in *Orpheus and Euridike,* the female roles of the time, including the New Woman, were the products of male fantasies (Keun 1989, 1990; Fleißer 1972; Theweleit 1988). In opposition to the latter, the Jewish women writers explored the condition of those who were most at risk in the new republics, including, in Kolmar's case, the threatened existence of animals in the modern world, a concern that was later taken up in Elias Canetti's notebooks and in the works of Rahel Hutmacher.

Race, Class, and Gender (Claire Goll)

The collaborative relationship between Claire Studer Goll and Yvan Goll was inspired by their mutual desire to inform the public of the atrocities of World War I.[11] In a review he had praised her devotion to the cause of pacifism, which she regarded as inextricably connected with feminism. She was convinced that women as mothers and educators had a special peace mission, as it was in their own interests to prevent men from becoming trained killers and thereby contributing to the escalation of violence against women and children.

Unlike many feminists who espoused certain aspects of the traditional binary view of gender championed by Freud and to an extent by Weininger, Claire Goll identified the segregation of men and women as the major cause of what she perceived as the schizophrenia in Western culture. Rather than defining gender in essentialist terms, she treated gender differences as socially constructed, and she shows humanity as a whole to be deformed as a result of artificially imposed norms. Some of Goll's female characters display considerable destructive potential, such as the mother figure in the autobiographical novel *Der gestohlene Himmel* (1990), which examines the author's relationship with her abusive and power-hungry mother. But Goll also portrayed female characters capable of love and nurturing. Nowhere, however, did she characterize suffering, self-sacrifice, or masochism as innate female traits. In her approach to the so-called Women's Question, Goll emphasized women's rational faculties and their potential for power in spite of the forces that hold them back. Goll represented patriarchal structures as the root cause of war, notwithstanding the complicity on the part of women who support military efforts and belligerent men (1989, 11). Hence the primary target of her criticism is the heroic masculine ethos of her time, uncovering its aggressive impetus for ethnocentrism in men and women. Her 1926 novel *Der Neger Jupiter raubt Europa* (1987) and 1931 novel *Ein Mensch ertrinkt* (1988) illustrate Goll's basic assumptions within the metropolitan setting of Paris. In addition, both works reflect the author's fascination with the racial melting pot.[12]

From a 1990s perspective, both novels make for uncomfortable reading due to their use of racial terms and inclusion of race as a major category. Bernhard Blumenthal, for example, decries what he terms Goll's "blatant stereotyping" (1983, 364). Central to both works are the physical and cultural differences of Europeans and Africans, discussed in the racial and ethnic terminology of their era; however, the racist stereotypes of colonial literature and the uncritical glamorization of Africans as musicians and dancers or as oversexed primitives are undermined.[13] Goll's novels reveal that, rather than expressing a new openness, the romantic images of Africans are yet another way to establish difference to ensure that Western culture and the European physiognomy would continue to be the measure of normalcy.[14]

Within the ethnic groups further under discussion, more subtle distinctions come into play, such as among Goll's Caucasian characters. The Parisians feel superior to the country folk, and they look down upon the Swedish protagonist in *Der Neger Jupiter* because she is too white and buxom (1987, 7). The Jewish characters in *Ein Mensch ertrinkt,* predominantly merchants, are accepted by neither black nor white society. They victimize members of both groups and are in turn victimized by both. In *Der Neger Jupiter* the binary opposition of black and white is already undermined by comments drawing parallels between Jews and Africans, such as when Jupiter states that perhaps his people are the "Black Jews of the twentieth century" (76).

As is to be expected under patriarchal systems, gender is the most obvious category within each ethnic group. It appears to have priority over race. In his marriage to a white woman, Jupiter Djilbuti occupies the dominant role, at least initially; so also does Babylas, in *Ein Mensch ertrinkt,* in his relationship with a servant girl. Goll seems to suggest that males, regardless of which race, have the upper hand. Yet, the plot of *Jupiter* does not play out this pattern. European males consider the title character's skin color and African features grotesque, but certain white women appreciate his exotic beauty and the sexual prowess they associate with it. After their honeymoon, the white woman perceives her African husband as a narrow-minded tyrant who hates all Europeans, including her, whereas the readers are called upon to interpret Jupiter's behavior with compassion because he is an uprooted man who resorts to desperate actions. In the course of the narrative he loses the quality of otherness—his anguish, the scorn on the part of white society, his wife's betrayal, and the loss of his child's affection lend him a tragic air that almost justifies the murder of his wife.

Goll shows that the European discourses on race and ethnicity are inappropriate to discuss the culture and psyche of an African man. Her novel is set apart from the colonial discourse that in contrast to her work stresses the lure and danger of black Africa from the European perspective: easy money, adventure, exotic women, and, as the other extreme, venereal disease and loss of identity. Many similar novels, written by authors such as Frieda von Bülow, Hanna Christaller, and Hans Grimm, warn white men against relationships with native women, which were actually quite common. Consensual intimacy between German women and black men was unimaginable to colonial writers, while Goll examines interracial relationships from the opposite point of view. With Jupiter as an example, she shows the extent to which European influences erode an African's integrity.

The allusion to *Othello* exposes the self-referentiality of racial discourses. Jupiter's notion that Shakespeare's "Super Negro" (*Überneger*) could help him if Othello were his ally, and his assertion that *Othello* is the only drama "written to glorify the dark race" (126) are so obviously flawed that they deserve closer scrutiny. Othello falls prey to the cunning of white men who manipulate his quick temper—he could not possibly act as an effective ally. If anything, he mirrors Jupiter's misfortune, which is actually greater than Othello's. Jupiter's identification with an African character, constructed by a white dramatist, shows that he has internalized the discourse of the colonizers almost completely. Having become an outsider of his own society without having been accepted into European culture, Jupiter experiences an identity crisis that causes him to mistake Othello, a scapegoat intended to satisfy the Elizabethan audience's sensationalism, for a positive black hero. White discourse fails Jupiter because it places him in the wrong cultural framework.

Class conflicts also come into focus in the course of Jupiter's and Alma's relationship. As an upper-class woman, Alma is in a position to keep her husband in check. In the proletarian and lumpenproletarian milieu of *Ein Mensch ertrinkt,* this is not the case. The protagonist of the later novel, the orphan Marie, a country girl at the bottom of the social scale, is Goll's case in point that class in social and economic terms supersedes race, ethnicity, and gender. Marie is exploited by the black chauffeur Babylas and by her Jewish employer. When she becomes pregnant by the latter and is dismissed from her job, she enters a downward spiral that ends in her suicide. As Marie is unable to care for her daughter, whom she refuses to give up for adoption, the child dies. The graphic images in which Goll describes the burning of the child's body in a mass crematory express the idea that proletarian women are destined for a life without hope.

Tracing Marie's demise provided the author with the opportunity to describe urban slums that she herself seems to have studied on location. Male and female characters contrasting with Marie's fate suggest that the two major factors in Marie's demise are her poverty and her gender. The exploitation of young proletarian women is shown to be a matter of course. Marie is taken advantage of by men of all races and classes and, as a domestic, by privileged women as well. Being a poor man is preferable to being a poor woman, and as the comparison between male and female prostitutes indicates, a male is safer than a woman in the same situation. Goll also reveals how the category of ethnicity intersects with that of class. One maid remarks to another, "Finally I worked for Jews" (1988, 127). The Gentile bourgeoisie does not mix with the Jewish middle class, and it occupies a more privileged status. Middle-class blacks are not mentioned at all, and black proletarians are segregated from the white working class—only occasionally do adventurous or ignorant women venture into the black dance halls (8).

In *Der Neger Jupiter raubt Europa* and *Ein Mensch ertrinkt*, the categories of race and status are questioned in such a way as to condemn the vilification of black people as well as the exoticism that celebrates them. In realistic terms Goll's black diplomat does not even come close to conquering his wife, let alone Europe—he plays a role assigned to him by white society and is destroyed as a result of violating the unspoken rules. Jupiter, who stands out as an exception in upper-class Paris, is distinguished from Babylas in terms of class, education, and degree of assimilation. His desire to conform, indicated by frequent quotes from European classical literature, helps him to gain access, but not integration. Babylas, on the other hand, an anonymous member of the masses, has no contact with the bourgeoisie except through crime, as a menial worker, or as a prostitute. His ambition to become a nude dancer—Josephine Baker is his role model—reveals furthermore that he has internalized Western racial iconography that stereotypes people of darker skin, including Jews, as feminine. Yet, his physical strength and his sadism toward women invalidates this cultural cliché.

In an examination of traditional Jewish stereotypes, Goll presents those who try the hardest to escape their underdog status as the most depraved, at least in their surface appearance. Like Babylas, the men who are disenfranchised because of their birth or occupation—the artist Mariati, the jeweler Delos, and the Jewish brokers and dealers—are portrayed as deeply corrupted. However, the episodes dealing with trade and commerce reveal the reason for their criminal behavior: the desire to succeed in the social Darwinist arena, where underprivileged males fight as if they were modern-day gladiators. In these episodes Goll exhibits the ground rules of capitalism, including the objectification of women and low-status males and the commercialization of relationships.

Ein Mensch ertrinkt reveals why the masses do not unite to combat the system: no matter how low the status of an individual, there is always someone more deprived. Holding out the promise of success, capitalism creates the illusion of opportunity, although there is no chance to achieve equality. *Der Neger Jupiter* explores the supposed prerequisites for integration: education and proper behavior. As the individual in question strives for perfection, the demands become ever more exacting—in short, assimilation is defined in such a way as to make it impossible to achieve. The categories of gender, race, and class are shown to have the function of preserving the status quo by preventing solidarity among the underprivileged. The heterosexual relationships in Goll's works reveal that men consider sexuality the key to a woman's psyche and use it to assert their power. Yet, Alma, in *Der Neger Jupiter,* who defies her husband, Didi, who practices birth control, and the two lesbians in *Ein Mensch ertrinkt* prove that subordination to a male is not part of a woman's biological makeup, nor is love necessarily a woman's fate. Rather, Goll configures sentimental love as a device to bolster the patriarchal system. All of her female protagonists have been conditioned to ascribe mystical powers to love. By examination, the commercial underpinnings of love and sexuality and constructedness of love and desire are made apparent. As the episodes involving the diamond traders disclose, masculinity, synonymous with dominance, is the attribute of the socially and financially strong, hence the desires involved in financial transactions assume a sexual character. "Abruptly he takes the envelope from his [the Indian's] long brownish fingers bent like the claws of a bird of prey and tears up his offer. He has the power to let go of the Indian. It is the true proof of his power to interrupt the sexual pleasure of bargaining right in the middle. He feels the excitement in his genitals" (1988, 51). Likewise, the sex act with which Marie pays for a necklace is prompted by her sensual desire for the pearls (61). The exchange reveals the basic pattern of capitalist economy: having dependent persons perform acts that violate their integrity. Privileged males and females have the power to make demeaning demands, forcing women of the lowest social stratum to perform menial work and sex acts they abhor, while the jeweler's wife has to tolerate her husband's unwanted advances but does not perform lowly tasks.

Goll portrays metropolitan culture as a network based on the oppression of one class by another, one race by another and, most of all, females by males. City culture has destroyed traditional patriarchy—the males in Goll's literary universe are no longer patriarchs. Refusing to bear the responsibility for their families and the children they sire, they act as capitalists who buy, rent, and use commodities. Clearly, the patriarchal discourse no longer reflects social reality but is an expedient means to rationalize power relationships.

Goll's analysis of big city culture bears a striking resemblance to that in Veza Canetti's novel *Die gelbe Straße* (1990) and Gertrud Kolmar's novella *Eine jüdische Mutter* (1965). All three works portray city culture as a lumpenpatriarchy. The old order has been replaced by a social Darwinism that is most hazardous for the weakest members of society, namely, women and children—not because of their innate characteristics but because they are kept in poverty. Kolmar, like Goll, characterizes the big city in which she lives, Berlin on the eve of the Nazi takeover, as a hotbed of racism and violence, but unlike Goll, she does not sidestep, as it were, the predicament of assimilated Jewry, the group most immediately threatened by the rise of fascism.

Mother and Daughter in Pre-Nazi Berlin (Gertrud Kolmar)

The economic and social problems in the new German and Austrian republics fueled left-wing and right-wing radicalism, both of which benefited from the trauma of the most devastating war of modern times and a widespread sense of humiliation caused by the Treaty of Versailles, in which Germany was charged with the responsibility for the lost war. The reparations imposed by the victors caused bitter resentment among the defeated population, who, reduced to poverty, were incapable of meeting the allies' demands. In addition, the prescribed reduction of the German military to a small fraction of its former size had profound implications for the sense of national identity, as Elias Canetti elucidates in *Masse und Macht* (1980b). In the absence of rehabilitation programs, large numbers of veterans found themselves jobless and unemployable. Many joined paramilitary groups such as the *Freicorps,* the Nazi storm troopers, or street gangs—it is important to note that the rise of the Nazi party and the gang wars of the American Prohibition were simultaneous events. Moreover, the newly instated form of government, democracy, added to the disorientation because it stood in direct contradiction to the conservative ideology that had dominated the Wilhelminian and Francis Josephinian high school and university curricula (Herf 1984, 61, 33). From their inception, the German and Austrian interwar republics were threatened by their own citizens, who questioned the viability of the states in which they lived. This was especially true for Austria, which was drastically reduced after the disintegration of the Habsburg empire. The peace treaty prevented the remainder of the former multination state, German-speaking Austria with Vienna as its capital, from merging with Germany, although a large segment of the population favored this option.

The products of authoritarian, rigidly structured monarchies, Germans and Austrians were unaccustomed to and to a large extent uncommitted to democracy, except for the socialists, who took the leading role in both republics. They faced a determined opposition on the part of militarist, fascist, and royalist groups. The power of the extreme right soon became manifest in a series of acts of terror and political assassinations, including the murder of Walther Rathenau, Germany's Jewish minister of foreign affairs in 1922, the pogrom in the Berlin Jewish quarter in 1923, the year of the coup d'état attempted by Hitler and Ludendorff, the murder of Viennese novelist and sexologist Hugo Bettauer in 1925 and that of Theodor Lessing in 1933. The reorganization of the Nazi Party in 1925, following Hitler's release from prison, and the reorganization of the SA, the party's militia, and the burning of the Palace of Justice in Vienna in 1927, followed by a shift of power toward the right, marked some of the turning points in the history of the interwar democracies. The closing of the stock exchange in 1931 left millions of people unemployed and further set the stage for the totalitarian regimes. In Berlin, the bank scandals were followed by anti-Semitic riots under the leadership of the SA and the formation of a conservative and right-wing *Volksfront*. By 1932, the membership of the SA had risen to 220,000, and in some key states such as Prussia, Bavaria, and Württemberg the NSDAP had become the largest political party.

These events were closely observed by German Jewish intellectuals, rightfully concerned about the effects of anti-Semitic propaganda. Calumnies such as the *Dolchstoßlegende,* concocted by Hitler and Ludendorff, consolidated the enemy image of "the Jew" and minimized the psychological impact of the defeat in 1918. Convinced that the invincible German military could not have been overcome except by foul play, the believers in the "Stab-in-the-Back" legend maintained that a Jewish conspiracy had foiled the German victory. Jewish authors responded in a wide variety of publications to these and other damaging allegations made by the anti-Semitic press, whose products included the widely read *Protocols of the Elders of Zion,* Theodor Fritsch's *Handbook of the Jewish Question,* and Julius Streicher's pornographic hate-journal *Der Stürmer.*

One of the first works scrutinizing the interplay of anti-Semitism and German-Jewish identity was the heartrending autobiographical account

Mein Weg als Deutscher und Jude (1921) by Jakob Wassermann, which portrays the difficulties faced by a lower-middle-class Jew whose goal was to become a German writer. Wassermann examined the deep-seated Judeophobia of German and Austrian Gentiles, as well as his dual identity. Less ponderous in his approach, Hugo Bettauer poked fun at the Nazis' ideology of ethnic cleansing in his 1925 utopian novel entitled *Die Stadt ohne Juden* (1988), which paints a satirical picture of life in Vienna under Nazi rule. The work conveys Bettauer's conviction that without Jews the Austrian capital would be a lackluster provincial town. In a more scholarly vein, Arnold Zweig in *Das ostjüdische Antlitz* (1920), Martin Buber in *Die Chassidischen Bücher* (1927), and Gershom Scholem in his studies on Jewish mysticism disseminated information about East European Jewry and Jewish thought. Blending fiction and history, Lion Feuchtwanger scrutinized German-Jewish relations from a Jewish point of view in his 1925 novel *Jud Süß* (1965), which debunks misconceptions disseminated by anti-Semitic publications. In 1927, Martin Buber's journal *Der Jude* devoted a special issue to the theoretical discussion of the coexistence of Jews and Gentiles, titled *Judentum, Christentum, Deutschtum*. In the same year, Joseph Roth's analysis of the Jewish diaspora in nineteenth- and twentieth-century Europe, *Juden auf Wanderschaft,* and Arnold Zweig's *Caliban oder Politik und Leidenschaft,* an essay discussing anti-Semitism in the context of politics and mass psychology, were published.

This extraordinary intellectual effort to interpret Judaism and Jewish culture to a Gentile and assimilated public reflects the twofold problem facing Central European Jewry. First, the almost complete absorption of many West European Jews into Gentile culture, according to Felix Theilhaber, was tantamount to the destruction of German Jews (1921). The other issue was, paradoxically, mounting anti-Semitism, which denied that any assimilation had taken place. The anti-Semitic press portrayed Jews as an unchangeable demonic entity, as the archetypal *Eternal Jew.* The effect was increased prejudice against immigrants from Eastern Europe, regardless if they were Hasids or socialists, on the part of the Gentiles and the Westernized Jews. In the face of this dual pressure, authors who rejected complete assimilation redefined or reinvented their Jewishness in a way that allowed for a dual German-Jewish identity. Monika Shafi observes that Gertrud Kolmar's pseudonym, the German version of her father's ancestral town of Chodziesen, conceals

the author's Polish-Jewish roots and solves her problem of not being allowed to publish under her family name (1995, 33). Jewish men, alarmed
by having their patriotism questioned, demonstrated their allegiance to
Germany in public events such as the rally of the *Reichsbund jüdischer
Frontsoldaten* (Imperial Association of Jewish Veterans), held in 1926,
and still others devoted themselves to a variety of progressive social and
political causes.

After Hitler's rise to power, Jewish authors, regardless of their persuasion, were silenced—forced into exile, imprisoned, or killed. A short
time later, in 1934, Austria's newly established Catholic dictatorship
began its campaign against the political Left. In addition, fascist and
Nazi ideology had a strong impact on the population of Austria and
other European countries that were systematically infiltrated by Nazi
agents. At the time of the annexation of Austria and the conquest of
Czechoslovakia, Poland, and France by the Nazi military, the ground-
work for a Nazi-dominated network of dictatorships had been prepared.
Many of the persons most directly threatened by these developments,
most notably Jewish intellectuals, recognized the significance of the
year 1933 for Germany and the year 1938 for Austria. In both instances,
the Nazi takeover was followed by a mass exodus of Jews and Leftists
into exile.

Unlike numerous members of her family and circle of friends, Gertrud
Kolmar remained in Germany until her own deportation on one of
the last transports of Jewish forced laborers from Berlin to Auschwitz.
Like Lasker-Schüler, she was highly acclaimed by the cultural establishment of the Jewish community. In Austria, Veza Canetti wrote for
the Viennese *Arbeiter-Zeitung* until her publisher succumbed to anti-
Semitic pressure and terminated his Jewish contributors, many of whom
were women. After the so-called *Anschluß,* Canetti escaped with her
husband to England. Living in Paris, Claire Goll was somewhat more
sheltered from the direct impact of the Nazi regime than were Kolmar
and Canetti, but she had firsthand knowledge of the reports of German
exiles.

Kolmar's novella *Eine jüdische Mutter* (1965), Canetti's novel *Die gelbe
Straße* (1990), her drama *Der Oger* (1991), and Goll's novel *Arsenik* capture the tense atmosphere preceding the Nazi takeover in the authors'
respective countries of residence. All four works are set in close proximity to the metropolis, but their characters' closed-in and limited sur-

roundings evoke the marginalized position of Jewish women at a time of radical androcentrism and ethnocentrism. The garden colony where Martha Wolg, the protagonist of *Eine jüdische Mutter*, lives with her child resembles the milieu of Brecht and Dudow's avant-garde film *Kuhle Wampe*, yet Kolmar's novella shows this environment without idyllic overtones and progressive spirit; rather, it reminds the reader of the treacherous country scenes in Alfred Döblin's *Berlin Alexanderplatz*. Here, like in *Eine jüdische Mutter*, the dilapidated semirural environment is associated with criminal activity, sexual abuse, and aberrant behavior. This is also the case in Canetti's novel and drama, both of which are set in Vienna's Second District, a more provincial environment than the Inner City. By focusing on one street of a specific neighborhood, Canetti places the focus on the lower-middle-class milieu. The atmosphere of this restrictive and authoritarian environment resembles Goll's stifling small-town setting of a village close to Paris in *Arsenik*.

Of the three authors, only Kolmar addresses Jewish issues directly.[15] Goll made subtle use of Jewish stereotypes in order to set her protagonist apart from the rural population, and Canetti, endorsing socialist and feminist principles, addressed gender, but no Jewish themes, perhaps because the latter would have disqualified her novel from being included in the *Arbeiter-Zeitung*. Significantly, Kolmar's novellas were not published during the author's lifetime. *Eine jüdische Mutter*, written in 1932, must be interpreted as Kolmar's literary stocktaking at a time when, at least for her, there can be no doubt that the German-Jewish symbiosis had come to an end. *Eine jüdische Mutter* and the novella *Susanna* (1994), completed shortly before her deportation to Auschwitz, are central to the works of Jewish authors examining the coexistence of Jews and Gentiles in Central Europe.

Kolmar's attitude differs from that of other intellectuals such as Martin Buber and Alfred Döblin, who in the early years of the Nazi regime believed that persecution offered Jews a unique chance for a cultural and spiritual renewal (D. C. G. Lorenz 1992b, 37). Rather, Kolmar was aware that Germany had ceased to be a safe place for Jews. In *Eine jüdische Mutter*, completed in 1932, the themes of rape and mutilation, betrayal, murder, and suicide, with a Jewish mother and her daughter as the primary victims, signal the end of the status quo, the more-or-less peaceful coexistence between Jews and non-Jews from the period of emancipation to the Nazi era. According to Marion Brandt, Kolmar's characters reflect the author's inability to take refuge in the traditional female roles, mother or wife. The author enjoyed a modicum of safety only in the role of daughter (Brandt 1994, 173–74).

In *Der jüdische Selbsthaß* (1930), Theodor Lessing discussed a widespread malaise among German-speaking Jews that, according to him, caused them to reject their Jewish identity. Lessing identified the desire to be German rather than Jewish as a form of self-hatred and established as its cause the internalization of anti-Semitic discourse. He claimed that the identification with Gentile culture and the attempts to erase traces of Jewishness had their origins in strategies designed to avert discrimination, which resulted in Jewish identity becoming devalued (30, 71). Kolmar's *Eine jüdische Mutter* addresses precisely this phenomenon, with which the author was familiar from her father's attitude, if not from Lessing's work. Kolmar's character study of a Jewish woman estranged from her community and her religion even anticipates Sander Gilman's recent argument in *Jewish Self-Hatred* (1986), according to which self-hatred is caused by the internalization of the enemy image that the majority superimposes on the minority. Unfamiliar with Judaism, Kolmar's protagonist Martha Wolg calls to mind Pappenheim's concern about the growing alienation of Jewish women. Martha, the daughter of East European immigrants, accepts a false group identity and buys into the defamatory myths created by anti-Semites. Her belief in her otherness enables her to avoid the actual confrontation with her opponents. Martha constructs her Jewish identity from hostile stereotypes in much the same way as described by Gilman: "We might assume that perceiving the fault as lying within themselves, outsiders would acknowledge their difference and cease striving for identification with that group which has labeled them as Other. On the contrary, however, while the unconscious sense of rejection is present, this rejection is projected by the outsider unto the world. Now the mechanism of stereotyping is brought full circle" (1986, 2–3). Using Martha as an example, *Eine jüdische Mutter* exposes the consequences of abandoning Jewish identity without a viable new German concept of herself and, more important, without having been integrated into the German *Volk*. In the absence of a community, real or imagined, Martha suffers self-doubt as to how to relate to herself, to her child, and to the outside world, which the narrator portrays as hostile or indifferent at best.

Martha Wolg, née Jadassohn, remains an outsider to her husband's family; even after marrying a non-Jew and bearing his child, the Gentiles consider the daughter of Jewish immigrants an alien, and she no longer belongs to her community of origin. Her mother and her dying father regard their daughter's union with a non-Jew as an outrage, but demoralized by sickness and poverty, they are too weak to oppose it. Aware that their daughter has already entered an illicit relationship with Friedrich, they hope that marrying a well-to-do Gentile will at least secure her future. Ultimately, it makes little difference whether Martha receives her parents' faint blessing or whether she is expelled from the fold of her family, as was the custom with daughters marrying outside the faith: Martha represents the archetypal stranger, whose image haunts Kolmar's poetry as well. She is a Jewish woman without ties to other Jews or to the Jewish community, her relationships with Gentile men are superficial and destructive, and there is no safe haven, no motherland, to shelter her and her daughter.

Martha's father-in-law does not welcome his daughter-in-law because of her background and her lack of money. The only tie between Friedrich and his wife is their initial sexual attraction; later he regards her as a wild woman and a liability. In that sense, Kolmar's story about the marriage of a Jewish woman and a Gentile man is a modern-day Medea myth, the major difference being the fact that Martha's husband dies and his widow continues to live as a stranger among his people. After Friedrich's death, the loose ties between Martha and her in-laws dissolve, and she moves with her daughter to the outskirts of Berlin.

Living in complete isolation, mother and daughter represent the most basic social unit on which Jewish identity rests. Their example shows the nurturing intimacy as well as the vulnerability of the matriarchal cell within a patriarchal and racist setting. As genuine as Martha's love for her child may be, it is corrupted by her—as it turns out, not unjustified—mistrust, which severely impairs her judgment. Living like a pariah causes her social skills to deteriorate until she withdraws into her own imaginary world entirely. People consider her an eccentric, not only in her home environment, but also at her place of work, where she develops into an accomplished animal photographer under the guidance of a woman photographer. Along with other details, Martha's profession must be read as an allusion to Kolmar's own recluse existence and her preoccupation with animals and as a hint that the author identified with her protagonist to a certain extent.

In the absence of a communal life, Martha establishes her and her child's identity on the basis of her notions of motherhood and Jewishness. Lacking the input of other people, she is unaware that she is increasingly affected by racism and Nazi ideology. For example, she allows her lover, Renken, to interpret her uninhibited sexuality as an ingrained Jewish trait and to define her Jewishness in terms of her blood (1965, 121). As Martha's discussions with her would-be savior show, she defines herself through stereotypes that resemble those propagated in Streicher's *Stürmer* and Hitler's *Mein Kampf.* Clearly, her isolation and her despondency have made her susceptible to anti-Semitism, and a revision of her misconceptions would be possible only in a Jewish environment.

Martha derives the license to kill her deeply traumatized daughter from this skewed image of Jewish behavior in conjunction with the doctrines of eugenics and social Darwinism, which she combines with a confused, homespun mythology of animal instinct and a Jewish mother's love. Only when she discovers a collection of racist journals on her lover's desk does she recognize which ideology actually is the driving force behind her actions, and she becomes aware of her unintentional complicity with her people's enemies. Beyond problematizing the mother-daughter relationship, Kolmar's novella reveals the failure of assimilation, symbolized by the unsuccessful relationships between a Jewish woman and Christian men, and the indifference displayed by Gentile characters toward a Jewish mother asking for justice (15–18).

Kolmar's narrative, furthermore, confirms Theilhaber's thesis about the immanent self-destruction of German Jewry by illustrating the elimination of the Jewish content from synagogue services. Among the examples mentioned are wedding sermons replete with allusions to German literature, concealing the Jewish ritual. " 'It was a marvelous sermon,' someone remarked afterwards, 'so liberal—as if it had not been held by a Jewish priest' " (44). These digressions about the larger community show that even if Martha had sought the support of other Jews, she would have found her own self-hatred reinforced. Rather than being an isolated case, Kolmar suggests, Martha represents only one of the many Jews corrupted by internalized anti-Semitism. Kolmar's protagonist finds herself in a no-win situation: there is no possible way to stop the erosion of Jewish life; nor is there acceptance by the Gentiles. The self-loathing and the hostility that she faces on a daily basis cause

Martha to vacillate between depression and grandiosity. Her imper-
sonal relationship with Renken is characterized by both of these modes,
which prevent her from opening up to him, and his racism; because
of this, he deems her less than human. He seeks an adventure with an
exotic woman; she wants to avail herself of his services by offering him
sex. Blinded by her unrealistic view of herself and her partner, she over-
estimates the power she has over him and his influence among Gentiles.
These and other misunderstandings illustrate that Jews and non-Jews
interact on the most superficial level, even in intimate relationships. A
few miles outside of the melting pot of 1920s Berlin, Jews and Gentiles,
and for that matter, men and women, continue to live in separate worlds.

There were many other authors who addressed the issues of gender and ethnicity in their works, in particular, Marieluise Fleißer in
Fegefeuer in Ingolstadt (1926) and *Pioniere in Ingolstadt* (1929) (both reprinted in Fleißer 1972, vol. 1). These two dramas expose the concept
of the New Woman in a society with double standards as a failure, and
Bertolt Brecht in a key scene of his 1938 work *Furcht und Elend des Dritten Reiches* (1967) shows the brittleness of German-Jewish relationships.
What distinguishes Kolmar's work is the fact that she combined both
issues in a discussion of social concerns and concrete physical existence.
Her approach, less ostensibly ideological than Fleißer's, as Monika Shafi
asserts, provides the basis for an uncompromising analysis and critique
of twentieth-century German society (Shafi 1995, 17). *Eine jüdische Mutter* shows that the metropolis did not create a new society but, rather,
a confusion of values, of which Martha's state of mind is paradigmatic.
Martha loves the German classics, but they offer her no comfort in her
time of need. Neither does Judaism, since she has forgotten her Jewish prayers. Kolmar's protagonist shares her predicament with the majority of German Jews, entrapped by a culture that had once endorsed
progress, enlightenment, and humanism, but that ended up destroying
them. Kolmar's novella leaves no room for a Jewish *renouveau*. Instead,
it suggests that those who abandoned their identity will end in destruction or self-destruction.

A few months before the Nazi takeover, Kolmar presented in *Eine
jüdische Mutter* her evaluation of the 150-year-long history of assimilation. Using the example of a woman who kills her daughter because she
believes the girl's life is ruined beyond repair, and who later commits
suicide because she cannot bear the consequences of her crime, Kolmar

suggests that Jews who naively consort with German nationalists and identify with the German mainstream inadvertently lend their support to anti-Semitism and misogyny, both of which appear already in tandem in Otto Weininger's *Geschlecht und Charakter* (1906). She argues in her novella that the corruption of Jewish values leads to self-elimination, thereby aiding the cause of the Nazis. Insofar as they accepted racism and eugenics, the assimilated Jews of Western Europe became the accomplices of the mass murderers.

Feminism and Socialism in Vienna (Veza Canetti)

Like Kolmar's novella, the works of the dramatist and novelist Veza Canetti were written with an awareness of radical politics, including the wider implications of the Nazis' rise to power. However, as an Austrian writer, Canetti viewed the situation as less inescapable than Lasker-Schüler and Kolmar. Veza Canetti's work and, for that matter, the author herself were forgotten after her departure to England in 1938. After her death in 1963, Elias Canetti dedicated his publications to her. Thus, she became known by name as one of the muses who inspire creative men. A few years before his own death in 1994, Elias Canetti began to publish his wife's works. Earlier, in *Die Fackel im Ohr,* he discussed the impression Veza Taubner-Calderon made on him at their first meeting in 1924 at one of Karl Kraus's readings. The then twenty-seven-year-old woman, already well known in the Viennese avant garde for her wit and critical judgment, played a key role in the development of her future husband, who was seven years her junior (E. Canetti 1980, 85).

The "beautiful raven lady" reappears sporadically in *Das Augenspiel,* the third part of Elias Canetti's autobiography, as a stabilizing presence in their Grinzing home, one of Vienna's privileged suburbs (1985, 86, 231ff.). Whereas Canetti elaborates his own views as a writer and critic, he does not discuss his wife's activities as an author and translator, and his introduction to her novel *Die gelbe Straße* reveals little more. Canetti maintains that she began writing in order to counterbalance the impact of his literary breakthrough on their relationship and to emotionally survive his creative efforts. According to him, she did not credit herself for her own work, out of consideration for him (E. Canetti 1990, 5).

Canetti underscores his wife's predilection for marginalized and victimized characters, particularly women, who are destroyed by bad marriages or in the service of others (6). Although certain elements of *Die gelbe Straße* and *Der Oger* (1991), the setting in Vienna's Leopoldstadt and the protagonist's Bosnian roots, reflect the author's background, Canetti does not admit the possibility that characters such as Mr. Iger's wife in *Die gelbe Straße* could be a reflection of Veza Canetti's own experience, as seems to be suggested by the emphasis placed on disabled characters. Instead, he emphasizes a less obvious aspect of her work, namely, the theme of altruistic service, and he does acknowledge the novel's feminist thrust, which he considers revolutionary for its time. At the same time, however, he characterizes Veza Canetti as moderate and feminine, claiming that she had an aversion to militant behavior as a result of her "admiration of beauty, seduction, and abandonment." "On the contrary, she had higher expectations of women, because she was convinced of their superior potential," he asserts (6–7).

Canetti's deference to her husband's work is characteristic of many women intellectuals of her time—so is her husband's unquestioning acceptance of her sacrifice. Like Claire Goll, she seems to have supported unconditionally her husband's aspirations as a writer. In view of the apparent similarities in both authors' works and the fact that Veza Canetti's prose appeared before Elias Canetti's novel *Die Blendung* was published in 1936, it must be assumed that her creative energy not only sustained but also shaped his work to a considerable degree. Veza Canetti published between 1932 and 1934; her career was limited by personal and political constraints.

The short story "Geduld bringt Rosen" in Wieland Herzfelde's anthology *Dreißig Erzähler des neuen Deutschland: Junge deutsche Prosa* (1932), published by the Malik Verlag in Berlin, one of Lasker-Schüler's publishers, contains Veza Canetti's philosophy in a nutshell. Urban culture, where abject poverty and undeserved luxury exist side by side, is examined from a social-critical perspective. The way in which the privileged compensate for their guilt by ostentatious sentimentality and worthless handouts to the poor is held up to scrutiny and ridicule. As a socialist—her views correspond to the tenets of Austro-Marxism—and as a Jewish woman writer, Canetti faced difficulties in finding publishers during those years. Her novel *Die gelbe Straße* appeared in the Viennese *Arbeiter-Zeitung* after she had received the first prize from the paper in a short story contest. Two additional novels are mentioned by Canetti in a biographical note, but they appear to have been lost (Göbel 1990, 172, 178).

The Viennese *Arbeiter-Zeitung,* Canetti's major publication outlet, had made its debut after World War I with contributions by socialists and avant-garde intellectuals such as Karl Kautsky and Viktor Adler. Over the years, the paper published texts by Albert Einstein, Yvan Goll, Jura Soyfer, Theodor Plivier, and Robert Neumann, translations of international literature, and reviews of social criticism, art, and literature. Furthermore, it included debates on issues such as the immigration of East European Jews, the pauperization of the working classes, and feminism.

After the Nazis' rise to power, Canetti's works could no longer appear in Germany; after the establishment of the Austrian *Christliche Ständestaat,* she lost her Austrian publishers as well. In the wake of the anti-Jewish boycotts and the book burnings in Germany, Austrian publishers became wary of their Jewish contributors. As Canetti explained in a letter written in 1950, she had to use as many as three different pseudonyms, because Otto König, the editor of the *Arbeiter-Zeitung,* cautioned her that too many contributions by her might damage his paper's reputation and hurt the cause of socialism. At the same time, he expressed his appreciation for her novels and short stories.[16] Canetti's unpretentious and witty style as well as the message of *Die gelbe Straße* fit extremely well into the feuilleton of the *Arbeiter-Zeitung,* whose readers were class-conscious blue-collar workers and left-wing intellectuals. Canetti's narrative voice is colored by a local flavor, achieved by the use of Viennese dialect, idioms from other languages of the former Austro-Hungarian Empire, and references to specific locations.

The setting is the multifaceted milieu of Vienna, which by virtue of its diversity is the ideal environment to illustrate the socialist ideal of internationalism. Canetti's readers are constantly reminded of the fact that one of the strategies of capitalism is to exaggerate the differences between the oppressed groups in order to keep them in check. At the same time, differences based on race, language, and ethnicity are shown to be less significant than the poverty and powerlessness that the underprivileged have in common. Rather than following one single plotline, the novel features a collective, the inhabitants of Yellow Street, which according to Elias Canetti was modeled after the Ferdinandstraße, located in the same district as the Prater, Vienna's amusement park, and the station of the Northern Railroad, which connected Vienna to Eastern Europe. The entire quarter was replete with open-air markets and coffee-houses, situated between the Danube River and the canal.[17] The latter is featured as a popular suicide site for desperate girls. Counter to the expectations raised in Elias Canetti's introduction, beauty and seduction are not factors in *Die gelbe Straße*. Rather, the novel addresses social ills in sober, concrete terms: every oppressor has a name and a face; behind every crime there is a definable perpetrator.

Each chapter focuses on a different set of characters that are connected through a network of plots. Featured in different parts of the novel, these literary figures provide continuity in an otherwise loosely knit narrative fabric. Identity is constructed by striking physical traits and easily identifiable phrases, such as the exclamation *Hàt,* habitually uttered by Mrs. Hatvany, denoting shock or skepticism. Canetti's narrative register includes the tragic, the tragicomic, the humorous, and the grotesque. Sudden changes in tone suggest that in modern urban culture tragedy can be averted by resolute action—in this respect, Canetti's antideterminist outlook is more optimistic than that of other critical authors of her time. In her work, personal initiative does make a difference, and even the most destitute individual has a choice. Hence her plots progress from bleak to hopeful as those destined to be victims begin to act rather than react.

The first three chapters of *Die gelbe Straße* portray the relationship between victims and exploiters; among the latter is a disabled woman devoid of remorse or pity. Deformed and despised, she considers herself a victim and believes that she is justified in tormenting other people. In addition, there are a husband who abuses his wife and children, and an employment agent who barters off women as if they were merchandise. In all cases, the aberrant behavior is motivated by a kind of greed that signals profound alienation. Rather than being attributed to the poor on whose part the desire to accumulate wealth would seem justified, it is individuals who have reached a secure position that are shown to be the most ruthless exploiters. In keeping with Marxist thought, Canetti attributes the most serious social abuses to the middle class, which she portrays as producing the most aggressive social climbers and business-people. Their ambition and addiction to material wealth are the central themes in *Die gelbe Straße*.

The last two chapters focus on female characters, a mother and a daughter, who are determined to fight the system. Like Lasker-Schüler in *Die Wupper,* Canetti suggests that women who want to take on the pillars of the community have to adopt the exploitative methods by which their adversaries live; it is made obvious that in a situation of oppression, compassion is out of place. Rather, Canetti argues through her characters that it is important to avoid emotional ties with the exploiters, lest oppression become enslavement. Tracing how gender-specific conditioning dovetails with unfair legislation, Canetti portrays that the most brutal forms of tyranny exist in the family, thereby characterizing patriarchal marriage as the ultimate stronghold of capitalism.

Die gelbe Straße reveals the way in which the institution of marriage bolsters the existing power structures. By assigning exchanges within the family to the private sphere, the dealings between a man and his dependents are exempt from the control required of business transactions. Denied legal and civil rights, women and children are left at the mercy of the head of the household. Possible actions of self-defense on the part of the wife and children to escape from abusive situations are foiled because of their economic dependence on the breadwinner. As the example of Mr. Iger reveals, by regulating the social contacts of the family unit and through his control over the persons whom his wife loves, namely, her children, the man manipulates her socially and emotionally. With a clarity that requires no elaboration, Canetti denounces the control mechanisms that empower men. But she also suggests that there may be an alternative route a woman can take that involves her detachment from a potential victimizer. The final episode of *Die gelbe Straße* deals with an exemplary case, that of a woman who prevails over her persecutor. To indicate that such a victory is, indeed, rare, Canetti portrays her as a heroine and a utopian role model.

Canetti's narrative techniques foreshadow those of her husband's in *Die Blendung* (1965); both authors favor dramatic effects and fast-moving action constructed from encounters and dialogues. They define their characters by their external features and language patterns—Elias Canetti later introduced the term *sprachliche Maske* (language mask). There are also similarities in their view of human nature—instead of portraying humankind as intrinsically good, they stress destructive human traits that, as they imply, are aggravated by modern urban culture. All too familiar with the opportunism of Vienna's petty bourgeoisie and its propensity for brutality, Veza and Elias Canetti are pessimistic about the future of Austrian society. In their depiction of cruelty, episodes such as "Der gute Vater" in Elias Canetti's novel *Die Blendung* resemble Veza Canetti's Iger story.

Yet, there are conspicuous differences between Elias and Veza Canetti's oeuvres as well. Remaining uninvolved in his characters' fate, Elias Canetti precludes any solution in his cynical portrayal of the perversions of city life. Veza Canetti's narrators, on the other hand, take the side of the disadvantaged, criticize the system, and expose legalized crimes, rather than merely insane behavior. Her concrete, case-by-case criticism of the capitalist system suggests that the underprivileged must —and within limits can—shed their shackles, if they make the resolve to overcome their misplaced loyalty, faith, and trust in authority. Veza Canetti's criticism is directed at capitalist practices that make a mockery of democracy, rather than at human nature itself. In its relentless criticism of irrationality and its call for emotional and sexual emancipation, Veza Canetti's work is the literary counterpart of Wilhelm Reich's 1933 exploration of fascism, *Massenpsychologie des Faschismus* (1974).

In particular, women living in isolation from one another, victimized by men and by male and female capitalists alike, must rely on their personal initiative in the absence of organized resistance. Canetti draws these conclusions from the collective experience of women since the early feminism of the French Revolution and, in Austria, the Revolution of 1848. Although some progress had been made since that time as far as women's emancipation was concerned, the right-wing revolution and the demise of feminism under Nazism put an end to it. This development parallels the experience of German and Austrian Jews— neither the feminist nor the Jewish emancipation movement was successful. Before their ultimate defeat, Canetti recommended subversive action rather than overt rebellion.

Canetti writes from the perspective of socialist and feminist rationalism, tempered by her own experience of oppression; both led her to take a hard look at the guises under which individuals in power operate. The shop owner in *Die gelbe Straße,* Ms. Runkel, is a case in point. Because of her disability, this character could have been used to evoke unquestioned pity as was customary in the popular press. Canetti, however, portrays Runkel as a greedy capitalist. Begrudging others their health and good looks, she attempts to destroy those more fortunate than herself; a prisoner of her own body, she tries to make everyone a prisoner of her money. By avoiding favoring Runkel's suffering, Canetti makes it impossible to use disabilities and other innate handicaps as a rationalization for unfair practices. Her tenets call to mind Claire Goll's unsentimental representation of war veterans or Elfriede Jelinek's and Jeanette Lander's criticism of former Nazi perpetrators, regardless of their physical condition or age. None of Canetti's characters, including Runkel, fits the norm, which does not make them exceptions—seen through Canetti's narrative magnifying glass, each individual is abnormal by definition. The entire collective of *Die gelbe Straße* is made up of unique characters, leading the fascist ideology of a homogeneous *Volk ad absurdum*.

On the contrary, Canetti intimates that normalcy is a construct, only possible if one takes a very superficial glance at people. Upon close examination, however, normal human behavior is an illusion. Canetti contradicts the therapeutic discourse as well as Marxist tenets by showing diversity and dysfunctionality, deviation from the norm in general, to be the rule. Not surprisingly, she refrains from portraying her characters in psychological terms. Examining them more closely is the reader's task outside of the narrative framework. Neither does she offer didactic commentaries, but her somewhat unreliable narrators do take sides, occasionally highlighting a character's endearing aspects or revealing shortcomings in the case of others.

Nonetheless, the individual episodes of *Die gelbe Straße* do provide instruction as well. For instance, the interaction between the characters reveals the underlying social hierarchy, and their emotions expose the degree to which any given individual is affected by ideological indoctrination. It is obvious from the attitude of the male consumers at Runkel's shop, for example, that young women are considered sexual objects. However, it is equally apparent that the men's behavior toward the shop girls is far less damaging than the rancor of the capitalist. The most dramatic case, however, is that of the wife abuser who brutalizes his family with impunity since his young and emotionally defenseless wife is unprepared to assert herself. Implied in these episodes dealing with oppression is a protest against the popular tendency to blame the victim for the brutality she suffers.

In addition, Canetti portrays in her novel the volatility of public opinion. Instead of being the carrier of a higher form of reason, the collective is shown to be in constant danger of turning into a mob whenever there is a potential instigator.[18] The author's distrust of the majority opinion reflects the disillusionment of an Austrian progressive intellectual and a Jewish woman who experienced the defeat of the worker's movement in 1927 and the steady rise of the fascist rabble. Canetti is aware that the radicalization of the public sphere affects first and foremost the weakest members of society: women, children, and the poor, as well as the one group that Veza Canetti cannot even mention in 1933 in a socialist paper that still rallies for popular support: the Jews.

Veza Canetti's drama *Der Oger* was neither printed nor performed during the author's lifetime. A comparison between the Iger episode, "Der Oger," in *Die gelbe Straße* and the drama *Der Oger* shows that different literary conventions govern the avant-garde novel and the social-critical popular drama. Geared toward a class-conscious proletariat, *Der Oger,* with its easy-to-follow conflicts, its overt revolutionary message, and its conventional dramatic techniques, is clearly didactic. The use of dialect and the references to specific locations identify the *dramatis personae* as products of a particular historical and geographical setting. The female protagonists in particular invite the audience to identify with them. Although highlighting the interaction between men and women, the drama addresses more comprehensive issues as well.

In order to discuss Canetti's feminist drama in terms of progressive popular drama, the term *revolutionary* must be redefined to include the struggle between men and women in the domestic sphere. As Canetti revealed in *Die gelbe Straße,* the power structures of the public sphere are mirrored and reproduced in private. Nonetheless, the concerns of women were minimized because of the limited access they had to public life. Moreover, treating the private sphere as separate from business and politics and leaving it seemingly unstructured meant that women and children remained without recourse. The domestic sphere, the last bastion of male domination, remained unassailed even by communists and socialists. Canetti shows that in precisely this sphere male violence goes unchecked.

Die gelbe Straße and *Der Oger,* with their moving portrayal of a woman's astonishing loyalty to her oppressor, reveal an intimate knowledge of devastating family dynamics on the part of Canetti—few authors have depicted the oppression of women as convincingly as she does. One is reminded of the prose works of Claire Goll and Gertrud Kolmar and, looking ahead, of Elfriede Jelinek's uncompromising indictment of the nuclear family. In *Die gelbe Straße,* the wife- and child-abuser causes his wife's insanity and death while he himself is sheltered by the law and public opinion. *Der Oger,* on the other hand, conveys the message that economic independence enables women to make autonomous decisions. Draga Iger escapes from her ruinous marriage, gains custody over her child, and has a second chance at love. Albeit to a lesser extent than in *Die gelbe Straße,* the anonymous environment of the modern city is portrayed as an opportunity for women, as a place that offers them a chance.

Draga's fate is exceptional: aided by those of her (male) friends who are no longer bound by traditional values, she survives a nervous breakdown and divorces her husband. As with Lasker-Schüler's *Arthur Aronymus,* the viewer is left with the suspicion that this ending is too good to be true, as the last lines of Goethe's *Faust* (part 1) resound in the comment made by the protagonist's sister, "Sister, you are saved," when Iger signs the divorce decree (98). Portraying a divorce as a happy ending suggests that after a transition period of increased domestic oppression, the disintegration of patriarchal values will ultimately work to the advantage of women. The crumbling of the old structures represents a turning point when women can slowly begin to work toward full social participation, and an emerging woman's network is portrayed to suggest complete liberation in the future. One of Draga's allies is her mother, who already expresses her dissent when her daughter's engagement is announced by her husband (7–8). In the confines of her native village, the mother cannot rescue her daughter, but outside Draga's sister is able to help. The play culminates by suggesting new ways in which men and women will be able to bond. The happy ending of *Der Oger* is based on a fundamentally optimistic view of human nature. In *Die gelbe Straße,* on the other hand, even the optimistic episodes remain ambivalent since only a few female characters display a capacity for altruism. *Der Oger* suggests no psychological difference between male and female characters—gender-specific characteristics are portrayed as the products of the dominant social structures.

Die gelbe Straße and *Der Oger* represent different aspects of Canetti's assessment of interwar Vienna. Yet, in both works the position of women is a crucial factor for the future of modern Central Europe—feminism is characterized as an issue of general concern. While Canetti's novel expresses a glimmer of hope at best, a solution through personal and community initiative appears not only possible but imminent in her drama. In effect, it is impossible to accept uncritically the happy ending to major issues of the early 1930s. Canetti's defiant confidence has the appearance of a last stand. Unless the drama is intended to reveal and thereby lament the opportunities squandered in the interwar period, the optimism of *Der Oger* must be read as a staunch refusal to capitulate.

Fascist Structures in Suburban Paris (Claire Goll)

Claire Goll's novel *Arsenik,* also entitled *Jedes Opfer tötet seinen Mörder* (1977), was written at approximately the same time as Gertrud Kolmar's *Eine jüdische Mutter* and Veza Canetti's *Die gelbe Straße.* Like Kolmar and Canetti, Goll focuses on the oppression of women and the demise of mothers and children, combining the action-oriented plot of her novel with a critical examination of social structures. The stark images suggest that a profound ideological overhaul is necessary to change the suicidal and at the same time murderous course of European history, but the magnitude of the suffering and the self-delusion of Goll's characters make it seem unlikely that a transformation will occur in time to avert the impending catastrophe.

Arsenik is set in Lavallier, a small town close to Paris. Removed from the bristling vitality of the metropolis, this dull provincial place epitomizes life in lower-middle-class France, the life of the majority of the population; the monotony of the rural town, rather than the glamour of the Parisian upper crust, typifies the experience of the average person. The narrator's unrelenting descriptions of directionless activity, of lingering and offensive smells and sounds, underscore the prisonlike atmosphere (1977, 92–93). The protagonists are members of the petty bourgeoisie, the class that the intellectuals of Goll's circle considered the backbone of fascism. Goll examines this class as it approaches the point of no return, an understimulated collective waiting for disaster to strike. The authoritarian structures discussed in *The Authoritarian Personality* by Adorno et al. and Reich's *Massenpsychologie des Faschismus* are characteristic of this milieu, where eavesdropping and scandal mongering about women's sexual conduct are the major forms of entertainment. The uneventful, latently explosive atmosphere foreshadows a work such as Albert Camus's *L'étranger.*

Goll's *Arsenik* and Kolmar's *Eine jüdische Mutter* explore the reasons why small-town and suburban populations displayed an inordinate propensity for organized fascism. Later, Peter Handke in his 1972 novel about his mother's life in prewar and postwar Germany and Austria, *Wunschloses Unglück*, shows how Nazi pomp and circumstance brought a festive spirit into an otherwise drab middle-class environment in Austria and instilled the repressed population with a sense of purpose and adventure. Moreover, the totalitarian system exploited the human penchant to control, spy, and inform on others, and holding up the promise of material gain, it manipulated the greed of the disadvantaged and their desire for advancement.

Goll, Canetti, and Kolmar highlight the malaise of prefascist society, including the alienation between men and women resulting from the legal and social double standard. The male characters' disregard for the female protagonists and the lack of protection for unmarried women are symptomatic of legalized gender inequality. The realization that they have been trifled with because they command no respect as women drives Goll's and Kolmar's protagonists to desperate action—both of them commit capital crimes. Their economic cares and the hierarchical structures from whose control they cannot escape even in their private lives contribute to their delusion.

Goll's and Kolmar's protagonists, as sexually active unmarried women, present a challenge to their coupled heterosexual societies. In addition, they stand out because of their exotic appearance—namely, their stereotypically Jewish features, although Susanne Amiel in *Arsenik* is not explicitly identified as Jewish. Both women are attractive, which makes them targets for a witch-hunt. In fact, Goll's narrator evokes the discourse on witches in the remarks about Susanne throughout the text. Her neighbors, for example, consider her hooked nose, her sensual upper lip, and her intense facial expressions as an indication of her passionate disposition (1977, 29–30), and most men, including the aging doctor, are enticed by her.

A factor contributing to Susanne's problematic standing in the community is her recent love affair with an upper-class man, who set her up in her millinery shop since he plans to marry a woman of his own social class. When he leaves Susanne, all men consider her sexually accessible (18), especially since she, like Kolmar's protagonist Martha Wolg, has no family to support her: she was orphaned early in life and raised by a guardian. Another similarity between Goll's and Kolmar's protagonists is the fact that both are enjoying a modicum of financial independence: Martha is a photographer, Susanne a shop owner. Yet, their problematic personal circumstances and their visibility have made them secretive and suspicious. To hide her insecurity and to avoid public scrutiny, Goll's Susanne cultivates a mask of impassivity under which she is aware of the envy she arouses among the small-town women and the desire of the men. Forcing herself to repress her spontaneous reactions, she projects an air of mystery, which heightens her seductive appeal.

The narrative perspective in *Arsenik* is designed to reveal the protagonist's frustration and her growing claustrophobia. The readers are aware that Susanne's lateral moves take her nowhere. When she sells her shop, she does so because she wants to flee from the memory of the past. Once she has moved, her urge to escape is transformed into a yearning for her familiar environment. As far as her neighbors' memories of her affair are concerned, Susanne's change of residence does not help them to forget the young woman's past either.

From a social and psychological point of view, the options open to Goll's protagonist are quite limited and decrease proportionately to her fear of losing face. Moreover, as her obsession with her unfaithful lover escalates, her compulsion to destroy her business rival grows. In the end, Susanne yields to her pent-up rage and commits multiple murders that do not, however, affect the man who took advantage of her. These developments are filtered through the protagonist's perceptions, which are colored by grief and infatuation. Susanne's loss of judgment is apparent to the readers who participate in her point of view but also see beyond her perceptions. They are made to realize that Susanne's dilemma, similar to that of Fanny Lewald's Jenny, is caused by her lack of opportunity, rather than her lost love—a fact of which Susanne herself is unaware.

Unbeknownst to Susanne, love had the effect of a drug on her—she was addicted to her lover, as he was her only distraction. His leaving is tantamount to shattering her dreams of a more rewarding existence. As long as she had a rich lover, she hoped that one day she would be rescued from her shop like a modern-day Cinderella. Unequipped to analyze the wider ramifications of her dilemma—the rules of patriarchy, class barriers, economic structures, and the bourgeois double standard—Susanne projects her suffering upon a person close to her, who not coincidentally is an unmarried woman like herself. The new owner of Susanne's shop, a widow approximately ten years her senior by the name of Gaby, represents what Susanne fears becoming: an aging, lonely, avaricious woman. Ignoring the similarities between her and her perceived rival, Susanne makes this likewise disenfranchised woman her scapegoat.

This constellation gives Goll the opportunity to juxtapose the situation of the fallen woman and that of the widow and mother. Albeit without direct male protection, both find themselves in a situation sufficiently different to preclude solidarity between them. Susanne commands less respect than Gaby, who has paid her dues to society. From a rational point of view, the social approval may seem insignificant, considering both women's common problems. Except for the patriarchal class and value system, there is no obstacle that would prevent them from becoming allies. Preempting Simone de Beauvoir's examination of women under patriarchy in *The Second Sex,* Goll reveals that women are conditioned to avoid bonding with one another—Susanne has not one single female friend (12–13). Trained to treat other females as rivals and to submit to male authority, each woman focuses on the other's weaknesses and uses them to her own advantage. Goll's portrayal of the conflict between two women is informed not only by the literature of her time but also by the ongoing discourse of Jewish authors who expose similar destructive and irrational behavior among Jews and members of oppressed groups in general.

The way in which Goll portrays relationships between women in the 1930s differs radically from her earlier description of same-sex love and bonding. In the urban upper-class environment of *Der gläserne Garten,* middle-class morality with its compulsory heterosexuality and compartmentalization of sexual practices is suspended. In contrast, the environment of the protagonists of her later work is designed in such a way as to veil the common bond of exploitation among the oppressed— they have no opportunity to learn how to act in their own interest. The authoritarian structures and the constant surveillance by their fellow citizens prevent Goll's protagonists from examining their predicament. Moreover, neither one is trained to think analytically; neither one comprehends that their shared beliefs, engendered by patriarchal indoctrination, prevent them from emancipating themselves. Trained to overrate their emotions and personal concerns, they remain ignorant of the larger social forces that shape them.

In masterfully concise prose, Goll traces the escalation of her protagonist's hatred. Initially, opportunism prevails over latent dislike, opening the door to a superficial friendship. Unable to curb her resent-

THE TROUBLED METROPOLIS

ment in the long run, Susanne comes to consider Gaby's avarice as a reason and a justification for murder. At first, Susanne's steadily escalating hatred kindles the desire on her part to make Gaby leave town; later it culminates in her decision to poison Gaby. This spiraling intolerance mirrors, among other things, an anti-Semite's ever-increasing hatred or, for that matter, an alienated Jew's self-hatred; beginning with the assertion that it is impossible to live with the Jews, it climaxes in the conviction that they have to be eradicated. Thus, Susanne's crime is one of passion; but rather than a spontaneous explosion, it is the result of sustained emotional battery and pent-up pain that impacts the protagonist's mental capacities. Susanne is obviously mad with despair when she gives herself over to the powers of a psychic whose shabby quarters alone indicate a lack of superior powers (33). Her insanity is furthermore suggested by the fact that the murder devastates Gaby's child, whom Susanne claims to love. Susanne's state of confusion resembles that of Kolmar's protagonist, who likewise resorts to murder, killing her daughter and ultimately herself. Yet, Susanne, like Kolmar's Martha, is unable to face up to the fact that her lover exploits her, for her infatuation with him has two distinct functions: shielding him from her rage and preventing her from breaking away from him.

In a brief episode at the church, Susanne's alienation from her religion of origin is revealed—like all women who embrace the ideology of love, she accorded her beloved the place of a divine being. Parallels between Susanne's delusion and that of an entire population placing its trust in a political leader are subtly suggested. Susanne's surrender to a man was as complete as the German submission to Hitler as their leader and interpreter of their collective psyche. It takes several murders, the intervention of the authorities, and a compelling confrontation with reality— she is arrested and imprisoned—to bring Susanne back to reality.

Goll combines the character study of a deranged killer with an examination of some aspects of the kind of mass delusion that was spreading in Germany at the time of her novel's publication. In the wider context, Susanne's madness mirrors the mass psychosis of the German population after the Treaty of Versailles, which had made Germany a pariah among nations. Her hysteria resembles the fanaticism fostered by the modern mass movements. On another level, Susanne's fate symbolizes the growing disorientation of the assimilated German Jews in the face of right-wing politics. In keeping with the discursive patterns of her time, Goll selects a female protagonist for the purpose of mirroring the dilemma of modern mass culture: both Nazis and Marxists, Hitler in *Mein Kampf* and Bertold Brecht in his poem "Deutschland bleiche Mutter," inscribe Germany and the German population as female. The use of femininity as a multivalent signal enables Goll to encode Jewishness as well as Germanness as feminine and thereby to simultaneously reproduce the standard practices of the traditional discourses on Jews and the *Volk*, the masses. Not coincidentally, Elias Canetti's novel *Die Blendung* and Hermann Broch's *Der Versucher* employ similarly ambivalent symbols to the same end.

Goll's narrative universe is constructed in such a way that it leaves no room for a nonviolent solution—the paranoia and the psychosis of her protagonist have progressed too far. In accordance with the novel's implied assessment of the political situation in Europe, Goll did not return to Germany and escaped from France in 1939. Her novel, as well as her actions, reveals a justified pessimism that was shared by a number of intellectuals. Wilhelm Reich maintained in 1933 in *Massenpsychologie des Faschismus* (1974) that the effects of the Nazi movement would be felt for generations to come, Arnold Zweig proclaimed the end of German-Jewish coexistence in *Bilanz der deutschen Judenheit* (1933), and Lion Feuchtwanger and Karl Kraus recorded the extent to which lives were being destroyed by the Nazis in their respective works, *Die Geschwister Oppenheim*, written in 1932–33, and *Die dritte Walpurgisnacht*, written in 1933.

Goll's work, however, does end with the protagonist's inner healing. After the destruction of her civilian existence and the loss of her property, Susanne is restored to sanity. Through the inner strength of her protagonist, the author herself seems to proclaim her resolve to prevail even—or particularly—if her country of origin denies her human dignity and her status as a citizen. Cast unto herself, a woman stripped of the external trappings of bourgeois life, Susanne's—and for that matter, Goll's—inner strength has become a force with which to be reckoned. As a member of the intellectual elite of her time, Goll, not bound by the German language, established her motherland in the culture of modernity, among cosmopolitans, travelers, and exiles.

Beyond Humanism

Reassessing Jewish Identity

The Nürnberg Laws (1935) and, even more so, the *Kristallnacht* (1938) forced the European Jews to reconceptualize their position. As Lion Feuchtwanger demonstrated in his documentary novel *Die Geschwister Oppenheim* (1933), anti-Semitism and the Nazi victory made the dual identity of German and Jew untenable (Horch and Denkler 1993, x). Regardless of an individual's self-identification, Nazi ideology, which shaped the legislation of German-dominated territories, excluded multiple allegiances. Those who, like Jakob Wassermann, had thought of themselves as being both German and Jewish were ultimately proven wrong. German Jews who refused to let their sense of identity be affected by Nazi politics, such as Gerty Spies and Grete Weil, continued to consider themselves Germans, even in the concentration camps and in exile. Others, such as Nelly Sachs, Elias Canetti, Theodor Kramer, and Ernst Waldinger, identified themselves as authors of German language, rather than as Germans or Austrians. For them, their native language or language of choice became the substitute for their country and culture of origin.

Socialists and communists, on the other hand, as well as members of other antifascist groups with a distinct ideological or religious framework, considered the defeat of the Nazis and fascists their first priority. The Marxists, in keeping with their movement's traditional cosmopolitism, considered matters of national and ethnic identity as being of secondary importance.[1] Only later, after the foundation of the postwar German-speaking states, did many test their Jewish identity against the official ideologies of their respective countries, notably Anna Seghers in *Karibische Geschichten* (1962), Stefan Hermlin in his short texts about the Warsaw Ghetto, Buchenwald, and Auschwitz (1980a, 1980b), and Peter Weiss (1968, 1963) and Erich Fried (1975) by focusing on the Holocaust and the Nazi past.

Among the authors accepting and redefining their Jewish identity was Gertrud Kolmar. Expanding her ideas of the early 1930s, she included artistic, political, and gender categories in her concept of Jewishness, without discarding her German identity. Nelly Sachs, whose 1921 collection *Legenden und Erzählungen* consisted of apolitical romantic vignettes characteristic of the circle of women poets around Helene Herrmann, likewise reconstructed or, rather, constructed a Jewish framework (1984, 7).[2] Reaching beyond the secular philosophy of the Enlightenment in which humanism and cosmopolitism, as well as racism and chauvinism, are rooted, and whose inner contradictions Adorno elaborated in the *Dialectic of Enlightenment*,[3] the works of Kolmar and Sachs highlight an intuitive visionary way of relating to reality exemplified by the spirituality of simple people, children and, in Kolmar's case, eccentrics and simple people. From the point of view of these characters, the perverse aspects of German postidealism are revealed, and a world unfolds of greater depth than rationalist and humanist values are capable of expressing. This alternative view of reality already emerges in the works of Lasker-Schüler. It is associated with a Jewish way of life in Kolmar's *Susanna* (1994), in Sachs's *Eli: Ein Mysterienspiel vom Leiden Israels* (1962), and, later, in Ilse Aichinger's *Die größere Hoffnung* (1974) and Rahel Hutmacher's *Wildleute* (1986). Texts such as these differ decidedly from Goll's and Canetti's social-critical novels, although it must be noted that some of Goll's later work is also set exclusively among animal characters, and that in *Die gelbe Straße* nonhumanistic perspectives are expressed in the final episode involving the relationship between a girl and her dog, but most of all in the sardonic last sentence: "For the human being has an upright stride, and the sublime features of the soul are burned into his face" (V. Canetti 1990, 168). These gestures of "becoming animal" signify, as Deleuze and Guattari maintain, an "absolute deterritorialization" (1986, 13) and, in the case of Kolmar, Aichinger, and Hutmacher, the rejection of the concept of humanity as traditionally defined.

Kolmar's last novella and Sachs's drama communicate serious doubt about humanity and human progress. Rather, these works suggest that in the face of the Nazi terror, extrahuman forces are necessary to safeguard humanity as well as the animate and inanimate world. Disillusioned by war and genocide, they question the benefits of reason and science, calling for a renewal of the emotional and visionary capacities of humankind as sources of strength and survival—if not as a utopia, then for the moment, and if not for humanity in general, then for the individual. Like Else Lasker-Schüler, Kolmar and Sachs scrutinize the Judeo-Christian hierarchy of values, religious and secular, and criticize its most basic assumptions.

A Requiem for the German-Jewish Symbiosis (Gertrud Kolmar)

After 1933 Gertrud Kolmar published two volumes of lyric poetry, *Preußische Wappen* in 1934 and *Die Frau und die Tiere* (1938). The reception of these works was limited to a Jewish readership. As Johanna Woltmann writes in her Kolmar biography, these poems were exceedingly well received by the *Kulturbund*, the Jewish Cultural Association, and the *Central Verein-Zeitung*. The poet herself was delighted by the reception of her work (Woltmann 1995, 224–25).

Kolmar's poetry had been read by Erna Leonhard-Feld in 1936 at an event featuring women's poetry, arranged by the *Kulturbund*. As a result, the withdrawn poet befriended other members of the cultural association, among them the poet and lawyer Jakob Picard, who brought her work to the attention of the New York *Aufbau*, the paper of German immigrants in the United States (Woltmann 1995, 207). Kolmar's novella *Susanna*, however, like *Eine jüdische Mutter*, did not appear during her lifetime.[4] Both works reflect some of the author's life circumstances in addition to the historical themes noted by Hilde Wenzel. Moreover, Kolmar's skepticism regarding the culture of Northern Germany, her ascetic bent, and, finally, her propensity toward Zionism are indicated as well (Wenzel 1960). Kolmar's correspondence confirms this proclivity: "Like in our prayer I keep my face turned toward the East. As you well know, rather than being a new fashion with me, this attitude started early. Not coincidentally I became the friend of Hilda Josan when I was approximately nine years old, and the Josans were very asiatic Russians. They had lived in Siberia and in China. . . . It seems that something prevented me from being an 'Asian,' and I would be happy if the obstacle, whatever it is, could be eliminated; as a European I would probably have an easier time to move westward" (Kolmar 1970, 25). Kolmar's fascination with the Jewish tradition and East European Jewish culture, which she characterizes by the term *Asian,* increased with the escalating anti-Jewish measures on the part of the German government. Like some of the leading Jewish intellectuals—Einstein, Feuchtwanger, Reich, and Kraus—Kolmar realized that the situation of the Jews in Germany was desperate, as is obvious from her poems in *Die Frau und die Tiere*, such as "Thamar und Juda," "Judith," and "Esther" (1938, 14–15, 69, 70–74).[5]

Kolmar's letters to her sister reveal the author's increasing loyalty to the Jewish community as well as her realistic appraisal of the political situation.[6] She deplores the shortsightedness of the Jewish middle class, most of whom thought that the Nazi regime would be of short duration. Unlike her more optimistic contemporaries, Kolmar was far from considering National Socialism an opportunity to regenerate the Jewish faith.[7] Her own spiritual renewal took place in private. For Kolmar it involved studying Scripture, keeping Sabbath, learning Hebrew, and writing for the Jewish community for as long as circumstances allowed.

The classical language and form of *Susanna* are characteristic of traditional mainstream German literature; avant-garde elements are conspicuously absent; or, as Woltmann maintains, her works lack the didacticism of Brecht's poetry, the musicality of the late Benn, and the experimentalism of Lasker-Schüler (1995, 12). What is striking about *Susanna* is the discrepancy between the conventional form and its unconventional themes and characters: with few exceptions, mainstream authors characterized Jewish characters as despicable, funny, repulsive, or dangerous, and they trivialized Jewish topics. The novella elicits precisely such expectations as it evokes classical, Romantic, and realist prose. In conjunction with the subject matter, a textual tension arises that is reminiscent of Heine, Kafka, and Lasker-Schüler.

Susanna addresses the dilemma of the Jews in Germany and Eastern Europe with greater subtlety than *Eine jüdische Mutter*. Compared to the stark *Neue Sachlichkeit* style of the earlier narrative, the later text seems deceptively harmonious. The smooth prose has an almost hypnotic effect and carries the reader, at least upon first reading, across the abyss of hopelessness, reflecting the author's own experience. The writing of *Susanna* coincided with the gradual shrinking of Kolmar's world; two weeks after *Kristallnacht* it was ordered that her parental house be auctioned off, and the author and her father were relocated to a ghetto house. Censorship of all her correspondence, her father's deportation to Theresienstadt, and forced labor mark Kolmar's life in the 1940s until her own deportation in 1943.[8]

Susanna contains numerous reminders of the author's life in the suburb of Finkenkrug and of her animals, among them a Barsoi, upon which Susanna's dog is modeled (1960, 553; 1994, 10, 14). In addition, Susanna and the narrator represent different aspects of Kolmar herself. Like the narrator, Kolmar was a teacher and, like her, hoped for a miracle so that she could leave Nazi Germany. Susanna, on the other hand, expresses Kolmar's qualities as a poet, a lover, and a Jewish woman proudly accepting her gender and her Jewishness. She is the only one in the novella who does not in one way or another reject her identity. Considered deranged because of the way in which she perceives and discusses reality, she is placed under the care of the narrator, an assimilated German-Jewish governess (Balzer 1965, 169). As alter egos, the pedagogue and the visionary poet represent two of Kolmar's personae.

In *Susanna,* the issues of racism and bigotry are discussed in an exclusively Jewish environment—only the novelistic frame relates to the historical situation with its alternatives, exile or extermination. Yet, the main plot implies that long before these extreme circumstances arose, the Jews of Europe had already been conditioned to destroy each other and themselves, as is exemplified by the narrator's prejudice against Rubin, expressed in racist language, the biases of the German governess against her East European co-religionists, and the intolerance of those with mental and physical disabilities, in this case Susanna and a young boy, by those who consider themselves normal. Instead of sharing Susanna's joy about being a Jew, the narrator tries to repress the "blemish" of her Jewish background (1994, 21).

Her physical beauty, her sensuality, her grace, and her childlike innocence let Susanna appear as the paragon of femininity, as celebrated by poets from antiquity to modern times. Secretly coveted by her guardian and her governess, Susanna represents both an object of desire and a scapegoat. The governess accepts the guardian's pronouncement that Susanna must not marry, convinced that only "normal" people have the right to procreate. Her view of eugenics coincides with Nazi doctrine, where the concept of life not worth living provided the basis for the extermination of the disabled as well as the Jews.

The example of Susanna illustrates the abuse of science by the arbitrariness with which the Nazis assess physical and mental health. Beyond the fact that Susanna has difficulty following and accepting certain generally approved ideas and that she does not fit the general mold, the text offers no clear evidence that she is, in fact, insane. Rather, Susanna's unusual way of relating to the outside world suggests the consciousness of a pretechnological age. It is fantastic, magical, and poetic, but by no means inconsistent or immoral. Her method of arguing resembles the comprehensive approach of the Talmud and the Cabala, while that of the narrator follows the linear patterns of modern Western culture.

Only much later, at the end of the novella, has the narrator come to appreciate Susanna's outlook. By adopting her dead student's point of view, the narrator demonstrates that she no longer endorses assimilation. Only when it is too late, when Susanna has died for lack of money to buy a train ticket, and the narrator, like Kolmar herself, is waiting desperately to leave Germany, does the governess realize that she herself, not Susanna, was in need of learning. At the brink of disaster, she gains an understanding of the Nazis' fanatical eradication of any group and ideology different from their own, which mirrors her and other assimilated Jews' intolerance of Susanna. Now that she is about to become a victim of fascist ideology, she examines the role she played in Susanna's death, be it an accident or suicide.

The novella portrays a spectrum of possible positions toward Susanna of which the most valid one is that of an uneducated woman, Seraphine, Susanna's former nanny, who refuses to disenfranchise her charge. However, those in power, including Rubin, the man Susanna loves, dismiss Seraphine's efforts to allow the young woman to exercise her basic human rights and approve of her being kept under lock and key.[9] From the narrator's retrospective point of view, the young woman's confinement appears doubly absurd, since the lovers, Susanna and Rubin, would have had at best eleven years together before their deportation to the death camps. The tyrannical attitude on the part of the governess and other assimilated Jews symbolizes the self-destructive impulses in the Jewish community. Susanna, who in a different era would have been considered an exemplary Jewish woman, perishes because of the neglect, the envy, and the prejudice of self-hating Jews.

Whereas Martha Wolg in *Eine jüdische Mutter* became vulnerable to Nazi ideology to the point of committing murder, Susanna, who lives in complete isolation, develops a rich inner life that distinguishes her from her Jewish contemporaries striving for assimilation. The novella's frame indicates that, even in the absence of external constraints, a one-woman attempt like Susanna's at safeguarding her integrity was doomed to fail in the long run; and yet, the success of Susanna's uncompromising pursuit of her convictions lies in the process rather than in the result. In that sense, Kolmar's novella, like Ilse Aichinger's *Die größere Hoffnung*, a work begun already in the 1940s, reflects a process-oriented philosophy.

Kolmar's novella traces the destruction of Jewish life at a time when it no longer mattered whether a Jewish person had achieved assimilation or not. Beyond the physical destruction faced by all Jews, however, Kolmar suggests that it did matter whether or not Jews aided and abetted anti-Semites and misogynists. By portraying racism and the belief in eugenics among Jews, *Susanna* exposes the corruption of Judaism as a result of uncritical conformism. In addition, Amy Colin refers to the unchecked instincts of death and destruction as the "sinister aspects of culture." According to Colin, Kolmar was aware of the fact that the impact of these phenomena would ultimately destroy the relationship between Germans and Jews (1994, 219).

In her examination of post-Enlightenment thought during the 1930s, Kolmar goes beyond a mere critique of fascist ideology. While examining basic Judeo-Christian thought, she touches on one of the core problems of Judaism, killing.[10] According to the regulations concerning ritual slaughter, the *shoykhet* is allowed only one attempt at cutting the animal's throat. If he fails, the animal lives. Furthermore, *milkhik* and *fleyshik* food must be separated in kosher households, and the laws regulating the processing of meat demand that it be prepared in such a way as to make it obvious that an animal was killed to provide the meal.

In *Masse und Macht*, Elias Canetti places killing and eating into the context of power, mass murder, survival, and the psychology of the paranoid leader, and he establishes the connection between oppression and ingesting: "Whoever wants to rule over human beings tries to humiliate them; to trick them so that they lose their power to resist as well as their rights, until they are powerless like animals. He will use them like animals; even if he does not tell them so; *he* knows at all times how little they mean to *him;* in the company of his confidants he will always refer to them as sheep or cattle. His ultimate goal is to 'ingest' them and to suck them dry; he does not care what is left of them" (1981, 231). Rather than distinguishing between human beings and animals, Canetti differentiates between creatures that exploit and kill others, and those who do not. In his notes, particularly in *Das Geheimherz der Uhr*, he suggests that the traditional differentiation between man and animal is unproductive, as in the following aphorism, with its peculiar use of the term *friend:*

"You do not have a single friend among the animals. Do you call that living?" (1993, 516). Similar notions pervade Canetti's entire oeuvre— for example, the gorilla featured in the chapter "Ein Irrenhaus" in *Die Blendung* (1965), an animal that is involved with human beings on all possible levels.[11] Critics tend to steer clear of Canetti's statements about animals or search for their metaphoric significance, although most of these passages leave little room for elaborate literary interpretations. At a loss as to how to deal with them, most critics react with embarrassed silence or superficial commentaries.[12] Most fail to come to terms with Canetti's statements that demand love and intimacy between human beings and animals, such as the following: "I never embraced an animal. I thought of animals with torturous compassion throughout my life, but I never embraced an animal" (1993, 480).

Gertrud Kolmar's animal imagery, the animal advocacy expressed in her animal poems, and her identification with animals are no less amazing than Canetti's statements. Indeed, they reveal a kindred spirit that is not surprising in view of their similarity in age and background, the educated European Jewish middle class. Both authors, profoundly affected by National Socialism, had to reassess their position toward life in general. A brief analysis of animal motifs in *Susanna* and selected poems of *Die Frau und die Tiere* reveals that the meaning of the animal images is more literal than metaphorical, and that their function is philosophical rather than poetic. A comparison between the use and significance of animal imagery in Kolmar's and Canetti's works shows the range and meaning of these themes.

"You know much about animals," says the governess to Susanna, whereupon the young woman replies, "But I am an animal." Startled, the narrator comments: "She said it without a smile, like a woman might respond in a conversation about nations: But I am a Polish woman" (1994, 19). Less than a page later, in answer to one of her teacher's questions, Susanna states: "But I am the royal princess. . . . I am a daughter of King David, or King Saul. . . . But many other people are not the descendants of kings. Only I am. Because I am a Jewish woman" (20). This seamless integration of the concepts *animal, woman, aristocrat,* and *Jew* in Susanna's response corresponds with Canetti's concept of transformation, discussed in *Masse und Macht* (1981) and, for that matter, Rahel Hutmacher's metamorphoses in *Wildleute* (1986). Canetti writes: "The body of one and the same bushman becomes the body of his father, his wife, an ostrich, a buck" (1980b, 378). While Claudio Magris is correct in extracting Canetti's fascination with transformation from Canetti's biography, the term can be applied in other than biographical terms as well (1985, 271–72).

One aspect of transformation is the metamorphosis from human to animal, and vice versa, which implies an interconnectedness between both as physical beings, a concept of cardinal importance in classical mythology and Eastern religions. In modern Europe, metamorphosis is of little significance except in children's literature, fairy tales, and science fiction. Yet, being an animal, rather than being *like* an animal, and speaking with the voice of an animal, rather than speaking *as if* with the voice of an animal, is the basic situation in Kolmar's *Rollengedichte* in "Tierträume" in *Das weibliche Bildnis* (1960, 141–215). These poems express empathy with the animal protagonists, but not in the usual patronizing manner in which animal fanciers discuss their pets. Kolmar's speakers take the side of the animals as equals—as creatures who are downtrodden like the Jews in Hitler's Third Reich. Those animals who are the most despised by human beings, amphibians and spiders, arouse the speaker's most ardent compassion—these animals, persecuted like herself, represent, so to speak, Jews among animals. To express the injustice done to them, Kolmar highlights those parts of animal bodies that resemble the human anatomy, particularly in its fetal form. For example, the hand of a dwarf is ascribed to the frog in "Teichfrosch," and in "Arachne" she perceives the "zwergige Hand," the dwarfish hand, of a spider (1960, 157, 155).

"Legende" expresses compassion with the dead animals and, invoking their ghosts, accuses the human race, represented by a man who lies sleeping in bed. A product of civilization, this man has made use of the parts of animal bodies to furnish his place—their hide, their wool, their feathers. These elements surround him in his comfortable bedroom (148–49). Similar to the vision of the killed animals in the *Bhagavad-Gita,* the murdered animals in Kolmar's work hold the man accountable for their suffering and their untimely deaths, and they demand satisfaction.[13] In the man's nightmare, animal products such as down pillows transform themselves back into the creatures they once were.

The wolf, flayed, skinned, bleeding-red,
Tore the small carpet weaved of fur

Trembling and gasping with bared teeth:
This was my garment! And this is why I'm dead?

The poem culminates in a comparison between the bodies of animals and the naked human body to demonstrate the animal nature of man along with his physical and psychological defects. Man is shown to be the most exposed of creatures and at the same time the most ferocious one, an exploiter and exterminator of his fellow creatures. Left to his own devices, it is suggested, he is physically inferior to the other animals (148–49), and his actions bespeak his moral inferiority. Man as a destructive force is also the theme of "Der Tag der großen Klage" (167–68), a poem about the "Judgment Day of Animals Tortured to Death," which ends with the ominous lines:

And a new Divinity spat like a dragon
The flame into a new horizon.

The new god, spitting fire like a dragon, and the fire image itself suggest an apocalyptic ending to man's reign and a day of reckoning that will be quite unlike the Christian judgment day, for neither God the father nor the son, but animals, shall sit in judgment. At the same time, the image of the dragon, an imaginary creature born of human imagination, suggests a synthesis between man and animal. Endowed with an animal's body, created by the human mind, and, as most legends allege, killed by a human warrior, the dragon, Kolmar suggests, must live and the warrior be overcome for the sake of global survival.

Like the poems discussed thus far, numerous other texts in "Tierträume" express Kolmar's condemnation of the use of animal products for food, clothing, and luxury goods, the capture of zoo animals, and the torture of animals for scientific experiments. More intensely personal yet are the texts in which the speaker assumes the role of an animal and speaks as an animal. This is the case in "Die Kröte" (159–60). The defiant challenge "Just come and kill me!" at the beginning of the first and third stanzas is made with the same self-assurance with which Susanna states that she is an animal, and with the same pride that she takes in being a Jewish woman. The poem climaxes in the lines:

You may consider me a disgusting pest;
But I am the toad
and I carry the jewel . . .

Still other poems are written entirely from the point of view of the animal, among them "Lied der Schlange" (161–62) in which the opening lines, strangely incommensurate with the traditional image of snakes, question human perceptions: "Nimbly I stepped through the wooden gate." These works call for a basic reassessment of the categories *man* and *animal*. Kolmar's point of view is based on a variety of experiences and influences. A teacher of disabled children and a keeper of animals, she also belonged intellectually to Walter Benjamin's circle, whose critical insights she shared and radicalized.

This is obvious in "Der Drache" (199–200), which begins with the dragon's complaint that he was driven from his (or her) native territory by human beings and which ends with a critical comment on the dualism inherent in Western philosophy:

You name the islands: Death, immortality.
Do you hear the life calling from the stones?
Do you see the spasms of the face of dust? [14]
You believe: Here is God's home — over there nothingness.
I am a third element. (200)

This third element represents the missing link in the Manichaeistic patterns of European thought, including Hegelian and Marxist dialectics. Kolmar's dragon asserts that a solution reaching beyond the binary and hierarchical patterns of Western philosophy must be found for the sake of global survival, about which Elias Canetti was to raise serious doubts: "Day by day humans become more impoverished. It might happen that they are left behind in complete emptiness and destitution." He goes on to lament the fact that no other animal species prevented the ascent of humankind (1993, 66).

Kolmar's line of argument follows Benjamin's observations on history, but it is more radical. Benjamin problematizes dominant culture because it is the product of barbaric acts, and he denounces the silencing of the victims and the socially weak for the perpetrators' benefit (1974, 693–704). Kolmar writes against the boundaries of Western philosophy and modern science by including nonhumans in the category of the oppressed. Aware that the European ideologies were formulated to serve those in power, she questions the concept of Man's superiority and its Judeo-Christian foundations. Her involvement with the problems of race, gender, and mental health opened her eyes to the fact

127

that twentieth-century biological and medical science was constructed to condone the persecution and murder of disabled persons, Jews, and women, as well as animals, to an even greater degree than had been the case in medieval church doctrine and popular superstition. Insofar as her animal characters reflect her experience of racist anti-Semitism, they are metaphors. Yet, they also articulate her concern for and identification with animals as fellow creatures and shed doubt on the assumed superiority of one species over another.

Kolmar's work shows that the disregard for life, no matter the form, is the first step in the abuses perpetrated by human beings against members of their own species. Particularly her later works, *Susanna* and *Weibliches Bildnis* (1960, 9–137) illustrate that the degradation of animals is the first step toward the degradation of human beings or, in other words, that brutality against animals is the last social and intellectual frontier. Kolmar's unspoken case in point is the Nazis, who considered Jews animals or less than animals—in Auschwitz, Jews, like the animals in Kolmar's "Gerichtstag totgeplagter Tiere," were reduced to raw material. Kolmar's urgent call for a third option to solve the impasse created by conceptualizing humans and animals as opposites is derived from her realization that the notions subhuman and animal open the door to the mass extermination of all lives deemed unworthy of living. The generally accepted hierarchy of values allows one race to claim superiority over another and offers intellectual tools to those who wish to justify their exploitation of other creatures.

Kolmar's call for a third option also questions what the Torah and the Christian Bible proclaim as God's command, namely, that Adam seek domination over the world and its creatures. Cognizant that the concept of humanity in Western tradition includes man's control over nature—conceptualized as the body, as woman, or as animal—Kolmar, unlike most other antifascist intellectuals, refrains from calling for more humanity. Ilse Aichinger, pursuing the same line of reasoning, expands Kolmar's perspective even further through her empathy with inanimate objects. Indeed, the history of anti-Semitism and misogyny, the medieval witch-hunts and cat hunts, and the extermination of entire species and the fast-progressing devastation of the environment illustrate that neither the Judeo-Christian religions nor the ensuing secular philosophies managed to instill their adherents with a reverence for life.

To illustrate the consequences of the prevalent attitudes, Elias Canetti wrote in 1979, "In a thousand years: a small number of animals of very few species, rare and fawned upon like gods" (1993, 455). He places his emphasis on the fate of the animals, since the racist and misogynist excesses of the first third of the twentieth century have already been the topics of much study and discussion, all of which failed to remedy the situation. Kolmar's texts imply that an improvement will not occur unless the protection of animals becomes an integral part of this debate. Neither she nor, later, Canetti exhibits any optimism regarding human and animal rights in view of the fact that killing is deeply rooted in Western culture. In their examination of the relationship of man and animal, they assert that a viable third path beyond the axioms of modern European civilization needs to be found in order to validate life, regardless of its form. Voices such as Kolmar's and Canetti's represent a minority point of view. Although animal rights concerns, raised in conjunction with Jewish topics, are not uncommon among German-Jewish writers, they have been dismissed and misinterpreted. In larger cultural debates, they have carried no weight, perhaps because they draw conclusions that touch on time-honored taboos and constitute an assault on man's creature comforts, consumerism, and love of gratuitous violence, but most of all, on man's arrogance—the same arrogance that caused Kolmar's destruction in the Holocaust.

Overcoming Destruction—A Spiritual Perspective (Nelly Sachs)

After the Berlin-born poet Leonie (Nelly) Sachs had received a summons for deportation in 1940, her non-Jewish friend Gudrun Harlan appealed for help to the Swedish Nobel Prize laureate Selma Lagerlöf, with whom Sachs had corresponded since 1907. Through the intervention of Prince Eugen, the brother of the king of Sweden, Nelly Sachs and her mother, Margarete, were admitted to Sweden after having been stripped of all their belongings in Germany (Strobl 1994, 126). Sachs's work as a writer and translator in Stockholm barely sufficed to sustain both women, but she provided for her aging mother until the latter's death in 1950. As a result of her economic insecurity, the author's first application for Swedish citizenship was rejected, but two years later she was naturalized.

Throughout her life Sachs suffered from health problems—presumably this was the reason why she was tutored at home and attended private schools (1984, 7).[15] In 1960, she had a nervous breakdown that was coupled with acute paranoia. She wrote to combat her condition, and from her sickbed she created some of her finest texts. In 1966, she received the Nobel Prize together with the Israeli author J. S. Agnon. Four years later she died after a cancer operation in her country of exile, having been apprised of Paul Celan's suicide.

Certain aspects of Sachs's biography bring to mind the lives of Else Lasker-Schüler and Gertrud Kolmar, the two poets with whom she is most frequently compared. Critics cite, for example, the three authors' common experience of persecution, uprootedness, and poverty.[16] Indeed, already in the 1930s the mutual affinity between Sachs, Kolmar, and Lasker-Schüler did not go unnoticed. At the already mentioned reading of women's poetry in 1936, arranged by the Berlin *Kultusgemeinde,* texts by all three authors were recited. At another such event in 1938, Fritz Rosenthal (Schalom Ben Chorin), Jacob Picard, Nelly Sachs, and Gertrud Chodziesner (like all Jewish authors, Kolmar was no longer allowed to use a pseudonym) were featured together (Schlenstedt 1989, 734). Beyond sharing the common fate of German Jewish women during the Weimar and Nazi eras, there are also concrete connections between these three poets, including a friendship between Kolmar and Sachs during the latter's last years in Berlin (Strobl 1994, 129).

Sachs knew and admired Kolmar, particularly her poems in *Welten* (1960), which she gave as a present to several friends. In a letter of 1943 to Emilia Fogelklon-Norlind, she characterized Kolmar as a "clairvoyant. Perhaps the greatest lyric poet . . . visions beyond all boundaries" (1984, 31). Sachs, who corresponded extensively with and about the intellectual elite of her time, shared acquaintances and friends with Kolmar and Lasker-Schüler, as is revealed by her inquiries about missing persons and her search for friends during and after World War II.

Her contacts also included prewar and postwar authors such as Hermann Hesse, Friedrich Torberg, Paul Celan, Alfred Andersch, and, after 1960, Ingeborg Bachmann, Hilde Domin, and Ilse Aichinger (355). It is more than likely that Aichinger, as an editor for Bermann-Fischer, publisher of her work and Sachs's, had become acquainted with Sachs's work in the immediate postwar era since Sachs's second volume of poetry, *Sternverdunkelung,* published in 1949, appeared at the time Aichinger worked for the publisher. Thus it seems no coincidence that Inge Scholl, the surviving sister of the anti-Nazi student organization *Die weiße Rose,*

(White Rose) and Aichinger's friend and collaborator, invited Sachs to visit the *Hochschule für Gestaltung* in Ulm in 1959. Sachs and Aichinger feature the White Rose in separate texts: Sachs in one of her letters (1984, 382), Aichinger in the short story "Nach der weißen Rose," published in *Kleist, Moos, Fasane* (1987).

The experience of persecution caused Sachs, who came from an assimilated Jewish background, to identify passionately with the Jewish people and Jewish history. Like Kolmar, who increasingly integrated Jewish customs into her daily life, Sachs was receptive to Hasidic spirituality.[17] Moreover, both poets led withdrawn and introspective lives, remained unmarried, and displayed an exemplary filial loyalty. Yet, Sachs refrained from questioning the basic assumptions of Judeo-Christian thought, namely, Man's unique status in the spiritual hierarchy, and the hierarchy itself. While Kolmar invalidated the Great Chain of Beings as a viable concept, Sachs derived her poetic power from the process of making distinctions, according to her a uniquely human and eminently Jewish faculty.

Sachs's 1943 lyrical drama *Eli: Ein Mysterienspiel vom Leiden Israels* (1962) and her poetry *In den Wohnungen des Todes* (1947) and *Sternverdunkelung* (1949) were written in exile. Her extreme sensitivity and her passionate disposition are manifest in her "Gedichte für den toten Bräutigam," published in *Fahrt ins Staublose* (1961), which reflect an unrequited love of her youth and the eventual deportation of her beloved. Other works were inspired by the poet's own experience of persecution and the loss of members of her family, fellow authors, and writers; still others by the accounts of Holocaust survivors and by Buber's *Chassidische Bücher* (1927) and the Cabala (Strobl 1994, 124, 127, 129). The Cabala fascinated Sachs, as it did many other German-Jewish poets of her generation. More significantly, however, these works constitute an attempt on the poet's part to construct an antiworld in opposition to her generation's fate and to affirm the values and heritage of Ashkenazic Jewry through the medium of the German language, both of which Sachs acknowledged as aspects of her motherland in times of extreme crisis.

Both the drama and the poetry, written simultaneously, reveal Sachs's reorientation toward Jewish spirituality and her disenchantment with modern Western culture. By emphasizing Hasidic themes, she embraces the most oppressed segment of European Jewish culture, thereby expressing her disapproval of the process of assimilation of which she herself was a product. Indeed, texts written and published in German by German-Jewish authors formed the basis on which Sachs explores Jewish and feminine ways of relating to the world. Inspired by her compassion for the most helpless of the persecuted, old women and children, and her admiration for persons who accept suffering with forbearance, Sachs transformed suffering into a religious and poetic experience.

The personae in her early poetry resemble those in Kolmar's *Die Frau und die Tiere* (1938). The poems in a section of *Fahrt ins Staublose* (1961) entitled "Grabschriften in die Luft geschrieben" (Epitaphs written into the Air)—such as "Die Tänzerin," "Die Schwachsinnige," "Der Marionettenspieler," "Die Malerin," and "Die Abenteuerin"—reveal Sachs's compassion with individuals who were marginalized because of their special talents, their lifestyle, or their disability. These characters are portrayed with affection on the speaker's part, and their own bearing is gentle and innocent, an attitude that reflects Sachs's resolve to accept the unacceptable, even the Holocaust, as divine providence.

The steadfastness with which Sachs rejected the concept of revenge separates her from poets such as Celan, although their poetic style and the superficial similarity of their themes and imagery suggest otherwise. The poem "Auf daß die Verfolgten nicht Verfolger werden" (1961, 77) articulates the concern that once Jews are drawn into the circle of violence, they might resort to the same brutal methods as their enemies and thus become just like them. For this reason, Sachs, who felt a strong attraction to the Land of Israel (125ff.) as the realm of the patriarchs and prophets, rejected Zionism: "I am not a Zionist the way in which the term is presently used, and I believe that our home country is located wherever the sources of eternity flow" (1984, 41). Much like Pappenheim, Sachs disapproved of the Zionists' goal to establish Israel as a military worldly power, but like the poet and scholar Margarete Susman (1872–1966), she conceded that the Holocaust had made a Jewish state a necessity.[18]

In contrast to the numerous authors and critics who considered the Shoah a tragedy of unprecedented proportion and character, Sachs portrayed the genocide perpetrated by Nazi Germany as one more chapter in the Jewish history of persecution. She claims this history as her own and, as did Kolmar and Lasker-Schüler, associates herself with the Jewish community of fate. Ingrid Strobl is correct in emphasizing that

Sachs's work expresses this affinity without any sentimentality and without endorsing the unqualified call for forgiveness and reconciliation articulated by many Gentile authors (1994, 119). Sachs employs several intersecting discourses to construct Jewish identity: the history of suffering, literary images of Jewishness shaped by authors such as Lasker-Schüler and Kolmar, and Jewish mysticism as transmitted to German readers of the 1920s and 1930s by Buber and Scholem. The legends celebrating simplicity, piety, and unrewarded selflessness, such as the myth of the thirty-six *Zaddikim*—just men—who by virtue of their suffering assume the place of the apocalyptic Messiah, proved to be a major influence on Sachs.[19] The book of *Zohar*, the central text of the Cabala, was a major source of inspiration for her mystery play *Eli*.[20]

Sachs was aware of the mass murders in Eastern Europe, but in 1943, when she began her work on her drama, she did not know the extent of the genocide, hence the utopian vision of a time "after the martyrdom." *Eli* is set in an East European soul scape; its protagonists are the survivors of a *shtetl* laid to ruins by the Germans. The pious Jews congregate to mourn and rebuild their hometown, an enclave surrounded by enemy territory. Notwithstanding the difference in form and genre, Sachs's assumption, that after the defeat of the Nazis a reconstruction of Jewish culture is possible, coincides with the message of other texts, including Friedrich Torberg's *Golems Wiederkehr* (1981), which is set in a distant future when Hitler's name will have been erased from memory. Like Sachs, Torberg also avails himself of Cabalistic tradition by utilizing the legend of the Golem as his frame of reference for relating a mysterious event in the Prague ghetto under Nazi rule.

Convinced of the play's significance, Sachs actively tried to market *Eli*. She writes, "I am possessed by the deep feeling that it had to happen, that Jewish artists would once again begin to listen to the voice of their blood so that the ancient source awakens to new life. It is with this in mind that I attempted to write a mystery play about Israel's suffering" (1984, 46). She tried to have the play performed in New York, Palestine, and Switzerland and consented to having the text set to music by Moses Pergament (46, 56). Working already on her second drama, *Abram im Salz*, she tried to arrange for a performance of *Eli* by the Jewish theater company *Habima*, then located in Palestine, whose performances Sachs had attended in Berlin before and after 1933 (62). Finally, in 1958, *Eli*, in the radio play version prepared by Alfred Andersch, aired on the *Süd-*

deutscher and *Norddeutscher Rundfunk,* and the opera version was broadcast on Swedish radio in 1959.

It is not unlikely that the devastating criticism of *Eli* and the ad hominem attacks on Sachs for presumably trivializing the Shoah by allowing it to be turned into an opera contributed to the poet's breakdown (Sachs 1984, 207). Echoing and misinterpreting Theodor Adorno, the critical establishment condemned the representation of the genocide in an aestheticized form, especially if the artists were intended Nazi victims or Holocaust survivors. Sachs's experience resembles that of Celan and Weiss. In her defense, Sachs referred to Hans Magnus Enzensberger, who maintained that there was a place for poetry after Auschwitz. Crediting only a few writers with the appropriate sensitivity and the literary talent to write about the Holocaust, Enzensberger had nothing but the highest praise for Sachs.

The mottos from *Zohar* and the Talmud preceding the poems written concurrently with *Eli* define Sachs as a mystic seeking enlightenment, rather than as a political author. Yet, her metaphysical message is empirical in that it is based in the material world, as shown in the poem "Ein Schuh" in the cycle "Chor der verlassenen Dinge."

A Shoe
Human measure lost; I am the solitude
For which siblings strive in this world—
O Israel, I am an echo of your feet's anguish
Crying out to the heavens (1961, 48).

Sachs's poetry as well as her drama emulates the perspicacious argumentation characteristic of the Talmud, and her imagery reflects a premodern, pretechnological view of reality. In *Eli,* the beauty of the natural environment, the forests and fields, is contrasted with the ravaged human sphere to reveal the indifference of nature to the destruction of the Jews, and thus the distinction between nature, God, and Man. Likewise, the prosperity of the land of the murderers shows the difference between the Gentiles and the Chosen People, whose task it is to accept and overcome suffering.

The human sphere as portrayed in *Eli* is a realm void of divine justice. Humanism as a possible source of decency is not even considered; instead, emphasis is on the laws to which the pious adhere in order to distinguish between human beings and nature, Jews and Gentiles.

These laws pose a special challenge, which is why the faithful are few in number, and their influence limited. A comparison between Sachs's and Kolmar's concept of animals evinces the fundamental philosophical difference between the two poets. In Kolmar, the boundaries between humans and animals are fluid; Sachs, however, perceives animals, their emotions and their suffering, as mysterious and separate from the human experience (Sachs 1961, 82).

Eli illuminates the difference between the human and the natural spheres, the special character of the Jewish fate as distinct from the path of the Gentiles, and the difference between men and women. It is implied that these distinctions, if properly understood, make it possible for the believers to come to terms with the Shoah. Therefore they must be maintained in order to prevent the surviving Jews from becoming entangled in chaos and being corrupted and ultimately destroyed like their enemies. Not coincidentally is there an emphasis on poetic and spiritual form and a deliberate disregard for mundane detail, signifying the priority of the spiritual over the material sphere.

The vagueness characteristic of *Eli* suggests the difficulty of imagining a new beginning after the nearly complete destruction of Ashkenas. Not only one *shtetl*, but the entire culture, must be reconstructed from shards and ruins. It transpires from the use of Yiddish and Hebrew names—Gittel, Samuel, Dajan, Jossele, and Mendele—and the syntax that echoes, rather than mimics, Yiddish sentence structure, that Sachs envisions the rebuilding of Jewish culture on the basis of the Eastern European heritage. Written in free verse, the most appropriate medium for re-creating Yiddish syntax in the German language, *Eli* avoids Yiddish vocabulary, which has negative connotations in a German context since Yiddishisms were traditionally used to defame Jewish characters in anti-Semitic literature and propaganda films. Instead, Sachs takes great pains to re-create a Yiddish timbre and an ambiance reminiscent of Yiddish literature and films.

Overall, the drama emphasizes the simplicity of Hasidic life. The anonymity of most of the characters and the lowliness of their occupations (among others, "a washer woman" and "a woman baker" are mentioned) set the realm of the believers apart from the world of capitalism and modern warfare. Within the Hasidic community, two characters stand out: the exulted child Eli, who was murdered by the invaders because he tried to save his parents from deportation by blowing his pipe, and

Michael, who is associated in name with the archangel and who, according to the poet, "is a secret servant of God, one of the thirty-six just" (1984, 208). The victim and the tool of divine justice are the focus of the mystery play.

The choice of free verse not only makes for a flexible poetic expression but also places *Eli* into the tradition of German classical literature. As is the case in Kolmar's *Susanna,* the finely chiseled form in conjunction with the Jewish content and the poeticized Yiddish German symbolizes the synthesis of German and Jewish culture. Sachs appropriates the classical meter in order to contextualize the suffering of the Jewish people under Hitler with the great disasters of European literature, celebrated and commemorated in the *Iliad,* the *Aneid,* the *Divine Comedy,* and Shakespeare's dramas. Three decades later, another author in Swedish exile, Peter Weiss, transformed excerpts from the transcripts of the *Auschwitz Trials* (1972–74) into the free verse of his Holocaust drama, *The Investigation,* obviously with the same intent.

The patterns underlying *Eli* are those of the history play and the spiritual drama, rather than tragedy. It is obvious from the new dresses, the music, the busy marketplace, and the New Year's service that the people of Israel have once again been saved (Sachs 1962, 31). The celebration is one of grief *and* joy, as is revealed by the dance of the old woman, who dances while remembering her daughter's death. This vignette calls to mind the significance of dance as prayer in Hasidic culture and the mystical powers of the miracle rabbi's dance. The survivors' naïveté signifies the peaceful character of Hasidism and confirms the victim status of the Jewish people, an important aspect of this work highlighting vulnerable individuals—old, weak, and disabled persons, including a crippled man, a blind girl, and a beggar. Through them, Sachs conveys the compassionate character of traditional Judaism: a nurturing community of meek and unassuming people with the strength to survive and to serve is the protagonist of Sachs's mystery play.

The survivors undertake the task of rebuilding with dignity, and in keeping with the Hasidic way of life, they do so thoughtfully as if steeped in meditation (23). From their comments it transpires that their life before the massacre was filled with serenity, contrasted in the text with the yelling and "wild laughter" of the conquerors, murderers, and rapists. Throughout the catastrophe and thereafter, the faithful preserve their innocence; they neither rebel nor question their fate; they humbly accept their sorrow and serve God with no less devotion than before. Nonetheless, they have become linked with the murderers by a spiritual bond established by the interdependency of crime and suffering, guilt and justice, and the slain innocents remain a part of their community, as if they were still alive (16).

Once again, the resemblance to some of Ilse Aichinger's works is striking. Sachs portrays the spirits of the dead as an integral part of life after the Holocaust: they hover over the Holocaust landscape, demanding to be integrated into the world of the living. Likewise, the landscape in *Eli* is alive with voices and signs, among them a chimney bearing witness to the fact that it was the last one to touch the body of Israel. By anthropomorphizing a chimney in a death camp, Sachs contrasts the innocence of inanimate objects with the guilt of the humans and amplifies this guilt by showing how humans abuse the material world for the purpose of killing.

In *Eli* the Nazi terror appears as a divine test that is followed by the redemption of the faithful. Notwithstanding this, Sachs confirms the responsibility of the perpetrators. However, her greater concern is for the Jews who experienced the genocide as children. Much like Else Lasker-Schüler in *Arthur Aronymus,* Sachs articulates concern that some of the men may have become permanently attracted to violence, and she addresses this possibility in the children's play. The girls dream of weddings, signifying that they continue to preserve the Jewish faith and culture, but the fantasies of the boy Jossele indicate that violence has entered the hearts of impressionable young males: Jossele wants to reenact a rape that he observed. Sachs's concern about the reproduction of violence is also implied in Michael's fate. The tool of divine justice, he must vanish once his mission has been accomplished lest violence stay in the world.

Michael, the fiancé of a woman who was raped and killed, faces a particularly difficult task; he is charged with finding Eli's murderer and delivering him to divine retribution but must refrain from personal revenge. In other words, Michael is to break the circle of crime and revenge. Throughout his quest, replete with miraculous occurrences and mystical signs, Sachs suggests that evil is as contagious as a virus and that the slightest wrongdoing requires redemption. Ultimately, Michael triumphs over the demons of untamed nature and human corruption, bringing about the victory of the *Schema Israel,* the words and spirit of

Jewish faith, over the perpetrators of the Shoah. The holiest of prayers and the divine law cause the collapse of the chimney and make nature rise to avenge the innocents. Among the perpetrators appear scientists, professors, orchestra conductors, and artists, representatives of the supposedly civilized society that conspired to slaughter God's Chosen People.

Eli illustrates that justice must be achieved without human intervention. Revenge belongs to the divine because men possess neither the power nor the measure to judge—only the knowledge of good and evil according to the commandments is human. Indeed, the world that Michael explores is full of ambivalence: the killer turns out to be a shoemaker like himself, the people in the enemy's town resemble those of the *shtetl,* and the Jewish boy Jossele and the son of the murderer are similar in that neither understands the principle of nonviolence. Although the past has left a mark on both children of the Holocaust, the *shtetl* differs fundamentally from the sphere of the perpetrators. The yearning of the murderer's wife suggests that she lives in a spiritual void, whereas the misguided Jewish males still are in the minority.

The ending of *Eli,* conceived prior to 1943, foreshadows the behavior on the part of historical figures such as Rudolf Hoess, the commandant of Auschwitz, before the courts of law. In the hope of justifing himself and being rewarded for his effectiveness, Hoess indicted himself in an autobiography that revealed his exact role in the genocide. In *Eli,* justice takes its course with Michael bearing witness: after the sudden death of his child, the murderer confesses his guilt in the hope of eluding justice. However, he disintegrates at the moment of his admission.

Eli, like Sachs's entire oeuvre, advances a radically pacifist philosophy. Already in the war years, the poet maintained that it was better to be among the persecuted than among the perpetrators, a view that is expressed after the liberation in Aichinger's novel *Die größere Hoffnung* (1974). The confirmation of the traditional *Galut* experience, the teachings of Hasidism, and the Yiddish language set Sachs apart from the way in which Zionists and socialists confronted and portrayed the Shoah.[21] From a religious and cultural Jewish perspective and a gender-specific point of view, her work focuses on the fate of the powerless. Sachs's humble female characters accept the divine will and abstain from violence naturally; although grief-stricken, they proceed with their lives without rebellion. To achieve such humility requires the male characters to have an exceptional inner strength, and those like Michael who are capable of such discipline are considered heroes and saints. Sachs also applies her concept of gender difference to the murderer's family: the father is the perpetrator, the son appears ready to follow in his footsteps, but the mother is portrayed as a victim of circumstance. To a certain extent, this configuration of male and female characters in *Eli* corresponds to traditional gender stereotypes, but it is also indicative of a feminist perspective in that Sachs suggests women's superiority to men.

Sachs's poetry deals especially with the suffering of women in ghettos and concentration camps. The poet was conscious of the fact that her beloved mother had escaped the horrors of the concentration camps by a hair's breadth. As in *Eli,* brutality is inscribed as a male characteristic, implying that the problem of violence can only be solved by men, hence men in particular are shown to be in need of spiritual principles to subdue their destructive impulses.

German and Jew

The Problem of Allegiance in the Holocaust Era

In interwar Germany and Austria, a diverse Jewish culture had emerged, which Ruth Beckermann in her study of Jewish life in Vienna of the 1920s, *Die Mazzesinsel,* describes as follows: "It was possible to be a Jewish Socialist or Communist, a Hasid at one of the 'Courts' that had immigrated to Vienna, a member of the small Sephardic community, or a Zionist. One could identify oneself as a Zionist and at the same time be an active Social Democrat, or one could consider oneself as an assimilated Viennese Jew and distance oneself from Eastern European Jews, but one could also abandon one's Jewishness and not even remember that one was Jewish" (Beckermann 1984, 13).

Hostile to modernity and the cultural and ethnic amalgamation of the big cities, the Nazis already called for a homogeneous national identity in their party program of 1920, as indicated in the following two items:

Item 4:
Only national comrades can be state citizens, and only persons of German blood, regardless of their denomination, can be national comrades. Therefore no Jew can be a national comrade.
Item 5:
Whoever is not a state citizen will only be allowed to live in Germany as a guest. Laws applicable to aliens will apply to such persons. (Broszat, Jacobsen, and Krausnick 1982, 255)

A national identity defining itself in such narrow ethnic and racial terms inhibits ethnic diversity. To this day, German identity is officially established by the *lex sanguinis,* by ancestry. As shown by Claudia Koonz in *Mothers in the Fatherland* (1987), the radically heterosexual Nazi gender ideology precluded sexual ambiguity and nontraditional gender roles such as the ones that evolved in Weimar Germany and the first Austrian republic, defining the role of women in restrictive terms.

Marxism and feminism were crushed in the earlier, German-Jewish culture in the latter half of the 1930s. After the Shoah, the majority of Jews and their children living in Germany and Austria were Displaced Persons from Eastern Europe. Initially, there was a consensus that the temporary postwar Jewish communities in Germany and Austria were to be temporary—the countries of the murderers were not considered appropriate for Jews to live in. Yet, over time permanent communities were established in the big cities. In addition, Jewish-identified persons, be it in terms of background or as members of the Jewish community of fate, live in today's Germany and Austria without officially registering with the Jewish *Kultusgemeinde*.[1] Sander Gilman argues that the Holocaust is the cornerstone of postwar Jewish identity (1986, 319). Confirming his view, Lea Fleischmann writes that the Jews in Germany are "unable to construct for themselves a German identity. They are state citizens with German passports, but they do not feel 'German,'" and even for the second postwar generation, "the 'Third Reich' is ever-present" (1994, 310).

The examples of Else Lasker-Schüler, Gertrud Kolmar, and Nelly Sachs have revealed that the basis for German-Jewish identity began to erode as early as the 1920s, and as many Jewish intellectuals hold, it was completely destroyed after the Nazi takeover.[2] At that point, a racial Jewish identity defined by German bureaucrats was imposed on individuals who up until that time had considered themselves Jews by religion or assimilated members of a culturally diverse society. To most German Jews, Jewish history, ethnicity, religion, and ancestry were only four among the many aspects of their multilayered identity, and not necessarily the most important ones. Nazi legislation rescinded all civil rights for Jews, and it imposed upon non-Jewish males a prescribed code of militarism and masculinity, relegating women to the status of housewife and breeder.

Faced with unrelenting physical and psychological attacks, many Jewish women and men internalized racist concepts and integrated Nazi terminology into their everyday language. It was common for concentration camp prisoners to adjust to the language of the camps and even to share some of the oppressors' prejudices against other ethnic groups, political views, and lifestyles (A. Reiter 1995, 104–6). Considering that middle-class education during the Wilhelminian and Weimar era had transmitted the very values that made the Nazi regime possible, it is not surprising that some of the most striking texts about the Holocaust were written by very young authors with little or no formal education, whereas women who appeared destined to become the chroniclers of their generation were oftentimes prevented from fulfilling this expectation because of their ideological baggage.

The Difficulty of Being German (Gerty Spies and Rahel Behrend)

Holocaust memoirs typically establish a particular narrative stance such as that of the victim or hero, with the hero being fashioned after the protagonists of German nineteenth- and twentieth-century literature (see Heinemann 1986). A case in point is the memoir of Elisabeth Freund, who represents herself as a privileged person in light of her past status and her ability to assert herself in the concentration camp. In the course of detailing the oppression of the Jewish community, Freund defines herself as a cultured, German-identified woman (Freund n.d.; D. C. G. Lorenz 1989). Her often critical perspective suggests a measure of insight, but her use of Nazi slang is startling. So are her positive attitudes toward Germany and Germans, including confirmed Nazis (Freund n.d., 172), and her prejudices against Sinti and Roma as well as the disabled. Like Freund, many women of her generation idealized German culture in spite of the barbaric reality they faced. They adhered to the values they had acquired in the humanistic preparatory schools (Humanistisches Gymnasium). Staunchly identifying themselves as Germans, these women derived a sense of superiority from their German heritage, ethnic or spiritual.

After years in hiding, even after the concentration and death camp experience, some women still felt a strong allegiance to their German culture and did not hesitate to return to their countries of origin. A few became involved in the Christian-Jewish dialogue, such as Gerty Spies and Hilde Burger, promoting mutual understanding between Jews and Gentiles (Schindler 1994, 184). Women who lived outside of Germany or Austria remained attached to their native language, writing and publishing in German, or teaching German language, literature, and culture in schools and at universities worldwide. Their loyalty belonged to an idealized, "better" Germany, a concept made up of German art, music, and literature, representing a motherland of which creative Jewish women could also feel a part.

Among the authors who returned from the concentration camp was Gerty Spies, who had become a lyric poet while in Theresienstadt. Much like the Theresienstadt poets Ilse Weber and Ilse Blumenthal-Weiss, Spies began writing for the sake of her psychological survival. Although in her autobiography she suggests that she had always had a penchant for literature, it was in the ghetto that she became an author. Through her intensive and painful efforts to express and transcend her anguish, she kept alert during endless role calls and her working hours at an armament factory. Poetry became Spies's first medium by necessity—she lacked the leisure and the paper to write prose. Since writing was punishable by death, she composed and memorized her poems during the day and secretly jotted them down at night. Thus she was limited to relatively simple forms and rhymes, and primarily four-footed iambic and trochaic meters. A perfectionist, Spies was painfully aware of her shortcomings as a poet and repeatedly expressed her desire to improve her literary skills. "Digging coal" (*Kohlen ausgraben*) is the term with which she describes her creative process. This allusion to a favorite motif of German Romanticism, mining and the miner, defines the basis of Spies's poetic theory. Influenced by the Romantics, she considered writing an activity of the intellectual elite. To her and her friends, poetry was a sacred mission that demanded the highest dedication. It was also a survival strategy to transform their reality.

Initially Spies's work was a solitary endeavor. Later, she connected with one of several circles of poets, artists, and intellectuals and used it as a vehicle for social exchange. She engaged in poetological discussions that helped her to fine-tune her literary tools. This is how Spies met her mentor, Elsa Porges Bernstein (pseudonym, Ernst Rosmer), who helped her to achieve a certain degree of fame in the ghetto.[3] A comparison of Spies's works with those of other Theresienstadt poets suggests that the ideals of her associates, all of whom were German-speaking members of the upper middle class, reenforced her traditional aesthetics.

Except in the brief period prior to the inspection of Theresienstadt by a Red Cross Commission in 1944, engaging in readings and discussions of any kind was dangerous. Yet, Spies mentions these hazards only in passing, stressing instead the significance of her poetry for herself and her friends: it represented a sphere of freedom and a respite from bondage. Moreover, the intimate ties between Spies and her friends functioned like an insulating wall between them and the Nazi-dominated environment and allowed them to maintain their intellectual autonomy. Spies and her friends opposed the Nazis by following an agenda of their own that, rooted in German culture, confirmed their German identity. In her memoir, "Ein Stück Weges" (n.d.), written soon after her return to Munich, and in her later autobiography, *Drei Jahre Theresienstadt* (1984), Spies focuses on her development as a poet. Surprising as it may seem in view of the political and ideological issues that had caused the author's plight, her work is an expression of her commitment to the German language and culture. In fact, her seemingly apolitical preoccupation with poetry is highly political: through it Spies confirms her position as a German Jew.

The narrative, interspersed with poems like a Romantic novella, relates how Spies was empowered through the process of creating poetry to cope with imprisonment and forced labor. The opening sentence of her memoir sets the stage by articulating the polarization of mind and body, art and reality, poetry and prose (n.d., 1). Working in an overcrowded factory, Spies experiences the exquisite alienation of a Romantic artist and removes herself emotionally from her savage environment. Convinced that being a poet makes her a special person, she trusts that she will prevail against any hardship. As is also the case in Ilse Blumenthal-Weiss's Theresienstadt memoir, "Im Auftrag des Reichskommissars" (1957), visions and intuition play an important role in Spies's work (n.d., 7). By translating oppressive sensations into visual and aural imagery, she overcomes the danger of paralysis.

Rather than being purely escapist, the preoccupation with language proved to be a viable coping mechanism for Spies and others who resolved to experience the world as language, among them Ilse Aichinger (D. C. G. Lorenz 1981, 34; Eich 1979, 19). Such a decision involved opting for a cerebral life as a result of which issues of race, gender, and the body were deprioritized. The ambition to become the best poet possible increased Spies's resilience. However, the subject of her poetry being life in Theresienstadt, she did not avoid reality. On the contrary, she described in great detail the agony of her fellow prisoners, older women like herself: the horrors of sleepless nights in overcrowded quarters and the agony of the sick and dying. With irony, humor, and sarcasm, Spies highlights the absurd aspects of this gruesome environment and overcomes despair. Love and tenderness involving other women are likewise a source of strength.

Despite focusing on Theresienstadt, "with its horrors, specters, and darkness" (n.d., 13), Spies's autobiographical narrative follows the linear structure of the German educational novel, the bildungsroman. The "time of terror" is configured as an opportunity for the protagonist/narrator to achieve her full potential; indeed, Spies reaches the apex of her poetic career in a concentration camp. Her delight in a poetry award she receives there is second only to the joy she experiences upon the arrival of the Allied troops. Nonetheless, the structure of the educational novel and Spies's actual story collide in a similar way as do the content and the form of her poetry. The author's life after her liberation was no happy ending: she has to stay in Theresienstadt and work in the camp kitchen during a typhoid epidemic until a shabby bus picks up the German survivors, taking them on a trip during which they realize the full extent of their home country's devastation. In Munich, Spies is informed about the death of most of her friends, and her encounters with average Germans make her understand that anti-Semitism still continues, as she relates in *Theresienstadt: Gedichte* (1948, 179). In addition, she notices that her accounts of her Theresienstadt experience are not appreciated by the general public. This not withstanding, she wrote and spoke in public about the Nazi crimes, admonishing her contemporaries not to forget and urging them to hold the perpetrators accountable. The disintegration of her later memoir toward the end reflects Spies's disillusionment with post-Holocaust Germany. After the destruction of the German-Jewish community, there is no audience for her to address. Rather than in Germany, Spies had to make her home in the German language.

The discrepancy between the narrative patterns preferred by German-Jewish survivors and the stories cast into these patterns becomes manifest in the structural problems of Spies's and other accounts, among them Rahel Behrend's *Verfemt und verfolgt* (1945), which later reappeared under the title *Ich stand nicht allein: Erlebnisse einer Jüdin in Deutschland, 1933–45* (Behrend-Rosenfeld, 1964), Lotte Paepcke's memoirs, *Unter einem fremden Stern* (1952) and *Ich wurde vergessen: Berichte einer Jüdin, die das Dritte Reich überlebte* (1979), and Ingeborg Hecht's *Als unsichtbare Mauern wuchsen* (1984). Dissatisfaction with their original reports seems to have caused these authors to rewrite their stories, some of them more than once, and under different names. This is the case with Rahel Behrend, whose fascinating autobiographies, with their fluid boundaries between reality and hallucination, danger and paranoia, reflect the profound disorientation of a persecuted woman whose identity has been shaken to the core. Other women waited for decades before they even found their voices and literary forms.

In the account of her survival in Nazi Germany, Rahel Behrend, née Elsbeth Rahel Charlotte Rosenfeld in 1891, who was raised Lutheran but registered as Jewish in 1938, defines herself as a German woman. The careful differentiation between Germans and Nazis enables her to sustain her loyalty to her native country. She bolsters her position by frequent references to the support received from Gentiles at home and abroad. The title change in the second version of her account is another indication of her view of the past. Originally entitled "Denounced and Persecuted," the later title reads "I Was Not Alone." Moreover, in 1964 Behrend published her memoir under the Jewish-sounding double name Behrend-Rosenfeld, which, along with the new title, must be read as the outward expression of her dual identity as a German and a Jew.

Verfemt und verfolgt begins a fictitious correspondence in the vein of the epistolary novel; later it changes into a diary addressed to the author's absent husband. Behrend, an inexperienced author, is profoundly influenced by the Nazi jargon and ideology. She uses terms such as *Jewish apartments* and *Jewish houses* without critical reflection and classifies other people according to racial stereotypes (1945, 128). The polarization between "good" and "evil" German becomes immediately visible in the first episode, which juxtaposes a brutal anti-Semite with a friendly German train conductor (6). This is not the only vignette illustrating that Germany has become the battleground between two opposing moral, if not cosmic, forces.

Behrend defines her narrative voice through her family history, her marriage (she was married to the Jewish lawyer Siegfried Rosenfeld, a member of the Prussian ministry of justice), and her own profession. As a young wife she helped her husband, a Social Democrat, along on his government career, which ended in 1932, when he became a target of persecution and lost his position. Almost simultaneously, her own position as a social worker was terminated. The Behrends are so severely affected by anti-Semitism that they decide to instruct their children at home. Completely disenfranchised from German mainstream institutions, the entire family goes on an odyssey through Southern Germany, with the narrator reporting one disturbing incident after another. The episodes of this trip are related in an allusive, subjective, and ambiguous manner, which creates a surrealistic ambiance. The *Kristallnacht* episode, on the other hand, in which Behend writes about her husband's being beaten and abused by the SA, is realistic and succinct. The great variety in the tone and style of the memoir suggests a loss of orientation on the part of a sensitive, but politically unaware, woman.

Initially Behrend seems so dominated by fear that she suspects everyone of plotting against her and her family. Desperate because her accounts of intrigues and attempts on her life are not taken seriously, she recounts her conversations with average Germans to prove that she has not lost her hold on reality. Her partly justified, partly irrational, fears and her and her daughter's psychosomatic illnesses reveal the stress to which fugitives and persons in hiding were exposed. Even in retrospect, the author is unable to reexamine her contention that she and her daughter were slowly being poisoned. In certain episodes perception and reality are completely indistinguishable, and the readers are drawn into Behrend's inner turmoil.

Throughout the first segment of *Verfemt und verfolgt*, fantastic and realistic events are intertwined, as are seemingly irrational and sensible reactions. Adding to the confusion is the fact that occasionally what seems like an exaggerated reaction proves to be correct, such as Behrend's insistence that their children return from a Zionist training farm—and they indeed have a narrow escape from being arrested. A marked change of pace occurs toward the middle of the account when her husband and the children obtain exit visas, while the narrator has to stay in Germany, living on a small fraction of her husband's pension in a collective home. Despite the external constraints, Behrend's narrative voice becomes stronger as her contacts with other people and her work obligations increase. She develops a keen sense of humor and a pragmatism that are surprising after the earlier confusion and melancholy. In particular, Behrend's descriptions of her dealings with state offices show that under duress her organizational talents, having lain dormant for so long, come to fruition.

In June of 1941, at the age of fifty, Behrend is drafted for forced labor. Working for the Jewish community, she is fast becoming aware of what actually goes on in Germany, and she takes sensible precautions, carefully separating fact from propaganda; not for a moment does she believe, for example, that the Poles provoked the German invasion

(1945, 9). Having heard that all Jews are to be shot at the beginning of the war, she makes herself as inconspicuous as possible. As was the case for Gertrud Kolmar during her forced labor experience, Behrend's self-confidence increases the more active she becomes, and she develops a sense of solidarity with her fellow workers and her supervisor (Woltmann 1995, 259). Even the order for Jews to wear the Yellow Star leaves Behrend surprisingly unconcerned, and she praises the smallest sign of compassion on the part of Gentiles.

The last episodes are evidence of Behrend's growth from a domesticated, frightened housewife to a determined survivor. Having once been spared deportation, she decides not to risk her life a second time. Rather than allowing herself to be shipped "like a piece of cattle," she goes into hiding and prepares for her escape (1945, 186). The boldness with which the middle-aged woman proceeds to save her life is remarkable. Realizing that civil disobedience is required to survive, she discontinues wearing the Yellow Star, and she networks with whomever she can to obtain false documents to get across the Swiss border.

Despite her profound attachment to Germany, being a Jewish woman was an equally important aspect of Behrend's existence. In contrast to Spies, who places the highest priority on being a member of the German intellectual community, national affiliation became a matter of indifference to Behrend when she was faced with deportation and death. Nonetheless, living in Great Britain from 1946 until her death in 1970, Behrend remained attached to the German language and never tired of expressing her appreciation for those Germans who helped her survive. At the same time, she lacked the passionate affinity for Germany of Spies and other Jewish men and women.

Opting for Jewishness (Ilse Aichinger and Cordelia Edvardson)

The Nürnberg Laws forced especially the children of assimilated parents to examine their identity in cultural, racial, and religious terms, perhaps for the first time. So-called *Mischlinge*, persons of mixed backgrounds, faced a particularly difficult situation. Regardless of their classification, they had to make a choice between Jewish and what was referred to as an Aryan identity.[4] Many Jews or half-Jews by Nazi standards had received a secular or Christian education and lacked the religious and cultural basis to establish a Jewish identity. Some of them, indeed, identified

with their oppressors; others refused to accept the alleged racial inferiority of their Jewish ancestors and maintained that they were as German
as any "Aryan." Not grasping the determinism of Nazi ideology, some
Mischlinge tried to renounce their Jewishness by redeeming themselves
through achievements or by converting, neither of which helped them
integrate into the mainstream but separated them from the Jewish community even further.[5] Being family members of non-Jews, the majority
of the *Mischlinge* identified with German culture even more closely than
German Jews. Many had been baptized and identified with the literature
and philosophy of the Enlightenment, classicism, and Romanticism,
being Christians, and, some of them, Marxists and socialists. Fewer of
them had been raised Jewish. Their autobiographical works for the most
part invoke the legacy of Germany's and Austria's great men: Kant,
Goethe, Schiller, Grillparzer, and Stifter.

The tragic situation of *Mischlinge,* whose self-confidence was crushed
as a result of being denied their German identity, has been frequently
discussed. There are, however, other cases where the opposite is true.
Peter Edel, the son of a Gentile mother and a Jewish father, for example, suffered considerable anguish because, according to Jewish law,
he was not a Jew; Ilse Aichinger and Cordelia Edvardson, despite their
Christian upbringing, identified with the Jewish Nazi victims. They expressed their position by dissociating themselves from mainstream Germany and Austria, fundamentally questioning the nations that turned
against them. The works of these authors are paradigmatic of the complex psychological processes involved in deciding which side to take.

Among the younger authors who rejected German identity as defined
by the Nazis, and who constructed their own position in solidarity with
the victims of the Holocaust, were Ilse Aichinger and Cordelia Edvardson, both of whom were classified as partly Jewish. With Aichinger the
process of forging a Jewish discourse in opposition to the Christian and
the fascist world view began with her family's breakup as a consequence
of the Nazi invasion of Austria. Edvardson's childhood, in contrast,
had already been overshadowed by the suppression of her partly Jewish
background and her grandmother's and mother's transgressions against
the bourgeois moral code. Her father and grandfather were Jewish, and
like her mother, the poet Elisabeth Langgässer, Edvardson had been
conceived out of wedlock. Langgässer tried to conceal this fact, as well
as her and her daughter's ethnic background. Whereas Aichinger solved

her dilemma by establishing for herself a radically individualistic identity as an outsider, a cosmopolitan, and an intellectual, Edvardson, after a long struggle, assumed a communal identity as an Israeli and as a Jewish mother.

Throughout her career, Aichinger scrutinized the ideological patterns imbedded in her native society and language. To illustrate her inner conflict, she employed experimental literary and Jewish themes and images reflecting her multicultural Viennese childhood milieu. Edvardson, having grown up under the spell of her mother's literary imagination, found her existence irreversibly disrupted by her imprisonment in Theresienstadt and Auschwitz. After her liberation, she worked toward creating a new identity for herself without mending broken ties. She abandoned the German language and became a speaker of Swedish and later Hebrew. Moreover, she left the Catholic Church, converted to Judaism, and moved to Israel during the Yom Kippur War.

Constructing a Post-Holocaust Jewish Identity (Ilse Aichinger)

Ilse Aichinger's works are linked by their language and their topics to the literature of Jewish women of previous generations, notably Else Lasker-Schüler, Nelly Sachs, Gertrud Kolmar, and Rose Ausländer. Despite her pronounced pacifism and her longing for reconciliation, Aichinger registers discord on all levels of existence—between men and women, Jews and non-Jews, different nations, and within nature. Her texts suggest that harmony can be achieved only in the moment, against great odds, and by only a few people. Her understated style reflects her need for privacy as well as her existential loneliness; by no means is the inaccessibility of her texts a manifestation of elitism or snobbery. Underlying her sense of the absurd is a fundamental hopelessness that she shares with Holocaust poets like Paul Celan. Not coincidentally, she has been compared to Franz Kafka, whom she claims to have read only late in her career.

Aichinger began writing during the war years and published her first prose texts in the immediate postwar era. Her descent—but more important, her rejection of Nazi ideology and anti-Semitism—excluded her from the culture of the Third Reich, although as a baptized "half-Jew," she had a status of privilege, which is problematized in her texts. It separated her from her mother's family and her friends and was a source of distress to her. She constructs a Jewish identity in opposition to the Aryan world in which she is marginalized, while at the same time she is an outsider to Judaism and the concentration camp experience.

Aichinger's situation resembles that of other Austrian survivors of the Nazi regime, namely, Friedrich [Friedensreich] Hundertwasser and Ernst Fuchs, the most prominent representatives of the *Wiener Schule* of art and Viennese Fantastic Realism. Fuchs, also classified as a *Mischling,* survived in hiding with his mother; Hundertwasser, the son of a Gentile father, had joined the Hitler Youth to save himself, while his mother's family was deported and murdered (Grunfeld 1981, 130ff.). Their formative experiences differ from those of the individuals who, defined as Jews internally and externally, went into exile or were deported. Their experiences also prevented them from identifying with the mainstream. There is an affinity between Hundertwasser's and Fuchs's ornate paintings and Aichinger's rich language, which manifest a dissimilation process from the literary and artistic programs of the postwar era. Linking up with surrealism and expressionism, both of which had been labeled degenerate by the Nazis, Fuchs, Hundertwasser, and Aichinger perpetuate the defamed and forgotten Jewish culture of the interwar period.

In the work of a multiply marginalized author such as Aichinger, national, ethnic, religious, and gender lines intersect. Ellen, the protagonist of Aichinger's novel *Die größere Hoffnung* (1974), best captures the author's position as an intermediary between cultures, age groups, and ideological factions. Ellen's situation reflects the problem arising from the increase in conversions and interfaith marriages and the reversal of the integration process as a result of Nazi legislation, which was designed to produce a pure race.[6] Arno Herzig points out that the "fourteen years of the Weimar Republic"—and interwar Austria—were "the only period of the history of the nineteen century-long history of Jews in Germany without separate laws, edicts, and policies pertaining to this minority" (1993, 1). After 1938, Aichinger's own father, like many "Aryans," had his marriage dissolved, causing his wife, the physician Bertha Aichinger, to lose her privileged status. Aichinger's twin sister Helga emigrated to England, but Ilse stayed in Vienna to protect her mother, who was exempt from deportation as the caregiver of a "half-Aryan" minor. The persecution of her friends and family members, including the deportation of her grandmother, and the experience of being disenfranchised and placed in jeopardy crushed Aichinger's confidence in the

German culture, hence her nonconformism and her distrust of any ideology and party politics.

After graduating from high school, Aichinger, barred from university study, performed forced labor. During this time, she began writing *Die größere Hoffnung* (1974a). Writing fulfilled the dual purpose of recording and processing her ordeal. The novel mirrors the author's escalating dissociation from Gentile Austria and Catholicism and her identification with the persecuted Jews, most visibly expressed by her protagonist Ellen's resolve to wear the Yellow Star without being forced to. Wearing the mark of disgrace, Ellen demonstrates her allegiance to her grandmother's people. In her later poem "Widmung," Aichinger articulates a similarly unconditional sense of belonging: "I write you no letters, / but I would find it easy to die with you." For many intended Nazi victims, including Anne Frank, whose diary Aichinger read after the war, writing was a way to preserve their sanity and dignity *in extremis*.[7] By writing, Aichinger articulated her feelings and constructed a vision of reality all her own in which she validates the legacy of her maternal culture, assimilated Austro-Hungarian Jewry, and repudiates the authoritarian structures of Nazi Germany her father had joined.

After the liberation Aichinger devoted most of her time to her literary pursuits. In 1951, alongside Paul Celan, she made her first appearance at the meeting of the Group 47, where her lyrical short story "Der Gefesselte" and Celan's poem "Todesfuge" (Death Fugue) created a sensation. In tone and mood, the works of these two authors of Jewish background differed from the terse and laconic literature of the so-called *Kahlschlag* (tabula rasa). Having had no involvement with Nazi culture, Aichinger and Celan neither distanced themselves from their pre-1945 existence nor placed any stock in the German efforts at reeducation. In opposition to the German postwar authors, who called for a start at point zero, Aichinger claimed the legacy of the authors whom the Nazis had defamed and destroyed. From her perspective, the end of the war was the time for the legitimate German language to reemerge.

In the stark landscape of postwar German literature, Aichinger's work stands out because of its ornate language and her frame of reference: the Bible, Martin Buber's *Hasidic Tales,* as well as legends, fairy tales, and folk ballads. She also established a link to German Romanticism at a time when this movement was dismissed by the critical establishment as a precursor of Nazi irrationalism.[8] Remembrance is an important aspect of Aichinger's work, blending personal recollections with references to critical and literary discourses, and her work evokes exceptional individuals as role models in the struggle against tyranny. Her work is an ongoing dialogue with authors who wrote about the plight of oppressed groups and individuals, including Nelly Sachs. At an age when German authors championed Ernest Hemingway, whose machismo was alien to Aichinger, she chose as her literary models dissenters and outsiders, many of them binational or multinational, such as Joseph Conrad, Samuel Becket, Hart Crane, and Henry and Arthur Miller. Aichinger's work is furthermore informed by her own experience, which is articulated with increasing directness. The anthology *Kleist, Moos, Fasane* (1987) contains themes and concerns already present in *Die größere Hoffnung*, but in the more recent work the author speaks directly, without a protagonist serving as intermediary. Yet, her childhood environment, depicted with great immediacy in *Die größere Hoffnung*, appears like a lost paradise in *Kleist, Moos, Fasane*.

The texts contained in the anthology have a dual focus that entwines the historical moment and subjective experience. In "Der 1. September 1939," for example, Aichinger reveals the confusion of average citizens like herself on the day of the Nazi invasion of Poland (Weilová n.d.; Winterfeld 1969). Rather than criticizing her lack of awareness as a young woman, she marvels at the naïveté that gave her the strength to enjoy life regardless of the circumstances. The process of memory is also explored in "Hilfstelle." The narrator, comfortable in her present state of prosperity, is almost unable to envision the past horrors until an empty space left by a bombed-out house enables her to visualize images of the past.[9] Even those, it develops, are not entirely without hope. Along with the devastation, the narrator remembers a support group sponsored by the Jesuits and, in another text, "Nach der weißen Rose," the resistance group White Rose.

The preoccupation with the past indicates that Aichinger's intensely felt separateness increased over time. There is a feeling of loneliness about *Kleist, Moos, Fasane*, caused in part by the speaker's individualism, in part by her loyalty to the murdered Jews. The protagonist of *Die größere Hoffnung* bases her decisions solely on her own perceptions, thereby positioning herself outside the accepted norms. Her alienation from society increases as each episode leads her to new insights and as her association with her Jewish friends deepens. In keeping with the

Talmudic precept that it is better to be persecuted than to be a persecutor, which is also the ethical basis of Nelly Sachs's work, Aichinger's
protagonist relinquishes her status as half-Aryan. Her destruction at the
end of the novel must be interpreted as a wish to perish with the people
she loves because their death leaves her extremely isolated. Later texts,
notably the poem "Dreizehn Jahre" in *Verschenkter Rat* (1978) and the
story "Rahels Kleider" in *Schlechte Wörter* (1974), confirm the earlier
commitment to Jewish culture and to the author's dead friends.

As early as *Die größere Hoffnung,* Aichinger's nonconformism is expressed through Jewish themes in conjunction with criticism of the
Christian world view, secular or religious, particularly asceticism. The
conditioning of children in order to renounce life is the subject of
numerous of her texts, such as in "Wiegenfest" (*Eliza, Eliza* [1965])
and "Rahels Kleider" (1974). She parodies Christian myths and legends
in "Mit den Hirten" (1965) and "Nachruf" (*Verschenkter Rat* [1978]).
Frequently, cynicism and blasphemy position her speakers outside the
Gentile world, as in "Einunddreißig," "In und Grimm," and "Jüngste
Nacht" (1978). All these texts convey outrage against a religion and a
god in whose name countless atrocities were committed.

The Jewish children and Ellen in *Die größere Hoffnung* oppose Nazism
by refusing to play victims' roles. Relying on her inner resources, Ellen
develops a highly personal reference system to withstand indoctrination from the outside. Contrary to Lawrence Langer's assertion that her
"fragmentary perceptions never fuse into a lucid whole" (1975, 140), she
is remarkably well equipped to cope with chaos, precisely because she
is a child, resilient and unafraid. Ellen defies the Nazis, including her
father, by disobeying their ordinances. Aware that the discrimination
against Jews reflects on the perpetrators, rather than on the victims, she
is not taken in by the distortion of Jewish symbols in public discourse.
A comparison between Ellen and the self-characterizations of women
who survived the Holocaust at a young age confirm Aichinger's representation.[10] Both in the memoir literature and in Aichinger's novel,
the narrator's identification with her mother is of great significance. For
Ellen, the internalized image of her exiled mother functions as a spiritual presence and provides the child with guidance and inner strength.

As early as her essay "Aufruf zum Mißtrauen" (1946), Aichinger called
upon the survivors of the Nazi era to subject their thoughts and motivations to a thorough examination (588). Although the rejection of

partisan politics and ideology was common among German-speaking authors after the collapse of the Nazi regime, the sources of Aichinger's distrust, culminating in her rejection of accessible modes of communication, differ from those of the World War II veterans. For Aichinger, detachment was a necessity, dictated by the dismissal of the Jewish point of view by the general public and the delayed effects of her survivor's trauma. While some Jewish authors left the German-speaking sphere altogether, although they continued to write in German, Aichinger left only her native Austria, but her attitude toward the language compromised by National Socialism and the authoritarian models of interaction prescribed by it was fundamentally critical.

In the 1950s, both Germanies entered the cold war, and Austria, having barely regained its autonomy, was remilitarized. The so-called minor war criminals were rehabilitated, and the new Western-style democracies became fertile ground for revisionist activities. Aware that hers was a minority position, Aichinger expressed her dissent quietly but participated in protests against the proliferation of nuclear arms and the Vietnam War. Her works convey discontent with media and governments that professed philo-Semitism in the absence of Jews but relegated Mediterranean workers to an inferior status.[11] Aichinger was unable to envision an end to oppression and genocide and was far from according the Allies a position of moral superiority, as her criticism of American racial politics reveals. In "Seegasse" (*Plätze und Straßen* [1954a]), for example, she suggests that within their respective cultures, the position of the African American soldiers resembles that of the Jews, and in the radio play *Auckland* she paints California as a social Darwinist jungle where brutal homosocial structures, racism, and misogyny are prevalent.

After the Nazi terror, the world was threatened by nuclear annihilation. Aichinger's pessimistic outlook suggests a lack of confidence in man's ability to cope with his destructive potential, a dilemma that the title work in *Rede unter dem Galgen* (1952) explores in a two-pronged fashion: like the Holocaust survivors and the Nazi veterans, the protagonist is granted an unexpected respite, and he is confronted with the difficulty of reentering everyday life. The hero and death cult of Nazi culture is juxtaposed to civilian living, revealing that survival is by its very nature an anticlimactic experience that requires greater moral fiber than killing and dying. Aichinger's protagonist, whose bombastic monologue calls to mind Nietzsche's *Zarathustra* and expressionist poetry, is reduced from a defiant hero to an average person.

In Aichinger's work the category of gender plays an important role. Only her female characters are rational; only they seem capable of self-discipline.[12] Older women in particular radiate a humble spirituality, reminiscent of Hasidic culture as portrayed in Nelly Sachs's *Eli*. In the short story "Der Gefesselte" (1953), Aichinger defines gender as a particular way of relating to reality: The female protagonist liberates the male protagonist in the assumption that his bondage causes him discomfort. It evolves, however, that he has no identity other than being the Bound Man and is unable to cope with freedom. With few exceptions male characters are portrayed as incompetent or destructive, and female figures who allow themselves to be dominated by their male companions come to harm.

In general, Aichinger's protagonists are not defined in terms of their biological function. Instead, the category of gender signifies more abstract qualities as well as opposition to patriarchal structures. Aichinger uses the term *motherland* to define the domain of her native language, regardless of political or ethnic boundaries. Conversely, the concept *fatherland* implies power structures. Her female speakers, residents of the motherland, are for the most part ignorant of the male-defined hierarchy governing them, but they reject it instinctively.

Aichinger's validation of otherness is inspired by her experience with Nazi rule and her disillusionment with postwar Austria and Germany. From a position of alienation, she portrays ethnocentrism, territorialism, and warfare as part and parcel of German *Gemütlichkeit* and its anti-intellectual conservatism ("Zweifel an Balkonen," 1974). Comparing the robust majority, contemptuously referred to as "the merry ones," to the small minority who support cultural values ("Liebhaber der Westsäulen," 1974), she makes it obvious that fascism's victory over the forces of freedom and culture has been nearly complete. Like Hitler's supporters—this association is initiated by the reference to freeway construction, which in Germany had been initiated by the Nazis—the public fetishizes youth, strength, and mindless progress, which Aichinger associates with brutality and exploitation.

Sensing that the past was but an overture to greater conflicts, Aichinger viewed the armistice of 1945 with caution. The ending of *Die größere Hoffnung* raised doubts about the future—there is not a hint that the liberators will do anything to support women and minorities. Ellen is a case in point. During the war years, she acts on her own, but on the eve of the armistice she is killed by an exploding shell while she is on a mission for an Allied officer. The love scene involving Ellen and this man portrays romantic love as a liability that requires the subordination of the female partner, thereby expressing in a nutshell Aichinger's outlook for the postwar era. The reconstruction of patriarchal society requires trading in the greater hope for freedom for the smaller hopes of capitalism. Aichinger's view corresponds to that of Helma Sanders-Brahms in *Germany Pale Mother,* a 1976 film about the experience of women under National Socialism, during World War II and during the postwar era (Weinberger 1992, 37–88).

In her introduction to the prose anthology *Der Gefesselte* (1953), Aichinger asserts that many writers of her generation are succinct to the point of falling silent (5–7). This statement applies to her own work, with its keen awareness of the limitations of language. The language problem in Aichinger is not only of a general philosophical nature; it also concerns German as a tool for a Jewish-identified author. Aichinger prefers gestures, imagery, scenery, and abstractions to direct commentary, and she frequently focuses on silence and being silenced. One of her most striking examples of the voicelessness of the victims occurs in "Port Sing" (1965), a story about the mass extermination of a nation of rabbits, which lends itself to be read as a parable about the Holocaust. The text problematizes historiography; writing for the benefit of the powerful, historians record what is in their employers' interest, whereas Aichinger explores the untold fates of the conquered.[13] To this undertaking, the teleological prose of patriarchy is inappropriate.

The narrator of "Rahels Kleider" (1974b) refuses to communicate altogether, rather than running the risk of being coopted by the wrong audience. Yet, the name of the title figure and the circumstances of her disappearance, as well as the imagery shifting from Christian to Jewish motifs, provide clues that establish a link between the narrator and the Shoah. These allusions, in turn, encourage the reader to investigate the history and the consequences of genocide.

The silence of Aichinger's victims and the wordiness of the perpetrators indicate that both act according to a different psychology, which produces different attitudes toward identical facts. The incongruity between word and fact, which is also shown in Peter Weiss's drama about the Auschwitz trials, *Die Ermittlung* (1964), is the theme of several texts by Aichinger. Particularly her later stories reflect her ongoing pursuit of honesty in language and her effort to articulate events and phenomena whose "unspeakability" has been asserted by writers and critics dealing with the Holocaust.

It has been noted that Aichinger emulates surrealist literature and the theater of the absurd. In contrast to the latter, however, her seemingly hermetic texts comment on historical problems by way of structural and associative analogy, and many contain Jewish subtexts. For example, the surface structure of Aichinger's best-known dialogue, "Französische Botschaft" (*Zu keiner Stunde* [1957]), purports to be a debate about stability and change, while a second layer of motifs makes it a parody of the angelic message the Annunciation. Contrary to the Virgin Mary, Aichinger's maid Marie realizes that eternity equals death, and she rejects the offer of the authority figure to eternalize her. The image of the prophet Elias in his golden carriage has Jewish and Christian connotations. According to Judaism, the Elijah will proclaim the coming of the Messiah; Christian tradition considers him a prefiguration of Christ. His golden vehicle, moreover, calls to mind the Greek god Apollo, the god of reason, who, according to Johann Jakob Bachofen, prevailed over the chthonic goddesses of the matriarchal world. The advent of Christianity and patriarchy is prevented by Marie's refusal to obey, which causes Elias-Apollo to pass by. The dialogue not only attributes power to the lowly woman but also contains a specifically Jewish message: it confirms that the Messiah has not yet come; thus hope must continue. In Judaism, this meaning is played out every Passover, when a goblet of wine is placed on the Seder table to welcome Elijah, who will enter when the time has come to announce the Messiah. The concept of the "Greater Hope," the title of Aichinger's novel, ultimately is the messianic Jewish hope, symbolized by Ellen, who dies still hoping for freedom.

After the publication of her novel, Aichinger increasingly engaged in a dialogue with the dead, her focus being the inscrutable realm before birth. In "Spiegelgeschichte" (1954b), which won the Prize of the Group 47, she portrays life as a brief emergence and death as a return to the original obscurity. Her concept of time and space as permeable and her meditative approach to reality call to mind the aesthetic and philosophical principles characteristic of the poetry of Rose Ausländer, who, like Paul Celan, was a native of Czernowitz. Ausländer's work, and possibly Celan's, are informed by Constantin Brunner's philosophy of motion, *Bewegungsphilosophie* (G. Reiter 1991, 169ff.), and there is an affinity between Aichinger's and Brunner's views as well. She shares his view that events and phenomena are preserved in and through language; thus in her texts the dead participate in everyday reality and articulate their anguish, which the living want to silence.

The presence of supernatural phenomena within contemporary reality is especially obvious in the vignettes "Plätze und Straßen" (1954a), where Aichinger subverts the antihistorical trends of the postwar era by portraying Vienna as the scene of untold crimes against humanity. All across the city, the speaker confronts memories of the Nazi-era: in the old Jewish quarter, at the site of the bombed-out "Philippshof," in the burned-out and rebuilt Gonzagagasse. She parodies the antiseptic language of technocrats to reveal their attempts at eliminating the perpetrators from their euphemistic discourse on mass murder and blends elements from a multitude of discourses, deliberately transgressing against traditional genre categories with the purpose of undermining established discursive practices. Aichinger's texts are constructed from interactive rather than psychological models; they expose the intersection between religion, ethnicity, and gender and highlight the conflicts between individual and collective, men and women.

In the radio play "gare maritime" (1974b), Aichinger revisits the concentration camp world with a focus on the connection between Jewish identity and gender. The text establishes a paradigm for overcoming the polarization of individuals and cultures under the auspices of feminist and Jewish values. The leadership role of the female character, Joan, a time-traveler like Stefan Heym's Ahasver, implies the surrender of male privilege and cultural feminization for the sake of global survival. Moreover, the pacifist ethos of both protagonists evokes traditional European Jewish values. The abuse of the two protagonists at the hands of guards and fanaticized youths is reminiscent of the situation of German Jews during the Nazi era. The fact that Aichinger's protagonists are puppets of varying shape and substance, but display a greater degree of qualities ascribed to human beings than the voices defined as human, draws secular Christian and humanistic concepts into question. "Gare maritime" juxtaposes the horror of the concentration camps with the power of individual resistance and love. When Joe and Joan are broken to pieces because those in power no longer consider them useful, they

state, seemingly paradoxically, that they are making progress. The radio
play radicalizes Aichinger's belief in nonviolence by suggesting that in
a society of oppressors it is best to be considered garbage.[14]

Beginning with her earliest works, Aichinger constructs a Jewish
feminine identity as an alternative position to the culture of German-
speaking countries after the Shoah. Too elusive to fit into a religious
framework, Aichinger's Jewish position is supported by her knowledge
and appreciation of the biblical tradition, her awareness of Jewish customs and thought, her acceptance and emulation of the discourses of
earlier German-Jewish writers, and her rejection of her native Gentile
culture. Its most important aspect, however, is Aichinger's identification with the victims of the Holocaust and her love for her mother's
Jewish ancestors.

"Am Israel Chai" (Cordelia Edvardson)

Like Ilse Aichinger, the journalist, poet, autobiographer, and novelist
Cordelia Edvardson was born into an assimilated urban environment.
Edvardson's self-constructed Jewish identity is rooted in the Holocaust
experience and the sensation of not belonging. "Still in Auschwitz, I was
unaware of the fact that I was a Jewish woman," she states (Koelbl 1989,
50). Edvardson made the decision to define herself as a Jew by leaving
the Catholic Church and joining the Jewish community in Stockholm
for moral and intuitive, rather than religious, reasons: she was convinced
that it was her duty to restore the children lost in the Holocaust to
the Jewish people, including herself. As the illegitimate daughter of the
well-known Catholic author Elisabeth Langgässer and a married Jewish man, Hermann Heller, who was killed in Spain in 1933, Edvardson's
childhood in Berlin differed substantially from Aichinger's (49–51), and
her recollections lack the intimacy of Aichinger's.

Langgässer had moved to Berlin in 1929 into a world her daughter
portrays as ambivalent and confusing. In her autobiographical account,
Bränt barn söker sig till elden (1984), translated from Swedish into the
German work *Gebranntes Kind sucht das Feuer* (1990) in 1986 and soon
thereafter distinguished with the West German Scholl Award, Edvardson unravels her past.[15] She surveys the stations of her life: her childhood, her detention together with other Jews and "half-Jews" before
their deportation to Theresienstadt and Auschwitz, the concentration

camp experience in which she refers to herself as the "child" and the "girl," her postwar existence in Sweden, featuring her as "the young woman," and, finally, her life in Israel under the auspices of motherhood. Edvardson's own need for mother figures and female mentors is expressed in the dedication of *Gebranntes Kind:* "To my mothers Elisabeth Langgässer, Berlin, Stefi Pedersen, Stockholm, Sylvia Krown, Jerusalem, and to my children."

A native speaker of German, Edvardson writes in Swedish, but her continued preoccupation with Germany and, after *Gebranntes Kind,* the reception of her work in the Federal Republic, places her work into the context of other post-Holocaust literature by Jewish women authors of German language and culture. When Edvardson wrote her autobiography, she had already published several works addressing her formative experiences in various genres, such as her poems about Auschwitz, *Sa kom jag till Kartago* (1958). Her work revolves around her multiple cultural and linguistic identity, her quest for Jewish identity, and gender issues. These concerns are addressed in her essay on women's rights, *Till kvinna fodd* (1967), her diary about her experience in Israel, *Om jag glommer dig . . .: En invandrares dagbok fran Israel* (1976), and the travelogue of her journey to Germany and her autobiography, *Viska det till vinden* (1988), translated as *Die Welt zusammenfügen* (1989). Similar to other survivors of the Nazi era and the Holocaust, including Ilse Aichinger and Mira Lobe, and male authors such as Bruno Bettelheim, Edvardson was interested in children and child psychology, and she wrote children's books. Her poetry anthology, *Jerusalems leende* (1991), translated into German in 1993 as *Jerusalems Lächeln,* deals with her experience in Israel. Edvardson's works have also appeared in Hebrew and other languages.

Gebranntes Kind sucht das Feuer confirms Edvardson's identity in terms of gender, race, religion, family, and nationality. The form of the literary autobiography is especially appropriate for the discussion of the multilayered identity of a multiply displaced person. Swedish, Edvardson's literary language, is a neutral anchoring point between the opposing forces of the author's German past and her Israeli present. It represents a compromise between that which she fears and wishes to avoid and that which she desires. Swedish differs enough from German, to which she is tied by love-hatred, to allow her the necessary space to be an author. Having immigrated to Israel at the age of forty-two, Edvardson does not trust her Ivrit enough to make it her literary medium.

Nonetheless, it is the language associated with her passionate personal commitment to Israel and her immersion into Jewish culture; neither one is without tragic overtones.[16] As she points out, in Theresienstadt and Auschwitz her German receded behind Yiddish, the lingua franca of the concentration camps. The greater the distance from her native language, the easier it was for her to shed her former persona. After her resocialization in Sweden, a new personality emerged, and did so again in Israel. When writing *Gebranntes Kind,* Edvardson was well on the road toward integrating herself into Israeli culture. She embraced Zionism and Ivrit as her language, while German, the tongue of her memories, tied her to the past, to Europe, and, most important, to her mother.

Even before the Holocaust the feeling that "something was wrong with her" haunted Edvardson, beginning in her childhood. Elisabeth Langgässer, a staunch Catholic, tried to conceal her and Edvardson's Jewish background. She vehemently rejected Judaism as she tried to atone for her and her mother's sexual transgressions.[17] Edvardson conjectures that Langgässer searched for an antidote to the "two Jewish men who had seduced and left her" (1990, 24). Considering the pretense and denial with which Langgässer raised her daughter, the impact of the Nürnberg Laws must have been devastating. They crushed Edvardson's identity and eventually threatened her life. Langgässer, who had been associated with a circle of poets that included Günter Eich, Ilse Aichinger's later husband, had written for the literary journal *Kolonne.* She tried various ploys to preserve her status as an author, including marrying a non-Jew in 1935, but as a so-called half-Aryan, she was excluded from the *Reichsschrifttumkammer,* the official organization of German writers, and was forbidden to publish. Even the commercials she wrote to support herself and her family placed her in jeopardy (41). The discrepancy between Edvardson's own perceptions and her mother's and grandmother's claim to status, which clashed with an environment that treated her family as outcasts, did not allow Edvardson to assess her situation realistically. Being the wife of the philosopher Wilhelm Hoffmann, who had been disowned by his family for having married a non-Aryan, and the mother of his son, Langgässer was in no danger of being deported (64). However, she was unable to protect her daughter. Notwithstanding Edvardson's Catholic upbringing and her Spanish citizenship, which her mother helped her acquire through adoption by a Spanish couple, Edvardson eventually was classified a "Three-Quarter Jew" (60). Edvardson describes Langgässer's surrender before the Nazi bureaucracy as the major turning point in her childhood. In the absence of her mother's unconditional support, she felt abandoned. Reminded by a Nazi official that she herself, a "half-Jew," might be deported, Langgässer did not stop Edvardson from accepting dual citizenship, Spanish and German, which deprived her of her immunity as a foreign national. As a consequence, Edvardson was separated from her family, imprisoned, and deported to Theresienstadt and later to Auschwitz (1990, 68). The examples of mothers who refused to leave their children under any circumstances clarify Edvardson's point of view: she blamed Langgässer for instilling her with a false sense of security, a false identity, and a false religion. Most of all, she is traumatized by the fact that her mother did nothing to prevent her deportation (89). The ensuing distance between mother and daughter, the older and the younger generation, is as unbridgeable as that between Ilse Aichinger and her father, expressed distinctly, but far more dispassionately, in Aichinger's poem "Mein Vater" (1978, 19).

Edvardson's ordeal is reflected in her autobiography, much more harshly configured than Aichinger's texts, as well as in her uncompromising life decisions, including her resolve to live as a Jewish woman in Israel. Much like Claire Goll's 1940s memoirs, *Der gestohlene Himmel* (1990),[18] Edvardson's *Gebranntes Kind sucht das Feuer* is a condemnation of the author's mother, portrayed as a sadist, hypocrite, and coward. Like Goll, Edvardson indicts her mother for being a sexual female, rather than a nurturer, and she configures her mother as the archetypal painted woman, the Great Whore.[19] Edvardson casts Langgässer with her "shining black hair and her red mouth" (60), as the embodiment of seduction and betrayal and attributes to her witchlike qualities. Edvardson and Goll, whose mother was murdered in Theresienstadt in 1943, describe the suffering their mothers inflicted upon them, and they expose their mothers' supposedly perverse sexual behavior. Edvardson does so in episodes involving Langgässer's and Hoffmann's crossdressing and sadomasochistic games in which "the girl" was forced to participate, albeit in a minor role. Moreover, Edvardson alleges that the abuse she suffered at the hands of her stepfather occurred with her mother's knowledge (31),[20] and she surmises that the atmosphere in her family predisposed her to the unbridled sexuality in which she engaged during her imprisonment (30–31). Goll's even more graphic memoirs cite countless examples of torment to which she, her brother, and her father were subjected by her mother, precipitating her brother's suicide (1990, 175f.). Both authors reveal the trauma of destructive mother-daughter relationships and the child's inability to let go, even after the mother's death. *Der gestohlene Himmel*, which Goll kept on revising and republishing, is perhaps the most explicit literary account of child abuse in the German language, but Edvardson's autobiography, vividly describing her mother's mental cruelty and ascribing to her the worst possible motives, is no less striking.[21]

Encouraged by the reception of *Gebranntes Kind sucht das Feuer*, Edvardson traveled to Germany in an attempt to overcome her misgivings about her native country and to come to terms with the past. Troubled by the intricate relationship between perpetrators and victims, she hoped to find out "what Germany was like" (Koelbl 1989, 52). *Die Welt zusammenfügen* (1989), written immediately thereafter, discusses her encounter with Germany more than four decades after the Shoah. Edvardson professes to have felt a frustration similar to Hilde Domin's two decades earlier. Domin, a native of Cologne, had been in exile in England and St. Domingo and returned to Germany in 1954. A comparison between Domin's semi-documentary novel *Das zweite Paradies* (1968) and Edvardson's *Die Welt zusammenfügen* reveals similar perceptions despite the authors' differences in age, approach, and outlook. Domin's work is poetic, subjective, and introspective, whereas Edvardson's is more direct and matter-of-fact, but both bring to light similar conflicts experienced as a result of the clash of subjective impressions with empirical fact.[22] The apprehension toward neo-Nazism on the part of Domin's protagonist is explained by the attitude of her German contemporaries toward the past and through flashbacks of the Nazi era. The latter are triggered by events in the present and newspaper articles, excerpts from *Der Spiegel* and right-wing publications such as *National-und Soldatenzeitung*. Two decades later, Edvardson expresses her dismay about the continued denial of the Holocaust and the neo-Nazi scene in the Federal Republic.

Both authors possess the cultural sensitivity of native Germans and an emotional distance caused by the experience of persecution and years in exile. As was the case with Rose Ausländer, who lived in the United

States from 1921 to 1927, or Hilde Spiel, who traveled back and forth between London and Vienna, the immersion into cultures and languages other than German produces bicultural or multicultural perspectives, precluding a unilateral cultural identity. Moreover, Domin's exile and Edvardson's concentration camp experience resulted in an irreversible estrangement from the German people and their language. Both authors question the background of every German they encounter, especially those old enough to have been adults or adolescents during the Nazi era, and they examine every statement for residues of Nazi ideology. They are extremely sensitive to potentially offensive remarks by average Germans. Obviously they, the intended Nazi victims, are tormented by the trauma of the past to a greater extent than the perpetrators.

For Edvardson, detaching from Germany and the German language required overcoming the stigma of her birth as a "non-Aryan" and as an illegitimate child, so being a pariah is a key motif of *Gebranntes Kind* (1990). The narrator traces her ejection from the fold of her family during the Nazi era, a family that deviated from the patriarchal family of the petty bourgeoisie endorsed by Nazi ideology: Langgässer likened her daughter's conception to the encounter between Zeus and Danae and discouraged conversations about Edvardson's father (1990, 14). Socialized in this bohemian matriarchal environment, Edvardson failed to establish a nuclear family for herself. Focused exclusively on her powerful, overbearing mother, she had no concept of paternal authority; matriarchs and lovers, rather than wives and mothers, shaped her character. Being conditioned to become a strong woman, she was better able to cope with life in the concentration camps, but it complicated her situation in peace-time living (22f.).[23]

By tracing Edvardson's separation from the German mainstream and her family, *Gebranntes Kind sucht das Feuer* shows the narrator's passive and active involvement in her unusual individuation process. As a "Three-Quarter Jew," Edvardson was ineligible for youth organizations such as the Nazi girls' association (BDM), and in view of the growing radicalization of the public sphere, she was dropped from her Catholic youth group. During a vacation in Bavaria, she was insulted as "a dirty Jew girl" by her host family, and eventually she was forced to wear the Yellow Star. Being made into a foreigner, interned in Berlin, deported, and, finally, tattooed with an Auschwitz number mark the phases of her path of humiliation.

In the dissociation process from her mother, however, Edvardson assumes an active role, rejecting her stepfather and her half-brother as intruders. All of these events coincide with the advent of her puberty, when a girl would be expected to detach from her family and to attain autonomy. Accompanied by other traumatic events, the violent break between Edvardson and Langgässer resulted in a lasting existential wound. Even prior to her mother's marriage, Edvardson had been plagued by feelings of inferiority: she felt that she lacked Langgässer's intelligence and beauty. On the spiritual plane, the most visible emblem of Edvardson's outsider status is a one-meter-tall crucifix over her mother's marital bed, which signifies to Edvardson that she, cast in Langgässer's work as the pagan Proserpina and the Jewess, could not be an integral part of a Christian home (1990, 64). Conditioned to interpret Langgässer's poetry as revelation, Edvardson is inextricably identified with her mother's work. The novella *Proserpina*, which centers on Demeter's sacrifice of her daughter to the god of the underworld (22, 60), has had an indelible impact on Edvardson, as is manifest from the way in which she explains her own experience. Only after her imprisonment is she confronted with a reality outside of her mother's fantasies, and she disentangles herself from them to a certain degree.

Edvardson's later avoidance of Germany not only signifies her rejection of the nation that planned her destruction; it also expresses her continued battle against her mother. Langgässer's image converges with Edvardson's vision of Germany, and the experience of marginalization within her family constitutes an analogy of the fate of assimilated German Jewry: an integral part of German society, they were also ejected and classified as people of a lower order. Thus, Edvardson equates her mother's disloyalty with the Germans' betrayal, and she holds her as much responsible for her fate as she does the Nazis. Only occasionally does she concede that Langgässer's own situation was precarious. On an emotional level, Edvardson identifies Langgässer with the Nazi henchmen, resenting her for having abandoned her Jewish child and her Jewish heritage. From Edvardson's point of view, it was the avowed Catholic Langgässer, portrayed as anything but Christian, who sent her child on the path to hell. Clearly though, both Edvardson and Langgässer engage in archetypical thinking. Edvardson does so especially in conjunction with her youth, in which case she interweaves religious, ethnic, and personal themes to expose an almost mythical pattern of betrayal.

In custody, a victim of depravation and physical abuse, Edvardson puts her childhood into perspective. Her new contacts include people whom she would never have met in her mother's circles; prostitutes, informers, small-time criminals, and desperados, some of whom become her lovers, and she savors the forthrightness of her new companions (1990, 70). It gives her the opportunity to develop conceptual models with which to deconstruct her mother's world. In the process, Edvardson's trust in other people is destroyed for life. Her emotional reaction to a nursery rhyme involving the tragic fate of a beetle reveals the extent of psychological isolation (48).[24]

Among the Jews and "half-Jews" with whom Edvardson is on intimate terms, there are some, as she writes, who love her and, more important, who give her the strength "to live and to breathe," helping her "frozen soul and heart" to thaw and to step out of her old identity. It is as much a gesture of regeneration as of compliance when she relinquishes her little silver cross and her large handbag to the Nazi official at Theresienstadt (75–76): Langgässer's daughter is at the verge of entering a Jewish world. In the camps, she learns about Jewish culture in a Zionist youth group. Their dances and songs, as well as the rudimentary Hebrew lessons, instill her with a new sense of communal belonging.

The second, and shorter, part of Edvardson's autobiography deals with her life in Sweden. Preceded by Goethe's famous verses about the inscrutability of the gods, who lead human beings astray only to abandon them to the consequences of their actions (97), it tells the story of her rehabilitation, a painful process full of disappointments and misunderstandings. Upon her arrival at Christmas time, Edvardson feels as if she has been transported to paradise (3). Soon thereafter, however, she finds out about the darker aspects of this seemingly tranquil world.

While Edvardson acknowledges the generosity of the Swedes for having admitted her and other survivors into their country, the most important events during her convalescence are her acquaintance with a Jewish woman from Berlin with whose help she comes to accept her Jewishness, and her continued struggle with her mother's influence. Upon Langgässer's request, she sends her information about her Auschwitz experience (114f.). The incident leads to a replay of earlier fiascos: Langgässer uses Edvardson's account, distorted beyond recognition, in one of her novels, *Märkische Argonautenfahrt* (1950). This episode provides some closure in the relationship between mother and daughter.

Edvardson does not even mention Langgässer's death soon after this event. Indeed, Langgässer's mystical novel bears no relation to Edvardson; it interprets the horrors of the Holocaust and World War II as a divine test and the postwar era as a pilgrimage. Using the example of a Jewish couple, she suggests that Judaism offers no salvation. She concedes that Jews were victimized, but she assigns the capacity for redemption exclusively to her Christian characters—to the Stalingrad survivor as well as to the former concentration camp prisoner (D. C. G. Lorenz 1992b, 162f.).[25]

Although Edvardson is painfully aware of her mother's tenets, she seems incapable of not duplicating some of her actions. Like Langgässer, she seeks salvation through a man who, notwithstanding his magnanimity, ultimately disapproves of her quest for a Jewish identity. Repeating her own experience with her mother, Edvardson withdraws into a world of literature, abandoning her son to his father's care. Only in passing, in the last chapter, does she inform the reader that the child died of cancer at the age of ten (1990, 130).

Moreover, Edvardson's version of the fairy tale of Hänsel and Gretel, through which she articulates her own fate, is a variation on Langgässer's Proserpina myth. In Edvardson's story, Langgässer figures as a queen held captive in Hades, she herself as Proserpina, and her children, a son and a daughter, as Hänsel and Gretel. Significantly, adult male figures are absent in Edvardson's story. By placing a pledge made by the God of the Torah into the queen's mouth, Edvardson, perhaps inadvertently, assigns her the supreme position (120). Much like the literary universe of Ilse Aichinger, Ruth Klüger, and Katja Behrens, Edvardson's frame of reference continues to be a world ruled by mothers.

The collapse of the would-be idyll and safe haven that Edvardson's marriage is initially configured to be hardly comes as a surprise.[26] It comes undone at the same time as the author begins to question Sweden's superiority. The decision to raise her children as Jews creates a conflict between her and the people around her, as is most pointedly expressed by the priest who disapproves of her wish to leave the church. His openly displayed anti-Semitism calls to mind the shocking confrontation of Else Lasker-Schüler's main character in *Arthur Aronymus* with the prejudices of his friend, the parson. "The old priest understood nothing. Irritated and annoyed he stared at her with misgiving, wringing his little paws, while his dry old man's voice crowed all his available arguments. Basically, they amounted to a single one: Jesus of Nazareth was the Messiah for which her stubborn people had waited but which it refused to acknowledge once he was in their midst. Their two-thousand-year-long wait had been nothing but the obstinacy of hard-hearted people" (Lasker-Schüler 1962, 2:121).

Edvardson experiences her journey from Sweden to Israel as a home-coming to a land, a people, and a history to which she had no inner con-nection. In her mind, Israel is *the* country where she will not be an alien, where she will overcome her alienation. The last chapter links Edvard-son's Jewish identity with her yearning for a normal life as a member of a religious, national, and ethnic community. Her exuberance recalls the sentiments of Lea Fleischmann prior to her arrival in Israel in *Ich bin Israelin* (1982).

The final section of *Gebranntes Kind sucht das Feuer,* "Am Israel Chai," is a three-page account of *Yom Hashoah,* the Day of Destruction, as Edvardson translates it. On this day, the sirens sound all across the land and the traffic stops to commemorate the Holocaust (127). The promi-nent position of this passage reveals that the Holocaust is the anchoring point for Edvardson's Jewish and Israeli identity. In Israel, she is free to remember and mourn her past in the community of other survivors, and it is here that she hopes to find healing. The Yom Kippur War was raging at the time of Edvardson's arrival, but it is mentioned as an event of secondary importance. In opposition to non-Jewish views, includ-ing her mother's, Edvardson differentiates distinctly between genocide and war.[27] In her observations about the still traumatized Holocaust survivors and the population of war-torn Israel, Edvardson asserts that the experience of war is qualitatively different from the fate confront-ing the Nazi victims. The European Jews were treated like objects, whereas the threat of the Israeli-Arab war "had a human face, the face of the enemy. It had to be combatted, conquered perhaps, but it could be recognized and respected" (129). Edvardson's account ends by confirm-ing the Israeli philosophy according to which the Jews must be a nation of fighters in order to avoid being victimized ever again.

Edvardson establishes her new identity in terms of religion, nation-ality, gender, and in opposition to her former victim status. Nonethe-less, she fails to overcome the chasm between her narrator persona and herself as a protagonist. Not even now does she forge an individual iden-tity. Rather, her switch from the first person singular to the first person plural characterizes her first and foremost as a member of a community, and she speaks of herself in the third person singular as a mother (130). Motherhood places her into the center of Jewish history, which Edvardson interprets as a never-ending cycle of birth, death, mourning, and restoration. The concept of motherhood allows her to overcome her problematic sexual identity with its multiple transgressions, androgyny, incest, homoeroticism, and promiscuity. It empowers her to proclaim in a prophetic stance the survival of Israel and her own victory over her mother's texts and over all those who design the destruction of the Jews.[28]

The Diaspora in the Diaspora

The Globalization of Fascism

World War II, the Holocaust, and German-Jewish exile caused many Jewish authors, as they became aware of the complexity of their situation, to question their earlier attitudes and values. A comparison between Anna Seghers's 1942 novel about the Nazi concentration camps and antifascist resistance, *Das siebte Kreuz,* and her 1943 *Transit,* dealing with the exile experience and the international rejection of refugees from Nazi Germany, demonstrates a remarkable development of an individual author's perspective in a relatively short time. Unlike the first work, with its clear ideological demarcation lines glorifying heroism and political activism, *Transit* depicts chaos and disorientation among a group of refugees from Nazi Germany in Marseille. As foreigners in desperate circumstances, the exiles trying to obtain visas are exploited by persons of every ideological persuasion, and the majority, rendered penniless before they can leave, are returned to Nazi Germany.

The realization that there was little compassion in the international community for the European Jews and the antifascist resistance destroyed the notions of a safe sphere some authors had harbored while still in Germany. The fact that German-Jewish refugees and dissenters were persecuted and even interned was proof that fascist thought was not confined to Germany. Bigotry, greed, and racism existed everywhere in the world, including in the countries that fought the Nazis. There was no simple way to determine friend or foe. As Germany advanced on its trail of conquests and made allies and satellite states worldwide, national boundaries became fluid, and nations that might have offered asylum one day did not do so the next.

Jewish women writers reacted to this discouraging global situation in a variety of ways. Authors with strong political convictions, like Anna Seghers, used their ideology as a protective shield against reality, as is the case in the 1946 narrative *Der Ausflug der toten Mädchen* (1979). The narrative devices employed by Seghers in this text configure German history in such a way as to facilitate a reconciliation with her native country and her fellow Germans. Other writers continued to use their customary literary tools to represent the changed situation. Often, these narratives and dramas disintegrated or remained fragmentary because of unresolvable textual tensions arising from the ineffectiveness of conventional literary forms and concepts when applied to multivalent international processes and from the failure of traditional poetic devices to convey the phenomena of the world war and the genocide. Nonetheless, because they reflect extraordinary experiences and communicate unconventional insights, works that appear weak from a literary point of view, unlike those of Seghers, also deserve critical attention.

The concept of the multination state, the legacy of the Habsburg Empire, continued to be a cornerstone of Austrian identity well beyond 1945 (Magris 1966, 40ff., 97ff.). Hence it is not surprising that many works addressing the globalization of fascism and the fragmentation of Central European culture as parallel phenomena were written by native Austrians who, in keeping with their tradition, asserted the validity of cultural diversity, individualism, and cosmopolitanism against the proliferation of totalitarian paradigms. Faced with the imminent threat of the cold war and the possibility of nuclear destruction, authors of the post-Shoah generations represented the experience of alienation in the framework of absurd or fantastic literature of which many of Ilse Aichinger's texts are characteristic. The increasing disenchantment with the human sphere and doubts about human achievement lead to fundamentally changed concepts of reality and a heightened sensitivity for the environment and animals. This is the case, for instance, in Rahel Hutmacher's narratives.

"Fascism Is Just Now Arriving in Our Parts" (Vicki Baum)

Despite their conventionality in terms of their form, the works of the Vienna-born best-selling author Vicki Baum (1888–1960) constitute a serious attempt at writing cosmopolitan German-speaking literature. Baum represents the expansion of fascism and the displacement of exiles from Nazi-controlled countries and survivors of the Holocaust worldwide as major problems arising as a result of World War II. "Fascism, after its failure in Europe, is just now arriving in our parts"; this state-ment of fact and warning by one of her characters in the 1947 work *Schicksalsflug* (1984, 104) would be a fitting motto for the entire novel.

Baum moved to Hollywood in 1931, where she gained international renown as a result of Edmund Goulding's 1932 motion picture *Grand Hotel*, based on her novel and play *Menschen im Hotel* (1929).[1] Here, as well as in all her suspenseful works, Baum addresses poignant issues, including the problems faced by women professionals in *Stud. Chem. Helene Willfür* (1928). Her flair for intrigue and superficial familiarity with international settings inspired works such as *Liebe und Tod auf Bali* (1937).

Schicksalsflug, a wartime adventure novel, provides entertainment and, at the same time, raises serious concerns about the danger of interna-tional fascism. Baum correctly characterizes Latin America as the site of a serious international power struggle. One of her more credible char-acters states, "But don't believe North American and British money is the only money which is used to buy influence in South America. The Germans sent us enormous sums and continue to do so. . . . Through-out this continent there are fascist cells, believe me" (1984, 103). Sens-ing, perhaps, that many perceived it inappropriate to discuss the spe-cial interests of a widely disliked group with a general audience, Baum does not raise Jewish concerns explicitly. She proceeds more cautiously, establishing the moral and ethical norm from the margins, through the character of an aging Polish woman pianist, Madame Manticka, for-merly the mistress of noblemen, who is identified with the culture of Strauß and Toscanini and subtly characterized as Jewish. So is this char-acter's companion, a Czech concentration camp survivor and partisan, Libussa, who is described as having a "narrow, long nose," black hair, "huge black eyes under heavy eyebrows" (16, 39). In conjunction with these physical stereotypes, Libussa's tendency to interpret her experi-ence in a biblical context, specifically *Exodus* (20), and her memories of the persecution of the Jews and the deportation of her mother estab-lish her identity as Jewish. Libussa's Jewishness, as was the case with Baum's, is visible and invisible, as the author proceeds in a way similar to that described by Sander Gilman with reference to Patrick Süskind's 1987 work *The Dove*: "His books are not received by their audience as highly political comments on European post-Shoah culture. But from the 'nasal' deformities of his prizewinning novel *Perfume* to the bizarre resurrection of the Wandering Jew in his most recent book *The Story of Mr. Summer* (1991), this theme is present" (1995, 68). Although Baum writes from a distinctly pro-Western perspective, endorsing the bourgeois ideals of democracy and individualism, she is far from sharing the anticommunist phobia that prevented the Western Allies from taking seriously the right-wing extremism outside the Nazi-dominated territories. Neither does Baum glorify the United States, realizing that Nazism was making inroads into American culture as well. In several novels, including *Schicksalsflug, Marion Alive* (1942), and *Hotel Berlin* (1944), she examines the threat of international fascism.[2]

Baum's position continued to differ from that of other Jews in exile, such as Hannah Arendt, who went to New York in 1941. A comparison between both authors shows Baum as a novelist with global humanistic concerns and Arendt as an intellectual with partisan politics. Baum rejected war on principle, except in extreme cases of self-defense; Arendt was affiliated with organizations urging the United States to enter the war against Germany and, with the welfare of the Palestinian Arabs in mind, opposing the creation of a Jewish state (Wimmer 1990, 263). As the director of the Commission of European Jewish Cultural Reconstruction (beginning in 1948), Arendt developed the concept of *totalitarianism* under which she subsumed both communism and Nazism. Arendt's 1951 study *The Origins of Totalitarianism* lent itself to the rationalization of the cold war by asserting the human and moral superiority of Western democracy.[3] Vicki Baum, also a conservative, although of a different, more tolerant kind, had been away from Austria for almost a decade when Arendt's sociological studies began to appear. As is obvious from *Schicksalsflug*, Baum's main concern was the intolerance faced by all refugees and survivors of the Nazi terror. Alarmed by the possible erosion of democratic structures, she portrayed right-wing extremism as the greatest threat to the free world and makes little mention of communism.

Baum's Libussa finds herself confronted with hostility and disbelief on the part of a variety of fellow passengers; some are outright fascists, whereas others are narrow-minded individuals who do not wish to be confronted with negative facts. Concerned for Libussa's well-being, Madame Manticka advises her companion to stop talking about her background and her past.[4] Her recommendation foreshadows the protective silence adopted by many Holocaust survivors who refused to disclose their experiences for decades. Baum seems to assume that Jews and antifascists are "at risk only if publicly identified as Jews," a notion that proved only partly correct in view of the Rosenberg trials and the experience of authors such as Bertold Brecht during the McCarthy era.

Schicksalsflug transcends the categories of class, ethnicity, religion, gender, culture, and political affiliation. Rather, the interaction between Baum's cosmopolitan protagonists is based on "elective affinities" of physical attraction and common convictions. Character is determined by moral actions, or as one figure puts it, there are "two nations, the good and the bad" (51). By making shared convictions the ultimate criterion for relationships, Baum discredits fascist determinism and questions the validity of blood bonds and family loyalty. Instead, she champions the decision of one of her protagonists to leave her husband once she recognizes that he is a criminal, thereby combining the criticism of fascism and patriarchy. She highlights oppressive practices inside and outside of Europe, including the hemisphere that during World War II was hailed as the bulwark of freedom, aware of the forces of extreme nationalism within the United States. The liberal-mindedness of Baum's positive characters, on the other hand, indicates that peace and international understanding may have a chance if the attitudes represented by them prevail. Their love of individual freedom and responsibility are a direct reflection of the values held by the enlightened middle class of Baum's own motherland, turn-of-the-century Jewish Vienna.

Woman, Jew, Scapegoat: The American Exile (Hilde Spiel)

Like Vicki Baum and her Madame Manticka, the protagonist of Hilde Spiel's 1965 novel *Lisas Zimmer* (1984) is tied to the Austro-Hungarian past, which in retrospect assumes a utopian character: Spiel's Lisa Leitner, as well as Spiel herself, is a product of the declining Danube Monarchy. The multination state, for which Jewish authors, including Kafka, had professed their solidarity as early as the beginning of World War I (Baioni 1994, 77f.), became for exile authors the object of an intense nostalgia after 1938.[5] Spiel considered interwar Vienna her beloved lost motherland, inclusive and mundane, in contrast to the petty provincialism she encountered in the postwar era.

Similar to Joseph Roth, Spiel uses the Habsburg myth as a cipher for tolerance and diversity. It stands for the ethical, constitutional state, embodied by its legendary last emperor, Franz Joseph, the emblem of legitimacy (Magris 1966). Not coincidentally does Lisa celebrate Christmas together with an African American family, a Latvian woman, and her illegitimate son under a tree decorated with ornaments from the "time of Franz Joseph's youth" (1984, 91). Lisa's background is identical to that of the assimilated Austro-Hungarian-Czech family featured in Alice Schwarz-Gardos's *Von Wien nach Tel Aviv*. Precisely because the Jewish world seemed safe within the Habsburg monarchy, Lisa's generation partook of the symbols and customs of both worlds, Jewish and Gentile (Schwarz-Gardos 1991, 50).

Spiel was born in Vienna in 1911 into an upper-class family, the daughter of converted parents, the scientist and *Kaiserlich und Königlich* (Imperial and Royal) officer Hugo F. Spiel and his wife, Marie, née Gutfeld. Spiel attended the exclusive girls' school of Eugenie Schwarzwald and began writing at a young age. In 1933, while a student of philosophy and psychology, she joined the Social Democratic Party (Heuer 1988, 93; Dick 1993b, 350). Having completed her Ph.D. in 1936, she emigrated to England, where she married the author Peter de Mendelssohn. Yet, throughout her career as a writer and journalist, Spiel remained attached to Vienna.[6] In 1955, she established a second residence in Vienna and tried several times to settle permanently in her native city, but her efforts failed because of the conflicts she faced in new Austria.[7]

Spiel's ambivalent identity as an Austrian woman of Jewish descent and a cosmopolitan is reflected in her memoirs *Welche Welt ist meine Welt?* (1992), as well as in her monumental study on one of Vienna's most famous salonnières, *Fanny von Arnstein oder die Emanzipation* (1962). The second work documents Spiel's fascination with Jewish women's history, which she considers central to European culture and with which she identifies.[8] The reversal of assimilation in the twentieth century left the heirs to Enlightenment, including Spiel, uprooted in a concrete and a philosophical sense. Similar to the Jews after the destruction of the temple, Austrian Jews who had relied on the Gentile-Jewish symbiosis were propelled into yet another worldwide diaspora.

Fanny von Arnstein examines the foundations of Jewish emancipation and the gains and the losses incurred in the process of assimilation. Rather than dwelling on von Arnstein's exceptional character, Spiel emphasizes the paradigmatic aspects of her biography, with an eye on the restrictions the famous salonnière had to overcome as a married woman, a Prussian in Vienna, a Jew among Gentiles, and an unconventional woman within her community. Like Arendt in her biography of Rahel Varnhagen (1962), Spiel highlights the issue of multiple marginalization and her protagonist's achievements.

Spiel's novel *Lisas Zimmer* (1984) features a female protagonist as well, the Austrian emigrée Lisa Leitner, whose life marks the end point of the process initiated by von Arnstein. Lisa reflects some of Spiel's own traits—her background, her indebtedness to the Enlightenment, her cosmopolitanism, and her love for Vienna (Kahn 1994, 285). Of Jewish and Gentile ancestry like Spiel, Lisa nostalgically remembers the sites of her youth to which there is no turning back. Her world has shrunk to the size of her room and includes her dwindling belongings, antiques and artifacts, the portable, eclectic rubble reminiscent of pre-Shoah Jewry. Lisa lives in New York, the world capital of exiles and immigrants. A rational, generous *femme du monde,* debonair, addicted to drugs, and promiscuous, she is an enigma to her petty bourgeois Latvian companion and her Midwestern husband, neither of whom are familiar with the forces that shaped Lisa's character and the impact of the experience of persecution on her psyche.[9]

Spiel focused on the "threefold curse," as Käthe Frankenthal calls it (1981)—the fate of being a woman, an intellectual, and an antifascist— in several other previous works, including *Anna und Anna,* a play about a Jewish woman in Vienna on the eve of the Nazi takeover. Compared to other morally upstanding protagonists, Lisa Leitner, an ambiguous figure, is an exception. Her merits must be inferred against the text of a self-righteous, unreliable narrator and against the views of bigoted Americans who consider the Austrian exiles failures, decadents, and de-generates.[10] The narrator, young, wholesome-looking Lele, has no dif-ficulty reaching her goal of becoming a good American, and she con-tinually compares herself to Lisa and her friends in terms of race, age, and physical fitness. Uncritical of Nazi ideology and American pre–civil rights norms, Lele resents Jews and discounts African Americans (1984, 34). Yet, Lele, the male-identified passive-aggressive woman, represents the future as she deals with the death blows to Lisa's complex, idiosyn-cratic existence.

White supremacism constitutes a natural affinity between Lele, Jeff, and his racist friend McColl. Their community of like minds includes Lele's ethnic-German friends, provided they do not find out about her

Russian ancestors (97). Something similar to the Nazi *Blut und Boden* ethos echoes in Lele's fervent declaration about her new home, California (184). Herself a concentration camp survivor, albeit an "Aryan" one, Lele has transplanted her European nationalism to the United States, where it merges with that of white lower-middle-class Americans. By showing that there is an affinity between European and American right-wing patriotism, Spiel, in analogy to the research conducted by German-Jewish exiles, suggests that the United States is a likely setting for a fascist *renouveau* (Adorno et al. 1950, vii). Such a turn of events seems all the more plausible since Jeff, Lele, and McColl do not learn from history, hence their naive belief in a new beginning after the war and Lisa's death (184, 105).

Compared to the starry-eyed idealism of some characters and the selling out to materialist values on the part of others, Lisa's eclecticism represents a middle path in that it avoids extremes. Indeed, from a rational point of view, relativism seems the only viable option in a world that has seen the breakdown of humanist norms. Only simple personal tenets such as the maxims Lele ascribes to Lisa make sense in a world void of universal values (128), but precisely because these tenets are not binding, they become ultimately dispensable like the objects in Lisa's room. Lisa's fragmentary moral precepts and her *objets d'art* symbolize the dilemma of the destroyed European culture, exploded by nationalism, racism, and ethnocentrism.

Lisa's own destruction parallels that of her cultural sphere. As a result of a global paradigm shift toward nationalism, her multiethnic identity is at odds with societal boundaries. So is her lack of ideological commitment in an increasingly dogmatic environment. For her survival, Lisa is dependent upon cosmopolitan values and individual rights. Although her vulnerability is not immediately apparent—she appears self-possessed and adaptable—she becomes immobilized as the result of her environment's increasing rigidity. An outsider to entrenched social factions, she is unable to acquiesce to any kind of dogmatism, and she is not "pure" enough, in any sense of the word, to be accepted by the "moral majority."[11] Up to a point, she is capable of associating with diverse groups of people, but she cannot abide any claims of exclusivity. Thus, her limitations are dictated by the intolerance of others, such as by her husband's refusal to tolerate immigrants and African Americans. Moreover, being generally perceived as untrustworthy, Lisa is prevented from committing herself to any group or person; no one gives her the chance to do so. Yet, in the postwar era, dominated by nationalism and lower-middle-class family values, the erotic Jewish woman cannot survive on her own.

Since Lisa only superficially blends in with her environment, her affiliations collapse as fast as they are formed. In that regard, she represents an emblem of the failed assimilation of the Jews as well as of the defeat of feminism. Just as Aichinger's Ellen, like Lisa, is a *Mischling,* Spiel's protagonist has neither a family nor an ethnic, religious, or cultural group upon which to fall back. More radically than Aichinger's *Die größere Hoffnung,* which opens up a perspective transcendental hope, *Lisas Zimmer* exposes the destruction of the individual as a result of a failed assimilation. Spiel's portrait of the larger situation corresponds to Lisa's microcosm: the United States is portrayed as a mosaic of distinct ethnic, class, and cultural strata, rather than as a melting pot.

In an international setting reminiscent of Baum's novels, Spiel examines "the epidemic of fascism" (Baum 1984, 104), which goes unrecognized by those "infected" because one of its symptoms is impaired judgment. The Europeans, rather than escaping their European fascism and their past, find them reproduced overseas. Critical exiles have neither the means to make their voices heard nor the right to vote, but they take the brunt of American politics, namely, Truman's election victory. Munk's arrest being one of the consequences of the Republican triumph, the vote cast by Lisa's husband is nothing short of a betrayal: "Jeff left and, as was the custom in his family, voted quietly for the Republican candidate. Lisa shrugged her shoulders, she had no intention of putting up a fight or mentioning Mr. Wallace and his third party" (Spiel 1984, 73). Beyond the specific political context, the concept of a third option is significant in Spiel's novel in general: precisely because there are only two alternatives in a polarized society, Lisa must perish, while Lele is pushed into the role of her antagonist; polarization requires competition, thus preventing reconciliation on a higher plane. On a personal level, as well as on a political level, the lack of a third option creates either-or constellations precluding rational solutions.

Lisas Zimmer appeared in 1965, three years after the Eichmann trial, one year after the Frankfurt Auschwitz trials, and in the same year as Peter Weiss's drama *Die Ermittlung.* These events sparked a renewed debate about the Nazi era, the Holocaust, antifascism, exile, and the upsurge of new Nazi activities (D. C. G. Lorenz 1992a, 80). Spiel's novel is indicative of the author's own position in that it portrays ethnocentrism and social Darwinism as global phenomena. The causal relationship between the Holocaust and exile is emphasized, both of which were brought about by fascism, with McCarthyism as their extension. Lisa's destruction during this era suggests that the principles of National Socialism did prevail. To further illustrate this point, Spiel avails herself of Nazi typology. Lisa's opponents are made up of self-righteous "Aryans," members of the lower middle class, who continue to spread bigotry, such as Lele:

> A few days later, they brought the Jews. . . . They shocked us when they came to the camp. They looked even worse than we did. And they did not change. Their barracks stank so badly that one could not go inside, and they were so greedy that they begged, traded, bargained, and stole all the time to get more food. We found them disgusting, but the Poles hated them. Nonetheless, they had the Poles to thank for getting more than the usual UNRRA-rations. . . . These Jews were the survivors. In order to survive they had to be wild, tough, and cruel. (Spiel 1984, 10–11)

A central motif of *Lisas Zimmer* is the anguish of exile, the "Europe disease," as Lele calls it. Spiel, like her protagonist, suffered from it all her life. Her statement, "I loved Vienna more than words can tell," expresses her longing for an empire, a city, and a culture that had ceased to exist (Khittl 1982). Even in an essay praising her old-new home, "Ich lebe gern in Österreich" (1981), she mentions that she was the target of anti-Semitic attacks by Austrian intellectuals. Spiel's and other Austrian exiles' unceasing attachment to Vienna may appear incomprehensible in view of the fact that more than sixty thousand Viennese Jews had been robbed of their property and sent to their death by Austrian Gentiles.

In the name of the Jews raised in postwar Vienna, Ruth Beckermann asks, "Why did you stay? Why did you return? . . . Why do you have to live among these people after all the outrage they inflicted upon you?" (Beckermann 1989, 97). *Lisas Zimmer* tries to come to terms with these questions by taking a close look at the life outside of Austria and by suggesting that there was no escape, neither from fascism, which under various guises continued to exist worldwide, nor from European and Jewish identity, which stigmatized the emigrés in the United States. In

light of 1950s' U.S. imperialism, the cold war, the anticommunist phobia, racism, and puritanism, the American panorama painted by Spiel is
no less bleak than the Austrian situation portrayed in Ingeborg Bachmann's much-debated novel *Der Fall Franza* (1981, written in 1965).
Both Austrian-born authors focus on misogyny, racism, and everyday
fascism through similar motifs; their protagonists are addicted to drugs
as an outward expression of the pressures acting on them as members of
ethnic minorities and wives of privileged, protofascist men. Spiel's Lisa
and Bachmann's Franza, women defined through their desires and sexuality, are exploited and "neutralized," a hysterectomy being the symbol
of defeminization in both cases. Other prominent themes are the socially
condoned marital infidelity on the part of the man and each female protagonist's subservience to white male power, expressed also in terms of
discursive agency. Although the narrator's unreliability is clearly indicated, Lele does write Lisa's story, making Lisa an object rather than an
active agent, and Jordan appropriates Franza's work as his own. Moreover, Franza's story is told by her brother, whereas Lele's text is published by Lisa's friend Bothe, who in his ironic afterword suggests that
Lele's assessment of Lisa is flawed.

Furthermore, the narrative tension, created by the inability of Spiel's
narrator to tell the protagonist's story, and the narrator's dishonesty call
to mind Gertrud Kolmar's *Susanna* (1994). Kolmar's narrator, however,
herself a Jew, does come to an understanding of the mysterious Jewish
woman, while the non-Jew Lele does not. In both works, the reader is
called upon to reconstruct the actual events. In Spiel's case, the narrator
writes to justify and glorify her own role. Lele trivializes her father's anti-
Semitism and her own destructive actions against Lisa. She casts herself
as a loyal servant trying to save her mistress. But once having gained the
readers' trust, Lele portrays Lisa as an Old World monster doomed to
succumb, thereby echoing the Nazis' verdict on Jewish culture.

The character of Lisa is the site where the discourses on gender, race,
and health converge. Lisa is neither good nor bad, healthy nor ill, Jew
nor Gentile, male nor female; hence her preference for androgynous
costumes and her hysterectomy. She is a nonconformist situated in an
authoritarian environment, a catalyst to play out the defeat of antifascism in the microcosm of an American postwar household. Rather than
the communist Munk, with his unbending principles, it is Lisa, with
her eccentric lifestyle and her independent thought and judgment, who

represents the antithesis to fascism. Her demise, the demise of a woman of Jewish ancestry and an individual without political affiliation, expresses the demise of the third alternative in a world painted in black and white, and in Spiel's view, the destruction of a sphere that had been established under the leadership of Jewish women.

Human Nature under Scrutiny (Alice Schwarz-Gardos)

Like *Lisas Zimmer,* Alice Schwarz's novel *Die Abrechnung* (1962) also grapples with the cultural and psychological fragmentation of the post-Holocaust era and problematizes traditional humanistic values in Israel, the land associated with the dreams of European Jews to an even greater extent than America, the "Golden Land," the *medine*. To the Israeli journalist Alice Schwarz (or Schwarz-Gardos, the name she later used),[12] a critical observer and reporter of the Eichmann trial, the relationship between former victims and perpetrators and the difficulty of establishing identity and assigning guilt are the focal issues. She writes in *Von Wien nach Tel Aviv* that the nationally publicized trial heightened her own "latent schizophrenia or ambivalence" in her relationship to the German language and culture (Schwarz-Gardos 1991, 193).

By way of numerous examples, Schwarz-Gardos demonstrates the special problems facing German-speaking Jews in Palestine, later Israel. Aside from having to adjust to an entirely different way of life, they missed the German-speaking environment (132–33). Fritz Kempe, Schwarz-Gardos's second husband, was one of the exiles who returned to Germany (183). She herself shares neither the Germanophilia of many German immigrants nor the rigor with which other Israelis refused any involvement with Germany and German culture.[13] Pointing out that the "Jews, not only in Germany, had traditionally been attracted to the German language" (237), Schwarz-Gardos argues that it is impossible to distinguish between a language and its content. Her view that native speakers (authors and readers) of a given language are unable to detach themselves from their mother tongue is confirmed by the practices of German Israeli authors, even those more critical than Schwarz-Gardos. Inge Deutschkron, for example, concludes her autobiography *Ich trug den gelben Stern* (1979) with the observations that in Germany former Nazis occupy government posts, that mass murderers go free or, if put on trial, find lenient judges, whereas those who helped persecuted Jews

are treated like outsiders. Although she sensed that as a Holocaust survivor she was not welcome in Germany because she represented a living
indictment (1979, 283), Deutschkron likewise continued to write in German, and her work as an author and journalist connected her to Germany. Margarita Pazi describes the dilemma of Israeli authors writing in
German: "The language in which they create their prose and poetry may
no longer be taboo, but it is without question associated with images of
inhuman cruelty, piles of defenselessly slaughtered people, and the symbol of horror: Auschwitz. Hence to the German-speaking immigrants
the language problem—the most difficult problem one faces when get-
ting acclimated to a country—was threefold: it was a practical, cultural,
and emotional problem" (1994a: 124). A similarly ambivalent attitude
toward Germany and Israel also characterizes the satires *Eine Seele aus
Holz* (1964) by Jakov Lind and *Der Nazi und der Friseur* (1977) by Edgar
Hilsenrath, natives of Austria and Germany, respectively. Like Schwarz-
Gardos, they spent the immediate postwar years in Palestine and, like
her, were familiar with the crises in the Middle East immediately following the armistice in Europe. All three authors view Israeli nationalism
and the role of Jews as fighters.[14]

Schwarz-Gardos's biography is marked by the partly voluntary, partly
forced crossing of political, cultural, and language boundaries. She was
born in Vienna in 1916, and grew up there and in Bratislava,[15] where she
attended the university and in 1939 joined a refugee transport to Palestine. In Haifa, she met Arnold Zweig and Max Brod, both of whom
encouraged her to pursue a career as a writer. After 1949, she worked
as a correspondent and journalist. Despite her commitment to Israel,
she maintained close ties to German culture and to her native city of
Vienna, where her parents lived (1984, 186).[16] The locations of her publishers, Germany, Austria, and Israel, are proof of the extraterritoriality
of her work. Pazi observes with regard to the goals of German-speaking
authors in Israel that they have no desire for a cultural *renouveau;* nor
do they wish to preserve the German language in Israel. On the contrary, many of them had to overcome emotional barriers before they
could write in German.[17] Schwarz-Gardos herself discusses the plight
of German-speaking authors in Israel. Her views coincide with those
of Hilde Spiel, who, at an international symposium on Austrian exile
also attended by Schwarz-Gardos, likened exile to a disease (Schwarz-
Gardos 1983, 11). According to Schwarz-Gardos, the Jews from Central

Europe were "split personalities for the rest of their lives," who never "got over their emigration, a topic which is simply not addressed" (11). Acknowledging that uprootedness is part of the human condition in the modern world, Schwarz-Gardos explains that the isolation of Israeli authors writing in languages other than Ivrit and, even more so, the solitude of German-speaking authors are historically specific phenomena. Indirectly she validates Else Lasker-Schüler's experience that nowhere did she feel farther removed from her motherland than in the land of Israel. In particular, authors in the German language suffer from a lack of younger readers; hence their texts are written without a future perspective. Schwarz-Gardos distinguishes between the older generation of authors like herself and more recent immigrants such as Lea Fleischmann and Henryk Broder, who do relate to the German public because they write about the situation of Jews in Germany (Schwarz-Gardos 1984, 13).

Schwarz-Gardos's works combine autobiographical experience, fiction, and documentary material. This is the case in the 1962 novel *Schiff ohne Anker,* a novel about the sinking of the refugee ship *Struma* off the coast of Turkey. It is based in part on notes taken by the author during her journey to Palestine and in part on press reports. The adventure novel *Versuchung in Nazareth* (Schwarz 1963) reflects Schwarz-Gardos's experiences in Israel. Other works focus on cultural issues, namely, her interviews with Israeli women, *Frauen in Israel* (Schwarz-Gardos 1979), and her sketches of everyday Israeli life, *Paradies mit Schönheitsfehlern* (Schwarz-Gardos 1982). Schwarz-Gardos's Central European background and her emotional ties to the culture of the Danube Monarchy are manifest throughout her work, particularly in her autobiography, *Von Wien nach Tel Aviv: Lebensweg einer Journalistin* (Schwarz-Gardos 1991), in which she discusses her own life in conjunction with her family history and the final years of the Habsburg Empire, the interwar period, the Nazi era, and the State of Israel until the Gulf war.

In contrast to authors who have discussed the trials against Adolf Eichmann and "minor" Nazi criminals with moral certitude and self-righteousness, Schwarz-Gardos displays a certain skepticism. "In 1951, immediately after the 'Law against War Criminals and their Collaborators' was passed, a kind of psychosis broke out. Many of the new immigrants who were survivors of the concentration camps and the Holocaust believed to recognize former Capos and Nazi-collaborators in the street, in the shops, but especially in the barracks of the transit camps" (162). In her assessment of Eichmann, Schwarz-Gardos shares by and large Hannah Arendt's point of view, and she characterizes the latter's portrayal of the trial as "outstanding and accurate," endorsing Arendt's term of the "banality of evil" (193). Less forgiving than Martin Buber and a group of Israeli university professors who petitioned for a pardon for Eichmann, Schwarz-Gardos was more lenient than Günter Anders, who maintained in his open letter to Eichmann's son Klaus, *Wir Eichmannsöhne* (1964), that fathers like Eichmann do not deserve to be respected and mourned by their children, regardless of their conduct as husbands and fathers, which Arendt had characterized as exemplary.[18] Many renowned personalities such as H. G. Adler, Gershom Scholem, Günter Anders, and Saul Friedländer contributed to the debate about Arendt's version of the trial, expressing indignation at her portrayal of the major perpetrator of the Holocaust in a psychologically understandable fashion, thereby demystifying him (Anders 1964, 5; D. C. G. Lorenz 1992b, 29, 341; Mitscherlich 1965, 78ff.).

The Eichmann controversy represented a turning point in the Holocaust debate. Issues such as guilt and innocence were problematized by the notion of complicity, an important theme, not only in Arendt's book, but also in Bruno Bettelheim's essay "The Ignored Lesson of Anne Frank" (1979). The sociological interpretations and the literature of the old and new Left, which increasingly dominated the fascism debate, blamed the disasters of the 1930s and 1940s on late capitalist structures, rather than on the crimes of individuals, and leftist authors exposed the pro-fascist propensities of the lower middle class and of big industrialists. Peter Weiss in his documentary drama *Die Ermittlung* (1964) and Edgar Hilsenrath in his satire *Der Nazi und der Friseur* (1977) emphasize the larger structures determining the actions of individuals.

Alice Schwarz-Gardos's novel *Die Abrechnung* (Schwarz 1962) is based on an actual case preceding the Eichmann trial, but it also addresses issues pertaining to the later show trial against the background of European Holocaust and pre-Holocaust history, the history of Israel, and authentic, but fictionalized, events (Schwarz-Gardos 1991, 163). Several narrative levels unfold, involving overlapping time frames and geographical settings. Also, the boundaries between different species, man and animal, become blurry in an attack on the most basic categories of Judeo-Christian thought and humanism. Whereas Baum and Spiel portray the problems caused by the expansion of fascism as played out by female protagonists, Schwarz-Gardos's central character is a man, the judge in a trial of a man accused of Nazi crimes. He is modeled after the defense attorney Doron, later Israel's ambassador to Vienna, who obtained an acquittal for the accused in a similar case in 1951 (164–66). Schwarz-Gardos, one of the few journalists to challenge the popular outcry for the death penalty, ascribed certain details from her own biography to her fictional judge.

Schwarz-Gardos focuses on the victimization of animals more graphically than that of human beings, and human gender and racial patterns are projected into the animal sphere. The discourse of masculinity and femininity in its traditional context and the racist discourse on Jews and Aryans are represented by dogs and cats, respectively. The cats are cast as female and, by extension, Jewish; the dogs are assigned characteristics traditionally associated with males—aggression, predatory behavior, and a soldierlike team spirit—and as they are trained to help satisfy man's hunting and killing instincts, they reflect Nazi characteristics.[19] The same categories are also applied to characterize different exclusively Jewish positions, that of the diaspora Jewry, Zionism, and traditional Judaism. To expose the constructedness of these discourses as well as their power to shape reality and to expose human agency, Schwarz makes transparent the exploitation of dogs, bred and molded to be subservient to human beings. The global victimization of animals as an important aspect of the human claim to power, more fundamental even than man's oppression of man, in Schwarz-Gardos's text suggests that ethnocentrism cannot be successfully combatted if oppression in any form is tolerated.

Schwarz-Gardos combines the call for justice for the victims of the Holocaust with a call for justice for animals. Her portrayal of the will to dominate, regardless of what or of whom, as a basic human trait implies that the problems of genocide, war, and interpersonal violence can only be solved on the most elementary level. An attempt to curb aggression against all forms of life is required. To underscore this point, Schwarz-Gardos recapitulates in *Die Abrechnung* the history of the interwar period, the Nazi era, and the Holocaust in conjunction with insights into the history of animals, suggesting that attitudes toward animals ultimately reflect the value assigned human life (Schwarz 1962, 248ff.). The digressions about the medieval persecutions of cats and cat crusades, the continued practice of drowning kittens, and the abuses at the animal shelter in Israel, similar to Lasker-Schüler's criticism, suggest parallels to the atrocities of the Holocaust insofar as all of these instances expose the mind-set of the perpetrators.

Schwarz-Gardos's concept of identity is dynamic. She conceives of human beings as neither fundamentally moral nor immoral but takes into consideration factors such as character development, partial, rather than total, guilt, and, most significantly, man's animal nature. Like Konrad Lorenz in *Das sogenannte Böse: Zur Naturgeschichte der Aggression* (1961), Schwarz-Gardos cites examples of aggression, violence, and the will to dominate in the animal world, thereby questioning the concept of human accountability for similar behavior and expanding the range of the so-called evil beyond man's rational faculties. In doing so, she indicates that the impulses that propelled the Nazis to commit genocide are identical to the ones that induce boys to torture animals, as well as to the ones that caused young Israelis to kidnap Hermon in an attempt to force him to pronounce the accused Ferdinand Valicek guilty. The same ingrained impulses prompt the workers at the animal shelter to expose Hermon's cat to the pent-up dogs and, in turn, cause the dogs to rail at the cat.

In opposition to Jewish critics who blamed the victims of the Holocaust for letting themselves be led to the slaughter like sheep, Schwarz-Gardos validates the pacifist tradition of Central European Jewish culture.[20] Inherent in the violent episodes involving Israeli citizens is a similar apprehension to that articulated by Nelly Sachs, namely, that Jews committed to fighting will end up acting like their enemies, that the persecuted will become persecutors.[21] Schwarz-Gardos advocates nonviolence as a central aspect of the discipline prescribed by Jewish law, which created among the Jews of Central Europe an evolved civilization, against which Schwarz-Gardos juxtaposes the brutality of the rural Czechs. The flashbacks into Hermon's and Valicek's childhood contrast the development of both protagonists in their respective cultural contexts. Loosely following the pattern of the fictional nineteenth- and early twentieth–century Gentile-Jewish double biographies such as Freytag's *Soll und Haben,* Raabe's *Der Hungerpastor,* or Dinter's *Die Sünde wider das Blut,* Schwarz-Gardos explores the forces shaping her protagonists.[22]

Her analysis shows that as a result of his Jewish socialization, both religious and secular, Hermon developed a sensibility superior to that of his militant contemporaries, Gentile and Israeli. He is a case in point used to illustrate that a complete cultural experience, rather than mere indoctrination, is required to repress destructive instincts. With his compassion and his distaste for brutality, Hermon, the European diaspora Jew, lives as if in exile among the gun-toting Jews of Israel. In the context of Schwarz-Gardos's novel, femininity and masculinity signify a civilized peaceful paradigm versus an aggressive militant one. Even in the presence of a female Jewish character, the European Jew occupies the female position, and the Gentile man and the youthful Zionists are configured as male. In opposition to the traditional discourse on Jews and women, Schwarz-Gardos places feminine qualities above male virtues.

Schwarz-Gardos also takes a critical look at the perpetrator awaiting trial and the Israelis, many of whom demand retribution rather than justice. Her assessment of human nature in general prompts her to portray the human race as a species of predators. From her perspective, it is impossible to separate the guilty from the innocent—pure innocence does not exist, not even in Hermon, who covets Valicek's wife, Milena. Matters are further complicated by the fact that Valicek, after years of living with his Jewish wife in Israel, is no longer—if ever he was—a fanatic Nazi and a murderer. The transformation over time, also an important aspect of Edgar Hilsenrath's satire *Der Nazi und der Friseur,* is addressed in *Die Abrechnung* as well. As the name changes indicate, neither the accused nor the judge has remained the same person. Even if Valicek, now a devout Catholic, is guilty as charged, he has changed so much that even the eyewitnesses have difficulty identifying him.

The humane verdict reached by Judge Hermon in defiance of public pressure and against his desire to win Milena, the love of his youth, seems anachronistic in the sensation-hungry media age. Critical of the commercial culture, which uses the court room as a stage for popular drama, Schwarz-Gardos casts doubt on her country's institutions. Israel in the 1950s is depicted as an anonymous mass society where the civilizing forces that shaped the *Galut* are absent. *Die Abrechnung* suggests that, ironically, Herzl's dream was fulfilled in more than one way; that, indeed, the Jews in Israel live in a state like any other. Schwarz-Gardos leaves her readers with the impression that in the trial at hand a fair verdict could be reached only by a representative of her lost motherland, and that if it was accepted by the media and consequently

THE DIASPORA IN THE DIASPORA

the public, it was by mere chance or, perhaps, because of a justice higher than human institutions.

Exiles from the Human Sphere (Rahel Hutmacher)

The awareness of a world out of control and of the powerlessness of the individual have caused the most diverse authors to question the concepts of individual responsibility and the superiority of human beings. Antihumanist and zoomorphic views play a significant role in the works of many Jewish women authors, most distinctly so in the works of Rahel Hutmacher, a Jewish author living in Switzerland in whose work animals figure prominently in a more than metaphoric or symbolic way. In addition, Hutmacher's view of reality includes legendary creatures and elements of the fantastic, as is also the case with Ilse Aichinger. Even more so than either Schwarz-Gardos or Aichinger, Hutmacher's narrative position transcends the human sphere and the community of men.

Hutmacher was born in 1944. A certified librarian, she became the director of a Zürich library. In 1976, she was appointed instructor for psychological discourse in Zürich and Düsseldorf. There is a stylistic and conceptual affinity between her and Aichinger, who has a loyal following in Switzerland. Despite their effortlessly flowing language, both authors' seemingly impenetrable texts resist cooptation by the dominant culture. Hutmacher's works reflect her professional interests: informed by a vast variety of discourses, they are set in archetypal landscapes void of historical markers, tracing processes of the individual and collective psyche. Hutmacher's preferred setting resembles that of Hermann Broch's *Bergroman,* a generic Alpine scenery with rivers, forests, and meadows.

Hutmacher's publications include prose published individually, as cycles, or as episodic novels. Her major works are *Wettergarten* (1980), *Dona* (1982), *Tochter* (1983), and *Wildleute* (1986). Her technique of encoding, coupled with ostentatious simplicity, again recalls Aichinger, particularly her later short prose. Both authors' calculated childlike directness masks complexity. Unlike Alice Schwarz-Gardos, Hutmacher does not comment on political and social issues, in spite of her interest in social attitudes. The indirectness in her narratives derives in part from her avoidance of these issues, which, in turn, is occasioned by a narrative perspective outside of the human sphere. From this vantage point,

humans appear as only one, and by no means privileged, species in-
habiting the earth. Seen from afar, the similarities among human beings
are more striking than their differences. Ignoring to an extent the techniques of conventional fiction, Hutmacher suggests that, rather than in
the social and political arenas, the decisive struggles involve natural and
psychological phenomena. Her use of fairy-tale motifs and magic for-
mulas as well as her defiance of recognized natural law point toward a
more comprehensive, more unified concept of the universe.

Hutmacher portrays the boundaries between humans, animals, and
plants as permeable. One of the episodes in *Wildleute,* for example, involves a Wild Woman, who defies her father's wishes and marries a
human man instead of a tree (1986, 86). By asserting the interconnectedness of all life in this way, Hutmacher points toward the autonomy and
complexity of all living beings. These basic tenets and concerns place
her work in the context of ecological feminism and postmodern environmental ethics. As Jim Cheney observes, "dismantling patriarchal discourse is not likely by itself to eliminate the forces of essentialization and
totalization," and he asserts that "a mythic, narrative, and bioregional
construction of self and community . . . has a close affinity with, and
relevance to, feminist postmodernist attempts to deal with the fractured
identities' of multiple female voices in the wake of the deconstruction of
patriarchal totalizing and essentializing discourse" (Cheney 1989, 133).

A closer reading of Hutmacher's narratives reveals furthermore the
presence of Jewish subtexts indicating that the author's particular sensitivity to power abuse and exploitation is linked to the Jewish post-Shoah
experience. In *Wildleute,* for example, a father mourns his daughter, who
marries an outsider, as if she were dead (1986, 87). Yet other aspects of
the work evoke Native American or African customs, the configuration
of animals as spirit guides, teachers, and friends or as the representation
of human characters endowed with animal features that underscore the
unalienable right of all variations of life to exist. In addition, the motif
of transformation points to their shared experience as living organisms,
as well as their ability to communicate with one another. The latter
themes also play an important role in the comparative anthropological
work of Elias Canetti, *Masse und Macht* (1981), where transformation is
represented as an attribute of the survivor.

Hutmacher's zoomorphism calls to mind the assertion of Gertrud
Kolmar's Susanna: "I *am* an animal" (1994). Like Kolmar, Hutmacher

assumes the voice of those who cannot speak out: oppressed human beings, animals, plants, and, by analogy, Jews in Nazi Germany. Her protagonists are residents of the realm of otherness to which European authors traditionally also assign non-European and non-Christian characters. Underlying Hutmacher's texts are radical antipatriarchal and anti-authoritarian tenets; every practice of Western Man is questioned by the norm-setting voices of outsiders, women and witches, reminders of a matriarchal tradition, whose exponents, like Jews and heretics, the Christian establishment demonized, persecuted, and burned. There are strong female role models in Hutmacher's texts, such as the protagonist of *Dona,* who defies her community to study with a female shaman. Female bonding and the transferral of knowledge from one woman to another cancel out the patriarchal hierarchy, and Hutmacher's portrayal of reality constitutes an open rebellion against the Linnean classification of plants and animals. Hutmacher's texts attribute speech and intelligence to women, legendary beings, plants, and animals, whereas men and the Judeo-Christian God play no significant role at all.

The irrelevance of the one male God undermines patriarchal concepts, including the traditional notions of knowledge and education, throughout Hutmacher's work. Relationships such as those between teacher and students, older and younger women, women and animals, and mothers and their illegitimate offspring—some sired by nonhumans— take precedence over heterosexual human unions and the bonding between father and child. Knowledge is acquired outside institutions, and the term *learning* refers to a great variety of activities: the development of skills such as weaving, tying nets, husbandry, and magic. The learning process is generally of greater importance than the result, hence the lament of the novice in "Lernen": "For how long have I been coming to you; and I am still learning and know nothing" (1980, 16). Unattached females figure as master practitioners, and the young girls who follow them become unfit for human society. Hutmacher's concept of training to become an outsider resembles Aichinger's concept of "unlearning" as the most significant educational process, because it enables the individual to detach herself from the trappings of her civilization (17).

The central role of female knowledge, acquired in communion with nature, the prioritization of female-female relationships, and the de-emphasis of blood ties are employed to support the theme of tolerance by exposing biases as a result of ethnic and cultural difference.

Supernatural and demonic figures, particularly those of women, have traditionally signified the uncanny in literary texts. Romantic literature abounds with such figures, which have been reconfigured in contemporary feminist literature. Ingeborg Bachmann explored a similar character in *Undine geht* from a feminist perspective, revealing her protagonist's anguish over her involvements with human men. Like Hutmacher, Bachmann identifies to a certain degree with the mythological woman figures that male authors have traditionally depicted as aliens. Heine's "Loreley" follows this pattern; so do most folktales and literary texts, including Felix Mitterer in his play *Die wilde Frau,* published the same year as Hutmacher's *Wildleute.*

According to Julia Kristeva (1990), death, unbounded instinct, and the female sex as the expression of the forces of death and instinct are the cause of phobias commonly found among men. Klaus Theweleit argues that male discourse desensualizes female figures, as they pose a threat to the ideological institution of masculinity (1988, 907). His observations explain why many women authors project their alienation into the figure of the witch, the Wild Woman, or the animal and why men tend to depict them as inarticulate or mute. Kristeva maintains that there is a link between the trepidation accompanying encounters with strangers, a mixture of fascination and rejection, and the political feeling of xenophobia. According to her, both threaten adult identity since they evoke infantile wishes as well as fear of the Other (1990, 208). Female authors, who themselves are objectified in male discourse, have a different relationship to these phenomena. Like Lasker-Schüler, Kolmar, and Aichinger, Hutmacher is drawn to the spheres of the fantastic and exotic, both of them vehicles of desire and contempt in texts by male authors; and like these other female writers, she aspires to the realm of the unknown.

Standing outside the male-defined structures, women and, to an extent, Jewish male authors do not share the majority's specific anxieties. Their apprehensions differ from those of the dominant group in that they consider that group itself fear inspiring. Women, Jewish and Gentile, speak and write from a position of otherness, as residents of Freud's proverbial Dark Continent, where men, by definition, occupy the role of strangers. Women may be excluded from the dominant discourse, but they can speak in and about the realm of the unknown. Portraying women as familiar, female writers demystify animals and unconven-

tional female characters, thereby assigning men the role of the inscrutable monstrous other. Not coincidentally, women in recent years have
produced an extensive body of scholarship, fiction, and poetry on wise
women and witches.

Rahel Hutmacher's *Wildleute* (1986) fictionalizes the interaction between human beings and the legendary Wild People of the Alpine region, who figure among the demons of folklore and fairy tales and to
whom Bächtold-Stäubli devoted a detailed entry (1935–36, 967–69). The
Wild People are said to roam the mountains and valleys, the men impish
or scary, the women graceful and goddesslike (970). The Wild People
may be kind and industrious, but they can also be malicious and may
lure children away from their parents. Wild Women are said to seduce
human males and become their spouses (974). The marriages to Wild
Women are described as advantageous to the human partner although
they are short-lived. In most cases, the man transgresses against a pre-
nuptial agreement, such as by beating his wife, by asking about her name
or her family, or by using profane language.

Hutmacher borrows freely from this rich tradition and constructs an
entire cultural panorama from the popular lore that she reinterprets,
revealing human xenophobia, sexism, and alienation from nature. The
stories involving Wild Women are the most intriguing, as they represent
otherness in terms of gender *and* species, as in "Herzbrechen," "Keine
Liebe mehr," and "Überwintern." In these episodes, Wild Women tell
of their experiences with human men, their captors, short-term partners, or spouses (1986, 86–99). The humans, male and female, also speak
for themselves, thereby allowing the readers to consider their point of
view. What come to light are insensitivity and self-centeredness causing unnecessary suffering. Similar motifs occur in earlier literary texts,
namely, Adalbert Stifter's 1847 work *Katzensilber* (1908), a novella about
the encounter between human beings and a "brown" girl of obscure origin. Here, the stranger is not physically mistreated, but abuse in subtle
psychological forms takes place.

The encounter between human beings and Wild People in *Wildleute* involves transcending the boundaries between the familiar and the
other. As both spheres are made transparent, it becomes obvious that
the emotional and intellectual similarities between both groups exceed
their differences, discounting their physical and cultural characteristics,
but the Wild People are smaller and weaker than human beings and

must therefore act with circumspection. Although aspects of feminist discourse enter into Hutmacher's texts, the Wild Women do not exclusively represent the condition of women. Rather, episodes such as "Herzbrechen" establish models of intimate encounters between different cultural groups and species. The plight of the Wild Women in a human environment corresponds to the fate of minorities or captured animals; these groups may be equivalent in view of the fact that until the eighteenth century Gypsies were hunted for sport and the humanity of women was in doubt. Although these discourses are interlaced, the discussion of gender is subordinate to that of prejudice. Hutmacher describes the culture of the oppressed in detail. In so doing, the traditional outcasts become familiar, and human men and male-identified female figures are placed into the position of aliens who act against the laws of nature and threaten the natural balance.

A psychotherapist, Hutmacher derives her most poignant images from dreams, the occult, and the psychology of Carl G. Jung. Rather than accepting the androcentric and ethnocentric bent of his psychotherapeutic discourse, though, she subverts it to use its culture-critical and feminist potential, most poignantly by constructing a consolidated human discourse. From the point of view of other species, Hutmacher suggests, the human race appears monolithic, working toward the destruction of the earth. Whatever internal dissent exists does not question human activity as such: there is no alternative movement to end the ongoing destruction. Whoever goes beyond the permitted boundaries, as do Hutmacher's rebellious women, is isolated and neutralized. Those who have the necessary distance to criticize human endeavor are too weak to assert themselves, while those who try to change the system from within are coopted. From the perspective of Hutmacher's Wild People, even the differences between human males and females are negligible.

Clearly, Hutmacher's works also reflect the author's position as a Jewish woman living in Germany and Switzerland: she is all too familiar with cooptation and marginality. These experiences inform *Wildleute* and undermine reader expectations. In "Herzbrechen," for example, romance plays but a minor role. There can be no doubt about the Wild Woman's love for her human husband. The couple's ethnicity—or, rather, the fact that they belong to different species—poses the problem: they think that they are compatible, but their communities do not.

It is the problem faced in almost all kinds of interfaith, intercultural, interracial marriages, even today.

In 1986, when *Wildleute* was published, the Holocaust received renewed attention as the result of a visit by the American president Ronald Reagan at the *Wehrmacht* and ss cemetery in Bitburg and again during the election campaign of Kurt Waldheim, a former Nazi who successfully ran for president in Austria. *Wildleute* reflects Hutmacher's awareness of the rise of anti-Semitism and hate crimes in Europe, and episodes such as the Wild People's abduction of human children must be read with this wider context in mind. The older generation refuses to learn from history—the human parents in Hutmacher's text continue to spread lies about the Wild People and perpetuate superstitions that do not allow for a peaceful coexistence between both groups. As the Wild Woman married to a human man finds out, the human race, incapable of accepting difference, is prone to hatred and destruction. Informed, perhaps, by Wilhelm Reich's *Massenpsychologie des Faschismus* (1974), Hutmacher portrays the Wild People's kidnapping of human children as a valid tool for transforming the human mind: nonhumans must come to the rescue of human children and expose them to sensually pleasurable experiences. This imaginary solution implies that nothing short of a complete reorientation of the human psyche can ensure the Wild People's future and, ultimately, that of the humans.

There are obvious parallels between Hutmacher's stories and the history of the European Jews. Moreover, with its open patterns, *Wildleute* can be applied to other situations involving coterritorial groups of varying strength. Hutmacher's work denounces ethnocentrism, misogyny, and the destruction of the environment. It also develops new patterns of understanding beyond the demarcation lines of cultures and species. Although she deals more frequently with disappointments than with successes, the fact that the attempt to overcome limitations is made at all, and repeatedly so, indicates a moderately optimistic outlook on the part of the author. The kidnapping episode in *Wildleute* suggests a different approach to parenting—a nonaggressive, fun-loving, and pleasure-oriented approach—to alter the deep structure of the human psyche and to effect a fundamental cultural and spiritual reorientation. It is important to note that the lessons Hutmacher's Wild People teach the human race and the kind of life they lead resemble the matriarchal structures attributed to Jewish culture by authors such as Lea Fleischmann and Katja Behrens.

ᴥ❦7❧ᴥ

Jewish Women Authors and the Left

The Legacy of Antifascism

Notwithstanding the affinities between the works of Jewish women authors in German-speaking countries, East and West, the qualitatively different experience of being Jewish in the Federal Republic, the German Democratic Republic, Austria, and Switzerland produced different literary styles. The stringent cultural programs and the planned economy under socialism, as well as the market-driven literary production in the West, had aesthetic and economic implications that are reflected in the works of Jewish women authors. After the foundation of the GDR, writers were called upon to produce socially responsible texts with positive socialist role models. Until the 1960s, the endorsement of socialist realism and the so-called Great Heritage—Enlightenment, classicism, and realism—as well as the rejection of modernist art and literature by the cultural establishment as formalist, left only limited room for literary experimentation.

The political dimensions embedded in these programs had significant consequences for the development of art and literature in the GDR. After World War II, a large number of exiled Jewish Leftists, intellectuals, artists, and writers settled in East Germany, in the hope of contributing to the foundation of a socialist state. Among them were Anna Seghers, Stephan Hermlin, Stefan Heym, Arnold Zweig, Peter Edel, and Barbara Honigmann's father, Georg Honigmann (Mayer 1991, 49–62). Most of them had been a part of the interwar avant-garde, and their work had been banned and destroyed as supposedly degenerate art by the Nazis, who had opposed anything but the crudest form of realism. Those who had the good fortune of escaping the Nazi regime continued to work abroad under exacting circumstances. Aside from financial problems, the European exile presses were threatened by the advance of National Socialism, of which the tragic fate of Emanuel Querido in Amsterdam is one example. A Social Democrat and an antifascist, he was the publisher of numerous German-Jewish authors. After the occupation of the Netherlands, he was betrayed to the Nazis and killed in Auschwitz in 1943.

Many blacklisted authors encountered disapproval in the GDR, where Jewish intellectuals were required to conform not only to a secular culture but also to a proletarian ethos, supporting the "Workers' and Farmers' State." Despite the fundamental differences in Nazi and Marxist ideology, literature was considered an instrument of mass education under Nazism and Stalinism alike, and both dictatorships prescribed similar aesthetic principles. The experimental styles and themes of the avant-garde, including expressionism and all abstract art, were considered elitist and decadent. What was called for instead was mimetic and easy-to-grasp art with mass appeal. Authors who wished to attain recognition in East Germany had to adjust; otherwise they risked being prevented from publishing at all. Nonetheless, many authors, including Seghers, adapted to the realism requirement only partially and not in all of their works. Hans Mayer points out that authors who like Seghers had spent their exile years in Western countries rather than in the Soviet Union came increasingly under scrutiny (1991, 199–200).

A large number of intellectuals expressed their dissent by defecting from cold war socialism, disheartened by its ballooning bureaucracy and the prevalent petty bourgeois mentality. Many of them did so, not because their political ideals had changed, but because they understood that these ideals would not be realized in East Germany. Dissenters who did stay faced the same fate as the interwar avant-garde in Prague, which Nadja Seelich depicted in her film *Sie saß im Glashaus und warf mit Steinen* (1992): stagnation, persecution, and marginalization. There can be little doubt that the Stalinist repression of modernism with Franz Kafka as its most prominent and most maligned exponent was motivated to no small degree by anti-Semitism. The "anticosmopolitanism" campaign in the USSR, launched by A. Zhdanov in 1946 "with ugly anti-Semitic undertones," as Lucy Dawidowicz maintains, dovetails with the propaganda defaming the avant-garde as decadent and bourgeois (1981, 75). In effect, the patriotic pitch of the Russian anti-Western campaign calls to mind Nazi chauvinistic *Blut und Boden* rhetoric: "We know that we have a glorious Motherland, which has its own glorious history, and we must not allow anyone to depreciate or debase it" (75).

Socialists of Jewish descent took the lead in shaping GDR culture as well as the legal and political structures, as demonstrated by the exponential roles of Hilde Benjamin as minister of Justice and Anna Seghers as president of the German Writers' Association. As Guy Stern points out with reference to Barbara Honigmann's background, antifascists who returned from exile formed a cultural elite and consorted only amongst themselves (1994, 337). The ensuing isolation of Jewish intellectuals was not unlike the situation of the Jews in the pre-Nazi era, whether the individuals involved considered themselves Jews or not. Although the GDR purported to champion a classless society, Jews continued to live in a social enclave. Precisely because Judaism or Jewish identity was not discussed in public, Jews were isolated or isolated themselves. Barbara Honigmann describes her parents' experience in *Eine Liebe aus Nichts:* "And finally they ended up coming to Berlin in order to build a new Germany; it was supposed to be different from the old one in every respect. For this reason, they preferred not to talk about Jews any longer. Yet, somehow none of this worked, and the day came that they had to justify even their choice of exile, why it had been a Western country rather than the Soviet Union" (1991, 34). Even compared to the small Jewish community in the Federal Republic—the number of Jews living in West Germany amounted to approximately 0.1 percent of the overall population, compared to 0.95 percent before 1933—the Jewish community in the GDR was minute. It was comprised predominantly of displaced persons from Eastern Europe, with only 350 registered members in 1985 (Richarz 1988, 13–31).

In keeping with the GDR's secular ideology, religious practices and political and cultural particularism were strongly discouraged, including Judaism and Zionism. Yet, Jews were recognized as Nazi victims, alongside antifascists and communists, and were compensated under the category of "Victims of Fascism" (20). Far from solving the problem of anti-Semitism or the "Jewish Question," as the Nazis had called it, the policy of silence fostered ethnocentrism. As texts by children of exiles and Holocaust survivors illustrate, their assimilation into the socialist state was incomplete at best; it prevented them from developing a Jewish identity, but it did not protect them from being placed into a position of marginalization and otherness.[1] As was the case in the other German-speaking countries, Jewish writing in East Germany can be considered a minor literature reflecting the experience and point of view of minority authors (Deleuze and Guattari 1986, 16–19). Xenophobia was curbed as long as the GDR existed, but it flared up after German unification, complementing the neo-Nazi scene in the West. In view of GDR history, these developments hardly come as a surprise; anti-Semitic tendencies manifested themselves in the purges of 1953 as well as in the official anti-Israel rhetoric after the failure of the Soviet Union to win Israel for the Socialist Bloc (Mayer 1991, 63–80; Lorenz 1992b, 349). Prior to the consolidation of the power structures in East Germany, a large number of Jewish Leftists, placing their trust in socialism, had enthusiastically embraced the concept of an egalitarian, progressive, and antifascist Germany. As the texts of Stephan Hermlin reveal, they did so as socialists, Germans, and Jews.[2] During the cold war, many reassessed their position as Jewish intellectuals. A few decades later, dissent arose among the women of the younger generation as well. They were becoming aware that legalized equality between men and women had failed to erode the entrenched patriarchal structures that kept them from realizing themselves in the public as well as in the private sphere. Generally suspicious of Western, especially American, feminism, they nonetheless received important impulses from the international women's movement, and by questioning their position as women, they came to scrutinize the political and social conditions under which they lived.

Betrayed by the Revolution (Anna Seghers)

Among the former exiles who chose to live in East Germany was Anna Seghers. Born in 1900 in Mainz as Netty Reiling, the daughter of the Jewish art dealer Isidor Reiling, she had joined the growing ranks of leftist women intellectuals early on. She studied philology, sinology, and art history in Cologne and Heidelberg, receiving her doctorate in 1924. Her dissertation on Rembrandt and Judaism combines an interest in art history and Jewish-Gentile interaction. Two years after her marriage to the Hungarian author Laszlo Radvanyi, Seghers joined the Communist Party, alarmed by the ascent of National Socialism. In 1933, she was arrested and immediately thereafter fled with her family to France. In 1941, two years after the Nazi invasion of France, Seghers escaped to Mexico, where she stayed until 1947, having survived a near-fatal accident in 1943. Then she and her family moved to Soviet-occupied East Germany, and she lived in East Berlin until her death in 1983.

Having participated in the antifascist resistance during her years in exile, her cultural and political involvement in the GDR was significant as well. One of the most influential East German authors, Seghers held prestigious offices, received literary awards, and represented the GDR in her travels to other Eastern Bloc countries and South America. Despite her ostensible leadership role in a system known in the West for its repressive practices, her work is not that of a dogmatist. Over the years, her relationship to her environment as it pertained to her own position changed. Her attitude regarding the issues of revolution and Jewish identity became increasingly complex.

Inspired by her trust in "communal strength" and "the strength of the weak" (Mayer 1991, 29), the topic of her earlier work, she wrote about the revolution, but in contrast to Rosa Luxemburg, Seghers treated it in a literary form. Later, she also examined the blind spots of Marxism. In her 1949 novella *Die Hochzeit von Haiti* (1976), which coincides with the founding of the GDR, she does so by way of Caribbean colonial history, and she returned to this topic in 1980 in *Drei Frauen aus Haiti*. In these works, race and racism are more than secondary problems, as they are defined in Marxist theory; they are shown to have dynamics of their own. The solution to these problems, Seghers suggests, is not merely economical, even though racism is entwined with economics.[3]

The 1928 publication date of Seghers's first novel, *Der Aufstand der Fischer von St. Barbara*, coincides with the author's joining the Communist Party. The novel, suspenseful and dashingly written, illustrates the official party line and the class struggle. This is also the case in her following narratives, including the 1930 work *Auf dem Weg zur amerikanischen Botschaft*, which call for solidarity among the oppressed. Faced with the threat of right-wing extremism, Seghers, like most German leftists, failed to differentiate between fascism and Nazism, with Nazism being primarily an anticommunist movement with anti-Semitism as a by-product. This is the case in *Das siebte Kreuz*, first published in the United States as *The Seventh Cross* in 1942, which immediately became an international success (A. Stephan 1995, 450). Seghers rarely emphasizes female characters; instead she expresses her views predominantly through male protagonists. Women's issues, as well as Jewish concerns, are not addressed, the assumption being that they will be resolved through the class struggle. In *Der Ausflug der toten Mädchen* (1979), this outlook is modified, although the story is by no means a feminist text. Surveying German history of the first half of the twentieth century, Seghers, although aware of the changing role of women, does not focus on the Nazis' repression of feminism and the decline in women's rights. Her portrayal of gender roles is conventional, generally speaking, as her female characters are cast as members of different collectives such as the family, the party, or the German people (Brandes 1992, 11). The changed outlook and the subtler character portrayal reflect in part Seghers's experience as a German exile in France. The autobiographical narrative *Der Ausflug der toten Mädchen,* written in Mexico in 1946 just prior to Seghers's return to Germany, showcases the author's attitude toward Germany and the Germans in such a way as to reveal her love for her native country, closely associated with the figure of her mother. The personal element in this short text is more pronounced than in her monumental 1949 novel about interwar Germany, *Die Toten bleiben jung,* precisely because its protagonists are women.[4]

Her choice of characters allows Seghers to construct a universe of victims in which even confirmed female Nazis appear relatively innocuous because they play a subordinate role in the Third Reich.[5] In general, women were not represented in the upper echelons of the Nazi hierarchy, and their role was distinct from that of the self-proclaimed protagonists of the *Männerstaat* heralded by Hitler and Rosenberg. Seghers's portrayal of women as a group oppressed and seduced by the Nazi regime corresponds to views common among early feminists, which came under scrutiny in the late 1970s (Frauengruppe Faschismus-forschung 1981, 9). More recent studies have uncovered women's complicity in the Nazi state, ranging from tacit approval and collaboration in typical women's roles as caregivers and nurturers to a more public kind of involvement in official capacities. Alison Owings, in the introduction to *Frauen,* her collection of accounts by German women of all walks of life, maintains that "by keeping the Nazi flame alive and/or the home fires burning, German women enabled German men to set the other conflagrations, those that burned ghettos, barns, countries, and corpses," and she raises the troubling question: "Why did the women behave the way they did? 'Fate' is too easy a scapegoat" (1993, xxv). In Seghers's narrative, however, the culprits are presumed to be the industrial and financial power brokers of late capitalism and their puppets, the politicians. Both remain behind the scenes.

The constellations in *Der Ausflug der toten Mädchen* allow for average Germans, male and female, to be configured as manipulated, misguided, and exploited, and hence not fully accountable. Even those who stand their ground as communists or who remain faithful to their spiritual principles do so because they have no other choice or because their particular position prompts them to do so. Leni is introduced to the leftist underground at a young age and marries an antifascist; not only are Lotte and Liese deeply religious, but there also seems to be a same-sex attachment between them; Fräulein Sichel and Sophie, both Jewish, are categorically excluded from Nazi society because of their ancestry, and Lore's promiscuity is incompatible with the Nazi ideal of womanhood. In all cases, extenuating circumstances are the key factors in the development of a woman's character and allegiances. In keeping with Seghers's overall representation of women, none of the women in *Der Ausflug der toten Mädchen* possesses the boldness of certain male characters such as Georg Heisler in *Das siebte Kreuz*. They also lack the independence of mind displayed by other male characters such as Michael Nathan or the stature of Toussaint in *Die Hochzeit von Haiti,* and their suffering is distinct from the martyrdom of Jean Sasportas in *Das Licht auf dem Galgen* (1962).

Der Ausflug der toten Mädchen is set within a narrative frame to tell, presumably, Seghers's and her former classmates' story, filtered through the experience of exile. The first-person narrator, a reflection of the author, as indicated by the name Netty, is recuperating from an illness that has intensified her alienation from her Mexican environment and her longing for the places of her youth. Her vision of the past, turned utopia, helps her to overcome her inertia. Mentally and emotionally Netty stands at a turning point: she reviews the past with uncanny clarity, while future tasks are approaching: "I felt an immeasurable current of time, undefeatable like the air" (1979, 82).

The recollection that reinvigorates the narrator is that of an excursion at the Rhine River with her high school class. The familiar German landscape and ambiance, a country inn on the river—almost identical to that of Hilde Domin's novel *Das zweite Paradies* (1968)—"her" street, her parental home, and the vision of her young mother express the narrator's nostalgia. The mood and imagery of the narrative imply that

Germany is a good country with basically good citizens. Replete with historical references, the narrative persuades the reader that forces beyond the individual's control have caused Germany's tragedy. Crimes as well as heroic deeds are mentioned as part of the fabric of German history, made up of loss, oppression, disorientation, and carnage, but also of heroism and valor. *Der Ausflug der toten Mädchen* is a plea to overcome the past so that young people of diverse backgrounds can, once again, live together in peace. Endorsing and seemingly believing in the power of reason and the basic goodness of mankind, Seghers attributes the catastrophes of the past to flawed political and social structures, rather than to the shortcomings of the human race or of the individual psyche. On this assumption she bases her confidence in a new beginning and a better future under the auspices of communism.

A person as politically astute as Anna Seghers would hardly have moved back to Germany for purely sentimental reasons—she had experienced the fanaticism of the Nazis and knew that it had been merely a matter of time before her name would have appeared on the death camp deportation lists. Yet, her conciliatory attitude toward Germany allows her to return to her native country with a sense of mission. To best accommodate the desire to return, *Der Ausflug der toten Mädchen* is set prior to World War I during the narrator's adolescence. This era, which countless European authors have described as an age of innocence, is not associated with pain and loss. Seghers's vignettes show future victims and perpetrators side by side, unaware of what the future holds. By focusing on their friendships and romances across ethnic, class, religious, and gender lines, Seghers illustrates that it was impossible to predict which girl would end up taking which side. The trauma of the war, the events of the 1920s and early 1930s, and radical politics are depicted as the major factors shaping individual fates. None of the protagonists occupy leadership positions, and their ideological orientations are determined by their personal choices. The character of Marianne, an icon of German womanhood and a symbol of the German fate, is a case in point; her morally upstanding fiancé is killed in the war—otherwise she would not have become involved with a Nazi. But, a conservative woman, she accepts her mate's politics as her own. By representing this key figure as politically immature, Seghers exonerates her to a certain degree. Moreover, her frequent references to Marianne's beauty and innocence as a young woman in love make the reader inclined to agree with the narrator (1979, 56, 64).

Yet, it is disturbing that Marianne's death in the rubble of her bombed-out house is discussed on the same narrative plane as the murders of antifascists and Jews in Nazi concentration camps. Characterizing herself as a double victim of National Socialism—an exile and the daughter of a woman who met her "agonizing, cruel demise in a remote village to which she had been banned by Hitler" (80)—the narrator arrogates for herself the right to forgive.[6] This presumption on the part of an exile writer is extremely problematic. Holocaust survivors such as Simon Wiesenthal in Die Sonnenblume (1969) have rejected the notion that any individual can "forgive" the extermination of a nation. In spite of the effort to obscure the differences between genocide, war, and civil disobedience for the sake of the future, Seghers's text reveals at which price the reconciliation is achieved. Her version of Nazi history, World War II, and the Holocaust is based on distortion and omission. To make her view of history plausible, she uses women characters, configured in a most conservative fashion. Dependent upon their fathers', lovers', and husbands' decisions and on the ideology represented by the organizations with which they are affiliated, they appear doubly disempowered. The text also suggests that German men of the middle and lower classes are powerless and hence not fully culpable.

Seghers's interpretation of Nazi history corresponds with the ideological assumptions on which the GDR was founded. Alleging that as a socialist state it was heir to the antifascist legacy and represented a morally superior Germany, East Germany disavowed all responsibility for the Holocaust. The apologetic stance in Seghers's story resembles, moreover, the narratives of certain West German veterans—Wolfgang Borchert, Heinrich Böll, and Günter Grass—who portrayed average Germans as victims of circumstance. The refusal to view history in specific terms and to discern between different levels of involvement and culpability made it possible for the citizens of the GDR and, for that matter, the majority of West Germans and Austrians to pose collectively as Nazi victims. In Der Ausflug der toten Mädchen, Seghers justifies the Germans' unwillingness to assume responsibility and to negotiate with Jews as Jews inside and outside of the GDR.

Indeed, dwelling on Germany's anti-Semitism would have been inconvenient and would have created ideological discord among German leftists. For this reason, many GDR authors, including Seghers, engaged in broadly conceived literary projects to enlighten the new socialists about the class struggle, fascism, and the role of communism. Pressing on into a brighter future provided Seghers with a stronger creative impetus than settling moral and material accounts with Holocaust survivors. To be sure, a serious accounting did not take place in any of the German-speaking countries, in spite of the urgent appeals made by Jewish-defined authors and intellectuals.

In 1962, having come to a fuller understanding of German socialism after fifteen or so years in the GDR, Seghers published *Karibische Geschichten,* containing the earlier novella *Die Hochzeit von Haiti* (5–60), *Die Wiedereinführung der Sklaverei in Guadeloupe* (61–120), and *Das Licht auf dem Galgen* (121–238), which first appeared in 1961 as a cycle. A variety of sources—biographical, historical, and literary—converge in these texts about revolution, the empowerment of the oppressed, and counterrevolution.[7] The historical material occasions the discussion of issues relevant not only to the eighteenth century but also the twentieth—revolutions, freedom fights against imperialist powers, the continued class struggle, political revisionism, and ethnic and racial strife. Excerpts of historical sources, included in the original edition, served the purpose of lessening the direct impact of Seghers's controversial discussion of the role of the Jews as a potentially revolutionary minority, regardless of their class affiliation.

Similar to Heinrich von Kleist in *Die Verlobung in San Domingo,* Seghers in *Die Hochzeit von Haiti* deals with the successful rebellion of the Haitian black slaves that led to the foundation of a black republic in 1804 (Kappeler 1994, 66). Unlike *Der Ausflug der toten Mädchen,* where Jewishness is inscribed as female, Seghers chooses the character of a merchant's son to explore the marginality of a liberal-minded Jew. Sima Kappeler's assertion that "the Jew, who is frequently used to represent the victim, emerges here rather as he who survives despite reversals" needs to be qualified (67). Seghers does link the fate of Michael Nathan with that of the black revolutionary Toussaint, stressing that the two men died at "approximately the same time," albeit in different locations and under different circumstances. Neither one dies a free man; Toussaint perishes as Napoleon's prisoner, and Michael Nathan, after the death of his black wife and child, withers away in London, having entered an arranged marriage with a Jewish woman. The fate of the former allies parallels that of the country for which they fought: Haiti ends up "impoverished, sucked dry, economically dependent upon the rich countries of the world. But she remained a Negro state" (1976, 60).

In Seghers's story the narrator's sympathies are different from those in Kleist, and an entire spectrum of political and social parties is portrayed, all of which can coexist in the absence of economic conflicts of interest. Seghers complicates the categories of race and ethnicity by exploring the multilayered relations between slaves and slaveholders, resulting in a third "race," the mestizos, who have their own political agendas. The race barriers are permeable, but economics and power struggles keep the "ethnic" groups apart (Kappeler 1994, 67). In analogy to the racially invisible European proletariat, the blacks are the most exploited group. The Jews are outsiders to all three groups—the black servants consider them "miserable 'small Whites'" (1976, 40). Yet, Seghers does not represent them as a monolithic group; she differentiates between Ashkenazim and Sephardim, men and women, rich and poor Jews, and she informs her readers about Jewish customs and Jewish history throughout her narrative.

Despite the overall discussion of other factors, race is the main category under scrutiny. The obtrusive use of stereotypes is provocative, since they are so obviously irrelevant to the actual story involving oppression, injustice, revolution, and love.[8] Yet, race dominates the thinking of the Haitians, as it did that of Seghers's German contemporaries, and for this reason alone must be emphasized. Haiti's three-race structure mirrors the European class structure. Poverty and blackness are synonymous in the Haitian context, the mestizos correspond to the European middle class (23), and the whites to the upper class and the nobility. As outsiders, the Jews can affiliate themselves with, but never be an integral part of, all races and classes. The interracial relations, typically involving men of a higher social class and more privileged racial group than the women, make the intersection of class, gender, and race visible.

The most oppressed group, the blacks, and the most marginal, the Jews, are shown to possess true revolutionary potential, although within the larger Jewish society revolutionaries are the exception. While the freedom fight of the blacks also involves their livelihood, the Jewish revolutionary is inspired by his sense of justice to fight slavery. The European gentry, holding onto their privileges, only flirt with revolutionary ideas, but Michael and the Jewish protagonist of *Das Licht auf dem Galgen*, Sasportas, take action as only members of a traditionally persecuted minority would. Michael's involvement with the rebellious slaves is intellectual, emotional, and, through Margot, sexual and familial.

The character of Michael Nathan serves to reveal paradigms of Jewish history. Nathan exchanges Judaism for the ideals of the Enlightenment and the French Revolution. He is the only one to put the egalitarian ideals of the Society of the Friends of the Blacks into practice; he alone takes the cause of racial equality seriously, being vulnerable to shifts in ideological patterns himself. Toussaint is as unprejudiced as Michael, but being a politician, he is more pragmatic: "Toussaint did not hate White people, no matter how much the Whites hated him. Neither did he despise the mulattos, even if they despised him. Already as a child he had learned that skin color was not the measure of a man" (1962, 34). The only other character who shares Michael's lofty ideals, albeit in a quiet, practical way, is his "ugly" sister Mali. The marginal position of the Jews, male and female, is captured in the image of brother and sister sitting alone at the dinner table "resembling one another and their father as much as ever" (58). This scene expresses the failure of the cosmopolitan ideal.

The tensions in Seghers's three Caribbean stories elude any easy solution. Although there is some overlap between the dialectic of race, class, ideology, and economics, no consistent ideology evolves, as it becomes obvious that the diverse ideological paradigms from the late eighteenth century to the mid-twentieth century engendered different sets of problems, none of which has been resolved yet. In periods dominated by cosmopolitan values, as in the one preceding the French Revolution, the issue of ethnicity and race are all but negligible. In such an atmosphere Jews can thrive, whereas the emphasis on national and ethnic patterns forces the individual back into his or her group of origin. The Jewish revolutionary, however, having left his community for the love of humanity, has no place to which to return. Seghers's narrator, beyond merely expounding the moral superiority of a cosmopolitan ethos, exposes the wider ramifications of the ideologies centering on race and economy, and the special interests intrinsic to both.

Karibische Geschichten also undertakes a redefinition of Jewish identity in view of the fact that in the long run assimilation has repeatedly ended up in an impasse. Although Seghers does not configure Jewish identity as a function of race, she shows that it can be interpreted according to racial, social, economic, or philosophical paradigms, thereby suggesting that whatever the internal definition of Jewishness, the secularized Jew is the odd person out when racism and nationalism reign supreme. This tragic conflict engenders the pure revolutionary impetus of Michael Nathan and Sasportes, which Seghers fails to encounter in her countries of exile as well as in the GDR. The position represented by her positive heroes is, in the final analysis, a Jewish one, associated with self-sacrifice and betrayal. It is most immediately expressed in Netty's dream about her mother and the sites associated with her fate: a German town near the Rhine River and a Polish village, synonymous with genocide.

From Antifascism to Judaism (Barbara Honigmann)

The image of the Jew as the revolutionary who questions existing structures, because he is excluded from them, but who never enjoys the fruits of his efforts, occurs also in the works of other GDR authors of Jewish descent, most notably Stefan Heym's *Ahasver* (1983). The novel was Heym's critical contribution to the Luther Year, honoring the reformer's five-hundredth birthday and an occasion for publications and symposia on Luther and the Reformation. Heym focuses on the barbaric, repressive, and petty aspects of the Age of Reformation, associating Protestant anti-intellectualism with the pedestrian attitudes of GDR technocrats posing as intellectuals. Drawing parallels between the official ideology in East Germany and the Reformation, Heym deconstructs the anti-Zionist rhetoric targeting the State of Israel. By exposing the connection between Lutheran anti-Judaism and the anti-Israeli sentiments in the GDR, Heym points to a continuum of German anti-Semitism affecting this supposedly antifascist country. At the time *Ahasver* was published, other GDR authors had already revisited Jewish history and Judaism in their works, but few did so in as broad a philosophical and historical framework as Heym. On the other hand, Barbara Honigmann, a child of returned exiles, provided a detailed subjective account of the condition of Jewish women in East Germany.

Herself a dramaturge, writer, and painter, Honigmann, the daughter of the renowned dramaturge Georg Honigmann, was born in 1949. She describes her parents' path as Jewish socialists before coming to East Berlin in her poem "Selbstporträt als Jüdin" (1992) as follows:

Vienna before the war
Berlin before the war
Paris until the occupation
London
Bombs on London
the Blitz.

Honigmann's father and his Bulgarian-born wife had engaged in antifascist activities in England, he in the European Service, she as a tool and die maker in an ammunition factory. They moved to Russian-occupied East Germany for ideological reasons. Barbara Honigmann grew up among the intellectual elite of the GDR. In her autobiographical novel *Eine Liebe aus Nichts,* she maintains that the activities of this group had very limited impact on average GDR citizens.

In East Berlin, Honigmann's situation as a Jewish woman was tenuous, not unlike that of Ruth Beckermann in Vienna. Unable to subscribe to her father's Enlightenment credo, Honigmann questioned his confidence in reason, equality, and brotherhood. Neither did she share his feelings of superiority—convinced that German Jews, "his people," had been the proponents of communism, he had little regard for East European Jews. Barbara Honigmann, in contrast, became increasingly disaffected with the GDR and alienated from her father, whom she portrays as a troubled individual, a man sitting "between two chairs," no longer a Jew and not quite a German. In her work, she traces the process leading her from an initial phase of skepticism and uncertainty to a deliberate detachment from the socialist state associated with her father, and it culminates in the construction of a positive Jewish position under the auspices of motherhood and women's spirituality.

Guy Stern characterizes Honigmann's texts as postmodern and apolitical (1994, 332). For Honigmann to reach this point required an act of rebellion against the system under which she grew up and that expected her to become a secular *artiste engagée.* Her turn toward Judaism has distinctly political dimensions. According to Dan Diner, Auschwitz, rather than assimilation, created a symbiosis between Jews and Germans, albeit a negative one. In analogy to this assertion, Honigmann maintains that Jews and Germans became "a couple in Auschwitz

209

which not even death can part" (1992).[9] It is precisely this involuntary union from which Honigmann seeks to extrapolate herself in order to overcome her dilemma as a German-speaking Jew.

In *Roman von einem Kinde* (1986) and *Eine Liebe aus Nichts* (1991), the narrator's relocation to France provides the necessary geographical distance. Yet, Honigmann concedes, "As a Jew I left Germany, but in my work, because of my very strong ties to the German language, I always return" (1992). Karen Remmler comments on the author's problematic relationship to her native language and culture: "Leaving East Berlin in 1984 became a necessary catalyst for writing about her Jewish identity in the former East Germany" (1994, 191). Obviously, Honigmann is not entirely successful in disentangling herself from Germany, and not only because her works are read primarily by the German-speaking public.

Honigmann's decision to join the Jewish community in the 1970s coincides with a worldwide movement of Jews in search of their roots. In order to accord Judaism a proper place in her life and to be able to provide her son with a Jewish education, Honigmann studied Hebrew and familiarized herself with Jewish traditions and customs. In contrast to Reich-Ranicki, whom he quotes extensively, Stern does not consider Honigmann's "adherence to a new faith" an exchange of a political credo for a religious one. Instead, he writes that "beginning with her ceremonial wedding to Peter Honigmann—one of the first traditional weddings in the GDR," Honigmann "journeyed step-by-step from an a-religious attitude to a comfortable embracing of Judaism" (G. Stern 1994, 340). Her individualism, her commitment to art as well as to women's rights, and her feeling of being a permanent outsider kept her from conforming to any party line and prevented her from giving herself unconditionally to a common faith. Stern argues that "by Jewish standards she can scarcely be labeled as Orthodox" (340).

Roman von einem Kinde was published prior to *Eine Liebe aus Nichts*, although the chronology of the events discussed in both works would suggest the opposite. As the novel reflects the processes that enabled the autobiographical narrator to liberate herself from her father's legacy in intellectual and spiritual terms, a basis is established from which to venture further out into the past. Coming to terms with her identity as a woman, a mother, and a Jew represents Honigmann's first steps toward examining her relationship with her father, inextricably connected to GDR history. She does so more than half a decade after his death and at the point when the GDR is about to be dissolved. At approximately the same time another Jewish author, Jurek Becker, who had also left the GDR, chose a similarly significant historical juncture to examine the relationship between the post-Shoah generations of Jews under socialism in his partly autobiographical novel *Bronsteins Kinder* (1986).

Roman von einem Kinde details the stripping away of the unessential and destructive elements in the narrator/author's life and the building of a foundation involving gender identity and religion. Her first pregnancy occasions an examination of her life so far. Fittingly, Honigmann's 1976 self-portrait *Schwangere* (Pregnant Woman) appeared on the cover of the first edition; for the later paperback edition, this image was replaced by one of Honigmann's less revealing self-portraits, showing a face rather than a pregnant nude. The use of the original cover in conjunction with the narrator's name, Babu, with which Honigmann signs her paintings, establishes an autobiographical relationship between author and text.[10] The birth of Babu's son Johannes represents a turning point—it signifies the narrator's own rebirth as a mother and as a Jew (1986, 15). Frustrated by the spiritual void she experiences in the company of her non-Jewish friends, she turns toward Judaism.

The problematic figure of the biological father, the narrator's as well as her child's, central in *Eine Liebe aus Nichts,* is bypassed altogether. Only the maternal voice, Babu's own and that of her mother, carries some authority. An attempt to introduce Gershom Scholem, the prominent scholar of Jewish mysticism, as a positive father figure fails. Scholem, who emigrated to Palestine in the 1920s, is shown to be still tied to Germany by his language, the Holocaust, and the tomb of his family at the Jewish cemetery in Berlin-Weißensee. His continued attachment to his native country undermines his own emphatic pronouncement that Jews, then and now, must not live in Germany (91). From the narrator's point of view, he is no less defeated by Germany than her own father— he dies soon after his visit. Although Scholem is buried in Israel, his name is added to those on his family's monument at the Jewish cemetery in Berlin in its German form, *Gerhard,* confirming Honigmann's impression that Scholem was unable to break the connection to his country of origin. On neither grave—not Scholem's in the capital of the GDR, nor Georg Honigmann's in Weimar, the city associated both with German classicism and with the fateful interwar republic—is there any reference to the disrupted Jewish lives. Babu and her husband choose a middle ground between Scholem's and Georg Honigmann's position: they leave Germany, but not Europe, and establish themselves as Jews among Jews in Strasbourg.

Roman von einem Kinde appeared at a time when anti-Jewish hostility and historical revisionism had caused many Jews of the post-Shoah generations to seek alternatives to renewed assimilation. These developments added considerable depth to Honigmann's examination of her relationship with her father, the Marxist legacy, and the ideological basis of her own secular upbringing. Similar to Seghers, she portrays World War I as having set in motion a process leading from the Weimar Republic to the present. Georg Honigmann's death is configured in such a way as to suggest that this continuum is drawing to a close.

Honigmann pays special attention to the role of women. She credits both her parents, as well as her father's third wife, for their contribution to her development as a painter and writer. Yet, her criticism of the employment practices at East German theaters, where she worked as a year-to-year dramaturge (G. Stern 1994, 331), and played the role of Alfried, the predatory male par excellence in *Eine Liebe aus Nichts,* is directed against the milieu that her father helped to shape. The more personal *Roman von einem Kinde* depicts a feminine sphere, highlighting the aspects of Honigmann's personality that were repressed in her father's domain. Both works support the conclusion that it is necessary for the narrator to separate herself from Germany. Strasbourg, her final destination, marks the beginning of her life in a Jewish community and as a member of a women's Torah study group, and it is suggested that Jewish existence within Germany's borders is by necessity transient (Remmler 1994, 197). In France, under the tutelage of a female Torah and Talmud scholar, the narrator establishes roots and a position of authority for herself in a Jewish context.

In both novels, the narrator's self-exploration occurs in isolation from her family and her native country. In *Roman von einem Kinde,* the almost mystical event of giving birth and the symbiosis between mother and child engender an increasing closeness to other Jews. The Seder celebration in East Berlin and the visit at the secret Hasidic community in Moscow represent counterpoints to Babu's German environment, whose attitudes to the past marginalize the children of exiles and Holocaust survivors.[11] In *Eine Liebe aus Nichts,* the key issue is the narrator's independence as the prerequisite for her inner restructuring on a political, aesthetic, and personal level, expressed by her official request to leave the GDR, her move to Paris, her studies at the École des Beaux Arts, and her struggle with financial and emotional insecurity. Honigmann describes the difficulty of detaching herself: "Now that my parents are dead, I am easily tempted to fall under the spell of these myths [exile, antifascism]. But I also hear the things that remained unspoken at that time and I see, or I believe I see, what has been concealed" (1992). *Roman von einem Kinde* begins on a note of hesitation and melancholy, but its ending is exhilarating. Being a mother instills in Babu a willingness to transcend her former self and assume new responsibilities. The last chapter expresses her openness not only to her mentor but to the entire world, while the intermittent chapters trace her progress. Strasbourg offers the narrator the opportunity to lead a serene and productive life within a vibrant Jewish community (1986, 116).

In contrast, the overall atmosphere in *Eine Liebe aus Nichts* is one of barrenness and futility. The designs of the older generation have come to naught, and Georg Honigmann leaves nothing behind but a trail of broken relationships, including the one with his daughter. His promiscuity and his inability to provide a home for his child stand in sharp contrast to the stability enjoyed by the members of the Jewish community in Strasbourg. Moreover, the entire young generation of GDR citizens is portrayed as bewildered and disoriented. Their exasperating cross-country hikes are an expression of their dilemma. Their endless disputes and their failure to bond in a meaningful way are directly related to Babu's illness, which, ironically, is cured in a stranger's house (1986, 70f).

The chaotic episodes in *Roman von einem Kinde* and the father's senility in *Eine Liebe aus Nichts* denote the end of an era. The defeat of the masculine ethos on which the GDR was founded is best expressed in the father's last year, when he requires his young wife's help to feed himself: "one spoonful for you, one spoonful for me, and one spoonful for your daughter, one spoonful for Bilbo [the dog], one spoonful for your Mama and one for your Papa, and one spoonful for the court bankers" [his ancestors] (1991, 94). Precisely because it is officially suppressed, Jewish identity is anything but a marginal issue in *Eine Liebe aus Nichts*. The chaos in the life of Georg Honigmann, the descendant of Jewish bankers, is in part brought about by his inability to resolve the contradictions between his family history and his socialist allegiances, his privileged status and his desire to live in a proletarian state; it is a form of self-hatred that deprived his daughter of her heritage.[12] It is not surprising that in *Roman von einem Kinde* a complete divestment of the Marxist and antifascist legacy takes place as the narrator embraces Judaism as her only true heritage: "Once I had a dream. I was with all the other people in Auschwitz. And in this dream I thought: finally I have found my place in life. But now I thought of the weak star and the rusty heavenly ladder" (1986, 28). With this statement Honigmann positions herself among Jewish exile authors such as Stephan Hermlin, Peter Weiss, and Erich Fried, who claimed the legacy of Auschwitz, the location that the Nazis had intended as their final destination, as their own (D. C. G. Lorenz 1992b, 145–52). Other Jewish authors born after 1945 — Lea Fleischmann, Nadja Seelich, and Ruth Beckermann, for example — relate to the Shoah in a similar way. Like Honigmann, they show that the psychological responses evoked by certain images and topics differ fundamentally among post-Holocaust Jews and Gentiles. Babu does not even consider the possibility of a Jewish renewal in Germany — according to her, "Elias, the Messiah, and God" cannot afford to show their faces in Berlin (Honigmann 1986, 26). Neither can they in Eastern Europe, which Honigmann portrays as a giant cemetery (71).[13] Instead, following Scholem's recommendation, Babu and Peter emigrate to a country where Torah is studied — "there is nothing more to learn" in Germany (94).

Unlike Lea Fleischmann, Honigmann shows no inclination to move to Israel. She does not focus on the Jewish State, nor is she, as the Jean-Marc and the Alfried episodes in *Eine Liebe aus Nichts* suggest, tempted to explore the United States or West Germany (104).[14] Considering the near-total co-optation of the former GDR by the West and the setbacks experienced by postunification East German women, Alfried's choice of taking up residence in Munich suggests that for men with a mercenary disposition, the Federal Republic of Germany would be the appropriate place. Living as a Jewish woman in France requires that Honigmann negotiate modern and traditional, revolutionary and conventional, values; the presumption of a woman's right to equal access and freedom within the traditionally patriarchal Jewish structures is as problematic as reconciling the empowerment of women in physical, spiritual, professional, and creative terms with motherhood and the nuclear family.

The individual segments of *Roman von einem Kinde* are structured like meditations on certain conflicts that the narrator resolves by drawing upon a whole spectrum of traditions and fields of knowledge. Blending the political with the personal, Honigmann's work stands in the narrative tradition created by Seghers, Hermlin, Heym, Bobrowski, Wolf, and Becker. Like Seghers, Honigmann makes the past part of the solution, rather than viewing it only as something to be overcome, as Lea Fleischmann does. The naïveté of Honigmann's paintings corresponds to her literary approach: nothing is taken for granted, and even basic facts are articulated with a directness that makes them appear new and surprising. The associative prose and the title link *Roman von einem Kinde* with the Romantic tradition—in a 1992 interview Honigmann suggested such a connection to Bettina von Arnim. Indeed, stylistically, Honigmann's narratives do evoke the childlike pose of von Arnim's *Briefwechsel mit einem Kinde* and *Dies Buch gehört dem König* (G. Stern 1994, 330); however, Honigmann achieves this naïveté *after* the Shoah. Her work comments on the genocide and proclaims that Jewish life continues in spite of it. An identity conflict such as Honigmann's is unknown to the Gentile women of the Romantic era. Rather than confirming Honigmann's many allusions to classicism and Romanticism, *Roman von einem Kinde* undermines and foils them. Ultimately, Honigmann places her work not into the tradition of von Arnim but rather into that of Rahel Varnhagen and Heinrich Heine.

By discarding the androcentric baggage contained in the heritage of her father's generation—classicism, Marxism, antifascism, and Zionism—Honigmann distances herself from all of these inherently heroic patterns. Instead, she reinvents reality from a woman's point of view, thereby outlining the possible basis for a newly configured motherland. Babu becomes the mother of a child as well as of her new self—hence the sometimes visionary tone. Having sifted through the debris of the past, Honigmann ventures into uncharted territory. Her attempt to create a holistic existence as a woman, a Jew, a writer, and a painter corresponds to the quest of other German-speaking Jewish women of her generation, unwilling to sacrifice their visions by conforming to the dominant cultural patterns.

Between Eden and Utopia

Jewish Women's Geography

Jewish and Christian geography differ insofar as the Jewish world traditionally extended across empires and nation-states. Most Gentile cultural centers happened to also be Jewish centers, because Jews lived in urban and metropolitan areas, but cities such as Vienna, Berlin, Paris, Amsterdam, and New York had their own significance for Jewish authors. In Eastern Europe, Vilna, Warsaw, Cracow, Lvov, Prague, Czernowitz, and other smaller towns were centers of learning and commerce, and as such they represented significant landmarks in terms of Jewish geography, although from a Western point of view they played no comparable role. Of the Jewish centers in the Middle East, Jerusalem had the greatest allure as a spiritual center for religious Jews and the intended capital of the Zionist Jewish State. Other locations were also surrounded by an aura more important than the place itself: America (referred to as the *medine* or the Golden Land), Galicia, the Bukowina, Vienna, Paris, Berlin, Vilna. Taking into consideration the associations attached to certain places, Irit Rogoff juxtaposes the concept site to the "rigid and natural" term *geography* and correlates it to the discourse of race and gender (Rogoff 1994, 259). *Site,* in conjunction with the latter two categories, represents an important component of identity.[1]

Texts of Jewish women authors have traditionally displayed a distinct disregard for political boundaries—they entice their reader to ignore, challenge, or traverse such boundaries. Jewish women authors regard them with the same matter-of-factness as did Glikl Hamil, who sent her sons all across Europe and who herself moved from place to place. In general, Jews regarded big cities as more hospitable than small provincial towns and villages. In their experience, language was not tied to a specific national or geographic setting. The Jewish languages—Hebrew, Yiddish, and Ladino—were extranational and supranational, regardless of a given speaker's country of origin or citizenship. Moreover, the transition from Yiddish to German contributed to Jewish deterritorialization, bringing about a simultaneous expansion of the range of the German language as the lingua franca of Jews of different nationalities and outlooks.

Many Eastern European Jews were bilingual or multilingual, whereas most assimilated Jews had only an academic knowledge of other languages and spoke exclusively German. Forced to adopt new languages in exile and in the Nazi concentration camps, most of them abandoned the language of the perpetrators, but writers and professionals whose linguistic and professional identity coincided found it hard, if not impossible, to switch languages and, by the same token, cultures. Both multilingualism and the inability of abandoning one's native language are reflected in the linguistic patterns as well as the themes of Jewish authors. Jeanette Lander's novels vacillate between Yiddish, German, and American Standard and Black English, each of which provides the protagonist with different frames of reference. The overlay of several sets of identity, expressed in terms of language, is also a recurrent theme in the works of Irene Dische, correlating identity with language and memory.

The immigration patterns of the last centuries created an international network of Jewish communities and established the larger context for Jewish authors. For them, the locations abroad and overseas associated with Jewish culture did not hold the exotic appeal they had for the less mobile Gentiles. In the wake of the forced displacement of entire populations during the Second World War, this international network became even more indispensable and extensive. Exiles and concentration camp survivors moved to destinations outside of Germany and Austria. Their postwar Jewish communities consisted largely of Eastern European Jews, who had experienced anti-Semitism most directly at the hands of local Nazis in their countries of origin. Few German and Austrian Jews returned—they and their children make up approximately 10–20 percent of the Jewish communities in present-day Germany and Austria. Leslie Adelson is correct in characterizing heterogeneity and diachronicity as basic elements of the identity search of Jews in West Germany (1994a, 312). According to Adelson, Jewish authors illustrate not only the rift between Nazis and victims by way of their fictional characters but also the lack of a single identity on the part of the characters. In the absence of a unified collective and individual Jewish identity, there can be no German-Jewish dialogue but only a "polylogue," Adelson asserts. In fact, some of Salman Rushdie's observations about English-language Indian literature, frequently subsumed under the term *Commonwealth Literature* and thereby simultaneously despecified and ghettoized, apply to the concepts of German literature and a Minor Jewish Literature in the German language: "One of the most absurd aspects of this quest for national authenticity is that . . . it is completely fallacious to suppose that there is such a thing as a pure, unalloyed tradition from which to draw. The only people who seriously believe this are religious extremists" (1991, 67).

The children of exiles were aware of, and at times intuitively committed to, their ancestors' countries of origin by curiosity, hatred, and a certain fascination. By the same token, the children of Holocaust survivors and returned exiles were intrigued by their parents' actual and possible countries of exile. Most post-Shoah authors envision an imaginary axis connecting the United States, Germany and Austria, Eastern Europe (Poland, Russia, the Bukovina), and Israel. Some connections reach as far as Australia and Asia, such as the work of Anita Desai, who was born in Delhi in 1937 the daughter of a German exile and a Bengali man. In *Baumgartner's Bombay* (1989), a novel written in English interspersed with German idioms and nursery rhymes, Desai focuses on the experience of a German Jew in India. In impeccable English that, when read out loud, retains the melody of Indian English, Desai reveals her and her characters' multiple identities and cultural displacements.

Most of the works by contemporary Jewish women writers are set in large metropolitan areas: New York, Los Angeles, Paris, Vienna, Berlin, and Jerusalem. These are, by and large, the same areas that have traditionally been important to Jewish geography when they came into focus as utopian sites for nineteenth-century immigrants and expanded the Ashkenazic motherland all across the globe. Although largely a site of Jewish emigration, Yiddish-speaking Eastern Europe and the *shtetl* culture occupied the imagination of Jewish authors as a source of inspiration for a Jewish renewal. In contrast to the older generation, the children of Jewish exiles who stayed in their parents' countries of exile and the Jews who were raised in post-Holocaust Germany and Austria and who left did so by choice. Among them are Jeanette Lander, who was born to Yiddish-speaking parents in New York and raised in

Atlanta, Georgia; the author and filmmaker Ruth Beckermann, born and raised in Vienna as the daughter of a Romanian survivor and an Austrian exile; Lea Fleischmann, who was born to Polish Holocaust survivors in a displaced persons camp close to Dachau and grew up in Frankfurt; Ronnith Neumann, whose parents returned to Germany from Israel in 1958; and Waltraud Anna Mitgutsch, born in Linz and raised Catholic but aware of her Jewish ancestry. Neither socially nor emotionally fully integrated, they made their parents' East European countries of origin, Israel, and, to a lesser extent, the United States the sites of their quest for identity. The search for a lost homeland in Eastern Europe or in Israel, which most of the post-Shoah authors knew at least superficially, must be interpreted in the context of earlier literary works and the accounts by the authors' parents, which contained nostalgic as well as horrifying descriptions of pre-Nazi and Nazi Eastern Europe (Zweig 1920; Birnbaum 1916; Döblin 1935). In his interview in *Die papierene Brücke,* Ruth Beckermann's father gives an idealized retrospective of the Habsburg multination-state, which he praises as a haven for all its nations (Beckermann and Aichholzer 1986). Similarly nostalgic images of Galicia's "multinational Eastern European cultural landscape" are also evoked in fiction and documentaries.[2] In particular, the capital of the Habsburg monarchy, Vienna, became mythologized in the process. Michael Pollak maintains that it was associated with social and economic advancement but, moreover, that in the minds of many Jews a direct path led from Vienna to Jerusalem (Pollak 1984, 26).

Post-Shoah literature still reflects these notions but only in an indirect way—Austria, Germany, and Eastern Europe have become the sites of trauma and mourning. Members of the older generation feel apologetic for having raised their children in the anti-Semitic environment of German-speaking countries. Their attitude seems justified in light of the autobiographical accounts of younger Jews, which typically follow a pattern that includes being raised in an urban Jewish community, the parents' being silent or secretive about their background, cautioning the younger generation against making statements that would expose them as Jews. Oftentimes, the members of the older generation were not interested in European politics but rather focused on Israel. In West Germany and Austria, most Jewish women were expected to marry young—to a Jewish man, of course—to have a large family, and to prove themselves in a high-profile career. The majority rebelled against these notions.

The post-Holocaust children's social awakening occurred around the time of the student movement of 1968. According to Dan Diner, the Left uncovered the repressed past and held the ostentatious philo-Semitism of the Federal Republic up to criticism (1986, 130). Seeing the children of former Nazis rebel against their fathers and governments, hearing the call for international brotherhood and, later, sisterhood, young Jews believed that this movement included them as well (Beckermann 1989, 121). Yet, it soon became clear that they were not included; anti-Semitism lived on under the guise of anti-Zionism, and as Wilhelm Reich had predicted in the 1930s, the old authoritarian structures outlived the collapse of Nazi Germany (1974, 225f.). Many Germans of the postwar generation embraced leftist politics in protest against their parents, who had been fascists. Most of them did so without scrutinizing their own authoritarianism and the impact of Nazi ideology on their thinking. Among the memoirs collected by Peter Sichrovsky in *Wir wissen nicht was morgen wird, wir wissen wohl was gestern war: Junge Juden in Deutschland und Österreich* is one by a Jewish woman, Edith, who describes her university experience with leftist professors hired after 1968: "Repeatedly we read texts which were clearly anti-Semitic, and not just covertly and vaguely, but crudely and stupidly" (1985, 141). Her protest against such required readings was dismissed as the neurosis of a psychologically deformed Nazi victim. Moreover, among German feminists, she encountered attempts to reevaluate the Nazi girls' and women's organizations as legitimate spaces for female bonding. The disenchantment with this intellectual climate prompted Jewish women writers to distance themselves from the West German Left and to reassess their position as Jewish women in terms of Jewish history.

Searching for the Land of the Fathers (Jeanette Lander)

Jeanette Lander's work is that of a world citizen in quest of an identity.[3] Prior to moving to Berlin in 1960, where she studied at the Free University, she had been awarded prizes for her publications in English and German. The multinational setting of her novel *Die Töchter* (1976) illustrates the global consequences of the Holocaust and the tenuous reality of Jewish women in Germany, Israel, and the United States.

Lander explores female Jewish identity from the margins—her protagonists' search for their father's tomb in Poland has strong autobiographical overtones. Having explored the position of Jewish immigrants in
the United States and between African American, Anglo-American, and
Jewish cultures in *Ein Sommer in der Woche der Itke K.* (1971a),[4] and the
interaction of Jews and Germans in post-Holocaust Germany by way
of the encounter between the daughter of Jewish exiles and her former
Nazi in-laws in West Germany in *Auf dem Boden der Fremde* (1972),
Lander emphasized the need for healing the wounds of the past by confronting the Jewish past in Eastern Europe.

The protagonists of *Die Töchter* are brought together by an event
of the past: the disappearance of their father, Jankel Lewandowski, in
1941, when he had left the unoccupied part of France to visit his father's
grave in Poland, defiant of the rumors about persecutions and pogroms.
Thirty years later, his daughters, unable to integrate themselves into
their current countries of residence (Germany, the United States, and
Israel), undertake a search for their father's tomb, which is, in fact, a
quest for their own identity. Julie, the Berlin-based sister, is frustrated by
the youth cult of the 1960s and the hollow phrases of the would-be revolutionaries of 1968; Hélène, a shop owner in Haifa, is increasingly unable
to reconcile her Polish Jewish heritage with Israeli culture, and her son is
drawn into the Israeli-Arab conflict; Minouche, a housewife in Atlanta,
rebels against Jewish life in the United States, which she experiences as
stale and artificial, and she comes to view American racial politics as intolerable. The sisters' quest does not yield concrete solutions to the protagonists' difficulties, but the search for Lewandowski's grave is a powerful symbol of their longing for roots as well as their own empowerment.
Die Töchter suggests new, woman-oriented ways of forming Jewish identity and a positive concept of the *Galut* in historical and current terms.[5]
By identifying Poland as the irretrievable fatherland of her protagonists,
Ashkenazic sisters and mothers, Lander points the way toward a reexamination of the almost-forgotten history of European Jewish women.

Leslie Adelson interprets Lander's first three novels as a "kind of trilogy," arguing that *Ein Sommer in der Woche der Itke K.* raises "vital questions regarding alternative conceptualizations of contemporary 'German' culture, as well as feminist models of minority discourse" (1993,
87). The same applies to *Auf dem Boden der Fremde* and *Die Töchter*. The
former is directly associated with the Holocaust discourse through a

reference to Paul Celan's "Death Fugue," "Death is a master from Germany"; the discussion of the poet's suicide in 1970 by one of the protagonists confirms the accuracy of Celan's vision of Germany as a land of the dead, a "Zombi-Deutschland," a "Dybbuk-Deutschland" (1972, 143). By exploring the protagonist's fate in her husband's country from her initial rebellious optimism to her resignation, *Auf dem Boden der Fremde* culminates in the realization that Germans and Jews are unable to bridge the rift caused by the Shoah. Lander's fourth novel, *Ich, allein* (1980), tests the conclusions reached in her earlier works in a situation of crisis: the protagonist's divorce in midlife, followed by isolation. She is forced to come face to face with herself without her ethnic, social, cultural, and sexual guises. Age being an important factor, the alternatives and escape routes envisioned in Lander's earlier works prove illusionary or simply irrelevant.

Die Töchter, preceding *Ich, allein,* reveals the causes for such extreme solitude—namely, the cultural and psychological identity explosion in the wake of the Holocaust and the exile experience and its consequences, radical individualism and a lack of community. The geographical settings involved in the individual biographies allow Lander to examine Jewish identity along the axis of America-Europe-Israel in its historical context: the exodus from Eastern Europe to the West, nostalgia for the *shtetl* culture, the conflict between assimilated and nonassimilated Jews, and the Shoah, causing complete destruction in Central and Eastern Europe and creating a new diaspora in different parts of the world.

Despite the fragmentation of the protagonists' family, a strong bond exists between the three sisters, even though all are at the verge of emotional and spiritual bankruptcy due to the lack of viable alternatives in their respective countries. All three have reached the point where they need to uncover those aspects of their identity that they had to bury in order to cope with everyday life.[6] Their trip to Poland is the outward expression of a spiritual and cultural pilgrimage that, tragically, leads into a vacuum: the Ashkenazic heritage has been destroyed, its remainders plundered by the victors. There is no indication that Lander's protagonists, demoralized and few in number, can provide a substitute for the land of their father. The only sign of hope is the intimate encounter between the children, a modern German-Jewish girl and her Israeli cousin, which provides a modest perspective toward the future.

The novel also addresses the relationship between Jews and Germans in the post-Shoah world. The fact that the German husband joins the sisters implies that there is a chance for reconciliation between Germans and Jews. Coming face to face with the sites of destruction is shown to be the prerequisite for true German antifascism, and it is necessary for the rehabilitation of Europe, torn by wars and ethnic strife. The exclusion of the Jewish-American husband from the pilgrims, on the other hand, suggests that the United States of the 1960s, whose ethnic discord Lander exposes elsewhere as well, is an unlikely site for Jewish rejuvenation. However, merely visiting or even returning to Eastern Europe will not result in an inner healing for Jews who reject their Ashkenazic origins; they are portrayed as persons who have lost their core. As the example of the sisters implies, the path toward an integrated Jewish existence requires a reassessment of the history in light of the traditional Jewish pacifist and cosmopolitan views denigrated by Zionism. The fate of Lewandowski, who went to Poland to visit his father's grave at the time of the Shoah, is set up as a cipher for a mentality and a decision incomprehensible to later generations, but consistent with the traditional Jewish way of life.

The protagonists' family history not only provides a survey of Ashkenazic culture *in nuce;* it also exposes the conflicts between East and West that set the stage for the daughters' rebellion against traditional boundaries. Lander suggests that the alternatives seemingly offered by these two cultural spheres never existed. One sister's memory of a French transit camp, entwined with Treblinka as the final destination of the Jewish prisoners, reveals that all of Europe participated in the Holocaust, and the encounters with Polish anti-Semites and would-be capitalists in the present debunk the socialist myth that at least in the Eastern Bloc a better world order has been established (Lander 1976, 175). Julie's experience, moreover, shows that the French Resistance, like other antifascist movements, was infected by anti-Semitism. Rather than offering a solution, *Die Töchter* reveals the all-pervasiveness of the problem, signifying that whatever measures can be taken are individual and personal — conformism, even for the sake of a good cause, is shown to be destructive and inhumane.

Lander's female characters are radical individualists, questioning and resisting, each in her own way, official policy. The male figures, on the other hand, are portrayed as dependent on superstructures that they try to force upon their spouses. Thus, Lander differentiates between an

ideological masculine approach and a more autonomous and spontaneous feminine approach to reality. Ideally, her novels suggest, a person's emotions and actions are in harmony, as is the case when Julie har-
bors her beloved enemy. She is, in Lander's terms, the optimal soldier
(14). Also, Hélène is at one with herself when taking care of herself and
her family. Yet, both women lose their spark when their personal engagement gives way to acquiescence and they submit to external constraints.

Written at the time that Lea Fleischmann published her farewell to
Germany, Lander's novel *Ich, allein* (1980) reads like an epilogue to *Die
Töchter,* confirming its conclusion. An exacting, and at times gloomy,
anticlimactic self-reflection sets the tone, perhaps the only possible
follow-up to the journey to a grave that was never found. *Ich, allein* is
the story of an isolated woman. Unlike the protagonists in *Die Töchter,*
the writer Harriet Wende in *Ich, allein* has no sisters with whom to quar-
rel and neither the means nor the energy for an all-out identity search.
Approximately the same age as Lander, Harriet is undergoing a crisis, as
her name *Wende,* meaning "change" or "reversal," suggests. A middle-
aged divorcée in a man's world, she finds herself increasingly marginalized, facing depression and age-related discrimination.

The issues central to Lander's earlier work, Jewish identity and the
Nazi past, are irrelevant in *Ich, allein*. Rather, a woman's survival outside of the traditional roles is the central issue. Harriet no longer fits
the roles of lover, mother, and wife, into which younger, sexually active
women slip without difficulty. She must come to terms with her aging
body, her loneliness, and the lifestyle changes they force upon her. The
geographic range in *Ich, allein,* as well as the possibilities, is limited,
illustrating a woman's reduced opportunities after years of married life
and with diminished options available to middle-aged persons. Unlike
the energetic protagonists of Lander's earlier novels, Harriet does not
even consider exploring options outside of Germany.

Ich, allein is propelled by a rigorous individualism that reflects also
the changes of the political climate during the late 1970s. Narrowing
her perspective, Lander makes a woman's situation the criterion for the
quality of the social system at large, and she exposes the unpreparedness
on the part of the general public to accommodate female professionals.
Although with a different focus, Lander's highly subjective text expresses the kind of frustration that prompted Lea Fleischmann to move

to Israel and Barbara Honigmann to go to France in search of a fuller Jewish life.

At this point Lander abstains from a renewed, specifically Jewish quest. By examining her protagonist's emotional and intellectual life, she makes a woman's psyche the primary site of the search for identity. Only a little later, however, under different auspices, did she venture out to examine postcolonial reality in Sri Lanka and the ethnically motivated civil war. Her novel dealing with this experience, *Jahrhundert der Herren* (1993), focuses on a set of issues related to that in her previous work. Instead of escaping the problem of gender- and culture-related oppression, the narrator confronts it in a postcolonial context where indigenous cultural problems intersect with others caused by the advent of Western capitalism. Similar to Ingeborg Bachmann's *Der Fall Franza,* Lander's last novel reveals the ever-present power hierarchies as it focuses on the plight of women and underprivileged men who are doubly victimized: within the context of a Third World country left in shambles by its colonizers, and as a result of the fast-spreading global economy.

*Between Israel and Germany (Lea Fleischmann
and Ronnith Neumann)*

Numerous factors, including the airing of the American television series *Holocaust,* which was received by the German-speaking public with great interest, sparked a renewed discussion of the Nazi past and the Holocaust in the late 1970s (D. C. G. Lorenz 1992b, 30–31).[7] At the same time, the teacher Lea Fleischmann, born to Polish Holocaust survivors in 1947, prepared to move to Israel in order to escape her dilemma as a Jewish woman in Germany. In her much-debated autobiographical account, *Dies ist nicht mein Land: Eine Jüdin verläßt die Bundesrepublik* (1980)—Atina Grossmann calls it "a kind of coming out for a postwar generation of Jews"—Fleischmann establishes clear fronts that leave no other recourse but to remove herself. She portrays Germans as former and potentially future perpetrators and Jews as victims, past and future. In her account, the Germans are made to appear peripheral and foreign to her existence, while Jewish life and culture are the center into which she positions herself (Grossmann 1986, 172). Nonetheless, like Cordelia Edvardson, Fleischmann remains connected to Germany through her language and her readership.

Fleischmann wrote her book about living as a Jewish woman in Germany in or around 1978, immediately prior to her emigration, and it appeared two years after her arrival in Israel. In order to build a case against Germany, Fleischmann traces her experience from her Jewish home environment among Holocaust survivors, who taught her about two categories of people, Jews and Nazis. Belonging to the former group, she felt out of place in Germany, except for a brief period as a university student when she opened herself up to her Gentile fellow students and to leftist politics. In retrospect, she considers the liberalization during and after the student movement of 1968 a mere fluke: neither it nor the Social Democratic government had any lasting impact on Jewish life in Germany (76).

Much like Theodor Adorno and his coauthors in *The Authoritarian Personality* (1950), which informed, among others, Klaus Theweleit's study on German Wilhelminian and Nazi culture, *Männerphantasien* (1977), Fleischmann characterizes the rigidity, intolerance, and pettiness, which she considers as German, as psychosocial phenomenona beyond the individual's control. She polemically configures Germanness as the opposite of Jewishness, defined by her as a humane way of life, thereby perpetuating the binarism of the traditional discourses on Germans and Jews, pro-Jewish in Jakob Wassermann's *Mein Weg als Deutscher und Jude* (1921) and anti-Semitic in Otto Weininger's *Geschlecht und Charakter* (1906). Considering that Jewish identity, the characteristics of women, and social and ethnic otherness have been configured similarly, it is only to be expected that the categories of gender and ethnicity intersect in Fleischmann's polemical work as well. In Israel, Fleischmann detects some of the hated German traits in herself when she, an Ashkenazic woman, interacts with Middle Eastern and African Jews in Jerusalem.

Fleischmann's sense of geography is structured according to bipolar categories as well, as the opening chapter of *Dies ist nicht mein Land* reveals. The inner landscape to which she relates as "home" is an imaginary *shtetl* in Poland where she and her parents might have resided, had she been born only ten years earlier (1980, 8). Fleischmann envisions a simple rural life close to nature (7–10), which calls to mind the motifs of Heinrich Heine's *Der Rabbi von Bacharach* (1956), Else Lasker-Schüler's 1932 drama *Arthur Aronymus,* and Isaac B. Singer's prose. The nostalgic vision ends abruptly with the German invasion, at which point Fleischmann's child-persona is confronted by the German war machine, a mass

of men in "black boots, a uniform and a cap" (1980, 12). The enemy
image of the Nazis intensifies the narrator's identification with the Holocaust experience. She has absorbed her parents' memories, transmitted
to her through survivors' accounts about "murders, humiliations, and
suffering" (25). In addition, Fleischmann is familiar with Holocaust literature and scholarship. Through the act of visualizing her and her parents' deportation to the gas chambers, she claims the fate of European
Jewry as her own, and like other children of survivors, she refers to
Auschwitz as the site from which she derives her identity (12, 21; Zipes
1980, 155–76). Similarly, Frank Stern describes Jewish geography in contrast to that of most Gentile Germans: "The future of German historical
consciousness, I would contend, will reorder the European map. On this
map, Auschwitz will be for most Germans just another site of World
War II, while for the Jews and, no doubt, for others it will forever remain a place of historical singularity and centrality" (1994, 58–59).

The teleology underlying Fleischmann's autobiographical work precludes more than a sporadic glance at Poland: her parents' country is
cast as a lost paradise turned into a wasteland to which there is no return. Fleischmann mourns the home of her alternate self but does not
wish to explore it. Rather, she presses onward and forward to Israel.
Having established her loss in historical and personal terms and defined the perpetrators, she subjects West Germany to a critical examination. The Germans, she argues, reaped the benefits of the Holocaust,
hence the collective refusal to confront the past. Her stocktaking leads
her to conclude that Germany is not an appropriate place for a new generation of Jews. Israel lies at the other end of Fleischmann's spectrum,
conceived as everything that Germany is not: a place where she will not
have to live as a member of a mentally and spiritually marginalized minority. Fleischmann writes: "My mother lived under the Germans for
five years, and I lived with them for five years [i.e., as a professional,
student and teacher]. It is enough" (1980, 250). Although Fleischmann
avoids Zionist rhetoric, her expectations do reflect Herzl's ideal of a free
Jewish nation. Hence her portrayal of Israel is free of the imagery of aggression surfacing in Ronnith Neumann's *Heimkehr in die Fremde* (1985).

The qualities Fleischmann attributes to Israel are a synthesis of her
imaginary Polish motherland and aspects of 1970s Europe acceptable to
her. It is a land made up of hopes and dreams. Peter Werres aptly observes that it was not until "Fleischmann had lived in Israel for some

time that she also wrote, in her considerably toned-down second book, of the possibility that some of her disaffections with Teutonic ways were in part rooted in the idiosyncrasies not of German, but of typically Western modes of socialization" (1994, 308). It is important to note that Fleischmann's book, with its "highly emotional outcries and the occasionally blanket statements," is as much an autobiographical account as it is a polemic "that hit a raw nerve in Germany because of its frontal assault on the German self-image" (313). By the same token, articulating the specificity of Jewish experience, Fleischmann proves the continuity of Jewish life in Germany (Fleischmann 1994, 309). Her voice is that of only one individual who, critical of her parents' decisions and disenchanted with the German Left, decides to leave, while other Jews will stay. Later, in *Gas: Tagebuch einer Bedrohung: Israel während des Golfkrieges* (1991), Fleischmann articulates her emotions and concerns as an Israeli woman, but her language of publication remains German.

The dissatisfaction about Germany expressed in *Dies ist nicht mein Land* resembles the sentiments of the poet and prose writer Ronnith Neumann, the daughter of German-Jewish refugees, who has no intention of leaving Germany. Her novel, *Heimkehr in die Fremde,* expresses the threefold desire of overcoming her longing for Israel, where she lived until she was ten years old, of confronting the old familiar sites and her acquaintances, and of reaching a more positive evaluation of Germany, which, in fact, she does. She resolves to live in Germany with the long-term goal of fighting nationalism and ethnic strife and working for world peace and environmental issues.

Neumann was born in Haifa in 1948. At the age of ten, she was forced to leave Israel by her family's return to Germany. In her examination of her German existence, threatened by xenophobes, anti-Semites, and neo-Nazis, Neumann reveals the barriers faced by a Jewish woman in Germany—her circle of friends consists of exceptional people (1985, 51). It is obvious that Neumann feels completely comfortable in neither country (55). Twenty years later, Neumann visited Israel and, like Fleischmann, recorded her impressions in an autobiographical narrative. *Heimkehr in die Fremde* is an affirmation of the tradition of the *Galut* and the German-Jewish experience before and after the Shoah. The motto preceding Neumann's account, "My soul is, I believe, many thousand years old," implies the immutability and continuity that German-Jewish writers have often ascribed to the Jewish people.[8]

228

The references to Queen Esther preceding the main text and the poetry about the murder of her grandparents at the center establish Neumann's link to Jewish history, ancient and modern (31–35). The Holocaust, exile, the Bible, and Ashkenazic culture form the basis for her search for identity, first conceived as a dual self, Israeli and German. With these elements as her point of departure, Neumann situates herself within Jewish post-Shoah reality. From there, she branches out into other areas, including ecology. Her narrative *Nirs Stadt* (1991), published after German unification, blends Holocaust themes with impressions of impending global depopulation and destruction.

Like Fleischmann's first-person narrator, Neumann's persona in *Heimkehr in die Fremde* represents the author's point of view, but in a circular, rather than a teleological, fashion. Chance and victimization, rather than decision making, are key elements in Neumann's text: her grandfather fails to establish himself in Palestine; alienated by life in the Middle East, he causes his entire family and their Israeli-born daughter to move to Germany, only to experience further turmoil. Like Fleischmann, Neumann emphasizes the older generation's struggle to come to terms with their distrust of Germany and the Germans, as well as her own difficulties with her German schoolmates (1985, 36–37). To a certain degree, Neumann acculturates herself, although she never gives up some Israeli habits that make her seem odd in Germany. Conversely, she notices her alienation from Israel upon her return to Haifa. She perceives the people and places of her childhood through the eyes of an adult tourist, and it takes her a while to uncover the person she might have been, had she never left. Then she explores her alternate self in a love affair with an Israeli man of a background similar to hers. In contrast to Fleischmann's *Ich bin Israelin,* where such a relationship leads to marriage and even stronger ties to Israel, Neumann's narrator leaves with the certainty that in spite of her deterritorialization her place is in Germany.

The wavering between the cultures creates an anxiety that is reinforced by other narrative patterns—the seemingly unrelated, associative segments of *Heimkehr in die Fremde* reflect the protagonist's state of fragmentation; each of the isolated narrative units examines one particular concept. The overall plot proceeds chronologically and causes the images relating to the various themes to collide, as the narrative voice travels between Germany and Israel, past and present. Oral history, Jewish tradition, survivors' accounts, and Holocaust literature merge into a web tied together by reflections on the Holocaust debates since the Eichmann trial as well as on more recent discussions about Jewish identity. Neumann, outraged at the self-exoneration of former Nazis and contemptuous of the German discourse on *Vergangenheitsbewältigung* (coping with the past) and *Trauerarbeit* (labor of mourning), assumes nonetheless a position that allows her to live in Germany (85).[9]

Fleischmann ventured out into German society when she was approaching maturity. She had been prepared for conflict by her Jewish community, which had provided her with a distinct sense of identity. Neumann, on the other hand, socialized on the fringes of the German mainstream and was plagued by feelings of inferiority (1985, 61–62). While Fleischmann perceived the Germans as different, Neumann internalized the perspective of the German majority. To be sure, she mentions a few Gentiles who helped her overcome her self-loathing, among them the daughter of former Nazis, who came to live with Neumann's family. The latter episode is momentous for the narrator's psychic healing (81–83). Not surprisingly, no similar experience is mentioned by Fleischmann, whose negative encounters with German Gentiles confirm her mother's uncompromising assessment: "These are no democrats. They are little, miserable subordinates, and the most ridiculous and downtrodden among them were the greatest slaughterers and, if ordered, they would slaughter again" (1980, 246).

Both Fleischmann and Neumann visualize a childhood prior to the Holocaust, but their visions could not be any more different: Neumann describes a nightmare in which blond Vikings in brown uniforms, ss men, and their dogs pursue her. The words *concentration camp, Auschwitz,* and *gas chamber* have already extinguished the images of a serene family life when she awakens (1985, 58). Moreover, her dreams elicit uneasy questions: Would she have defended herself or gone to the slaughter like a lamb, as the Jews were said to have done in accounts that accuse them of lethargy? Such questions were, in fact, asked by critics such as Bruno Bettelheim in "The Ignored Lesson of Anne Frank" (1979, 246–57). Fleischmann's portrayal of Jews and Jewish culture is free of such reproaches—there is neither self-hatred nor the tendency to identify with the aggressor. Instead, the narrator admires the Jewish parents' dignity and their concern for their child, as they prepare for their own death (1980, 13–17).

Neumann has no appreciation for the quiet steadfastness of pious

Jews. Rather, she blames them for their supposed fatalism and criticizes the failure of apolitical and conservative Jews to take up arms and defend themselves. The socialist resistance fighter David Levin provides her with a positively configured symbol of a modern Jew: he survives, but his passive co-religionists die in Auschwitz (1985, 60). The Levin episode, with its implied blaming of the victims, and the correlation between survival and the correct political conviction reveal strong leftist influences on Neumann, as well as inner inconsistencies: the concept of the socialist fighter is no less incongruous with Neumann's radical pacifism and the Green Party perspective from which she criticizes Zionism and the Israeli military.[10] Precisely because of her inability to integrate her theoretical knowledge into her emotional economy, Neumann's protagonist fails to achieve an inner balance. She lacks Fleischmann's self-assurance as well as the defiantly experimental "wait-and-see" attitude championed by Nadja Seelich and Ruth Beckermann.

Neumann's decision to return to Germany rests upon an ecological perspective transcending national boundaries as well as the dichotomy of German and Jew. By way of prioritizing environmental problems, Neumann develops a global perspective that enables her to relativize the Middle Eastern conflict as well. Under the auspices of her apocalyptic world view, the Arab-Israeli conflict appears minor, but Israel is configured as a demonic Western power (85–87). Moreover, from a microperspective focused on Israel, the Jewish State with its multitude of languages has the appearance of a modern Babylon (87)—Neumann had apparently hoped to find the Garden of Eden of her childhood (7). Irritated by Israeli bureaucracy and the harshness of daily life, she finds Israel no less annoying than Fleischmann did Germany. Together with her old friends, Neumann enjoys Israeli country living, which is also eulogized in Alice Schwarz-Gardos's *Hügel des Frühlings* (1984, 359–61). At the same time, however, Neumann's narrator is painfully aware of the fact that her friends' peaceful home environment is bought at the price of war, of which armed soldiers are a constant reminder. Through her images of aggression, particularly the leitmotif of the machine gun, Neumann correlates Israel and Germany.

Without considering Israel's complex position in the Middle East, Neumann casts it as the epicenter of aggression. She does so by revealing disagreements between Israeli civilians and the military, Israel and her neighboring countries, Israelis and German-identified Jews. Her most important theme, however, is the threat to the integrity of the Holy Land posed by technology. In this context, Israel embodies Western civilization amidst lesser-developed countries. From such an ahistorical perspective, Germany seems the lesser of both evils. Contributing to the narrator's preference for Germany is the fact that in Israel she is treated as an outsider and forced to acknowledge her German identity, to which Israelis and American Jews react with suspicion (39). By the same token, she is unable to accept inclusion: she is offended by the consensus implied in the collective "we" of Zionist discourse. Opposed to militant secular Judaism, she confronts it in the language of religion. In a prophetic voice, Neumann proclaims the problems of her world: "When will the Messiah come? When the sheep graze side by side with the wolf? When Christians graze side by side with Jews, Moslems, the Greek-Orthodox, and Buddhists? When the East grazes side by side with the West? When all of us fly together through the universe into the infinity of your arms? God, your Messiah had better hurry, if he wants to have sheep graze side by side while the wolf is still in this world" (11–12). The authority Neumann arrogates as a woman and her use of blasphemy constitute transgressions against traditional religious discourse and a direct assault on the perceptions of most Israelis.

In the summary of her own development from a believer in Israel's responsibility to fight for her rights into a pacifist, Neumann combines her contempt for militant nationalism with a green agenda: she discusses the ecological impact of war and suggests connections between armed conflict and real estate speculation. In both cases, she identifies personal gain as the primary motive. Furthermore, she explores the drive to kill and dominate, differentiating between human and animal violence—deliberate and instinctual killing—of which her vindication of the snake is a vivid example. Her arguments echo some of the basic assumptions of Eastern teachings, the *Bhagavad-Gita,* for example: "An animal can kill without sin because he is bound by the modes of nature. But if a man kills he is responsible" (xxxi). Like Elias Canetti and Gertrud Kolmar, Neumann considers the desire for willful destruction and the construction of an entire killing machinery an exclusively human trait (1985, 26). According to her, these basic instincts are the cause of racism, anti-Semitism, the destruction of animals, the extinction of species, war, and genocide.

Avoiding oversimplifications such as the ones that occasionally flaw the works of Lander and Weil, Neumann is cognizant of the complexity of Jewish life in Israel, including alternative lifestyles. She portrays life in the city, in the country, and on a kibbutz, taking Israel's multiethnicity into consideration (37). More radical than other authors interested in animal rights or ecological issues, Neumann's criticism of education and development is diametrically opposed to the views of Schwarz-Gardos, for example, who expresses delight about the progress that an Israeli delegation brings to underdeveloped parts of the country (Schwarz-Gardos 1991, 146).

Neumann's rejection of patriarchal structures embedded in Judaism manifests itself at the holiest of places, Mount Sinai, through her criticism of the Jewish religion (93). Influenced, in all probability, by Buddhist or Hindu thought, she focuses on the commandment not to kill and makes it her ultimate criterion for determining the merit of individuals or entire cultures. Judged by this standard, her lover, an Israeli soldier, does not measure up.[11] As a contrast figure, Neumann introduces a German man, the son of a Nazi lawyer, committed to the same principles she upholds. Regardless of their history, tradition, or gender, she alleges, their mutual desire for peace and their pacifist, environmentalist mission make them citizens of the world.

Neumann ultimately opts for an association of like-minded individuals trying to transcend their culture and history. Her adherence to an individualistic, cosmopolitan paradigm stands in direct contrast to Fleischmann's and Honigmann's decision to place themselves into a specifically Jewish communal context. Neumann, trying to maintain her cross-cultural identity, is unable to commit herself to one specific nation; instead she assumes the role of an intercultural ambassador and mediator.

Geography and History (Ruth Beckermann)

In the works of the Viennese journalist and filmmaker Ruth Beckermann, history and geography converge, as she ties Jewish identity and Jewish memory to specific locations: Vienna, Czernowitz, and Jerusalem. Both her texts and her films, where she occasionally appears, are gendered in an unobtrusive way. In the films *Wien Retour* (1983), *Die papierene Brücke* (1987), and *Nach Jerusalem* (1990), as well as the autobiographical culture-critical study *Unzugehörig: Österreicher und Juden nach 1945* (1989), Beckermann situates herself within the larger context of Central European Jewish history, thereby implying the continuity of pre-Shoah Jewish culture in Vienna, represented by Friedrich Torberg, Joseph Roth, and other Jewish intellectuals of the interwar period as her source of inspiration. Until 1938, Vienna had been a center of secular and religious Jewish culture, and Austria's cultural achievements would have been unthinkable without Jewish authors, artists, philosophers, doctors, and scientists. The Vienna in which Beckermann grew up was, as Hugo Bettauer had predicted in his satirical novel of 1925, a "city without Jews" (*Die Stadt ohne Juden* [1988]). The international debates about the Shoah and the destruction of Ashkenazic culture avoided dealing with Jews who, like Beckermann's parents, took up residence in German-speaking countries. Their decision was considered politically incorrect by the Jewish public worldwide; conversely, their unwillingness to assimilate incurred the disapproval of the Austrian establishment.[12] According to the official verdict on both sides, Jewish life in Austria after the Holocaust was impossible and indefensible.

When in 1945 the first services were held at the City Temple, Vienna was considered a transit station for emigrants to Israel or the United States. Until 1938, approximately two hundred thousand Jews had resided in Vienna, a city with twenty synagogues, one hundred prayer houses, and Jewish schools, seminars, and newspapers. The *Israelitische Kultusgemeinde Wien* had been one of the largest and most heterogeneous in the world. Only approximately five thousand Viennese Jews survived the Holocaust. The majority of the Jews who settled in postwar Vienna were East Europeans.

Ruth Beckermann was born in Vienna in 1952, the daughter of a businessman from Czernowitz and his wife, a Viennese woman, who had fled to Palestine, served in the Israeli army, and did not intend to return to Austria prior to her marriage. Although some prominent Jewish intellectuals and artists lived in Vienna, a Jewish *renouveau* was out of the question. The majority of exiles did not return; nor did the Austrian government invite them back. Jewish writers who assumed a specifically Jewish point of view were met with hostility. In the 1980s, a debate about Austria's participation in the genocide began, which sparked interest in Jewish topics. Literary works on Jews and Jewish history continued this trend from the early 1980s into the 1990s, including Brigitte Schwaiger and Eva Deutsch, *Die Galizianerin* (1982); Peter

Henisch, *Steins Paranoia* (1988); Robert Schindel, *Gebürtig* (1992); and Renate Welsh's 1994 work *Das Lufthaus.* Until then, Beckermann states, it was impossible to talk openly about the Nazi crimes and the continued injustice perpetrated against Jews in Austria. "Prior to that time, one had arranged oneself with the outside world, each one in his or her own way" (1989, 121). Many Jews of the postwar generation wanted to live in Austria without being absorbed into the mainstream. They positioned themselves outside of Austria's traditionally Catholic culture and distanced themselves from the conservative Jewish religious community. They searched for an alternative to Zionism, religious Judaism, and assimilation. Without the inner torment and indecision evident from Neumann's work, Beckermann traces the quest for a secular Jewish existence in a paradigmatic fashion.

In *Die Mazzesinsel: Juden in der Wiener Leopoldstadt* (1984), Beckermann reviewed Vienna's Jewish past by presenting historical photographs and texts. The Leopoldstadt, the site of the second Viennese ghetto until the expulsion of 1670 and home to Jewish refugees from the pogroms of turn-of-the-century Russia, is the focal site of this photodocumentary that reconstructs Jewish history and creates intellectual and emotional spaces for contemporary Jewish readers. The text selections by twentieth-century Jewish authors open up a spectrum of Vienna's Jewish life, demonstrating that this city had been a site for assimilated and religious Jews, the "transformed" and the "untransformed" (1989, 124). Beckermann explores this panorama with an eye on the past, but also to test the potential this past may have for the future.

The feature film *Wien Retour* (1983) explores Vienna's Jewish history in more specific terms. Embedded in the interview with the antifascist Franz Weintraub/West are images from socialist, "red" Vienna of the 1920s. Weintraub/West's own fate, his exile in England, his return to Vienna, his work with the Austrian communist paper *Die Volksstimme,* and his protest against the Communist Party's endorsement of the Soviet invasion of Prague are configured both as a testimony and as a model for a European secular Jewish existence. Set in Vienna's Second District, a center of immigration during the interwar era, *Wien Retour* establishes a link to Austrian Jewish culture and works such as Veza Canetti's *Die gelbe Straße,* as well as to the Shoah. Departing from the collection site at the Aspangbahnhof, the transports to the death camps left Vienna via the North Station, traversing the Second District. Beckermann and Josef Aichholzer, her collaborator since 1977, reveal these contexts in *Wien Retour* through the account of their interviewee, supported by original historical footage. Under discussion are the burning of the Palace of Justice in 1927, which, marking the end of an era, is the key event for the developments leading up to the Holocaust, the destruction of the organized antifascist opposition, the conservative revolution of the Catholic regime, and the Nazi takeover.

The major coordinates in *Wien Retour* are geography and history. When the film opens, the camera, situated on a train, approaches Vienna from the North East until it stops at the North Station. Then the frames alternate between Weintraub/West's narrative and this neighborhood; his apartment and historical photographs and film footage, until the film ends at a modern Viennese subway station on the Danube Canal opposite the Second District. The switch from the larger train to the local transit system suggests a narrower scope and the provincialization of a once cosmopolitan city, but the direction is still the same. The subway also moves toward the West, suggesting both the increasing hegemony of the Western powers, relegating Vienna to the status of a local transit station, and the direction of the traditional escape route for Jews: coming from or via Vienna, they traveled West. Some, like Roth, Celan, and Améry, went to Paris; others continued on to England or the United States. Beckermann herself followed this direction by studying in New York in 1975–76 and commuting between Vienna and Paris in the 1980s and 1990s. As the train gains speed, Weintraub/West reads, as if it were a *Kaddish,* the names of his expelled and murdered relatives.

Beckermann's film *Die papierene Brücke* (1987) involves a quest for the lost culture of the filmmaker's father in Eastern Europe. Having considered Israel, her mother's safe haven, never more than a summer vacation site and study site, Beckermann accords it a few flat images and sound bytes in her film. In contrast, Romania possesses an aura of mystery, conveyed in images of seemingly endless, foggy country roads. Czernowitz, Beckermann's destination, is never reached, because the Iron Curtain has not yet opened, but her father, Salo Beckermann, speaking with nostalgia and the highest praise in an interview included in the film about his former home city, transforms it in his daughter's and the viewer's imagination into a mythical site. Although the filmmaker

236

knows better, she and her viewers expect to find nothing short of a lost paradise.

The beginning of *Die papierene Brücke* resumes the melancholy ambiance with which *Wien Retour* ends. The setting of one of the first frames is the attic of an old house in the process of redecoration, the actual location of Beckermann's apartment in a formerly predominantly Jewish inner-city district close to the first ghetto—Beckermann situates herself, quite literally, within Vienna's Jewish past. The renovation implies that tradition is preserved but also adapted to the needs of a modern Jewish woman, signaling a Jewish future. While the tools lying around suggest activity, the feeling of inwardness implies that the past must be overcome psychologically. Much like the view from the moving train in *Wien Retour,* the panorama in *Die papierene Brücke* from an attic window, draped with a light curtain, reveals only contours, while the narrator tells a story of hope and trust. In a German context, the main symbol of the short narrative, a bridge made of cigarette paper, seems oddly unlyrical, but it is consistent with the Yiddish folk tradition. The veil before the attic window and the cat sitting on the sill gender the space as feminine and evoke the secrecy of the occult, witches, and witch-hunts, while the voice-over articulates the experience of an invisible Jewish woman living in the center of Austria's capital. In addition, the following trolley car ride around Vienna's Ringstraße in actual time, replete with images of average Austrians, filmed in such a way as to appear grotesque, suggests the narrator's longing for a time, a place, and a language that, if they still existed, she could call hers. Her alienation motivates the following quest for the Jewish past in Eastern Europe.

The opening image of a plane in foggy weather with only the red warning lights visible and the accompanying noises of a shortwave radio connote adventure, mystery, and hope, whereas the actual journey ends in a wasteland. The explorer, Beckermann, at times in full view, finds only fragments of the past: communities at the verge of extinction— those who have the strength, leave—an ancient *mikve,* turned into a steam bath for local farm women, abandoned cemeteries and, on the other side of the border, in Yugoslavia, an artificial Theresienstadt, built especially for Herman Wouk's monumental television series *War and Remembrance.* Beckermann interviews the extras of the filmic venture, Viennese Jews from all over Europe, Israel, and the United States. They debate about Jewishness, the appropriate place for a Jew to live, Zionism, and tradition. In between the at-times feverish discussions empty spaces emerge: muddy roads lined with trees, a primitive cart drawn by a horse, ice drifting on the river Drina, the clouds in a low sky, and, symbolizing the dying Jewish communities, the half-cut tree without foliage and branches.

These images communicate why Beckermann decided in favor of Vienna, apart from the love for her home city, which she expresses early in the film, characterizing Vienna as the place where she is "at home like nowhere else, and where I know every stone." She lacks a deeper affinity for Israel, and Eastern Europe, the graveyard of Ashkenazic Jewry, does not offer her any alternative. For this reason she opts for Vienna, in spite of its continued anti-Semitism, of which the attacks on Jews by Waldheim followers are but one example. One segment of the film, shot with a video camera, shows a demonstration at St. Stephan's Square. Shortly before Ruth Beckermann's camera is smashed by angry Austrians trying to avoid having this scene documented, Salo Beckermann is shown as insults are being hurled against him. In one of the stories in his collection *Papirnik,* Doron Rabinovici alludes to the same incident (1994, 60–73).

Unzugehörig, based on Beckermann's childhood memories, discusses the author's position in more theoretical terms. Beckermann defines herself as a "miracle child" of the 1950s, stating that every Jewish child in postwar Vienna was a miracle, hence the links among contemporary Jewish authors in Vienna, such as Beckermann, Seelich, Schindel, Menasse, and Rabinovici. Rather than attempting to provide a rational explanation as to why her parents established themselves in post-Shoah Austria, Beckermann demonstrates that she herself faces life in Vienna without any illusions about the past or the present. Unlike Jewish intellectuals of previous generations, including Hans Weigel and Friedrich Torberg, she casts herself neither as a victim nor a cultural mediator: "The children of the survivors do not want to be silent any longer, nor do they want to enter into debates with anti-Semites or plead for compassion," she writes (1989, 10–11).

Reflecting a different historical and different cultural situation, *Unzugehörig* conveys even a bleaker picture than Lea Fleischmann's *Dies ist nicht mein Land* ten years earlier. Beckermann, in her attempt to cope with her and her parents' life, "here, after all the atrocities these people have perpetrated," confronts her own inability to separate herself from

Vienna in light of that "boundless Jewish sentimentality" that caused many Austrian Jews to conceptualize the Nazis as German and to exonerate the Austrians (39). Beckermann, in contrast, has only criticism for the country whose former National Socialists, such as Kurt Waldheim, made such a smooth transition to postwar democracy.

The silence of former Nazis has been the topic of many critical studies; not so the silence of Jewish survivors. Beckermann writes that although she and her peers observed the effects of the past in their parents' and older relatives' mannerisms, there was never an in-depth discussion (120). She remembers living in a dual reality, forbidden to mention family matters or her Jewish identity outside of the family circle: "We even changed our language," she writes. By the same token, any attempt to share Holocaust accounts she had heard in the "outside world" was frustrated by the Austrians' refusal to listen (118). Hence, Beckermann felt a similar isolation as Lea Fleischmann, and it led her to rebel against her parents' secluded life in a community of survivors. Like Fleischmann, she disappointed her family's expectations by not marrying a Jewish man and starting a large family and by not choosing an academic career (104–5). In the 1960s, she writes, she was almost convinced that the alliance between Jewish intellectuals and the Left could bring about an understanding between young Jews and non-Jews (121). Realizing that the anti-Zionism of the Left was an ill-concealed anti-Semitism, Beckermann, like Neumann, Fleischmann, and Lander, came to the conclusion that the views of the children of Holocaust survivors and those of the rebellious Nazi children were irreconcilable.[13]

Focusing on the monument of Alfred Hrdlicka commemorating the fiftieth anniversary of Austria's annexation, Beckermann illustrates the rift between herself and "the Austrians." According to her, the monument, located at the Albertinaplatz in Vienna,

accommodates the opinion of all those who unthinkingly balance victim against victim: the victims of war against the victims of National Socialism—Jews, Gypsies, homosexuals, mentally disabled persons. . . . Whatever this monument is intended to tell the people of Vienna, it tells me: you lay in the dust. You crawled on your belly. And this is our image of you today. Fifty years after the fact we form you in this image. As a pious old man. That touches the heart and places the victims at a comfortable distance; it suggests that the Jews were a senile, wretched old people, whose natural death was imminent (14).

Denouncing the hypocrisy of the inscriptions on Hrdlicka's monuments, which in retrospect ascribe a higher meaning to the extermination of the Jews, Beckermann refutes the notion that the Jews gave their lives for the liberation from Nazism or for the sake of the Second Republic. "Their death made no sense at all," she states emphatically (13–16).

Seeing herself from a dual perspective, from her own Jewish point of view and that of the Gentiles, Beckermann relates to her environment and herself with ambivalence. Much like Fleischmann, she is used to measuring herself by the degree of integration she has achieved and by the impression her parents make on Gentiles.[14] Yet, both authors' self-conscious attitude must not be mistaken for Jewish self-hatred. Both authors distance themselves from Jews who disavow their identity, and Beckermann has nothing but contempt for anti-Semites, including Jewish anti-Zionists. Her objections to using the term *Jew* as a metaphor for any oppressed minority and the globalization of events pertaining to Jews seem directed at Erich Fried, a Viennese Jewish exile in England who, embracing a Marxist point of view, made himself the spokesperson of the Palestinians. "The Blacks in South Africa, the trees, the women, became Jews, but most of all, the Palestinians. They became the Jews of the Jews," Beckermann comments (125).

Transforming the images, visual and aural, of *Die papierene Brücke* into critical prose, *Unzugehörig* conveys the same message as the film, albeit in a different medium. With its extended silences, the film is sensual and lyrical, whereas the prose text shows Beckermann as an astute critic. Similar to Lea Fleischmann and the filmmaker Nadja Seelich, who drew criticism both from the Jewish and non-Jewish public for exposing uncomfortable facts, Beckermann also faced disapproval. One review of *Die Mazzesinsel* and *Die papierene Brücke* does not even mention *Unzugehörig* and attacks Beckermann for her critical views on Israeli politics (Reischer 1990).

In 1990, Beckermann completed the film *Nach Jerusalem*, which she considers the last part of her trilogy on Jewish identity and geography.[15] Like *Wien Retour* and *Die papierene Brücke*, *Nach Jerusalem* is a filmic travelogue. The "century-old longing FOR JERUSALEM," as it says in the brochure, collides with images of contemporary life in Israel among

East European immigrants, cab drivers, and soldiers. Beckermann's film, eminently secular, full, and fast, deconstructs in only 121 frames and twenty-three individual stories the dream of the Jewish State by exploring the unrealistic expectations associated with the Holy City and the Holy Land. In order to capture the stress to which Israel's multicultural population is exposed, Beckermann filmed the highway from Tel Aviv to Jerusalem. The sounds of airplanes and car engines, of excited, angry voices and gunshots, suggest psychological and social tensions at the center of which lies Jerusalem. So do the fragmentary plotlines, the disjointed scenery, and the statements made by individuals at the roadside end at the city walls—the camera never enters into the Old City. In conjunction with the chaos and randomness, the inability to gain access to Jerusalem represents a comment on Zionism; it succeeded insofar as the Jewish State was founded at all, but it fell short of its high-minded ideals. Indeed, a variety of images suggest that the Zionist dream was impossible to realize: Israel, with its Arab workforce, its diverse Jewish population, strongly defined by Western culture, is not a Jewish State.

Instead of letting the known attractions for tourists and pilgrims pass review, Beckermann shows images of Arab workers who, like the foreign workers in Austria and Germany, perform menial labor. Much like in Neumann's *Heimkehr in die Fremde, Nach Jerusalem* exposes injustice, guilt, and the daily threat of terrorism. Only in the end does religion come into focus, in conjunction with a group of Hasids wandering about in the midst of tourist buses. Here, rather than at the Western Wall, a Jewish religious leader speaks to Beckermann and her camerawoman. His message, almost drowned out by the background noise, is the last one heard, but it seems irrelevant and anachronistic in light of the unmanageable reality.

Traveling is a vehicle to create different moods in all of Beckermann's films. The external movement opens up inner spaces in which multiple alternative identities unfold and allow Beckermann's films and her prose to move between the established genres. Clearly, her work belongs in the international context of postmodern literature and film. In an era of increased nationalism and ethnic and religious strife, Beckermann's secular outlook, derived from the history of Central and Eastern European socialism, reflects the experience of a generation deeply affected by their parents' pasts. Simultaneously attracted to and repulsed by the countries that her parents had to leave, Beckermann's ongoing search for stability is an indication of a persistent feeling of transience.

Notwithstanding Austria's sinister past, which Beckermann explores in a film project occasioned by an exhibition on the atrocities committed by the *Wehrmacht,* the regular German military, she does not view Israel as a viable alternative to Austria (Blümlinger 1991). In fact, Beckermann's observations in *Nach Jerusalem,* which was filmed a few months before the outbreak of the Gulf War, are confirmed to a certain degree in Fleischmann's diary of the war, *Gas: Tagebuch einer Bedrohung,* an indictment of the international warmongers and a cry for help for the Jews of Israel. In Beckermann's opinion, Israel offers no substitute for the lost community into which she would have been born, had there been no genocide.

As is the case with Fleischmann, Beckermann's work ultimately relates to the lost Ashkenazic motherland whose memory continues to provide her with creative impulses. For Beckermann, it is Vienna, the city of Jewish intellectuals such as Weintraub/West, Friedrich Torberg, and Hans Thalberg, that provides her with her role models. At the same time, *Wien Retour* and *Die papierene Brücke* reveal that Vienna is an impossible space for Jews of the post-Holocaust generation.[16] *Nach Jerusalem* returns to Beckermann's point of departure: after her journey to Jerusalem, Beckermann is, once again, thrown back upon Vienna. Having experienced Israel as a country at the point of breaking apart, she doubts that the efforts to create a safe and harmonious Jewish state will succeed. More important, however, is the realization that the spirituality that Jerusalem represents can be approached only in the manner of the Hasids, which excludes Beckermann, a modern Jew and a woman. Rather than the imminent coming of the Messiah, she notices only fragments, chaos, and conflict.

Although Beckermann has lived in Paris for several years, Vienna remains the site of her intellectual involvement. Ideologically, she is closest to the Austrian intellectuals who, like Roth, Zweig, and Spiel, were the most Austrian the farther they were removed from Austria. Like these authors, Beckermann states no irreversible positions but allows for change in her attitudes as well her texts. "There is, in fact, no narrative where the question: how did it continue is not justified," writes Walter Benjamin, distinguishing between narrator and novelist (1974, 453). Asking such questions about the development and the expansion of ideas and images is an appropriate approach to Beckermann's work and the quest it documents. For Beckermann, finding a space means moving away from it.

A Jewish Woman between Frontlines (Anna Mitgutsch)

In the works of the critic and author Waltraud Anna Mitgutsch, a Ph.D. in literature, different kinds of marginality converge, indicative of the author's multilayered identity and her exposure to different languages. Mitgutsch was born in 1948 in Upper Austria to a family of Austrian and Jewish background and, like Ilse Aichinger and Cordelia Edvardson, raised Catholic. Her recent conversion to Judaism is the external expression of her identification with her grandmother's legacy, as is her decision to abandon her German-sounding Christian name Waltraud. Similar to Aichinger's and Edvardson's works, Mitgutsch's texts reveal ambivalence and seemingly mutually exclusive allegiances, the root cause of which is the dissimilation process beginning in the Nazi era.

In her last and most complex novel, *Abschied von Jerusalem* (1995), set in Jerusalem during the *Intifada,* this multidiscursive city—with distinct yet permeable neighborhoods and diverse ethnic and religious groups— is the emblem of the biographical and psychological confusion of the protagonist/narrator Hildegard. Her newly assumed name Dvorah expresses her desire to be Jewish and her intention to make a clean start. She is, however, unable to elude the history of her country of origin, her family history, and her own past. Influenced by the silences in the home of her Jewish grandmother and her Christian grandfather, who never articulated the difference between Jews and Christians (69–70), on the one hand, and by the explicit racism of her father's relatives (72) on the other hand, Hildegard/Dvorah lives in a state of alienation, unable to trust her intuitions. Her insecurity regarding her background—she even doubts her mother's identity—and her ambiguous status in Israel cloud her perceptions even further. Superficially conversant in several languages, she is an outsider to all the groups with which she comes into contact, unable to decode their cultural signals in their proper context (116). For lack of a reliable instrument to gauge reality, Dvorah makes her body and her feelings the touchstone of authenticity, but this seemingly direct approach to her environment does not help her to understand the processes into which she becomes implicated. In contrast to Aichinger's

Die größere Hoffnung, where random encounters and a strictly empirical approach to reality lead to the protagonist's individuation, isolation and panic are at the end of Hildegard/Dvorah's experiment. Isolated in an interrogation room while waiting to be questioned by Israeli security officers, Mitgutsch's protagonist—who claims to be Jewish despite her mixed ancestry and her Catholic upbringing, who has only an imperfect command of Ivrit, and who placed herself between enemy lines, having become involved with an Arab—symbolizes the cultural and linguistic deterritorialization of the descendants of European Jews in the post-Holocaust era.[17] The earlier observations about Jewish women's geography also apply to Mitgutsch, who spent extended periods of time in Israel, England, Korea, and the United States. From 1979 to 1985, she taught German language and literature in Boston. She returned to live in Linz, Austria, the same year in which her first major novel, *Die Züchtigung* (1985) was published. Her subsequent work includes the novels *Das andere Leben* (1986), *Ausgrenzung* (1989), and *In fremden Städten* (1994).

Abschied von Jerusalem depicts marginality and exclusion from a woman's point of view in all the major groups present in Jerusalem: Jews, Europeans, Arabs, Armenians. Mitgutsch's perspective reflects the author's personal observations and is influenced by the feminist discourses of the last few decades. Because of her interest in and experience with mental illness, disability, physical and emotional abuse, and cultures in contact, women's issues, although important in Mitgutsch's work, are portrayed in a wider context, and she has occasionally been criticized for reproducing traditional women's images (e.g., Gerhards 1986). Until recently, the Jewish perspective played only a minor role in her work. Maria-Regina Kecht's interview with the author, as well as her perceptive article about Mitgutsch's attitude toward women's problems, issues of alienation, women's language, and women's silence, does not address Jewish themes (Kecht 1992a and 1992b). Before the publication of *Abschied von Jerusalem,* Mitgutsch used her female and male characters of diverse backgrounds to explore the situation of women and to question the boundaries of patriarchal and ethnocentric structures. Like Hannah Stern in Seelich's film *Kieselsteine* (1982), Mitgutsch's female narrators and protagonists are too detached from the society in which they live to conform to its basic rules and values.

In *Abschied von Jerusalem,* identity in terms of gender, nationality, and religion is the central issue. These three concerns are entwined, revealing the linkage between the discourses of masculinity and femininity, national power and weakness, friend and enemy. Already in Mitgutsch's earlier works, problems of gender were not played out in binary oppositions. *In fremden Städten* concentrates on other related problems, modifying and expanding the discourse of power associated with gender. Occasionally, Mitgutsch discusses the issues of power and dominance among women, such as in *Die Züchtigung,* a novel about three generations of women in a dysfunctional, abusive family situation, grandmother, mother, and daughter.[18] In *Abschied von Jerusalem,* she explores power and dominance among women of different ethnic backgrounds.

Mitgutsch writes about socially sanctioned emotional and physical abuse as explicitly as does Elfriede Jelinek in *Die Klavierspielerin* (1983), which portrays a destructive mother-daughter relationship. Moreover, Mitgutsch's literary universe is similar to that of numerous other Jewish women writers in that it is predominantly female. In her second novel, *Das andere Leben,* she prioritizes relationships among women over heterosexual or all-male allegiances. Compared to the symbiotic relationship between two women protagonists, with one protecting the other, the involvement of both characters with the same man is little more than a catalyst for the women's interaction. An even closer symbiosis is that between mother and child, as in *Ausgrenzung,* a novel inspired by the author's experience with her own son. Indicting the intolerance of those considered normal, the work shows the increasing isolation of the two protagonists, mother and child. The patterns that emerge in Mitgutsch's earlier novels remain characteristic also of her later work: broken relationships, solitude, exclusive one-on-one relationships of deceptive intensity, the ultimate strangeness between the partners—lovers, couples, and mother and child.

In light of her latest novel, the Jewish subtext of Mitgutsch's entire work becomes apparent. In the complex cosmopolitan settings of her last two novels, *In fremden Städten* and *Abschied von Jerusalem,* themes of her earlier works are resumed and transposed into new contexts, including different geographical settings. Similar to Jeanette Lander in *Auf dem Boden der Fremde* (1972), whose Jewish protagonist marries a German man, Mitgutsch situates the protagonist of *In fremden Städten* between two geographic and cultural spheres, Austria and the United States. She does not identify with Austria, having left it because of its narrow confines in the hope for freedom and romantic fulfillment, or with the United States, from which she eventually returns, disillusioned by the prevailing puritanical and materialistic attitudes. Karl-Markus Gauß suggests that if there is any home for Mitgutsch's protagonist, it is the Austrian-German language (1992, 89–91), but not even her native language prevents the bicultural protagonist from vacillating between past and present, Austria and the United States. "The rip in her life would remain; time would not heal it, she knew it. Two lives, neither one of them unreservedly hers, two languages, she had to look for herself in between. Two enemy camps each one of which made sense only in isolation" (Mitgutsch 1994, 9). Numerous statements express the protagonist's exclusion from the fold of her husband's family, from any fold at all: "You are the archetypal stranger," made by the protagonist's American husband (30); "You are a cosmopolitan," by an American woman (8); and the protagonist's observation that in her husband's family she has played the role of "a foreign woman whose major characteristic was her foreignness, who is always a little uncanny, never quite trustworthy enough for a personal, open and direct conversation" (18). Indeed, she confirms these notions by leaving her husband and her son.

Yet, in this text, and even more explicitly in *Abschied von Jerusalem,* correlations are established linking the protagonist to the unreachable sphere of her Bohemian grandmother, who is defined as Jewish. While the narrator's cultural identity beyond being Austrian is not made explicit *In fremden Städten,* her inability to settle down, to assimilate, and to acquiesce, as well as the repeated allusions to her foreignness, both in Austria and in the United States, seems to denote Jewishness. The disorientation of the protagonist in *Abschied von Jerusalem* is unequivocally linked to the Holocaust; during this period her grandmother had to conceal her Jewishness, but she attempts to return to Judaism on her deathbed, much to the dismay of her Christian in-laws (1995, 70). In addition, Mitgutsch establishes a connection between the Israeli-Arab conflict and the Holocaust, which neither the Arab Palestinians nor the German-speaking tourists in the novel are interested in investigating. Dvorah's former husband, Alwin, an Austrian Gentile and, as it becomes apparent during their trip to Israel, an anti-Semite, is only one example (135–38). "Only the injustice of the Jews in Palestine, the country they took supposedly illegally, released him from his oppressive ever-present feelings of guilt," the narrator comments (156).

Mitgutsch's protagonist comes under scrutiny in the course of her extended vacation in Israel, during which she interacts with individuals of diverse backgrounds. Unlike Alice Schwarz-Gardos's not necessarily hostile, but distanced, portrayal of Arabs and Arab culture—with a clear Western bias, she portrays them as part of the background scenery in *Versuchung in Nazareth* (Schwarz 1963) and *Die Abrechnung* (Schwarz 1962)—Mitgutsch portrays the representatives of all ethnic groups in equal terms. Dvorah's official acts of defining herself as a Jewish woman—after her divorce she joined the Jewish community in Austria—are undermined by her inability to stay within the confines of the Jewish sphere, quite literally, in geographical terms, but also in linguistic and ideological terms. Choosing to treat the indoctrination by her friends with skepticism, Dvorah moves naively all across Jerusalem, half a tourist, half an insider. By doing so, she transgresses against the rules of conduct pertaining to Jewish women. Ignorant of the codes of the different ethnic, religious, and political groups, she violates the norms guiding group interaction, but being a Jew and a European tourist, she enjoys the full support of the law; with the luck of a fool, she avoids serious clashes (95). All this changes when she enters into a sexual relationship with a man much her junior, an Armenian, as he claims, but equally likely an Arab, involved with the *Intifada* on the side of Fatah or Hamas. As his lover, Dvorah compromises her privileged status and is forced into an untenable position between the warring factions. She gradually comes to realize that she, like all Western women, is considered easy prey by the males of all groups (97). Being Jewish and a Western traveler are privileges that apply only to men and break down in a case such as hers. The graffiti in the Arab quarter spell out the power structures of patriarchy: "We fuck your women, they say as the ultimate humiliation of the enemy" (11).

Mitgutsch's protagonist, positioned between Austrian Jewish and Israeli history, proves incapable of matching her desires with her externally defined identity as a single, middle-aged woman traveler. Other women characters serve as a foil to make Dvorah's dilemma visible; Anahita, a businesswoman, left her family but lives in a convent to safeguard her reputation, and Nurit, "a rebellious, intelligent woman" (49), according to Dvorah, resides outside of the city and wears long black dresses because, as she says, "they despise women, also their own" (96). Although she refuses to live like a recluse or to conform to the "us-them" mentality of even her most open-minded Israeli friends, Dvorah is nevertheless incapable of preventing the view she has of herself from being affected by the reactions of others; their clichés, warnings, and prepossessions. Acting against their rules and her presumed status, no less a prison than it is a privilege, places her into a conflict that is aggravated by an unstated age and gender code. Dvorah knows that her friends, were they apprised of her romance, would consider her a traitor and a harlot. Her paranoia increases proportionately to the weakening of her rational capacities: "Did my crime simply consist in having fraternized with the enemy? Or in demanding what only men have the right to demand for themselves, namely, taking a summertime-lover twenty years my junior? Was this my actual offense, the provocation for which I had to be punished?" (92). In her discussion with a relatively liberal Israeli friend, Dvorah recognizes that she has discredited herself as a woman, a Jew, and a European, and she internalizes his condemnations: "Every bomb that tears apart an overcrowded bus may have been planted with my help, I may be accountable for anyone murdered through an act of terror. I have no reason to feel that I belong" (175).

The object of Dvorah's desires appears randomly selected, yet he is well suited to her in many respects, despite the cultural and age-related disparities. Like her, Sivan is a multilingual individual of many names and changing identities, a man of possibly mixed ancestry, who reveals little of himself and who seems as insincere about the relationship as Dvorah. Focusing on the doubts she has about him, she is not prepared for his declaration of love and the invitation to meet his family: "I imagined his parents, barely older than myself, his curious siblings and the horror: what do you want from this woman, who is she, perhaps they had already found a girl for him to marry, a young girl from their neighborhood, her face gentle and her eyes cast down" (203). The degree to which Dvorah herself is prejudiced becomes obvious when she rejects Sivan's plans for a life together in the United States or in Israel. Moreover, she dismisses the possibility of living among Arabs as preposterous.

In an episodic form, *Abschied von Jerusalem* reveals a continuum of prejudices and resentments of which the Nazi past is one aspect. The latter is kept alive all across the world, by Alwin and by the seemingly Americanized wife of the narrator's American host family, who still mourns her ss husband (177). Then there is the Palestinians' hatred of the Jews (205), whose historical connection to National Socialism Mitgutsch fails to explore. Dvorah negotiates between these fronts, concealing the fact that she was baptized and raised Catholic from her Jewish friends, her Jewishness from her Austrian friend Irene (117), and from all of them her involvement with Sivan.

Abschied von Jerusalem is open-ended, leaving it to the readers to imagine the outcome of Dvorah's interview with the Israeli authorities and to speculate if she will eventually establish a more fully integrated identity for herself. Moreover, the question arises if the postmodern fragmentation still allows for identity formation at all, Jewish or otherwise, or whether ethnicity and religion are not merely the markers of randomly chosen positions. Of all the categories scrutinized in Mitgutsch's novel, gender seems the most deeply ingrained.

In the second post-Holocaust generation, the institution of the patriarchal family and fatherhood have been repeatedly drawn into question by Jewish authors such as Becker and Hilsenrath. They showed that in the chaos of world wars, lineage was impossible to establish. While they assert the breakdown of patriarchy, the hallmark of identity in Christianity, Mitgutsch, not unlike Neumann, undermines the concept of motherhood, thereby questioning the cornerstone upon which rests Jewish identity. Dvorah travels to Jerusalem, motivated by her desire to meet with her mother's cousin Martha, whom she suspects to be her real mother, but her inability and her lack of determination to find this woman suggest that an undertaking such as this ultimately may be irrelevant. Rather, understanding what triggers the protagonist to react in certain ways in the present rather than to ascertain her biological lineage becomes increasingly important. No matter which history and identity Dvorah may construct for herself, they do not change the person underneath.

In her encounter with Sivan, Dvorah meets another individual as uprooted as herself, although due to different political circumstances. Like her, he has no country, no language, and no name on which to base a permanent identity. Like her, he gets by, telling half-truths, and his feelings, as much as they can be ascertained, are of a similar ambivalence. *Abschied von Jerusalem,* portraying an equally fragmented panorama of Israel as does Beckermann's *Nach Jerusalem,* reveals the extraterritoriality of the postmodern world with the Palestinian Arab and the Austrian Jew as paradigms of fragmentation, and the prison cell as the only possible place of containment.

⊶ 9 ⊷
Encounters and Confrontations

Jews, Germans, and Austrians

The relationship between Jews and non-Jews in post-Shoah Germany and Austria has not been normalized, nor is it likely to become so in the foreseeable future. As Lea Fleischmann writes: "Ambivalence toward Germany is characteristic of the Jewish postwar generations, along with a keen historical perspective, an awareness of continuity. In many families, all relatives were murdered. The young generation was directly confronted with mourning and sorrow. Whether their parents discussed their experiences freely during the time of persecution and in the concentration camps, or whether they remained silent, sparing their children the psychological burden, the past could always be sensed" (1994, 311). Every work written by a Jewish author must be read against the background of the Shoah and anti-Semitism, especially the works published in the German language, addressing the German-speaking reading or viewing public, the perpetrators and their children. Jack Zipes mentions that in the 1976 work *On Jews and Judaism in Crisis,* Gershom Scholem "refuted the existence of a productive German-Jewish symbiosis" because, he maintained, the European Jews' love of things German had always been "one-sided and unreciprocated" (Zipes 1994, 144). There remains, nonetheless, the impression of a strong affinity between Jews and Germans, regardless of the fact that in postwar Germany, as in Elizabethan England, whose most brilliant poet created the figure of Shylock, there is virtually no Jewish presence, as Ruth Klüger points out (1994, 9). The affinity, real or perceived, is evinced by a host of critical and fictional works by Jewish and non-Jewish authors portraying the duality "German and Jew" and the interaction of "Germans and Jews," conceptualized as a pair of opposites that remained constant throughout German-Jewish history. Already Martin Luther in his anti-Jewish pamphlets refers to "Germans and Jews" (rather than Jews and Christians),

250

and Germans and Jews have once again been described by Dan Diner as partners in a "negative symbiosis, constituted by the Nazis" (Diner 1986, 9; D. C. G. Lorenz 1994b, 3).

Non-Jewish authors in post-Holocaust German-speaking countries, including feminists, perpetuated Jewish stereotypes. In light of recent history, however, the majority of them connoted Jewish stereotypes as positive until works expressing anti-Jewish biases from a leftist perspective became increasingly more frequent in the 1960s (Klüger 1994, 23ff.; Améry 1982). On the other hand, texts by Jewish and Jewish-identified authors depicting encounters between Jews and Germans have used racial clichés satirically, even if serious topics are addressed. This is the case in Bruno Apitz's 1958 Buchenwald novel *Nackt unter Wölfen,* Jakov Lind's grotesque about the euthanasia program, *Eine Seele aus Holz* (1964), and in Edgar Hilsenrath's *Der Nazi und der Friseur* (1977), a satirical novel about a mass murderer turned Israeli citizen (D. C. G. Lorenz 1992b, 279ff.). All of these works represent Nazis in much the same way as do American and British films and television series, as bungling, unsavory characters. Beyond that, Hilsenrath and Lind explore the causes of "Jewish behavior." Lind, in his short story "Der fromme Bruder," suggests a structural and ideological affinity between right-wing Catholicism and National Socialism by the ease with which the protagonist slips from his Nazi identity into that of a Jesuit. A fatal love-hate relationship of these two groups with the people they persecute the most, the Jews, is implied, symbolized by the Jesuit's ultimate identity change into a Hasidic Jew. Jewish women's writing likewise employs satirical and grotesque elements when depicting non-Jews, addressing the situation of contemporary Germany or Austria, or writing about encounters between Jews, Germans, and Austrians. Some do so deliberately and pointedly, such as Ilse Aichinger, Elfriede Gerstl, and Elfriede Jelinek, all of whom were associated with the Viennese avant-garde of the 1950s and 1960s and the Vienna Group (Gerstl 1982).

Jelinek resumed the techniques of Jewish interwar satirists, defining the "work with language and criticism of existing conditions with the help of language" as a fundamentally Jewish undertaking (Berka 1993, 129). In contrast to her earlier more cautious and pessimistic statements,[1] Jelinek stresses her affinity to Karl Kraus and the Jewish Cabaret of the interwar era in her 1993 interview with Sigrid Berka and through her references to Hilsenrath and Schindel, as well as Farkas's and Waldbrunn's Jewish Cabaret (Veigl 1992). She claims her own Jewish identity as the daughter of a Holocaust victim, her father, thereby suggesting that there is a continuity of Vienna's Jewish tradition (Berka 1993, 137f.; Gilman 1995, 3).

Nazis, Existentialists, and the Petty Bourgeoisie (Elfriede Jelinek)

Prior to confirming her bond with the Jewish tradition, Elfriede Jelinek had made no secret about her alienation from and scorn for her fellow Austrians and Austrian society. She did not usually feature Jewish characters and Jewish issues but rather mercilessly scrutinized Gentile Austrian culture. Born in 1946, in the Styrian town of Mürzzuschlag, Jelinek, who now lives in Vienna and Munich, is familiar with both rural and urban Austria and treats them with a similar venom as did the late Thomas Bernhard. Jelinek explores the contemporary power structures in Austria before the background of the Nazi past and from a feminist point of view. Sander Gilman aptly characterizes her as the most radical Austrian feminist author "on the fringe." Being a feminist of Jewish background, Jelinek faces a dual predicament; not only were Jewish topics marginalized during the 1960s and 1970s, but women's problems were as well. Elke Frederiksen uses the term "point zero consciousness" to define the political and social situation of women in the early 1970s, suggesting a parallel to the tabula rasa sensibility of the immediate postwar years (1989, 87). Margret Eifler maintains that feminist voices were not heard until the revolutionary mood of the 1968 students' movement gave way to a new conservatism, at which point feminists were considered "bothersome," drawing defensive reactions from the male establishment that safeguarded its traditional bastions (1989, 2). Among other reasons, it may have been Jelinek's desire to avoid the marginalization to which women's discourses tend to fall victim that she, like numerous other German-speaking women writers, never identified herself as a feminist, and she proceeded with similar caution as far as her Jewish background was concerned.

Jelinek does not make her Jewish identity the central issue of her work —it is seemingly subordinated to her feminism, although she is popularly received as a "cultural Jew" (Gilman 1995, 3). Important elements in Jelinek's feminist cultural criticism are interwar Austro-Marxism and the literary styles of that era. An heir to the legacy of authors such as

Veza Canetti, Jelinek examines sexual politics, the socioeconomic problems of women, gender issues, the female body, and sexuality in the context of class and power structures. Her novel *Die Liebhaberinnen* (1975), a cult book in the late 1970s and early 1980s, demonstrates that women's problems can be solved only by equal access to education and employment. The novel portrays the position of a woman at the conveyer belt as preferable to that of a housewife—in contrast to the wife, the worker has an economic basis, albeit limited, to develop self-esteem. At the same time, Jelinek takes on popular culture whose function is, according to her, to program women in such a way as to prevent them from recognizing the nature of their problem. In a similar position are the workers, whom she finds, as Heinz Sichvrovsky puts it, "degenerated from Marx to Elvis." Like the women who have bought into the myth of femininity, they also stand no chance of liberating themselves (1979).

Jelinek's feminism is based on Marxist theory with which she became familiar as a participant in the 1968 student movement, during which time she lived in a Maoist commune in Berlin and became a member of the Austrian Communist Party (KPÖ).[2] In keeping with the theses of Engels's essay *On the Origin of the Family, Private Property and the State,* she portrays women as the most exploited group of human beings since they are subject to oppression in all social classes. No matter what their status, they are controlled to such a degree that a serious attempt on their part to emancipate themselves seems futile. Jelinek portrays male-female relationships as between slave drivers and slaves: raw, brutal, uncompromising. She reveals that capitalist society is set up in such a way as to prevent men and women from becoming equal partners: women are locked into their position by their upbringing and cultural indoctrination, their poverty, and their supposed inferiority.[3] They are, moreover, prisoners of language patterns, acoustic stimuli, and sound bytes reinforcing the status quo. The media totalitarianism renders police terror and concentration camps obsolete as methods of forcing groups and individuals into submission. The "systematic moronization of children and adults," as Herbert Marcuse calls it (1965, 83), is one of Jelinek's foremost topics.

Jelinek's attitude—detached, cynical, and without a trace of sentimentality—is that of an individual who, because she does not identify with the mainstream culture, is able to hold its every foible up to criticism. This is also true in *Die Ausgesperrten* (1985), a novel about a former Nazi and his family in Vienna of the 1950s. Although the novel is not intended as a documentary, there are parallels between Jelinek's fictional work and the case of a seventeen-year-old high school student who killed his parents and brother, inflicting on them 180 injuries (Sichrovsky 1979). Jelinek transposes the events of the 1960s into the previous decade, a time when Austria underwent a cultural crisis because of its refusal to deal with the legacy of Austro-Fascism (McVeigh 1988, 117f.) Robert Menasse observes that "no country in the world has problematized and fundamentally examined itself as little as Austria" (1993, 12).

Coupling her youthful killer with a twin sister allows Jelinek to develop a gender-specific dual perspective, while the representation of all social strata by specific characters provides a class-specific perspective. The portrayal of members of different age groups expands the historical panorama to the demise of the Danube Monarchy. The names of two of Jelinek's characters, Hans Sepp and Sophie Pachofen, refer to Robert Musil's *Der Mann ohne Eigenschaften,* establishing a sense of continuity from the Habsburg era to the present as they transpose the social conflicts depicted by Musil into the postwar era. With gender, class, and history as her coordinates, Jelinek paints a differentiated portrait of her own formative years, which continued to be dominated by fascist attitudes. *Die Ausgesperrten* reveals that the popularized existentialism of that time, as well as the anarchistic individualism and the beatnik attitudes, represented merely emotional safety valves, rather than real alternatives. Certainly it afforded no escape from the real power structures, which, as Lind also surmises, remained virtually unchanged since the collapse of the empire.

By exploring psychological processes, particularly of the would-be gangster and murderer Rainer Witkowski, the son of a Nazi and his oppressed wife, Jelinek uncovers the effects of National Socialism on the postwar generations. The lower-middle class or, rather, lumpenproletarian men, Rainer and his father, carry on the legacy of the mass murderers. For lack of an appropriate mass organization, they transpose this legacy into their private sphere.

Old Mr. Witkowski's sadism calls to mind the portrayal of the Nazis by Apitz, Lind, and Hilsenrath. He is a former SS officer and an invalid, obsessed with pornographic photography, for which he uses his wife as a model. Apart from being a cynical comment on Nazi sexuality, the motif calls to mind Hitler's lewd drawings of his fiancée Geli Raubal, who committed suicide. Using this unwholesome nuclear family as her test tube, Jelinek also destroys the myth of women's otherness. Anna and her mother have been more thoroughly brainwashed than Rainer and his father. They are victimized by both males, but in no way do they represent contrasting figures. Functioning as the perpetrators' support system, Jelinek's women characters represent the female version of the fascist prototype. The child of a wife abuser and a codependent mother, Anna, incapable of resolving her inner conflicts, also possesses a sadistic streak that comes to the fore when she believes she is in control. Only then does her usual passivity turn into aggression—her feminine socialization has not equipped her with the capacity of expressing her repressed rage. Therefore she encourages her brother's brutal behavior as well as the small-time crimes he and Sepp, a working-class boy, commit, and she accompanies them on their exploits, where she commits less obtrusive small-scale atrocities on her own. The males treat her, as they do all females, as a sex object, and to Sepp she represents a stepping-stone toward social advancement.

By contrasting the psychology of a male and a female Nazi child, Jelinek reveals patterns the postwar generation shares with its parents: inferiority complexes, feelings of social displacement, and a fierce ambition frustrated by the social hierarchy. Despite her fashionable veneer, her interest in Schönberg and existentialism, Anna is steeped in social shame and sentimental yearnings. With her aggressions turned inward, she develops a speech impediment and an eating disorder. Rainer and his father, on the other hand, use women and persons of lower status to take out their frustrations and aggressions. The ultimate reason for their mental and emotional deformity, including Mr. Witkowski's sexual perversion and the fury that causes Rainer to murder his entire family, is their inability to escape a substandard life. "Anna is enraged against all people, which is bad, because it clouds one's perspective and blocks one's access. To be sure, Anna has little access to the finer things in life anyway, because it takes money to pay for them," the narrator sarcastically comments (1985, 11).

Jelinek states that her "literary technique does not allow for a positive counter model" (Hoffmeister 1987, 111). Far removed from the privileged class, the Witkowskis have no idea where to direct their hostility; neither do the proletarians without class consciousness. Sepp's mother, on the other hand, a communist of the old school, has the necessary awareness, but the party to which she belongs is small and impotent. Her dilemma resembles that of Jelinek, who remained committed to the insignificant кРö longer than most of its occasional intellectual members. Both the petty bourgeois characters and the aspiring proletarians are oppressed by a mass culture that diverts the general population from their true interests—only the upper class is in touch with capitalist reality. The blatant inequality makes the criminal activities of the under-privileged seem only natural—the have-nots' crimes are a mirror image and consequence of the crimes of the powerful.

Implied in the 1950s setting is a reference to the experimental literature of the *Wiener Gruppe* and the performance art of the *Aktionismus,* neither of which developed a political program or came to terms with the Austro-Fascism, despite their ostensible avant-gardism. Their protest remained diffuse at best, and at worst, it imitated aspects of the Nazi terror. Often their behavior involved brutality: surrounding a theater audience with barbed wire and throwing water on people, killing and mutilating animals on stage, defecation or urinating on fellow actors, particularly women. The atavistic carnage caused by Jelinek's teenage protagonist resembles the fascist rage, termed "white terror" by Klaus Theweleit, and it calls to mind the bloody excesses of the "aktionists" of which Weibel and Export's anthology gives a good impression (Theweleit 1980; Weibel and Export 1970). Like the men in Theweleit's Nazi case studies, Rainer is unaware of his motivations; his apolitical high school education has caused him to consider politics and history unworthy pursuits for an intellectual.

Jelinek's omniscient narrator is seemingly uninvolved in the events at hand. Like the chorus of a classical drama, she elucidates the forces guiding her characters. Privy to and yet detached from the social meta-language, she positions herself as an outsider who, having studied the hidden blueprint of postwar Austrian capitalism, is able to reveal the falsity of its promises of individualism, freedom, and equal chances. She shows that they are illusions, fabricated to keep the oppressed divided and ignorant of their abject condition: the apparent chances are no chances, and what is called education is an infusion of useless information to prevent social change. Jelinek's narrator speaks from outside the mass culture with a cynicism equal to that of the engineers of her society, and like them, she is not affected by the insidious mass-produced sentimentality that represents the foremost barrier to understanding. Thus, she purports to be able to expose the disabling collective discourse and the reactions it prescribes by causing sensations without there being any occasion for them. Jelinek's is a Jewish voice, insightful and critical like that of Claire Goll and Veza Canetti, and yet unable to make a difference.

Jews and Nazis (Lea Fleischmann)

In contrast to Jelinek's narrative strategy of detachment, Lea Fleisch-mann speaks passionately with her own voice—she is the central char-acter of *Dies ist nicht mein Land* (1980), her account of why she left the Federal Republic. Jews and non-Jews are present in her exasperated re-port of her life as a Jewish child and young woman in West Germany. Although ostensibly a factual publication—the book appeared in Hoff-mann and Campe's series *Bücher zur Sache*—Fleischmann's techniques place her works alongside Jelinek's *Die Ausgesperrten*. The reflections, anecdotes, and memories, not necessarily the author's own, as well as the imaginary alternative childhood biography, add aesthetic dimensions to the bare facts. The timbre of Fleischmann's nostalgic passages is reminis-cent of Yiddish authors and Jewish memoir writers, whereas her depic-tion of German Gentiles as Nazis and crypto-fascists resembles those of Jelinek and, for that matter, Nadja Seelich. Fleischmann's identity, like theirs, is constructed from elements of the past—her parents' memories and her knowledge of history. Filtered through these, she depicts the insurmountable distance between Jews and non-Jews in Germany.[4]

Dies ist nicht mein Land struck a cord with the German public in the 1980s. For young Jews, the past was a cause for mourning, long-ing, shame, and pride and had to be explored further. Moreover, rising xenophobia and anti-Semitism necessitated the construction of a Jew-ish identity. By the same token, the increasing awareness of the Jewish tradition provided alternatives to non-Jews in disagreement with the dominant culture. Fleischmann's Polish *shtetl*, as well as her utopian vision of Israel, expresses the desire for a spiritual home outside of Ger-many (8). From her point of view, the Germans appear as agents of destruction, be it the Nazi storm troopers, who invade Poland, or the petty-minded teachers, her colleagues, who crush the creative spark in children. She portrays the Germans as stereotypes, proceeding in a man-ner similar to German authors who depict Jews as immoral elements from whom one had best keep one's distance.[5] Constructed from anti-

German clichés, Fleischmann's characterization of Germans is unabashedly hostile. Likewise, her portrayal of Jews is not free of stereotypes; she tends to idealize them, except when discussing specific situations and individuals.

Fleischmann's attitudes reflect in part her parents' experiences and views. Her family lived in Frankfurt as if in a voluntary ghetto because, she states, "Jews are not afraid of Jews" (1980, 25, 31). Thoroughly entrenched in her Jewish environment, Fleischmann scrutinizes the outside world critically and suspiciously, registering what separates her from the Gentiles. The major difference is caused by culture-specific associations, similar to the ones discussed by Honigmann, Beckermann, and Seelich. Fleischmann portrays her inner world in detail, juxtaposing it to what she perceives as typically German thought and behavior patterns. She contrasts, for example, her parents' tolerance and tenderness with the Germans' strictness and discipline. Greed, pettiness, and the absence of feelings are ascribed to the Germans, whereas the Jews are characterized as relaxed, indifferent to material goods, generous, and forgiving. The essentialism implied in Fleischmann's categories corresponds in part to the sociological studies of the Frankfurt School; in part it reflects the author's experience. Clearly transcending objective cultural criticism, the stereotypes are used to express the author's inability to reconcile herself to a life among people who would have sent her to the gas chamber four decades earlier.

Like Jelinek's works, Fleischmann's account had a calculated shock effect on the German majority. While not specific to Germany or Austria, many of the negative qualities identified by both authors can indeed be observed in the postwar republics, where they are not registered in the public consciousness. By way of example, Fleischmann tries to persuade her readers that her observations are based on more than a marginalized individual's paranoia, and she cites instance after instance of rigid authoritarian attitudes toward women and children in German society. She also examines the social hierarchy, showing that it fosters ethnocentrism and attitudes similar to the ones from which sprang National Socialism and from which it might again arise, regardless of West Germany's democratic surface structures (Mosse 1979; Heyen 1967). Furthermore, the traditional German primary and secondary virtues and their negative sides are revealed—among others, the sadomasochism inherent in a system based on control and subordination and the Germans' avarice, anal retentiveness, and repression of emotions are held up to ridicule. Moreover, Fleischmann, like Lander, suggests that the idolization of genital sex in the wake of the sexual revolution and the supposedly revolutionary lifestyle of the 1968 generation represent a mere reversal of traditional behaviors into their opposite. Fleischmann contrasts, not without comical effects, the German scoring mentality with the more relaxed social patterns of the Jewish and the foreign workers' community.

The polarization of Jewish and German characteristics is necessary for Fleischmann's construction of identity. Her concepts of Jewishness and Germanness are interdependent, designed as contrasts. In spite of their obvious artificiality, these opposites are rhetorically effective in that they parody the traditional anti-Semitic binarism of German and Jew. It is important to note that in a context where the construct of Germanness is irrelevant, Fleischmann also bypasses the concept of Jewishness in *Ich bin Israelin* (1982), for example, as well as in the short stories in *Nichts ist so wie es scheint: Vierzig Jahre war Isaak und andere Erzählungen* (1985). In exclusively Jewish settings, Fleischmann's narrators and characters are individualized, and only casual culture-specific references indicate the Jewish context. Unlike *Dies ist nicht mein Land* (1980), these texts do not configure Jewishness as an essentialist quality, and it stands to reason that the inclusion of the German counterfigure, the image of the other, is the element that makes it impossible for Fleischmann to create more differentiated characters, Jewish and Gentile. The awareness of the Nazi legacy in post-Shoah Germany seems to prevent her from perceiving the humanity of both Jews and Germans, hence her need to leave Germany. The use of German and Jewish stereotypes similar to the ones in *Dies ist nicht mein Land* is a distinguishing feature in the work of another daughter of Holocaust survivors, Nadja Seelich.

Home in the Avant-Garde (Nadja Seelich)

The films *Kieselsteine* (1982), written by Nadja Seelich, and *Sie saß im Glashaus und warf mit Steinen* (1992), written and codirected by Seelich, have as a theme the search for a post-Holocaust, post-Stalinist European Jewish identity, distinct from Zionism, religious Judaism, and assimilation. Seelich, born in 1947, was one of the first members of a large German-Bohemian-Jewish family to grow up speaking Czech. Many of her relatives were Holocaust survivors and resistance fighters. After the violent suppression of the "Prague Spring," Seelich left Czechoslovakia.[6] Since that time, she has lived in the United States, Switzerland, and Austria. Much like Beckermann's work, Seelich's films are anchored in specific localities: Vienna in *Kieselsteine,* and Prague in *Sie saß im Glashaus.* Seelich uses coffeehouses, restaurants, bars, private apartments, parks, and neighborhoods to represent atmospheres as they relate to her protagonists' search for self-realization.

The language of her works of the 1980s, including *Kieselsteine* (1981), a film examining the interaction between children of Holocaust survivors and non-Jewish Austrians and Germans, and several children's movies, is German.[7] In certain ways, these works reflect the filmmaker's own experience of marginality. Set apart from the mainstream by their background and fate, their abilities and their convictions, Seelich's protagonists engage in a quest for alternative realities that leads into absurd, tragic, and ambiguous situations. Yet, the filmmaker has a flair for tempering disaster with irony, especially so, as Ursula Kubes-Hofmann observes, in *Sie saß im Glashaus und warf mit Steinen* (1991), a documentary film and a carefully composed work of art.[8]

Sie saß im Glashaus, Seelich's most personal film, examines a woman's aesthetic and moral position in conjunction with Prague's transformation from socialism into a Western-style democracy and pays tribute to the dissenters who were affiliated with *Divoke Vino* (Wild Wine), the literary magazine of *Klub Mlada Poezie* (New Poetry Club), for which Seelich had worked as an editor in the late 1960s while a student at the Prague Charles University. At that time, she met the poet and critic Jana Cerna (1928–81), the daughter of Franz Kafka's friend Milena Jesenska and the architect Jaromir Krejcar (Kubes-Hofmann 1991, 17).

Seelich and her coproducer Bernd Neuburger capture Prague's vanishing predemocracy culture at a time of transition in personal narratives and in simple, but striking, images of people, objects, and locations that reveal problems inherent in the ongoing gentrification of Prague. In the film, philosopher Egon Bondy expresses his ideological reservations indirectly, by relating that Jana Cerna's main reason for not moving to Austria was her misgivings about a country where former Nazis occupied prominent positions.

Sie saß im Glashaus traces the lives of Prague's underground dissenters, surrealists, and anarchists, who remained outsiders after the fall of the Iron Curtain—it seems too late for them, if they were so inclined, to become respectable capitalists. By examining the fate of Jana Cerna and her associates, Seelich, who prepared Cerna's publication *Adresat Milena Jesenska* (1969) for publication, explores her own position as an exile who is returning, at least part-time, to her native city. She does so indirectly, by lending her protagonist her own voice in her impassioned readings of excerpts from Cerna's works.[9]

The language of *Sie saß im Glashaus* is culturally and politically significant. With the exception of a Czech-speaking prison matron, everyone speaks Prague German, an idiom that links them to Bohemia's multicultural heritage and the Habsburg Empire. This almost extinct language, according to Deleuze and Guattari, already was deterritorialized in Kafka's times (1986, 17), and recurrent historical motifs define the featured artists and intellectuals as members of a lost generation. Indeed, now that Cerna and her friends are no longer threatened by a totalitarian regime, their works may already be obsolete.[10] On the other hand, they may speak to future generations after the dust of the Velvet Revolution settles.

Already in her earlier film *Kieselsteine,* Seelich emphasized separateness, produced by the long-term effects of the Shoah. Too young to have been directly involved, her protagonists are nonetheless shaped by their parents' past. *Kieselsteine* exposes Vienna's thriving Nazi legacy, widespread anti-Semitism and homophobia, both of which are of immediate concern to the filmmaker. Her deliberately biased character studies reveal the aftermath of the past as it affects Jews, Germans, and Austrians of her generation, and she depicts the brutality toward marginalized groups and individuals in pre-Waldheim Austria as related to the Nazi legacy. *Kieselsteine* shows that the Shoah produced different collective memories. Focusing on encounters between children of perpetrators, bystanders, and victims, the cultural fragmentation of Central Europe is inseparably linked with the Holocaust. So is the deterioration of traditional values, exemplified by Seelich's Jewish protagonist, the daughter of Holocaust survivors, and her counterpart, the son of a German Nazi doctor. Their inability to come to terms with events that they neither understand nor control causes them to enter into a destructive relationship.[11]

The blunt articulation of biases that German and Austrian bigots express only in the company of people who share their point of view lends

Seelich's film a most remarkable quality. The secret rhetoric of every-day fascism and neo-Nazism is exposed from the perspective of a Jewish woman who is neither religious nor assimilated—Seelich's protagonist Hannah Stern has no intention of forgiving or forgetting the crimes of the past, nor does she desire to leave Austria.[12] In contrast to many of the Jewish protagonists in contemporary German texts, Hannah is neither a victim nor a villain. In her struggle to be recognized as a Jewish woman, she turns the tables on her opponents and makes Germans and Austrians the objects of her unmerciful gaze, stereotyping them as radically and unfairly as anti-Semites would do for Jews. This particular technique lends the character of the German man a cartoonlike quality. With the critical detachment of a satire, Seelich's film exposes everyday fascism, matter-of-course xenophobia, and the deliberate abuse of any-one considered different, coupled with a disregard for animals and the environment.

In *Kieselsteine,* Seelich establishes her artistic approach, which is to measure the quality of a society by the condition of those living at the margins. Her children's films, likewise, portray society from the point of view of the socially underprivileged—old people and children, poor and eccentric persons.[13] *Sie saß im Glashaus* represents a different phase of Seelich's career. The film was produced in Prague, the city of Kafka and Rabbi Loew, to which Seelich continued to feel a keen attachment during her years in exile, and whose Jewish tradition, Jana Cerna's and Seelich's background, is evoked in numerous scenes. Cerna, the daugh-ter of a Jewish father and a Gentile mother, was so intensely identi-fied with Franz Kafka that she considered him her father. For Seelich, commemorating Cerna means commemorating the lost legacy of Cen-tral European modernity, embodied by Kafka, which at present seems threatened by extinction more than ever. The fall of communism, it is suggested, ushered in an era of cultural indifference that may prove to be intellectually more destructive than the cultural dictatorship that af-fected Cerna's fate (Seelich n.d., 3).

Nonetheless, the dead poet and bohemian, inscribed with the terror of Nazism and World War II, as well as the chaos within her family, provides also a symbol of resistance against repression, and her texts at-test to her integrity. There are parallels between Cerna's plight and the position of the women poets of the World War I era, torn between bour-geoisie and *bohème,* socialism and individualism, Jewish and Gentile culture, Else Lasker-Schüler and Claire Goll. Cerna's rebellion against the ideologies of her time by her lifestyle and her poetry resembles theirs. Expressing dissent drove Cerna into an existential loneliness that is conveyed in several leitmotifs, such as the figure of a girl standing underneath Prague's mighty bridges, cut off, as it were, from the city and nature alike.

The Nazis labeled the production of the interwar *bohème* as degenerate and persecuted its members. A few years later, the Stalinist regime in Czechoslovakia, whose cultural program bore a remarkable resemblance to Nazi aesthetics, persecuted anyone attempting to revive the legacy of the 1920s. Juxtaposing surrealism to fascist and socialist realist art, *Sie saß im Glashaus* contrasts two diametrically opposed experiences of reality. The powerful image of a taciturn man on horseback, riding back and forth, points to the dialectic processes underlying art and history. His appearances, alternately on a black horse and a white horse, correspond to the pendulum motion of the metronome overtowering Prague, an edifice erected at the former location of a Stalin monument. The perpendicular movement of the red hand underscores the structure of the entire film: Bohemia's position between right-wing and left-wing extremism and Eastern and Western Europe. The metronome's and the rider's seemingly perpetual motion signifies the temporality of every condition, including the present one. The movement pertains to Cerna's life under two supposedly different political systems, each one of which, nonetheless, demanded total surrender.

The forces that shaped Cerna's perceptions are revealed in carefully selected images: a military cemetery in Russia to evoke World War II and Nazi aggression, the Jewish cemetery and the Altneuschul to represent Prague's Jewish culture and its annihilation during the Holocaust, and the polluted industrial landscape on the outskirts of Prague to characterize the legacy of communism. All of them are part of Cerna's surroundings, the strongest of them being her identification with the Jewish fate. Cerna's and her friends' excesses, it is suggested, must be interpreted against the background of the Shoah to fully appreciate their radical pacifism and their passion for life, which made them heroes in their time and models for the filmmaker.

The film's carefully balanced narratives and imagery form an aesthetic unit that is neither reassuring nor harmonious. As was the case with Vienna in the setting of *Kieselsteine,* Prague's spectacular scenery is bypassed. Rather, the city is shown from the perspective of a well-informed outsider who is too familiar with the sites to be taken in by their glamour, but not familiar enough to avoid them entirely. Even the opening scenes of *Sie saß im Glashaus* convey the conflict between new and old. The soundtrack includes the noise of detonations and drills to signal the rapid change: amidst the debris of the past and the soon-to-be debris of the present, an erasure of history, more complete than after World War II, is taking place. The energy with which the business of laying the past to rest is conducted and the eagerness to import whatever the West has to offer suggest a complete disregard for the ancient city, which the camera scans over and over again. The breathless whistling and the jazz version of the French song "La blonde" evoke, and abandon, not only the possible associations of French and Eastern Jewish culture, but also the image of the idealized blonde mistress in contrast to Cerna as Seelich remembers her, "a large, solid woman, with a fat stomach and sagging breasts, dressed in men's trousers, with straggly dark hair, soft full lips, a squint, and wearing spectacles," as it says in the film brochure.

Seelich's underground heroes are a group of aging Jewish and non-Jewish beatniks, all of whom assumed conspicuous Jewish-sounding names in order to protect their Jewish colleagues from Stalinist anti-Semitism. As the film progresses, viewers revise their initial impression that these marginalized intellectuals and artists, survivors of two dictatorships, have been defeated, as their tenacity and courage become obvious: their solidarity, their untiring search for freedom, which they retain even after liberty has supposedly arrived. To properly assess the situation after the fall of the Iron Curtain and the bustling new Prague, their perspective, the only one providing continuity, must be taken into consideration. For them, who were cut off from the free world for forty years, nothing has changed—neither their status and standard of living, nor their opportunities. Like the anonymous thirty-six Just Men of Jewish tradition, they represent the secret history of the free spirit. In the hidden pockets of society, among the survivors of state terrorism, Seelich envisions a possible future and a motherland for Jewish nonconformists like herself. In this alternative environment away from the centers of power, utopia seems possible: the harmonious interaction of Jews and non-Jews, and the intellectual and sexual self-realization of women.

The Hidden Jewish Identity (Irene Dische)

The exile experience and the Shoah also shaped the work of Irene Dische, who was born in New York in 1952, the daughter of German Jewish immigrants (Remmler 1994, 186). Her work reflects several different levels of alienation: her parents' separation from their native culture and religion, her own difficulties in negotiating issues of identity—she was raised Catholic in a neighborhood that "might have been Jewish," but she went to school with white Anglo-Saxon Protestants (185). As is the case in Jelinek's and Seelich's work, Dische's portrayal of German, American, and Jewish culture and the relationship between Jews and Germans is pointed, sarcastic, and satirical. Her writing is seemingly crude, and her provocative use of clichés leaves many of her readers and critics unsure of her intended meaning. Remmler, for example, maintains that "Dische's apparent subversion of typical Jewish bodies in her texts through a reinstatement of anti-Semitic representations of them is actually overlooked by a reading public that is as much invested in constructing her work as Jewish and non-German as it is in maintaining negative images of Jewish men and women. Rather than disrupt Jewish stereotypes, Dische's work appears to incorporate them" (201). When reading Dische one must keep in mind Zipes's observation that "hilarity becomes a nomadic means of questioning majority culture and of reversing identities so that understanding between different groups can be generated" (Remmler 1994, 36; Zipes 1994, 36).

Although Dische's narrative strategies are designed to create a distance between the author and her protagonists, autobiographical elements do enter into her stories, captivating the flair of Washington Heights, formerly a center of German Jewish immigration and Dische's childhood environment. Other stories move between an American setting and contemporary Berlin. Dische's comments regarding her relationship to Judaism are no less ambiguous than the multiple personalities of her literary characters. Although she writes about issues facing post-Holocaust Jewry, she refuses to define herself as a Jewish writer, perhaps because identifying herself in such a specific way seems artificial to her, since it implies the exclusion of other, equally viable aspects of her experience. At the same time, Dische focuses on the necessity of acknowledging one's personal, cultural, and family history.

Like Fleischmann's and Jelinek's prose and Seelich's films, Dische's aggressive, satirical texts decry the deception with which she grew up. Dische portrays the immigrants' *Marrano* existence as a defensive response to the exclusion from the dominant culture and satirizes the compulsive need to belong, even if it is to the incorrect group. Beyond the calculated confusion prevailing in most of Dische's texts, there are hints that apart from all subterfuges there may be a path toward an authentic existence. In most cases, the quest for authenticity leads past the ethnic, religious, and gender codes of any given group or community. The "frequent portrayal of Jewish figures in Dische's works and her Jewish ancestry became catalysts for German reviewers to identify her as a Jewish writer," writes Remmler (200). Dische's language, choice of residence, and places of publication indicate a position between German and American, Jewish and Gentile culture: Dische lives in Berlin, writes in English, and has her works translated into German.[14]

Like Jeanette Lander, Irene Dische is concerned with the effects of exile: involuntary multiculturalism, the dilemma of acculturation, and the impact of the cultural displacement on the next generation. Although both authors problematize the American exile experience in different ways, they view the affiliation to more than one culture as an essential part of twentieth-century Jewish identity. Dische focuses on the situation of German-speaking Jewish refugees in the United States, and she introduces Jews of other backgrounds only to fine-tune the characterization of her German-Jewish protagonists. As in Lander, language as it relates to an individual's cultural and personal experience is an important topic in Dische. Layers of language surround Dische's exiles like a protective shield, which dissolves in moments of crisis or in old age. Whereas Lander illustrates multilingualism by blending sociolects, ideolects, and languages, Dische, like Anita Desai, does not mix languages, but she interpolates German, Yiddish, Polish, and Russian sayings and phrases into her prose.

Frequently, Dische portrays the alienation of converts and children of converts who, like herself, were raised Christian, but who nevertheless would have been exterminated by the Nazis. The awareness that their escape is due to lucky circumstances permeates her work and is a source of guilt, shame, and self-hatred. Rarely does a story end as optimistically as *Pious Secrets* (1991), whose protagonist achieves an inner healing by facing up to the destruction of her family and their culture. By doing so, she is released to grieve, and her children are able to establish an identity

of their own. In other instances, moments of truth are achieved by senility, through the process of unlearning. Old people, having lost their
short-term memory, are thrown back into the world of their youth and,
once again, come face to face with that phase of their lives that they most
want to repress, their European Jewish past and their shattered dreams.

Like Hilde Spiel's *Lisas Zimmer*, Elfriede Jelinek's *Die Ausgesperrten*,
and Nadja Seelich's *Kieselsteine*, Dische's stories exclude the possibility
of a German-Jewish *renouveau*, least of all in Germany. The children of
exiles who, like Charles Allen in "The Jewess" (1992), travel to Germany encounter a familiar language but cannot comprehend German
culture, which including the legacy of the Jews, has been taken over by
the descendants of the Nazis. The character of Margerete, alias Esther
Becker, who passes herself off as a Jewish woman in order to exploit
German and American Jewish guilt, is a case in point.[15] "The Jewess"
provides no more information than necessary for a satirical effect. The
protagonists appear one dimensional and grotesque, "thus drawing attention to the dominant discourses about Jews and gender in German
society" (Remmler 1994, 202). With her black humor and an eye for incongruity, Dische holds the young American man's disorientation up
to ridicule—long before he does, the readers have taken the hint that
Esther/Margerete is not Jewish.

Set in the perplexing panorama of post-Shoah Europe and the United
States, with protagonists too flat to allow for reader identification, "The
Jewess" highlights the materialism and the absence of moral values in
contemporary Germany. The character portrayal of the false Jewess,
aside from being reminiscent of Hilsenrath's *The Nazi and the Barber*,
calls to mind Fleischmann's contention that it is a Gentile, rather than
Jewish, tendency to reduce relationships, emotions, and memory to
their monetary value. Germany's commercialization constitutes an unbridgeable gap between the prewar and postwar generations, Jews and
non-Jews. Dische makes no attempt to define Jewish and German identity, regardless of whether the setting is Germany or America; these
categories have lost their meaning, as the story reveals. In contrast to
Lander, whose topic was identity, Dische, like Hilsenrath, writes about
dissimulation. Whereas former victims and their children, deprived of
the chance to articulate themselves, conceal their past victimization, the
descendants of Nazis pose as Jewish survivors.

In "The Jewess," Dische's most controversial story, individuation occurs at a time when the persona crumbles. The process of unmasking involves Charles Allen, alias Allerhand, the son of German-Jewish exiles, and the false Jewess Esther Becker. The setting, Berlin, and the time, 1988, the fiftieth anniversary of *Kristallnacht*, add symbolic dimensions to the conflict. Like Seelich's *Kieselsteine*, "The Jewess" involves a replay of historical events on an individual level, albeit with a new ending. After Charles has discovered Esther's true identity, he rapes her, but he loses his innocence—quite literally his virginity—in this act of violence.[16] Much in the same way as the misconceptions of Seelich's protagonist Hannah are shattered, as she sets out to "destroy" the son of a Nazi doctor and is eventually raped by him, Dische's protagonist is freed from his obsession with his father's native land. In both cases, the violent act breaks a spell and liberates the individual. In Seelich's film, a German male rapes a Jewish woman. The viewers' initial interpretation of this rape is foiled by the fact that Hannah, after cleansing herself, walks off fully dressed, leaving her opponent, Friedrich, cowering on the floor, nude. Moreover, her final gesture of turning up her coat collar, deliberately staged to call to mind the pose of Humphrey Bogart in *Casablanca* after he kills a German, suggests that the Jewish woman has come out the winner. In the context of the *Kristallnacht* commemoration, the rape committed by Charles Allen also signifies a Jewish victim's belated revenge for the German crimes against his parents and for his loss of identity. It is a victory, since Charles, unlike his father, breaks the hold Germany had on him. Although playing this theme out between two individuals, male and female, is problematic in either case, Remmler's interpretation, which ignores the obvious satire, is not convincing: "Unfortunately, the shifting of identities from one body to another in actuality reinstates the negative image of a Jewish male violating a German female body" (203).

The identity problems in "The Jewess" must be seen in a historical context. Despite his country of residence, Charles is a product of German-Jewish culture, an extinct culture, as is made obvious by his stay in Berlin. He arrives at a time of rising anti-Semitism; according to Beckermann, in 1986, a virulent "anti-Semitic mud-slinging" campaign began in conjunction with the Bitburg scandal, the Waldheim affair, and the so-called Historians' Debate (1989, 114). In her description of the *Kristallnacht* remembrance, Dische captures the tension between Germany's official policies and the activities of the radical right wing over-shadowing the event.

> It proved a magnificent crowd of emotional people but not many Jews among them, they had stayed home in fright. . . . The procession halted when it reached the front of the community house, dissolving into a crowd plied by policemen and a contingent of nicely dressed, earnest young men distributing leaflets about the Auschwitz lie. The crowd grew silent when Rabbi Schwarz appeared on top of the stairs of the Jewish community house. Everyone knew he had lost his parents and all his siblings in Auschwitz. He raised the huge seven-armed menorah high over his head with its candles blazing. Silhouetted in black on the rooftops behind him lay the police sharpshooters. (1992, 54)

Since the publication of *Fromme Lügen* (1989), the issues raised in "The Jewess" have gained added momentum. The date 9 November is a prime example of the ambiguity of German history: it marks both *Kristallnacht* and the collapse of the Berlin Wall, providing the opportunity to neutralize and, ultimately, erase undesirable memories.[17] For some Germans, Jews and Gentiles, 9 November is a day of mourning, and for others, it is a day of national pride, marking the fall of the GDR, socialism, and the legacy of antifascism.

Dische's characters illustrate the connections between individual lives and Germany's history. "The Jewess" is constructed like a detective story; the narrator, reader, and protagonist are involved in solving a mystery. In the course of the fact-finding, the reader is repeatedly misled. What initially promises to become a narrative about a man's quest for his father's legacy in the vein of Lander's novel *Die Töchter* gradually evolves into a detective story with Esther, the title figure, at the center. During Charles's initiation into German society, truth and honesty become central themes. Esther's dishonesty as a businesswoman is readily apparent, but not so her lack of personal integrity. As the latter comes to light, one of the initial assumptions, namely, that honesty can be compartmentalized, is debunked—Esther's fraudulent business practices fall in line with her equally fraudulent persona. Ironically, though, superficially her strategies resemble those of Mrs. Allerhand on her way to America. She, too, changed her family members' names and adopted new customs and new religion. The difference between the transformation of the Jewish exiles and that of the former Nazis lies in the fact that Mrs. Allen, being serious about her conversion, lacked Esther's deftness, that of an emotionally uninvolved operator. The religious denomination Mrs. Allerhand chooses has been traditionally stigmatized in the United States—religious freedom was still withheld from the Catholics after it had been granted to the Jews. More important, however, Mrs. Allerhand's deceit is intended to place the family on an equal footing with the rest of society and to conceal a fate she considers dishonorable. Dische shows the victims of National Socialism as being ashamed of their past—they have internalized the dehumanizing images their persecutors constructed of them—and the perpetrators and their children as having no scruples whatever. Furthermore, Dische's female characters appear more adroit at changing identities than males. Charles and his father are too rigid. For both, the German language constitutes the ultimate prison: it prevents Mr. Allerhand from making the transition into the United States; his son Charles is recognizable by his German accent as the son of immigrants, whereas in Germany he is identified by his fluent German as a Jew. Even with their new identity made up of clichés, the Allerhands do not fit in.

But whereas Johannes Allerhand has a country to which to return, his son Charles does not. In the postwar generation, the multiple transformations develop a momentum all their own: Charles, the hidden Jew, and Esther, the hidden Nazi, react to each other's respective personae and to their hidden identities.[18] The attraction between Charles and Esther involves the traditional stereotypes and transcends them as well. In her untransformed form, Esther/Margerete is the kind of woman Charles may well fall for—he prefers blondes. At the same time, her age, her ostentatious "Jewishness," and her black hair have an exotic appeal for him as a supposed non-Jew. Esther, not surprisingly, seems unlike any Jewish woman Charles has met before. On a conscious and a subconscious level, she represents the forbidden fruit. As a result, Charles is entrapped in a vicious circle of exploitation and erotic suggestion, the objects of satire throughout the text. The insights into Allerhand's life in Germany further complicate matters, since they reveal that Esther's predilection for Jewish men is not only pragmatic but is also based on an emotional affinity. Charles, with his protective mother, and the overbearing Esther, who equates love with complicity, are suited for one another in a codependent way. Only when Charles realizes that he has been duped by a woman who, under different circumstances, would have sent him to the death camps is he released from her spell.

"The Jewess" is replete with references to rebuttals of discourses on the relationship between Jews and Germans, including Reich's thesis that in the absence of a thorough reeducation, authoritarian and fascist paradigms will prevail in Germany for generations to come (54). Concurrently, the concept of a collective German amnesia is debunked—average Germans recognize and dislike Charles Allen precisely because they know who he is (3–4).[19] The pervasiveness of anti-Semitism is indicated by the fact that Charles does not pass as a real American, but Esther/Margerete's Jewish persona goes unquestioned. Since it seems so unlikely for a Gentile to pose as a Jew, tinted black hair and a few stereotypical traits suffice to mark her as Jewish. Charles, having internalized his mother's self-hatred, is taken in by Esther's disguise as well. Similar to Hilsenrath's *Der Nazi und der Friseur* (1977) and Lind's "Der fromme Bruder," "The Jewess" suggests that only a German can enact the image of the *Stürmer* Jew, the epitome of anti-Semitic stereotyping.

Esther's unmasking calls for a reassessment of the text as a whole; the narrator's anti-Semitic statements must now be read as critical of the mind-set of the German public. Whether in Cincinnati, Oregon, New York, or Berlin, Charles feels that he must hide his Jewishness, but old—not former—Nazis such as Mr. Nadler, whose name recalls a famous Nazi literary scholar, still command authority in public (4–5). Nazi victims live in fear, but a German woman can afford to pose as a Jew because she knows how to manipulate the anti-Semitic prejudices of her fellow Germans in such a way as an actual Jew never would. Being more than just a conglomerate of crude clichés, Esther also serves as a vehicle to satirize opinions set forth by scholars and critics. She says: "We Jews have no taste. I read an article once on why. It comes from generations always having to move on. We don't form attachments to furniture" (18). Similar notions do in fact occur in historical and sociological studies. By having a highly unreliable source such as Esther reiterate them, Dische suggests that these facile notions, even if presented as objective or sympathetic, are anti-Semitic nonetheless. In the same way that Esther, the false Jewess, stands between Charles and the truth about his father and himself, such stereotypes, in whatever type of text, make a mockery of Jews and Jewish history.

Partly confirming, partly revising the conclusions following "The

Jewess," the short novel "Pious Secrets" portrays three generations of refugees from Nazi Germany, the Bauer family. Not unlike the Allerhands, the Bauers are exiles wishing to become absorbed into the American mainstream. Their names, Carl, Connie, Sally, and Dicky, are symbols of their ambition, but their lifestyle reveals their repressed cultural identity. In tone, "Pious Secrets" differs considerably from "The Jewess," but certain themes are present in both works. What little is shown of the New World is so dismal that it makes the Bauers' self-deception appear pathetic as well as endearing. The work environment of Connie Bauer at the New York City morgue is no less inhospitable than Allerhand's pawn shop in Berlin. In both texts, an opportunity for inner renewal is occasioned by the death of the protagonist's father, which Dische's black humor prevents from appearing tragic. Yet, contrary to "The Jewess," with its two grotesque protagonists—Charles and Esther—Connie and her father are the targets of a persecution campaign and are fleshed out enough to arouse sympathy. In the end, Connie establishes her humanity by revealing the well-guarded family secret, her Jewish descent.

The more that is revealed about Connie, the more she loses the features that made her seem bizarre at the outset. For the most part, her eccentric mannerisms are caused by her and other assimilated German and Austrian Jews' attempt to be like everyone else. As a result, they are measured against the wrong cultural paradigm. Until the end, Connie's children are unaware of their background. "We wanted to spare the next generation the shame of knowing. Not all knowledge is desirable," Connie explains (146). The Bauer's well-intended "pious lies" are proven a mistake; rather, the narrative reveals the destructive power of ignorance. The case in point is a scandal resulting from little Sally Bauer's confiding to her mother's lover that she suspects her grandfather of being Hitler. In the outset, Dische's incommunicative characters, seemingly arrested at different phases of adolescence, do not call for an emotional involvement on the part of the readers, but Mr. Bauer's death causes Connie to undergo an emotional transformation. Forced by the slander campaign, she speaks up, embracing her Jewish heritage. "And she told her family history with affection and familiarity until the characters, called back as spirits by recollection, seemed to join them in the living room. Connie allowed them to speak, prompting them like a souffleur. They came in, in order of disappearance" (143).

The title "Pious Lies" is ironic, as is "The Jewess." The secrets of Connie's family may harm no one but the victims, but by denying their history, the Bauers kill their dead one more time. Their view that it is shameful to be a victim empowers the perpetrators and diminishes the next generation's sense of self. This is the case with the Bauers, whose judgment has become eroded to such a degree that they would rather have Connie be the mistress of a mediocre Gentile American than the wife of a Jewish Nobel Prize winner. To add insult to injury, in spite of their efforts, there is nothing mainstream about the Bauers. Their accent, their tastes, and their dachshunds are reminders of the Old Country. Similar to the American husband in Hilde Spiel's *Lisas Zimmer,* Connie's Gentile lover is configured as a latent fascist who takes up with Connie, not suspecting that she could be a Jew (1). Initially, the disparities in Connie's personality seem erratic: her extreme dependence on her mother clashes with her professional self-confidence; her insecurity seems incongruent with her openly displayed sensuality and her sudden resolve to get married. Her partner of choice, a Polish Jew, reveals the degree to which Connie vacillates between the cultures, European, American, Jewish, and Gentile. Stanislav Reich, her estranged husband, represents the one; the American macho Ronald Hake, whose name alludes to the American cowboy-actor president Ronald Reagan, the other extreme. Connie is incompatible with both, hence her inability to sustain either relationship. Ironically, Ronald is even more attracted to Connie when he suspects her of being Hitler's daughter; indeed, the deviant ways in which he tries to expose her father disclose his affinity to Nazi practices. Driven by psychosexual Hitler fantasies, he undertakes skull measurements, engages in underhanded detective work, and writes pedantic reports. The motif of a man's enjoying a woman's favors while plotting against those closest to her and the proximity of lust and betrayal are combined with cultural difference in a novel of deception and self-deception. All characters display similar foibles, but the Bauers most blatantly exhibit self-deception. Blinded by their desire to belong, they do not realize that the Yale graduate Ronald Hake considers them just as inferior as they do East European Jews.

When Connie integrates her Austrian Jewish and her American identity, she is no longer out of context. Assuming her proper position —socially, historically, and subjectively—she gains a new dignity and ceases to be a funny character. In Dische's text, what separates the European Jew and the white Anglo-Saxon Protestant is the century-old history of persecutor and persecuted, to which the text alludes throughout. Admitting that these boundaries can be overcome in exceptional cases — of which the trust between the Bauers and their Austrian employee, Gerda, is an example—Dische posits that the Holocaust remains a dividing line between groups and individuals (145). Like the survivors, the American man also has a secret inner life, but his is truly a dirty one, "swaddled in layers of pity": he could live with the daughter of Hitler, but not with the child of Jewish Holocaust survivors (147). The boundaries between the Bauers and the Hakes, rather than being drawn along religious and ethnic lines, are ultimately shown to be a matter of history, culture, and conditioning.

Toward a New Jewish Women's Literature

(Re)Constructing the Motherland

During the 1980s Jewish and Jewish-identified women created a considerable body of German texts—literature and film—that broadened the basis for a new Jewish women's literature, most of which explores the events of the late 1980s and early 1990s—the reorganization of Europe, the fall of the Berlin Wall, the unification of Germany, and the democratization of Eastern Europe. This literature reflects the fact that the Jewish community in Germany and in Austria "has begun to restructure itself as a living integral part of both German and Jewish culture" (Gilman 1995, 2). Included among the women authors involved in establishing this new Jewish literature are members of the generations born before 1945, whose recollections encompass the time of persecution and exile. Many of the younger authors, some of whom have already been discussed, deal with the past as well, recasting it, as it were, as their personal and literary genealogy.[1]

It is obvious from the previously discussed works of the 1980s that the literature of Jewish women authors in Germany and Austria is anything but homogeneous. Despite the differences in style and focus, however, there are shared core topics and categories, such as the emphasis on the relationship between mother and child, the body as the site of conflict, the concern with geography and history, particularly women's history, and the search—successful or unsuccessful—for an intellectual or spiritual anchoring point, a new motherland, as it were. Typically, such a search involves the examination of traditional Jewish positions and concerns—religious Judaism, Zionism, and feminism, as well as Marxism and the leftist tradition, the relationship to Israel, Europe, and the United States, and the Shoah.

On the surface, the formidable political changes of the late 1980s had only a small impact on Jewish women's writing. Already established authors continued pursuing their previously established course, perhaps modifying their perspective to acknowledge the new situation in passing. In other cases, few as spectacular as Ruth Klüger's, these events in conjunction with personal experiences inspired memoirs or critical essays examining the authors' situation as Jewish women. Already the Historians' Debate of the mid-1980s, which called into question the significance of the Holocaust, had caused numerous writers to define themselves as Jews, both in their texts and in personal statements (Fleischmann 1994, 311; Beckermann 1989, 32). German unification made it even more necessary for German-speaking Jews to find their own voices and assert themselves in view of the danger of having the Jewish experience be subsumed under the triumph of German unity (D. C. G. Lorenz 1992b, 9). As Fleischmann comments, "The Germans are in the process of discounting the 'Final Solution' chapter of their history in order to integrate the 'Third Reich' into their history. As far as the Germans are concerned, this resolution is too convincing as to even mention the crimes of the Nazis in the Treaty of 'Reunification,' despite massive Jewish protests" (1994, 312).

Many of the publications by Jewish authors following the Historians' Debate, the commemoration year 1988, honoring the victims of the *Kristallnacht* and those of the annexation of Austria, and, even more so, the spectacle of German unification and the fall of the Iron Curtain, confirmed earlier-held positions. None of these events engendered radically new perspectives; nor did they elicit a unified Jewish response, which, in view of the diversity of the earlier debates, could hardly be expected. At the same time, Jewish culture is receiving unprecedented attention by the German public, obvious from recently instated Jewish studies programs, Jewish museums, and high-profile cultural events. Rafael Seligmann correctly attributes the promotion of Jewish culture in Germany at least in part to the German intelligentsia's fear of being associated with the nationalist and xenophobic forces in the Federal Republic, "although a full-scale renaissance" is impossible (1994, 182).

In view of the dearth of "genuine" Jews among the Jewish-identified authors in Germany, Y. Michal Bodemann uses the term "professional almost-Jews" to characterize some of the participants in Germany's new Jewish culture. "It is important to see then that to a considerable degree, Jewish culture is being manufactured, Jewish history reconstructed, by these Judaizing milieux—by German experts on Jewish culture and religion," she writes (1994, 57). While this and similar notes of caution against a search for Jewish authenticity in Germany or, for that matter, in any post-Holocaust country are justified, it must be kept in mind that since emancipation the construction and reconstruction of German-Jewish identity has been an ongoing process, paralleling the construction of German identities during approximately the same period. Establishing identity and cultural positioning have always been important aspects of texts written in the German language by Jewish women.

The continued "inability to see Jews as part of contemporary German culture," although self-identified Jews do play a prominent role in the cultural life in Germany and Austria (Gilman 1995, 33), more than justifies the continued pursuit and study of a Minor Jewish Literature and culture in both Germany and Austria. Jean Améry expresses the predicament faced by Jewish-identified individuals in contemporary Germany or Austria: "If being a Jew means sharing a religious creed with other Jews, participating in Jewish cultural and family tradition, cultivating a Jewish national ideal, then I find myself in a hopeless situation. . . . If being Jewish implies having a cultural heritage or religious ties, then I was not one and can never become one" (1986, 81). Yet, Améry insists, as does Edgar Hilsenrath in his novel *Das Märchen vom letzten Gedanken,* lest a racial ideology be adopted, identity can and must be modified by acquiring languages, discourses, and customs, which makes it to a certain degree a matter of choice or discourse (D. C. G. Lorenz 1990, 204). Améry comments: "Who would possibly prevent me from learning the Hebrew language, from reading Jewish history and tales, and from participating—without belief—in Jewish ritual, which is both religious and national? Well supplied with all the requisite knowledge of Jewish culture from the prophets to Martin Buber, I could emigrate to Israel and call myself Yochanan. I have the freedom to choose to be a Jew, and this freedom is my very personal and universally human privilege" (1986, 81).

Anne Carmny-Francis argues that "sexist discourse defines, describes and limits how men and women must act in order to be considered masculine and feminine, how to be 'real' men and 'real' women in a patriarchal or male-dominated society, anti-Semitic as well as a dogmatic Jewish discourse prescribe how a person has to think and act in order to qualify as a Jew" (1990, 1–2). As do feminist authors, who construct within their texts a "feminist reading position" (205) in an attempt to liberate themselves from externally defined codes and stereotypes, Jewish women writers construct positions within their work that address Jewish readers in particular. These must be taken into consideration when reading Jewish texts. Beyond that, the German-language literature written by Jewish women negotiates Jewish, German, Austrian, or Swiss issues, whichever the case may be, as well as women's concerns, all of which, intersecting and running at cross-purposes, produce unresolvable tensions and undercurrents.

Recasting Tradition: Personal Memory and Judaism (Grete Weil)

The experience of Grete Weil, born in 1906 in Rottach-Egern into an assimilated family, spans the most decisive decades of German twentieth-century history. Her writing reflects elements of the major intellectual movements in the Federal Republic since the end of the war. Existentialism left a noticeable mark on her earlier work, the student movement informed her negative view of American culture, as it did that of Lander and Mitgutsch, for example, in *Happy, sagte der Onkel* (1968), and the impact of the women's movement is apparent from her representation of female bonding and same-sex relationships in *Generationen* (1983).[2] Weil examines her position as well as those taken by other survivors of the Nazi regime from her point of view as a woman educated in the humanist tradition, which fostered German nationalism and an affinity for Greek antiquity and the classics. Weil's German humanist education is evinced by her unwavering loyalty toward Germany, past and present; her love of the Greco-Roman legacy is demonstrated by the setting and characters of *Meine Schwester Antigone* (1980). Weil's accounts of her life prior to the Holocaust disclose the contrast between her carefree bourgeois background and her present condition. In *Meine Schwester Antigone* she describes herself as a single older woman leading a modest, health-conscious life.

Before the publication of *Der Brautpreis* (1988), Weil had not addressed specifically Jewish topics. When she did so in the 1980s, she chose a historical setting, namely, ancient Judaism and the Bible. Even in her treatment of biblical themes, her post-Shoah perspective prevails: she seeks access to Jewish history from the point of view of a survivor of Nazism, a modern woman, and a feminist. In an interview, Weil characterizes her relationship to Germany and Judaism: "I have not been raised in the Jewish tradition. My parents always believed in the German-

Jewish symbiosis, as did most everybody at that time. And I always identified with German culture—with Goethe and Schiller" (Koelbl 1989,
256). Throughout her career, Weil has tried to come to terms with the
broken Jewish-Gentile synthesis and her own traumatic and uncomfortable memories of her years in exile, including a failed attempt to escape,
which she and her husband, the dramaturge Edgar Weil, undertook before the Nazi invasion, his arrest, his death at Mauthausen, and her work
for the Jewish Council in Amsterdam before she went into hiding in
1943. There was, however, never a moment's hesitation about her return
to Germany in 1947, at which time Weil established herself as an author.

The autobiographical novel *Ans Ende der Welt* (1949), set in Nazi-
occupied Holland, already addresses some of the conflicts emphasized
in Weil's later work, articulated with an authority and a precision equal
to the works of H. G. Adler, Giorgio Bassani, and Arnost Lustig. Weil
describes the effects of the Nuremberg laws on the Jews under Nazi
control, their loss of rank, name, and identity. The experience of being
confronted by fanatics who have an utter disregard for humanist values
and are propelled by lust and greed is a theme frequently revisited in
Weil's later texts. Contrary to most popular postwar authors, Weil, in
keeping with her conviction that the individual and his or her moral
values take priority over group interests and identity, portrays criminal behavior not only among the Nazis but also among Nazi victims.
From the beginning, she writes from a feminist perspective. In contrast
to male Holocaust authors, Weil ascribes agency or a sense of control to
her female characters, manifest also in their sexual desires and aggressions. These qualities are portrayed as factors that enhance a woman's
ability to survive.

Meine Schwester Antigone (1980) combines autobiography, mythology, and fiction. Gender and cultural identity are explored by way of
the Antigone myth and, highly topical, from the perspective of the Jewish survivor. Published three years prior to Christa Wolf's novel *Kas-
sandra,* which deconstructs male mythmaking by recasting the story of
the Trojan War from the point of view of the woman prophet, Weil's
Antigone reconfigures Greek mythology in close identification with her
protagonist.[3] The antique subject matter is recast in such a way as to elu-
cidate the post-Shoah fate of women dissidents who, like Weil herself,
survived a male companion being killed by the Nazis. Furthermore, she
projects into Antigone, a woman torn between two hostile brothers,

her dilemma as a German woman of Jewish descent who has difficulty positioning herself between German Gentiles and Jews.

Meine Schwester Antigone and *Der Brautpreis* are written from the perspective of a woman whose body is affected by old age, while her long-term memory is becoming increasingly lucid. Incompatible with her alert mind, her aging body creates for her unsolvable problems and imperious feelings, including the craving for affection and her grief about the loss of her companions, most recently her dog. Her female identity poses another problem, as does her relationship to Judaism. The latter two are entwined: she speculates, for example, if she might have had children, had the Nazis not come to power (1988, 146). The blurring of the time lines causes the narrator to remember her male friends and lovers of the different stages in her life with equal immediacy, and Vienna, the city of her youth, Holland, her place of exile, and Frankfurt, her present residence, are integrated into a network of perceptions reminiscent of the states of mind portrayed in Irene Dische's narratives about older refugees from Nazi Germany (53). Weil's prose crosses boundaries that include gender, sexual identity, and the categories of humans and animals. Moreover, her prose expresses bisexual desires for men and women and transcends species lines in the portrayal of her relationship with animals (147).[4]

Antigone, the protagonist, provides Weil with a foil for her own dilemma of being a woman of problematic ancestry, who was torn from a princesslike existence. Through this experience, the author became attuned to Antigone's destructive and self-destructive tendencies, her incestuous passions, and "the arrogance of the martyrs who consider themselves, rightly or wrongly, better than the others" (10–13). Weil uses the Greek myth to overwrite it with her own memories, thereby transforming it to provide a paradigm to interpret the failure of the German-Jewish synthesis. Through this approach, she places her work into a discursive continuum from antiquity to the present. Greek mythology, having retained some of its character as the universal European system of communication, bridges the generation gap between Weil's narrator and her goddaughter; it serves as a medium through which the two women can discuss otherwise taboo topics, the Nazi past and the Holocaust.

In *Der Brautpreis,* the autobiographical and cultural aspects are even more tightly interwoven. For Weil, the biblical setting requires greater distance than the Greek myth. For this reason, the text ostensibly moves away from the author's own story to explore Jewish tradition in cultural, existential, and personal terms. The first phrase, "I, Grete," followed by a disclaimer of the author/narrator's "Christian" names, Margarete and Elisabeth, indicates a repositioning similar to that intended by Mitgutsch's name change from Waltraud to Anna (1988, 7–9). Since Weil has neither Zionist leanings nor a religious faith, her concept of Jewish identity is based on the experience of persecution. Oppression and suffering are also major aspects of Weil's concept of being a woman in the Gentile as well as in the Jewish context (70–71, 167). This aspect of her work is particularly pronounced since her novel, similar to Ruth Klüger's autobiography, is directly motivated by her direct confrontation with her own mortality as a result of her physical frailty, disease, and aging. Weil's literary attempt at coming to terms with her identity by expanding her understanding of Jewish culture occurs as she is recovering from a stroke (72–73).

Since Weil finds it difficult to relate to modern-day Jews such as the Americans and the Sephardim whom she met on her trip to Jerusalem—she feels as distant from the Jews in Israel as she did from the indigent Dutch Jews being rounded up by the ss—she approaches Judaism through the Bible and the figures of David and Michal (219). Her journey to Israel has provided her with some insights into Jewish history and the incentive to write a Jewish novel based on Scripture. Since Weil's work is informed by a wide variety of sources and impulses, several irreconcilable constructs of Jewishness collide. From a philosophical point of view, the persecuted Jews of Europe are given preference over the victorious Jews of the Bible and in Israel, but intuitively the narrator feels closer to Michelangelo's heroic statue of David. Throughout the novel an attempt is made to synthesize the two divergent aspects of David, the one expressed by Michelangelo's idealized sculpture, the other in a more realistic Rembrandt painting (236).

In conjunction with her version of the story of David, Weil recounts her development, beginning with her father's humanist legacy, symbolized by Michelangelo's statue of David, an image that left no room for Jewish reality, but the Jewish faces painted by Rembrandt did (11). Inspired furthermore by the homoerotic poetry of August von Platen, Weil had formed an enticing, larger than life-size image of David when she was a teenager. These associations are preserved in *Der Brautpreis.*

David's requiem for Michal's brother identifies the relationship between the two men unequivocally as homosexual (90). By revealing these and other possible facets of the David myth, Weil offsets the patriarchal ideology of the biblical text and configures a framework that she finds easier to accept.

Der Brautpreis discloses how persons of Weil's generation and background had been indoctrinated. As a result of Jewish history not being discussed in her circles, she was prevented from identifying her hero David as a Jew, and she placed him on the same level as the heroes of classical German literature. This kind of naïveté, fostered by her education at home and in school, was a breeding ground for Jewish self-hatred, which affected Weil, as it did many of her German-socialized Jewish contemporaries. She preferred her German high school classes to Hebrew school and the patriotic German cultural and historical instruction to the traditional Jewish teaching style by rote. Because of her learning experience and her early encounters with anti-Semitism, she wished to be German rather than Jewish (9). Reviewing her life on the occasion of the 1988 *Kristallnacht* commemoration, she reaffirms her decision to live in Germany, although it is the country of her husband's killers; she never had the desire to leave the realm of her literary language, even though her trust in her native country had been severely undermined (163).

Weil's discussion of Rembrandt's representation of David, modeled after a Dutch Jew, reveals her ambivalence toward the biblical story. Unsure whether David is a criminal or a hero, Weil projects certain aspects of her own experience onto him, including her self-doubts regarding her work for the *Judenrat* in Amsterdam. Michal and the anything but likeable Bathsheba represent yet other facets of the author, namely, her association with the fate of the perpetrators from whom she is unable or unwilling to distance herself. In this respect, she uses her characters to stage a literary psychodrama. Michal, the daughter of Saul, twice married to David and one of his widows, embodies wisdom, humanity, and powerlessness, while David, whom she loves and despises, is corrupted by desire, power, and greed (13). Moreover, the character constellations in *Der Brautpreis* are configured in such a way as to accommodate the author's concerns as a bisexual woman in post-Shoah Germany, as well as the German-Jewish problematic, both of which are interconnected in the novel.

Similar to *Meine Schwester Antigone, Der Brautpreis* is organized around the opposing poles of art, love, and pacifism on the one hand, and zeal, ambition, and destruction on the other. Power and sexuality cause Weil's David to betray his better self, embodied by Michal and Jonathan. In opposition to biblical law, Weil, through the eyes of Michal, portrays passion and luxury as positive and the heroic male virtues condoned by the Scriptures as destructive. The mass murder of the Philistines instigated by David to win the hand of Michal marks the end of her physical attraction for him.

This episode of indiscriminate violence in biblical times is used to suggest parallels between Jewish and German history. Through Michal's alienation from David and her open dislike for his and Bethsheba's son, the exulted king Solomon, Weil expresses her own ambivalence toward the Jewish as well as the German past. In her search for an alternative tradition within Judaism, she confronts, as she did in the myth of Antigone, paradigms that entail male violence and the oppression of women. To expose these characteristics of patriarchy, Weil lends the oppressed her voice and psychologizes Michal and other female characters. Michal's two marriages, her sexual prowess, and her appetite for love are portrayed in positive terms, although they constitute violations of the laws that regulate women's lives.

Weil's lack of interest in the traditional motifs of the David story shows that her main agenda is inscribing biblical tradition with a perspective that allows her to position herself into this tradition as an emancipated modern Jewish woman. In conjunction with her psychological portrait of David and his contemporaries, Weil creates a version of the biblical text that allows for female agency. Along with her literary project of appropriating Jewish history goes an antipatriarchal discourse opposing ancient and modern cultural practices. The David presented in Weil's novel is a calculating opportunist and a mass murderer: his sanctimonious speeches show him to be a master of crowd manipulation, and his character traits combine the seducer's sexual allure and the tyrant's brutality. He possesses the intense appeal of a sex symbol, but his frigidity rules out sustained intimacy with him—these very traits have been attributed to Hitler. By way of a Jewish text, Weil probes the roots of genocide, ethnocentrism, and the domination of women.

Ultimately Weil's narrative analysis leads to the conclusion that the patriarchal structures of Judaism contain the roots of imperialism and genocide. Reflecting the author's middle-class sensitivities, the obscure charismatic adventurer, David or Hitler—rather than the established tyrant Saul—is portrayed as the real danger, someone who ruthlessly exploits the advantages that traditional patriarchy offers to an ambitious male. The traditional patriarchal values, Jewish and Gentile, are portrayed as the lesser evil, but they present a threat because they are easily radicalized. To express it more pointedly, in the context of Weil's novel, the much-debated *Sonderweg* leading to Nazism, rather than beginning in nineteenth-century Germany, started among Jews at the time of David.

Establishing a link between her own fate, her flight from Germany, and the arrest and murder of her husband allows Weil to produce an internally consistent and hence persuasive text to illustrate her underlying argument. Countless statements applying to both David's rule and the Nazi era (1988, 50) suggest that being a Jewish woman has never been a matter of positive choice but, rather, a condition superimposed from the outside. Being identified as Jewish rendered Weil's own love of the German language and German culture irrelevant—her definition by others was more important than her self-definition and socialization (51).

Although an entire system of literary signals in *Der Brautpreis* associates Weil's text with the works of other Jewish women authors, her novel is distinct from German mainstream literature, and its multiple contradictions are inconsistent with the works of most contemporary Jewish authors as well. The allusions to Paul Celan's "Todesfuge," for example—namely the lines referring to German and Jewish female identity, "Your golden hair, Marguerite/ Your ashen hair, Shulamith" (Weil 1988, 56)—position Weil's work within the Holocaust discourse (Celan 1952, 37–39). Ironically, however, these lines also effect the opposite: they contain a reference to the author's given name, Margarete, thereby assigning her to the German context. Similar to Ronnith Neumann's *Heimkehr in die Fremde* (1985), Weil's *Der Brautpreis* revives the pre-Nazi German-Jewish discourse with all of its contradictions.

Der Brautpreis represents the attempt of an author more identified with German tradition than with the Jewish heritage to transform biblical characters and motifs in such a way as to bring them closer to her own situation. The emotional and cultural differences that must be overcome are too great, and the experiment fails. Weil can endorse the Jewish legacy only by deconstructing it, and she can affiliate herself with Germany only by remaining at its margins, hence her focus on a powerless, marginalized woman character. By making the attempt to place herself in the position of Michal as well as David, Weil attains a better understanding, not of Judaism, but possibly of herself. Her biblical novel is a unique literary enterprise, the document of an author's struggle to come to terms with both her German and her Jewish heritage in religious and historical terms at a time that does not allow for neutrality.

A Universe of Terror (Ronnith Neumann)

Ronnith Neumann's science fiction narrative *Nirs Stadt* (1991) is in many ways paradigmatic of the literature exploring the position of Jews and women after the fall of the Iron Curtain and German unification. *Nirs Stadt* portrays a universe without alternatives, foreshadowing dire consequences at the hand of a victor whose identity remains unspecified. The basic outlook of the narrative, as well as its major themes, resembles later works such as Katja Behrens's *Salomo und die anderen* (1993). Neumann's reconsideration of the Shoah, evoked in stark images, connects her text to the autobiographical literature of Grete Weil and Ruth Klüger, whereas the emphasis on global destruction places *Nirs Stadt* into the context of ecological science fiction literature. The latter connection is problematic insofar as it links her work to the blatantly anti-Semitic views, expressed in "Violence against Women and Children" (1990), published by the Green Party.[5] The anti-Semitism pervading the most socially progressive German party makes it difficult for Jewish authors committed, like Neumann, to a Green Party program to maneuver between a politically correct feminist and offensive anti-Semitic agenda.

In *Nirs Stadt,* Neumann circumvents this conflict by selecting an ahistorical abstract setting. In a surrealistic representational style, the narrative links visions of disaster reminiscent of Lea Fleischmann's Gulf War diary, *Gas: Tagebuch einer Bedrohung* (1991), with stark concentration camp imagery. The grim outlook for the future, suggested in both works, mirrors an atmosphere that Kizer Walker describes as "a sense of a hopelessly shattered German Left in the aftermath of the Gulf War" (1994, 149). Neumann's narrative cosmos resembles the totalitarian male-dominated setting of Margaret Atwood's *The Handmaid's Tale* (1986), portraying misogynist, fascist, and totalitarian structures taken to their extreme. Unlike Atwood's protagonist, the main characters in

285

Nirs Stadt, an imprisoned woman left to starve in a dungeon and her daughter, who watches her die from outside her cell, are too far removed from the centers of power to form even an impression of what lies beyond the boundaries of the concentration camp in which the jail is situated. Limiting the narrative perspective predominantly to the perceptions of the girl Nir causes the impression of an immense distance between the powerful schemers behind the scenes—if they actually exist—and the tormented women.[6] Additional insights are provided into the confused thoughts of Nir's starving mother, who is in touch with her daughter on an intuitive level, as well as into the psyche of the camp commandant and the guards. There are also occasional comments by a third-person narrator, elucidating the situation from a seemingly objective point of view. All of these insights are directed in such a way as not to detract from the camp's oppressive monotony. Nowhere, except in the women's memory and Nir's imagination, is there a hint that there may be a peaceful world outside, a private sphere that would allow for personal fulfillment. Nir's inner dialogues, involving the allegories of War and Peace and other imaginary figures, show that the children are already lost between escapist dreams and a horrific reality.

Similar to the protagonist of Ilse Aichinger's *Die größere Hoffnung* (1974a), Nir uses her creative resources for her emotional survival. She struggles to form a coherent vision of the world, an antiworld to counterbalance her experience. What seems like child's play, her building a city of dirt and stones, is a constructive activity similar to the sand play used by Jungian therapists to help their clients to integrate the disparate elements of their fragmented psyche. Nir's attempts to create a sphere of well-being and serenity, a safe place for women and children, is a religious undertaking by which she forges a space for herself and her fellow prisoners to live in peace. Her work mirrors the post-Shoah woman author who writes of a Jewish text in the German language, a text that by its very existence defies the lessons of history and her own experience of a world at the verge of destruction.

Like the narrator, Nir reflects almost incessantly upon her and the other prisoners' plight in order to find a solution, even if it ends up being one uniquely suited to only one person. Neumann's text, similar to Aichinger's radio play *gare maritime,* re-creates the concentration camp universe in a radicalized form by combining elements from historical studies, fiction, and personal accounts. Portraying a universe populated by victims and perpetrators, *Nirs Stadt* emulates different genres of Holocaust literature and different literary styles—realistic, fantastic, bizarre, and absurd.

Only the most rudimentary information necessary to establish the circumstances under which the protagonists live is provided in *Nirs Stadt,* fleeting impressions of a war in which the men of the defeated country were killed and the women and children rounded up, imprisoned in concentration camps, and ordered to build roads (46). As in the Nazi concentration camps, the women wear uniforms, have their heads shaved, and perform slave labor. The camp structure—including the barracks designed for a variety of purposes, an *Appellplatz* for role calls, the electric barbed wire fence that some prisoners use to commit suicide, the anonymity, and the daily routine, with the life of the women is compared to that of ants in an anthill—resembles that of Auschwitz-Birkenau, with the exception that no mention is made of mass exterminations and that children are allowed to live. They are even the objects of a certain benevolence on the part of the guards (46), calling to mind Rudolf Hoess's portrayal of his interaction with Gypsy children in Auschwitz (Hoess 1961, 141).

Similar to Kafka's culture-neutral descriptions in *The Penal Colony,* Neumann's narrative is rich in detail, but not enough so to connect it to a specific era or location. The references to extreme temperatures suggest a continental climate, the monsoon a subtropical climate (1991, 46). The camp installations and the guards' equipment belong to the technological age, but the prisoners live under the most primitive conditions imaginable, signifying the difference between victors and victims and characterizing the preeminence of the instruments of destruction over the institutions of civilized society. Except, perhaps, for the women's dark eyes, no ethnic or racial differences between oppressors and oppressed are alluded to (146). Gender is the first, age the second, distinguishing category among the individuals in the camp. The openness of Neumann's narrative calls for interpretation on a multitude of levels, but the most obvious one involves gender, the category according to which the characters are grouped.

The insights into the camp commandant's psyche reveal that the prevailing misogyny and sadism are rooted in destructive childhood experiences. Apparently the reasons for women's mistreatment by the men are deep-seated psychological and cultural, rather than political, causes (65).

The need to sublimate for his rejection by women other than prostitutes and the cruelty at the hands of his mother have filled the commandant with a craving for power, best expressed through his relationship to his machine gun, which he treats as if it were a woman: "The machine gun lay in his arm. It lay warm and trusting in his arm. It had no fear. . . . What now, my friend, he thought, what's your decision? — Do we want to show them [the women]? If you love me, you'll show them" (97). The males in the novel are without exception shown to be incapable of normal sexual relations; they rape, and the commandant engages in acts of mutilation and murder. His sexual behavior is of such violence that Nir is unable to grasp what is going on — she interprets it as a manifestation of her most ferocious imaginary enemy, the wolf (36–37).

By contextualizing elements of contemporary pornography, such as the fetishization of breasts and segments of the female body as the site of sadistic fantasies and practices, with the concentration camp scenery and murder, Neumann, similar to Jelinek, links the exploitation of women through pornography to criminal and fascist practices. Nir's mother, whom the commander uses to frighten the prisoners into obedience, is left to die under the man's watchful eye. His fascination with having absolute power over her is spelled out directly: "HE — yes, he — HE had the power. Yes, he wanted to think of the woman, of course. With her, he had the upper hand. He liked that thought" (106). The psychosexual entanglement of the male in authority with the tortured prisoner also involves attempts on his part to take control of the woman's daughter: he feeds her and tries to invade her imaginary city; when he fails to win her over, he sets her free to face the world outside the camp, depopulated and devastated (171).

The motto by Peter Handke — "Time heals everything/ But what if the time itself / is the disease?" is taken up in the guard's musing: "We are all sick, he thought, including the children. . . . Only we do not know it" (168). The statement provides a key to the events: the male characters are demented as a result of living as loners, "wolves," unable to bond with other persons, female or male (129, 25). The male hierarchy of rank and power is depicted as a system that utilizes the propensity for sadomasochism to regulate the interaction among men through domination and submission, expressed by giving and receiving orders. As far as women are concerned, men control, intimidate, and violate them (107) because men perceive women as a species distinct from their

own. The women, in turn, respond in the manner of a subjugated hostile crowd, calling to mind Elias Canetti's image of the double crowds,
Doppelmassen (1981, 66–71). The males are excluded from the women's
inner circle of nurturing.

Although the women end up fighting, opposing the men in an unsuccessful revolt, they are not real warriors. As desperate mothers, the
narrator stresses, they confront and even terrify the professional killers
(137). Unlike the males, however, they have reasons to fight. Contrary
to the men's gratuitous brutality, their hatred, like their exuberance, is
elicited by specific events (139). The women's excesses are characterized
as being the result of prolongued imprisonment and frequent battery;
their cruelty springs from the knowledge that their fight is futile. The
fact that their rebellion instills the pride of fighters into their children is
viewed as a tragedy because it entails abandoning the commitment to
peace. Only Nir remains unaffected by the new militant attitude (144–
45).

Neumann's concept of masculinity as disease goes beyond the traditional criticism of patriarchy. The social structures of her concentration
camp universe may be dominated by males, but they are not patriarchal; the males in *Nirs Stadt* assume the total power, but none of
the patriarchs' responsibilities. Cast as predators, similar to the name-
less marauder in Marlen Haushofer's novel *Die Wand* (1968), the male
characters represent individualism taken to the extreme. Eradicating the
memory of the past and the hope for the future, Neumann's men are
the ultimate expression of a society overcome by homocidal and suicidal tendencies.

Compared to Neumann's earlier novel *Heimkehr in die Fremde* (1985),
Nirs Stadt represents both a radicalization and a universalization of
views expressed earlier. Structurally, the situation of Nir, deprived of
her nation's and family's legacy and sent on her way into an uninhabit-
able world, resembles that of Neumann's earlier autobiographical narrator, who is alienated from Germany as well as Israel. *Heimkehr in
die Fremde* suggested the possibility of global devastation and criticized
the hero-and-fighter ethos among Jews in Israel. Nir's solitude is even
greater than that of the Jewish woman who stands between the cultures,
the legacy of the Holocaust and the prospect of an apocalyptic future.
Unlike the woman, who ends up placing her hope on a young German

idealist, Nir is left with a bird of prey circling over her head as her only companion.

In 1991 the U.S. intervention in Iraq, "Operation Desert Storm," provided a graphic preview of a modern-day apocalypse shortly after the rehabilitation of the nation that engineered the Holocaust. These events account for the bleak outlook in *Nirs Stadt:* the heroic rhetoric of the Germans, the wave of anti-Semitism that swept all across Europe in the late 1980s and early 1990s, General Norman Schwarzkopf's swagger of bravery, and the beginning of ethnic cleansing in Eastern Europe, conducted by means of slaughter and mass rape, form the background of *Nirs Stadt.* The devastating images of Eastern Europe published after the fall of the Iron Curtain, showing a polluted wasteland, may have been an additional source for Neumann's portrayal of a homogenized and impoverished world. Without naming the Shoah, *Nirs Stadt* incorporates the language and the images of the genocide that shaped the author's outlook as a Jew and as a woman and the events of a time when anti-Semitism was once more becoming acceptable in public discourse and when the progress made by the feminist and ecological movements was fast eroding.

The image of Neumann's fictitious land, overrun by enemy forces and sectioned off into concentration camps, suggests that without the checks and balances that the presence of a political alternative in the Eastern Bloc provided, women and children are most likely to become the victims of exploitation on a global scale. The vision of a future dominated by social Darwinism resembles the description of greed and brutality in Edgar Hilsenrath's 1964 work *Nacht,* a novel set among ghetto prisoners. Like Hilsenrath, Neumann questions the values to which the Federal Republic subscribed after the demise of Nazism, and like the older author and Holocaust survivor, she attributes to women exclusively the necessary qualities to safeguard the survival of the human race (D. C. G. Lorenz 1994b, 221). By depicting the abject conditions in an exclusively male-dominated society, *Nacht* and *Nirs Stadt* indict the androcentric social organization of the Western world. In a 1990s context, Neumann's novel makes a strong critical statement about German unification and the global restructuring under the auspices of Western-style democracy.

Also underlying Neumann's narrative is a Jewish subtext. In *Heimkehr in die Fremde,* Jewish identity is gendered as feminine, and the

290

oppression of the dark-eyed women in concentration camps by sexually repressed military men in *Nirs Stadt* ties in thematically with the
critical studies on the authoritarian personality, fascism, and the construction of masculinity and femininity. These elements call for a reading of Neumann's text as a commentary not only on female but also on
Jewish identity. Similar to early Holocaust texts, *Nirs Stadt* juxtaposes
two attitudinally and ethnically distinct groups, victims and perpetrators. Separatist feminist literature configured a similarly polarized view
of women and men.[7] In both instances, fundamental constitutional differences were attributed to the two opposing groups. In *Nirs Stadt*,
these difference are suspended during the armed rebellion. "Like a pack
of dogs in a chase, they ran toward the women. The women yelled at
them with a single voice. They raised their arms holding clubs, sticks,
and stones and ran toward the men. Like two hunting packs they ran
toward each other and collided in the middle of the square" (1991, 133).

In this scene, and even more so through the impact of the fight on the
children, the distinction between victims and perpetrators breaks down.
Nelly Sachs's concern that the victims become perpetrators seems confirmed, even if only temporarily and in self-defense; in the iconography
of Nir, War has swallowed Peace. Similar to Beckermann, who suggests
in *Die papierene Brücke* (1986) that traditional Jewishness and militant
Jews are a contradiction in terms, or to a character in Nadja Seelich's
Kieselsteine (1982), who maintains that by adopting Zionism traditional
Jewry created its own final solution, Neumann also deplores the demise
of Jewish pacifism. Without denying the courage of the rioting women,
she suggests that for the sake of future generations acquiescence is preferable to taking up arms because confrontation entails conforming to
the enemy's way of life. Signifying that she has understood that the myth
about the Jewish victims' going to the slaughter like lambs is as incorrect as it is demeaning, Neumann nonetheless objects to any entanglement of victims and perpetrators, least of all in an armed confrontation.
To avoid being caught up in dynamics that turn the formerly oppressed
into oppressors, Neumann champions unconditional pacifism.[8]

Memory and Autobiography (Ruth Klüger)

Weiter leben (1992), the autobiography of the scholar Ruth Klüger, a
native of Vienna, represents a landmark between earlier and more re-

cent discussions of the Holocaust and Jewish identity in the German language. The book is a personal document, written under the author's maiden name, Klüger, rather than her professional name, Angress. Like Weil's autobiographical prose, Klüger's account is based on firsthand experience and a broad-based perspective from which it challenges major trends in Holocaust literature, to which her title, a variation of Jean Améry's *Weiterleben* (1982), establishes an explicit connection. Similar to Améry, like herself a Shoah survivor, and other Jewish autobiographers, such as Peter Weiss, Manès Sperber, and Elias Canetti, Klüger represents subjective experience and historical processes as intimately intertwined. Yet, her focus being the present and feminist, her account, unlike theirs, is free of the nostalgia that Michael Fischer attributes to the traditional search for an ethnic identity in autobiographical texts (1994, 92). At a time when the younger generation of Jewish women defined themselves as writers, filmmakers, and intellectuals in such a way as to compromise neither their Jewish identity nor their status as emancipated women, Klüger established a tenuous link with Germany, reclaiming her native German language as a Jewish writer.

The account of a survivor of Theresienstadt and Auschwitz written in the late 1980s and published in 1992, *weiter leben* marks an end point in the tradition of survivors' correspondences, memoirs, and Holocaust scholarship, and a new beginning in that it documents a Jewish émigrée's return to the German language to discuss Jewish concerns.[9] With some notable exceptions, sophisticated superstructures are uncharacteristic of survivors' memoirs. The complex patterns of *weiter leben,* a prose work interspersed with lyric poetry, the earliest of which dates back to Auschwitz, the latest to the time prior to the completion of the book, show Klüger as an accomplished author and critic. *Weiter leben* is a contribution to both the ongoing attempts to deal with the past and a Jewish feminist's attempt to integrate her separate biographies. The work demonstrates that the Nazi legacy concerns not only the German mainstream but also Jews who must come to terms with their history, the Holocaust, Germany, and the Germans.

Weiter leben documents healing and self-affirmation despite its focus on the attacks on the narrator's and author's individuality, freedom, health, and life. Vienna, Theresienstadt, Auschwitz, and Groß-Rosen are the sites of Klüger's ordeal; Bavaria of the 1940s and Göttingen of the 1980s are those of her physical and emotional recovery. Klüger is conversant with German and international Holocaust literature against which she measures her own experience. She bypasses the debate about the representation of the Holocaust and the ability of language to convey its horrors (Hilberg and Söllner 1988, 175).[10] Her deliberate avoidance of this discourse suggests that she does not consider theories forged by critics with only secondhand knowledge of the Holocaust relevant to her work, as she expressed earlier in a review of Claude Lanzmann's film *Shoah*.[11] Klüger sets her experience apart from the views of writers whose lives were affected by, but who did not experience, the death camps.

The museum culture that has sprung up around the concentration camps is based on a sense of *spiritus loci* which I lack. What was done there could be repeated elsewhere, I have argued, conceived as it was by human minds, carried out by human hands, somewhere on earth, the place irrelevant, so why single out the sites that now look like so many others? I don't go back to where I've been. I have escaped. Lanzmann goes back to where he has never been. . . . Like all survivors I know that Auschwitz, when the Nazis killed Jews there, felt like a crater of the moon, a place only peripherally connected with the human world. It is this "otherness" of the death camps that we have such difficulty conveying. But once the killing stopped these former camps became a piece of our inhabited earth again. (R. K. Angress 1986, 250)

What distinguishes Klüger's writing from that of exile writers and the younger generation of Jewish authors is the fact that she was at the places that they try to imagine. Hence, Klüger does not search for her lost culture and the death camps. Having survived and left the country of her oppressors, she knows that memory transcends time and space, and that landscapes and buildings have neither spirit nor language. Lander, Honigmann, and Beckermann come to the same conclusion *after* their trips to Eastern Europe. Klüger does not repeat known descriptions of the concentration camps that have been elaborated by Käthe Starke, Gerty Spies, and many others. However, the texts of these and other women authors constitute points of reference for Klüger.

A feminist, Klüger is often in disagreement with the ideological thrust of traditional Holocaust literature. Aware that the discrimination of women is common to all Western societies, she contends that misogyny is the reason why even prominent Holocaust authors omit or

distort women's experiences or represent them with voyeuristic overtones or as outright pornography (1992, 236). Consequently, the intertextuality Klüger establishes is between her work and the ongoing discourses by women authors dealing with issues of memory—she shares
their concerns about German and Austrian culture and the search for
an appropriate position. Klüger has achieved greater distance, albeit
not greater impartiality, than the younger authors, but her memories of
growing up among persecuted adults, her encounter with genocide, and
her own development are immediate and intense, as are her discussions
of the historical background for her and her family's suffering.

Klüger's convalescence in Göttingen after a near-fatal traffic accident
represents the biographical and narrative anchoring point for the entire
text. The collision with a young man on a bicycle elicits old memories of
her encounter with the German soldiers invading Vienna in 1938, a collision of existential proportions: "Metal, like spotlights across the barbed
wire, I want to defend myself, push him back, both arms stretched out,
the collision, Germany, a moment like a brawl, I am losing this fight,
metal, once again Germany, what am I doing here why have I returned,
did I ever leave? . . . And this notion or perhaps only imagination that
this sixteen-year-old drove into me out of aggression. Not out of aggressive thinking, but out of an aggressive instinct" (272). Passages like
this one, scrutinizing multiple layers of facts, manifest the complexity
of Klüger's narrative. On one level, the accident represents a replay of
the past; on another, it does not: the boy causing the accident is Viet-
namese, the adopted son of a German couple. Similarly, the portrayal of
Klüger's childhood from an adult point of view involves different degrees of insight and varying time frames.

Klüger's autobiography stands in a class by itself because of its literary merits. With a sensitivity for nuances, it evokes contexts, emotions,
atmospheres, and characters. Austrian expressions, the Viennese timbre,
and occasionally Yiddish vocabulary are employed to evoke the atmosphere of the conservative Viennese Jewish middle class of the 1930s.
Within, and in contrast to this environment, Klüger portrays herself as
a rebellious young girl, attracted to Zionism and insisting on changing her name from Susanna to Ruth to better express her personality
(40). Integrated into the personal experiences is an abundance of critically processed material. The result is a highly reflective text. During
decades of silence, Klüger achieved a unique mastery of her material as

well as the confidence to draw conclusions without arguing every point. She states her positions with unerring certainty regarding, for example, the question whether writing poetry after Auschwitz was possible and legitimate. She emphatically answers in the affirmative, since she considers every attempt to articulate the unspeakable as significant (36).

Having been denied access to writing tools in the concentration camps, Klüger does not even take the material basis for her work for granted and is keenly aware of the problems of authorship. She reflects on the processes of writing and remembering as well as on her means of production, formerly the typewriter, now the computer (25–27). By revealing the many details upon which she depends as an author, she shows that creativity is dependent on a great many factors, including community and language. Klüger discusses her experience with Austrian German, Yiddish, English, and German, the four major languages in her life.

Klüger's native Viennese dialect links her to her childhood; Yiddish is associated with the Holocaust—she picked it up in the camps as a tool for survival, acquiring through it a persona that she later wanted to suppress (176). It evokes the extinct *shtetl* culture, the tenderness and the wit of Eastern European Jewry, but, above all, the genocide (208–9). English and Standard German are the media of Klüger's profession. The latter, her official language, is the idiom in which she confronts the German intelligentsia of the 1980s. Exposing their fragmentary knowledge of Nazi and Holocaust history, their specialized vocabulary and body language reserved for these topics, Klüger illustrates the failure of the German project of dealing with and thus overcoming the past (269). On the other hand, she concedes that she herself might not have reached her present degree of insight without first distancing herself from her country and language of origin. The confrontation with the language of the perpetrators was one precondition for writing her memoirs; the accident in Göttingen and the convalescence period was the other. It represents the "tableau," as Fischer terms the dramatic event from which flows the autobiographical text (1994, 105).

Weiter leben simultaneously engages the readers' intellectual and emotional faculties. The contrasting modes of poetry and prose captivate the imagination in different ways. Sudden switches from a global to an intimate perspective, from reflection to irony, are other frequently used devices. In her opening sentence Klüger establishes an unsettling ambiance that she sustains throughout the book: "Death, not sex, was the secret about which the adults whispered and about which one would have liked to hear more" (1992, 7). Klüger's use of perspectives can best be described in terms of shifting camera angles. The panoramic views and fluctuating moods create images changing in color and lighting, while stark closeups bring perceptions and ideas into focus. Characters such as the narrator's father are singled out from the larger spectrum and examined in detail. Flashbacks and previews enable the narrative voice to travel between different time frames and cultures. The chronological structure suggested by the list of contents is merely a blueprint on which a network of associations and cross-references is superimposed. Klüger likens her approach to the "unerase" capability of a computer, which makes it possible to recall information as long as it has not been overwritten with new information (271). Priorities are implied in this metaphor: Klüger's childhood memories and the Holocaust experience remain intact because no later event was powerful enough to overwrite them.

At no point are the narrator's identity and the authenticity of her insights questioned. The person telling her story may have changed over time, but she has remained one with her earlier selves, hence her certainty. Her lack of self-doubt is surprising in a postmodern environment that problematizes identity as few others have. The basis for Klüger's self-confidence is her Jewish identity. She describes her background as "emancipated, but not assimilated," stating that before Göttingen, she had lived "not exclusively, but to a large extent" as a Jew among Jews—mainly women—be it in Austria, in the concentration camps or in the United States (61, 269). This experience gave her the certainty of belonging, rather than, as Hannah Arendt defines the status of Jewish women in German society, playing the role of a "pariah" or a "parvenu." Jewish identity does not pose a problem: it is a given, rather than a "question."[12] Klüger finds her views confirmed by her acceptance by other Jews and the hostility of anti-Semites. In this respect, Klüger's experience differs from that of assimilated Jews or women of mixed parentage. She experiences gender and ethnicity as positive forces that shape her political views, her sense of justice, her compassion for the oppressed, and her rejection of violence.

Being a woman is the next important category defining Klüger's position. Neither the Holocaust nor the experience of aging (283) has eased her resentment against Jewish religious and social practices that relegate women to an inferior position. She deplores the fact that, as a woman, she is denied the right to say *Kaddish,* the prayer for the dead, for her father, and she denounces the Jewish gender code, which reduces women to the status of domestic helpmates (23). Citing numerous examples, she exposes the double standard that denies women their sexual freedom and a social experience equal to that of men. Yet, her criticism is that of an insider; its goal is change. Rather than internalized anti-Semitism or self-hatred, her pain of being discriminated against sparks the desire for reform (214). In this spirit, she sets her own feminist interpretations of biblical texts against orthodox views and questions patriarchal norms.[13]

After her concentration camp experience, Klüger's description of her acculturation in the United States reads almost effortlessly. She minimizes the rejection she encountered as an immigrant woman—she expected it. Neither it, nor the acquisition of a new language, poses a serious problem. Klüger reports that after her admittance to New York's Hunter College, she took up writing in English. Her later career as professor of German demonstrates her ability to overcome cultural and gender barriers and evidences the more egalitarian structures of her new society (231). The memory of the Holocaust, a basic element of her personality, is also an integral part of her new nationality and continues to shape her relationships, such as the love-hate relationship between Klüger, her mother, and her stepsister, a life-long codependency caused by the shared trauma. The disputes within this exclusive group do not preclude emotional closeness, whereas Klüger maintains, the misunderstandings between Jews and German Gentiles, "die Deutschen" (23), occur because they lack a common ground. Yet, she asserts that the barriers between German Gentiles and Jews are not indicative of a moral difference—being victimized does not presuppose superiority—but rather they signal a difference in outlook and sensibility. While Auschwitz, Klüger explains, was not a training ground for humanity and tolerance, it did create two categories of people, intended victims and perpetrators. She sees both as still separated from each other as if by a "rusty barbed wire." The Holocaust survivors and the students in today's Germany speak a different language.[14]

In Klüger's portrayal of women concentration camp prisoners and guards, her feminism comes to the fore. She differentiates between male and female behavior, asserting, in contrast to Fania Fénelon (1981), that sadism was rare among women. Examining gender roles among prisoners and perpetrators, she exposes the stereotype of the brutal female Capo (women prisoners put in charge of other prisoners) as a male fantasy. At the same time, her notions about women differ from the idealistic assessment of Hanna Lévy-Hass (1979) and Joan Ringelheim (1985), who portray mutual nurturing and love as innate female characteristics. Klüger points out that mutual support did increase the chances for survival, particularly in the neglected women's camps, but she rejects the notion that there is a biologically determined feminist impulse. Rather, she places women's endurance and cooperation into a sociological context. Similarly, she approaches the problem of anti-Semitism with a critical attitude, refuting misapprehensions about Jews and Judaism still held by mainstream Germans, but she also rejects the simplistic view that the Nazis were primitive barbarians, which fails to take into account the reality of the 1930s (1992, 24, 48).

Klüger writes with affection about her residence of choice, California, but she is emotionally more involved with Northern Germany. For her, a reevaluation of her life in light of the "jüngste Vergangenheit" (the "most recent" past)—a German euphemism for the Nazi era—was indicated by her stay in Göttingen at the time of unification. In her daily contact with Germans speaking High German, the language associated with Prussian militarism and German National Socialism, Klüger explored the nation that had perpetrated the destruction of the European Jews. The positive reception of *weiter leben* proves that in spite of everything that had been written about the Nazi era and the Holocaust until this point, experiences such as Klüger's continue to be debated in postunification Germany. Within a few weeks, *weiter leben* was discussed on German television, and Klüger was invited for readings and interviews in Germany and Austria and awarded prestigious prizes.

Despite the imposing intellectual and emotional force behind this autobiography, a remarkable humility is associated with the experience of survival; Klüger explains her fate in terms of luck and coincidence (73). Her awareness of human frailty provides an intellectual honesty and spirituality that gives *weiter leben* an aura of grace, reflected in her tolerance toward her former enemies (184). Rather than calling for an indiscriminate reconciliation between Jews and Germans or an unqualified "forgiving and forgetting," as the German public and many Gentile authors do, Klüger, Frank Stern points out, insists on historical accuracy, demarcations, and difference, which, if adhered to, could bring about the kind of tolerance that Moses Mendelssohn advocated two centuries ago (F. Stern 1994, 55; D. C. G. Lorenz 1994c, 220).

Coming Out Jewish (Esther Dischereit)

There are distinct parallels between the motifs and topics of Katja Behrens, Anna Mitgutsch, and Esther Dischereit stemming from the authors' perceptions of being at the margins of their respective societies. Like the above-mentioned two authors, Ruth Klüger and Ronnith Neumann, Dischereit is also of mixed parentage. Born in Heppenheim, in 1952, the daughter of a Jewish mother and a non-Jewish father, she was raised Lutheran, conscious of, but never discussing, her mother's background as a Jewish Holocaust survivor. Only after she and her mother moved to Frankfurt following her parents' divorce was it possible for her to reveal the well-guarded family secret. By November 1988, Dischereit had joined what Gilman defines as "the ranks of the canonical 'Jewish' writers in Germany"; however, he writes that "being Jewish" for Dischereit meant "to identify herself as religiously Jewish, celebrating the Sabbath and the High Holy Days and attending the *Gemeinde*, but not very often" (Gilman 1995, 64, 58).

Dischereit's autobiographical reflections about "being Jewish, being a woman and being decentered in German society" (Gilman 1995, 61) in *Joëmis Tisch* (1988) appear to have been occasioned by the fiftieth commemoration of *Kristallnacht*, which also inspired Irene Dische's satire *The Jewess* (1992). Dischereit examines German society from a dual perspective, expressed by an antithetical arrangement of text sequences. Her narrator is as well informed as anyone born and raised in Germany, and her literary models are "clearly those from post-Shoah modernist German high culture" (Gilman 1995, 61). Her convictions, however, are distinct from those of the German mainstream. In the 1990s, dissenting views such as hers are as much a part of German identity as the image of diversity that this culture wishes to project about itself. Nonetheless, a keen observer like Lea Fleischmann and Katja Behrens, Dischereit uncovers a host of disconcerting qualities in her native country that the general public denies or ignores. Through her writing, which is "political as well as aesthetic," she positions herself as part of the Jewish cultural presence in Germany as well as of German literary culture, and she participates in the debates and schisms that "reveal a living and breathing cultural entity," one that, Gilman asserts, "is virtually unique in the contemporary world" (69, 59).

In *Joëmis Tisch,* Dischereit reviews her experience of growing up as the daughter of a Jewish woman in West Germany. This experience ultimately motivates her to establish herself as a Jew. After her stocktaking in *Joëmis Tisch,* Dischereit moved from Frankfurt to Berlin, where she wrote the narrative *Merryn* (1992). From the vantage point of different historical junctures, both texts explore the narrator's difficulty of being a Jew in Germany and her ambivalence toward the gender roles available to her in German as well as in Jewish culture. In *Merryn,* more than in her previous book, Dischereit seems convinced of a continuity of "the Jewish past in Germany, with the inheritance of the Shoah" (Gilman 1995, 62).

Having established her personality in a symbiotic relationship with her severely traumatized mother, Hannah, the narrator/author of both works defines her Jewish identity as female and casts it as a mother-defined realm. Even though Hannah's existence was destroyed by Nazi racial politics—she lived as a marginalized and abused woman until her suicide—she nonetheless possesses memories of a time of relative stability and of her own bourgeois childhood. Unlike her daughter, Hannah, the child of a decorated World War I officer (1992, 91), had known and identified with pre-Nazi Germany. This knowledge provides her with an emotional anchoring point. Her daughter, however, has to construct, rather than reconstruct, a Jewish position for herself in the German context. This task can only be accomplished on the basis of Hannah's experience, although, paradoxically, it exemplifies to a large extent the failure of assimilation and the impossibility of living as a Jewish woman in Germany before, during, and after the Nazi era.

The narrator's memories reveal that neither the much-discussed *Wiedergutmachung* (restitution) nor a reintegration occurred for the Nazi victims after 1945—the destroyed communities could not be restored, and the survivors remained uncompensated for the loss of their family members and friends, as well as for their mental and physical suffering. As the narrator points out, the gap between Germans and Jews seems to be widening. If she chooses to stay in Germany, it is because she considers it the least unacceptable option available to her.

In her loosely knit prose text, Dischereit touches upon a multitude of factors leading up to the narrator's decision to declare herself Jew-ish. Important steps in the process are establishing a link with earlier Jewish discourses, examining "bodies of remembrance," while at the same time problematizing "the act of remembering" (Remmler 1994, 188). The motto preceding Dischereit's narrative refers to postwar Ger-man guilt and injustice, as does her topic, her mother's suicide, which is reminiscent of and yet fundamentally different from Peter Handke's 1972 novel about his mother's suicide, *Wunschloses Unglück*. Dischereit sets her Jewish experience against this and other non-Jewish texts with a certain resignation, implying that since neither the past nor varying perceptions of the past can be changed, there will be no justice for her protagonist and her mother. This very realization motivates Dischereit to register as a Jew, thereby effecting a change in the present, regardless how small. Having identified for twenty years with workers' issues and, at an earlier phase of her development, having been a moderate Chris-tian, her membership in the Jewish community is the expression of her final surrender as well as a new start: she has found no other spiritual or social authority to turn to, no forum with which to identify.

Joëmis Tisch opens with a narrative frame detailing the bureaucratic formalities involved in the protagonist's religious and cultural decision and her reflections about the events leading up to it: her past denial of her mother's legacy, her acknowledgment of the fact that national iden-tity is an important issue even in secular German organizations, and her hesitation to discuss Jewish issues and the Holocaust with Gentiles for fear of having to confront anti-Semitism. Faced with the alternative of assimilation, which would invalidate her and her mother's experience, or accepting her Jewishness, the latter is the only way to preserve her integrity.

The technique of reconstructing key events by way of tangible evi-dence such as notes and letters, also employed by Nadja Seelich and Ruth Beckermann, enables the narrator to formulate her priorities with increasing specificity. Her direct, colloquial, yet artful, diction is appro-priate to the display of subjective involvement. Rather than proceeding in a linear pattern, *Joëmis Tisch* is organized around themes and charac-ters, as is Dischereit's second book, *Merryn* (1992). In both texts, the plot lies hidden under layers of reflection and strands of interlocking epi-sodes. Dischereit's associative approach follows no chronological order, and the reader is forced to establish the course of events. This technique slows down the reading speed and mirrors the disorientation caused by the absence of a conventional narrative subject. The guesswork the readers are forced to undertake imitates the process of positioning on the part of the narrative voice within a perilous environment, and readers trace the process of memory. Gilman notes that Dischereit's writing is a "self-conscious attempt" to come to terms with her multiple identity. Addressing the non-Jewish public, the text takes into account the "non-Jewish audience's difficulty in identifying with her central problem—how to construct an identity as a Jew in post-Shoah Germany" (1995, 59–60).

Despite references to planting trees in Israel, religious holidays such as Hanukkah and Purim, and customs such as the lighting of the Sabbath candles, the Holocaust is the major element in the narrator's Jewish identity. It is evoked in images of cattle cars, transports, allusions to works such as Hilberg's *The Destruction of the European Jews,* and in the plot itself (Dischereit 1988, 31). The long-range effects of persecution and the survivors' trauma are manifest in the panic reactions that overwhelm the narrator in her daily life, as they did her mother (19). Remmler points out that her "trembling hands are an image of the denial of proper burial, of a missing farewell to a loved one, a gesture of distancing and dismissal," since in Dischereit's text "the hands embody silenced memories" (1994, 196). Moreover, anti-Semitism, historical and contemporary, is a key element shaping the narrator's identity—it defines her as other. Among the numerous instances cited are the telling of anti-Semitic and Holocaust jokes by her fellow workers and the harassment by a fellow student. Such incidents are glossed over or excused by the authorities so that the perpetrators enjoy immunity (Dischereit 1988, 64). Latent anti-Semitism is also mentioned in conjunction with the seemingly well-intentioned German tourists roaming Israel. Many of them seem to have been motivated to undertake their journey by a perverse psychosexual curiosity (50).

Dischereit's novel is subdivided into prose segments of one to three pages in length that facilitate the sketching of characters and events and the construction of a rudimentary plotline to explore specific topics. Because Dischereit includes such a wide variety of issues, her narrative range expands continually. Seemingly insignificant episodes illustrate, for example, the methods Germans have developed to avoid dealing with the Shoah or how irrational impulses, triggered by a survivor's guilt, have become part of the narrator's psychological makeup. The digression about the Austrian death camp survivor Jean Améry, with notable parallels to Ruth Beckermann's essay "Jean Améry and Austria" (1994b), places the reactions of the narrator's mother and the narrator herself into a larger context. The narrator's joyful relief upon crossing the French border and seeing non-German soldiers recaptures Améry's relief upon escaping from Nazi Germany to Belgium, only to find out later that "the world approved of the place to which the Germans had assigned us, the small world of the camp and the wide world outside, which but rarely, in individual heroic instances, arose in protest when we were taken at night from our homes in Vienna or Berlin, in Amsterdam, Paris, or Brussels" (Améry 1986, 85). Dischereit's protagonist repeats the survivor's experience under changed conditions a few decades later, but the outcome is similar (Dischereit 1988, 35).

The codependency between mother and daughter portrayed in *Joëmis Tisch* evolved as a result of persecution, life in hiding, poverty, and continued discrimination. The close physical and emotional proximity with her mother foils the narrator's own individuation—her every experience is conditioned by the mother's reactions. Gertrud Kolmar's *Eine jüdische Mutter* (1965), Barbara Honigmann's *Roman von einem Kinde* (1986), and Ronnith Neumann's *Nirs Stadt* (1991) revolve around similarly close and confining mother-child relationships, developing the motif of the Jewish mother and daughter as the elementary family unit in a hostile environment, the true nuclear family in all of its positive and destructive aspects. In their works, as in *Joëmis Tisch,* Jewishness is gendered as female, which facilitates the uncovering of parallels between the persecution of Jews and the oppression of women.[15]

In Dischereit's text, historical and cultural specificity is provided by juxtaposing the protagonists' fate with that of non-Jewish females. Her novel's larger framework addresses the persecution of German Gentiles, prisoners of war, non-Jewish displaced persons, and dissenters such as the clergy of the *Bekennende Kirche* in order to differentiate between the fate of these groups in contrast to the wholesale dehumanization of the Jews (1988, 55, 70, 83). The reasons for the narrator's inability to cast off her Jewishness despite her superficial ability to blend into the German mainstream are explored in a variety of environments, the leftist scene being one of them. Initially, the narrator experiences the revolutionary culture of the 1960s as liberating, but her submersion into it ends in the same disillusionment as is did for Jeanette Lander and Ruth Beckermann. In addition, she is disappointed by the ideology dominating her field of study, German literature—Dischereit criticizes the anti-Semitic representation of Jews in the works of Gerhard Zwerenz and Rainer Werner Fassbinder, the commercialization of the Nazi past and the Holocaust by the German media, and the historical revisionism that emerged in the Historians' Debate. A further complication to the positions outlined is caused by the narrator's ambivalence toward Israel. Like Ronnith Neumann and Katja Behrens, Dischereit belongs to the left-leaning intellectual Jews "who consider the strong identification Jews in Germany feel toward Israel as a form of 'substitute identity'" (Kaplan 1994b, 86). This outlook explains her growing disaffection with Jewish and Zionist culture: she realizes that the spontaneous attachment she felt as a child is incompatible with her opposition to imperialism and racism—her former image of Israel as the ultimate refuge does not match with what she perceives as Israeli expansionism. But she also finds it impossible to meet the expectations that the German and Jewish public have of her as a Jew; nor can she define herself as a German woman.

Joëmis Tisch provides an alternative view of Judaism through a comparison of the Jewish cemeteries in Fez, Prague, and Warsaw. The vitality of the North African community, a non-European Jewish culture, stands in contrast to the ghettos that the narrator associates with Germany and Poland (11). The multiculturalism of the Moroccan community—intermarriage, shared holidays, and symbols common to all the religions of this Moslem-Yiddish-French melting pot are mentioned—signifies a different Jewish life, a ray of hope, in spite of the narrator's limited ability to participate. In her attempt to conceptualize a Jewish culture other than the one of whose tragic history she is a product, Dischereit examines the history of Sephardic Jewry, only to have to confront the expulsion of Jews and Muslims from Spain. Her portrayal of the persecution suffered by both groups at the hands of the same oppressors, encapsulated in the image of a triumphant and malevolent Virgin Mary, signals her dismay about the animosity between them in the present. If the title *Joëmis Tisch* (Joëmi's Table) is, in fact, intended as a reference to "The Table," a major section of the Qur'an containing moral precepts, stories, and prophesies, it would express on yet another level structural affinities between Jewish and Islamic culture, which Michael Fischer also observes in his article on autobiographical voices and memory (1994, 95).

The nonlinear structure of Dischereit's novel and its language—at times poetic, at times archaic—is reminiscent of "The Table," as is its intent, to define righteous living under the auspices of the final judgment for Jews, Muslims, and Christians. By revealing the claims of exclusivity inherent in each religion, Dischereit points her finger at the cause of the power struggles that continue to divide them (1988, 13–14). The digression about Franz Werfel, who dreamed about a Jewish-Catholic reconciliation but who died in exile, establishes a case in point.

In contrast, the community of women consisting of the narrator's grandmother Rose, her sister Meta, the narrator's daughter, aunts, friends, and acquaintances is based upon a feminist model. Without idealizing women, the narrator shows by way of example that her mother's support system in times of need was comprised exclusively of women. In contrast, the narrator's father, entrenched in his culture's humanistic discourse, Hannah's second husband, inconsiderate and brutal, and the grandfather in America who rejects his black grandson are indicative of male mentality—abstract, distant, and unbending. In *Joëmis Tisch,* true Jewish spirituality evolves in the community of women. The options presented to the narrator, assimilation or emigration to the United States or Israel, are viewed, as they are by Beckermann and Neumann, as antithetical to Jewish life. Since Dischereit's narrator, not without a tinge of self-hatred, follows the line of leftist anti-Zionist rhetoric, Israel is not given much positive consideration.[16] With that in mind, the only site at which she can realize her Jewish identity is Germany.

In her postunification novel *Merryn* (1992), Dischereit focuses more specifically on women's issues. The work revolves around the same basic situation as *Joëmis Tisch,* albeit from a different point of view. The protagonist's psychological and intellectual destruction is emphasized as it progresses during puberty through alcohol, drugs, and promiscuity. These abuses occur as a result of her estrangement from her recently remarried mother and her unfulfilled yearning for love. Merryn's ambivalence toward her Gentile stepfather (107) resembles that of Cordelia Edvardson in *Gebranntes Kind such das Feuer* (1990). The time span between the narrator's loss of her innocence and her reconstruction, involving her move from Frankfurt to Berlin as the mother of two children, is reviewed in seemingly disjointed narrative segments. The oldest part chronologically speaking, the narrator's diary, appears at the end of the novel, preceded by the episode about Merryn's relocation to Berlin after the collapse of the Berlin Wall. Her attempts at claiming her grandparents' apartment and her establishing herself in their old neighborhood indicate an increasing interest in the Jewish legacy of which she, the daughter of a Jewish woman, is an heiress. Her walk across the Alexanderplatz, formerly the center of the Jewish quarter, the grocer's knowing remark about her child's "almost Jewish eyes" (79), as well as her reflections, rich in imagery, about the Holocaust and her ancestors' fate signify that Dischereit's protagonist is at the point of coming home.

Merryn's transformation through the experience of motherhood is no less remarkable, albeit less joyful, than that of Barbara Honigmann's Babu. Jewish Berlin, in contrast to Strasbourg, is overshadowed by the past, a "crying" that is only temporarily drowned out by construction noises (79). Yet, as suggested during a visit to the Jewish cemetery, the narrator does consider Berlin a site where Jewish memory is being kept alive, and her own fertility attests to the fact that there will be a Jewish future in this city. The last lines of *Merryn*, "All the king's horses / and all the king's men / couldn't put Humpty together again," taken from the nursery rhyme of "Humpty Dumpty," indicate that neither the woman, who in her formative years underwent a brutal awakening, nor the re-emerging Berlin Jewish community will ever be the same (118). Yet, there is reason for cautious optimism that, like the protagonist who rose from the ruins of her adolescence to become a Jewish mother, the community that emerged at the time of German unification will prosper.

Merryn is set partly in France, among proletarians, substance abusers, transients, and women outside of the patriarchal hierarchy, in a milieu reminiscent of Else Lasker-Schüler's 1906 play *Die Wupper*. These underprivileged characters seem mysteriously connected to one another, forming, as did the persecuted Jewish women in *Joëmis Tisch*, a separate subculture. Implying that there is greater solidarity among the socially deprived than among the privileged, Dischereit explores the community of the disenfranchised in ways that call to mind Neumann's *Nirs Stadt* (1991), the bohemian milieu in Seelich's film *Sie saß im Glashaus* (1992), and the uprooted protagonists of Améry's novel *Lefeu oder der Abbruch* (1974).

Merryn, a runaway teenager, and numerous other exploited female characters participate in a subculture diametrically opposed to the authoritarian structures associated with fascism. The oppression of these women as menial workers, medical guinea pigs, and sex objects by men of all social classes is exposed and connected to the women's experiences with the slave labor in concentration camps and to the abuse of medicine and science by the Nazis. By suggesting that in contrast to the French political establishment, including the white supremacist Le Pen as well as the socialist Mitterand, her characters represent the true antifascist resistance, Dischereit surmises that fascism has won, not only in Germany, but in the countries of the liberators as well; there is no escape from it.

The journal entries, written when Merryn was a young girl, are said to have been inspired by Anne Frank's diary (1992, 98). The journal shows that as a teenager, Merryn was able to express herself in a direct, simple prose style. The thematic similarities between Merryn's diary and the main text bring the protagonist's character development into focus: while in both texts the writer seems tentative and confused, the later narrative is far more sophisticated than the diary. As the novel shows, the narrator had to pay a high price for conquering the German language as her literary medium; it was her painful quest for self-realization that made her an accomplished writer.

Merryn's perceptions and the account of outside events mutually illuminate one another. Whereas Merryn considers her reactions as ordinary, they are viewed as unusual by her environment and set her apart from peers. Her mother, at times intimidated and confused, at other times persistent and courageous, plays a role in causing her daughter's ambivalence. Having been raised by a Jewish mother who hides her identity, Merryn has become secretive and paranoid. The text traces and reflects this development in the indirect way in which Merryn's story is told. Oftentimes, the effects of certain events, but not the causes, are communicated, calling to mind the approach taken in some of Ilse Aichinger's works.

Two poems form the frame of the narrative. The one preceding the novel places Merryn's story into a biblical context, albeit with sarcastic overtones. The reference to the bitter herbs calls to mind the Seder night, which commemorates the liberation of the Israelites from slavery in Egypt and the beginning of their migration. The poem suggests that the Jews' migration never ended and that their slavery was followed by eternal hellish suffering. The final poem is "Humpty Dumpty," followed by the sentence "I have been integrated into nature" (117), both of which signify a complete dismantling of Merryn's Christian and German childhood persona. Dischereit's protagonist has undergone an irreversible deindividuation process, the only possible point from which to construct a new self. Merryn's radical disintegration calls to mind Aichinger's concept of unlearning as well as similar processes in Honigmann's *Roman von einem Kinde* (1986).

Merryn's deconstruction begins when she runs away from home after the death of her mother. Living outside the social hierarchy, Merryn transgresses against social and moral standards. Fittingly, the novel begins with Merryn being casually deflowered in a rooming house (11). From a middle-class point of view, this encounter might seem reprehensible. Yet, the lewd verse about Gretchen and references to Goethe's *Faust* signify that male authors have traditionally configured such episodes as romance, casting women as the stepping-stones for a man's self-realization. Illustrating the gratification derived from a one-night stand from a woman's point of view, Dischereit undermines the bourgeois sense of propriety (88f., 12). At the same time, she questions the codes of high-class classical literature, including the works of women authors such as Rahel Levin Varnhagen, Bettina von Arnim, and Caroline Schlegel. The insidiousness of this heritage is revealed when the protagonist, overwhelmed by the processes of pregnancy, abortion, and birth, has nothing but male-defined discourses, rather than a text of her own, from which to take comfort. According to her society's ideology, however, even an emancipated woman will eventually pay the price for defying convention (37f.).

The narrator distances herself from the texts of Gentile women in a short satirical digression about Bettina von Arnim's account of her visits to the Frankfurt ghetto. Using "Die Klosterbeere" (von Arnim 1959) as an example, Dischereit exposes the difference between the Jewish and the Gentile point of view by ridiculing von Arnim for assuming the role of a benefactor of Jewish women to whom she takes flowers from a greenhouse outside the ghetto walls. Dischereit denounces von Arnim's presumption, showing that the German Romantic poet patronizes Jewish women much in the same way as Southern belles patronize their black slaves. Von Arnim's use of the diminutive *Jüdchen* (little Jewess) and the reference to the Jewish girls' "giggling" are held up to scrutiny: not only do they suggest that the oppressed enjoy their life because they do not know any better; they also suggest that the underprivileged are naive and childlike. The final image of the Jewish girls' recoiling behind the ghetto gates as if fleeing from the Gentile poetess implies that the

Jewish women reject a woman like von Arnim, seemingly so well intended and yet so insensitive.

Through a network of associations these gates of the ghetto are connected to the gates of the concentration camps and the fate of Jewish women a century later. While in the hospital, Merryn wakes up to a *Drachenschwester,* a "dragon" nurse hovering over her in a scene that elicits the image of a brutal-looking concentration camp nurse in Alain Resnais's film *Night and Fog,* a massive woman holding a needle (39). Here, and in other fleeting impressions involving the different fates of Jewish and Gentile women, Dischereit shows that tragedy is an ordinary event in the lives of the oppressed (13).[17] Since they are the norm, rape, the killing of fallen women, and humiliating sexual encounters are recounted matter-of-factly. Unable to bear this reality, the narrator seeks refuge in alternative cultures, the occult and zoomorphism: she refers to herself as the mother of "Rosemary's Baby" and claims to have given birth to a "young wolf" (16). This kind of imagery establishes a connection between *Merryn* and the works of Gertrud Kolmar, Ilse Aichinger, and Rahel Hutmacher.

Dialogue is an important narrative element throughout the novel, eliciting the reader's involvement. Much like in Honigmann's "Brief an Josef" (1986), Dischereit's first-person narrator addresses an unnamed "you." Moreover, this narrative device suggests the successful construction of a new persona, able to assume the role of a mother and a teacher who informs the presumably inexperienced person about the ways of the world from a Jewish point of view. Spelling out brutal facts in aggressive and deliberately offensive language, she exposes the contradictions within the dominant moral, religious, and legal codes. Providing her own interpretation of the New Testament, she points out that Jesus was an illegitimate child who would have been victimized along with his mother by the adherents of the very religion that co-opted him (1992, 40, 47). Christian morality is shown to be in conflict with human nature, as Dischereit's detailed description of male and female reproductive functions suggests. Parodying the accounts of the Nativity, the narrator once again confirms her outsider position. "Everyone would have loved your child, the Christians at Christmas Eve would have brought gold and myrrh. It would have croaked as a result," she declares mockingly (14).

Even after unification, the memories of Nazi terrorism, transmitted from the survivors to the next generation, are still a part of post-Shoah European culture, amplified by the memories of the silent horrors of postwar Germany with its more subtle forms of oppression. The dialogue character of Dischereit's novel and the detached review of her protagonist's past reveal that it is possible and necessary for a German-speaking Jewish woman to abandon her split, bicultural identity and to cease participating in situations such as the ones described in *Merryn*. Having reached this point, Dischereit's protagonist can, indeed, live in Germany, aware and secure in who she is. It is this position of hard-fought certainty that defines *Merryn* as a Jewish text, a position taken after the failure of the revolutionary movements since 1968, including the sexual revolution and feminism, and the consolidation of Germany.

Jewish Mothers and Daughters in Unified Germany (Katja Behrens)

Since her first literary publication, *Die weiße Frau* (1978), Katja Behrens has explored gender and race in a global perspective and has combined these topics with a close examination of her situation as a Jewish woman in West Germany. After German unification, she continued writing about these issues, focusing on the incompatibility of the children of former victims with the children of former Nazis, the continued presence of the protofascist structures after the breakdown of the Nazi state in Germany and worldwide. In the 1990s, Behrens's criticism of the situation of Jewish women in the Federal Republic, exemplified by the experience of her grandmother and mother, became as rigorous as the stance adopted by Lea Fleischmann. Contrary to Fleischmann, however, Behrens, not unlike Neumann and Dischereit, is unable to envision a more auspicious situation for herself outside Germany. Her stocktaking with Germany in *Im Wasser tanzen* (1990) and *Salomo und die anderen* (1993) includes equally critical analyses of life elsewhere —in the United States or Israel. Having explored other cultural and geographic options in her earlier works, including Latin America and Eastern Europe, Behrens, foiled in her search to discover alternative lifestyles, accepts her German existence without approving of it entirely. In her postunification work, she restates from a global position problems already defined by her and other Jewish women authors in Germany and Austria in the previous decade. Behrens is anchored in Germany, but she provides yet another variation of the "nomadic" approach to writing—

lost in darkness, wandering, searching, dangling, distressing, surviving at the margins—which Jack Zipes characterizes as a trait of Jewish writing in the Federal Republic and which, according to him, challenges the manner in which Jews and Germans have tried to contain Jewish identity (1995, 30). Behrens, like Neumann and Dischereit, universalizes the conditions in Germany to such a degree as to leave no imaginable room for escape. Her narratives demonstrate that no culture offers solutions to the problems of oppression and gender inequality. If at all, visions of a viable community arise from the alternative lifestyles of like-minded women on the fringes.

Katja Behrens's literary universe reflects her youth in her mother's and grandmother's matriarchal household. Outside the larger community, the three-women household, which later includes the narrator's daughter, constitutes a separate social and cultural unit with rules and dynamics all its own. With increasing age, Behrens's narrator becomes aware of the idiosyncrasies of her home environment, and she grows critical of it, only to find out later that the all-female Jewish cosmos is more nurturing and rational than the German mainstream, which she experiences more or less as an outsider. To appreciate her heritage, however, she must test and establish her identity as a Jew and a woman on the outside, in the absence of role models—neither the Germans' view of Jewishness nor her grandmother's and mother's experience suffices to do so. Zipes argues that, as in Dischereit's *Merryn,* Jewish identity in Behrens is shaped "through the narrative itself that challenges the expectations and categories of the reader" (1995, 31).

Born in Berlin in 1942, Behrens grew up in Wiesbaden and married soon after her graduation from high school. She is divorced and the mother of a daughter. After several career changes she became a translator and an editor, working for a publishing house from 1973 until 1978. Her travels since becoming an author have taken her to India, South America, the United States, and Israel. Now a well-known member of the German literary community, Behrens has received numerous awards. Her interest in German-Jewish and women's history is manifest from her novels and short stories, as well as her edition of *Frauenbriefe der Romantik* (1981b) and *Das Insel-Buch vom Lob der Frau* (1982).

Behrens's autobiographical prose fiction, *Die dreizehnte Fee* (1983) and *Im Wasser tanzen* (1990), deals with the Jewish heritage in the lives of women of different generations. The psychologizing portrayal of the characters reveals the influence of the Swiss psychotherapist Alice Miller, whose intellectual relationship with Behrens may complicate the author's view of Jewish culture; Miller recently launched an attack on Jewish male circumcision, labeling circumcised men as child abusers (Gilman 1995: 36).

Die dreizehnte Fee, a historical and personal novel, establishes the basis for Behrens's entire work. Constructed from the author's family history and themes from German, Jewish, and women's history since the late nineteenth century, the novel examines three generations of Jewish women; it is the death of the grandmother Mariechen that occasions the account of her daughter and granddaughter's story, which is told in such a way as to reveal the intricacies of gender and multicultural identity. According to Jewish matrilineality, Jewishness is gendered as feminine. Hence, gender, ethnicity, and religion intersect and allow the author to construct situations involving multiple marginality.

By entering a relationship with a Gentile man during the free-spirited Weimar era, grandmother Mariechen transgresses against the moral code of her family and culture. An outcast, she gives birth to another outcast, Hannah, the "Mamserte," who follows the paradigm set by Mariechen: she becomes involved with a Gentile man who leaves her and their illegitimate daughter, Anna. Matriarchy, configured as motherhood out of wedlock, survival in the underground, and the silent opposition against the German mainstream and Nazi culture provide the basis of the three women's antifascism and feminism. These are, in turn, associated with Jewish identity. Since Jewish identity is established matrilineally, Behrens and her narrators identify themselves as Jewish women in Germany (1993, 73). They refer to Israel as "land of my mothers, *schamaim*" (177, 180). In contrast to *schamaim,* the term "land of the fathers" (184), associated with the image of a German Shepherd dog, an Israeli family's pet, is associated with violence (185).

Behrens cultivates an associative, open style of writing that also emerges in the narratives in *Jonas* (1981a), some of which bear a certain resemblance to Aichinger's, Hutmacher's, or Fleischmann's short prose. "Jonas Achtundsiebzig," for example, combines the playful use of language, the reinterpretation of religious themes, and mythological or fairy-tale motifs, in this case the story of Jonas and the whale. Several of the narratives in *Von einem Ort zum andern* (1987), among them "Nach innen ausgewandert," which Zipes considers paradigmatic

of contemporary Jewish writing (1995, 30), revisit the topics and characters of *Die dreizehnte Fee,* namely, the protagonist, her mother Hannah,
and her grandmother Mariechen, the trauma of World War II (disabled
fathers, fragmented families, ruined houses), and the narrator's dilemma
of living in a historical vacuum signaled by the fact that the mother and
grandmother discuss their Jewish background only in English and retreat from their Gentile environment as much as possible. Only in retrospect does the narrator realize that they were trying to hide their background from their neighbors (1987, 7–25). The postwar era creates yet
another rift between the narrator and her fellow Germans. After 1945,
when everyone else falls silent, her mother and grandmother speak out
in an unsuccessful attempt to come to terms with the past. Their memories cannot be expunged; nor can their alienation from their neighbors
be lifted. Despite their move from Berlin to Wiesbaden, they remain
caught up in their memories of Berlin: the Romanisches Café, storm
trooper marches, Yellow Stars, and voices hurling insults.

In the title story, "Von einem Ort zum andern," Behrens discusses the
creative process involved in *Die dreizehnte Fee* in a self-reflective first-
person narrative about traveling and memory. She reports how external
events and disruptions have modified her intended topic, her grandmother's life as a single mother. Having witnessed the social ills and the
oppression of women outside of Germany—in Nicaragua, Ceylon, and
Italy—Behrens, much like Jeanette Lander, reconsiders her own family's
plight in a global context, and she discovers parallels to the history of the
Jews and Germans. However, of all the different sites, Lvov, the capital
of Galicia, becomes a place of great significance to Behrens because of
its connection to her own history, even though there is no living Jewish culture to be found there. She expresses her affinity to pre-Shoah
Poland through her use of Yiddish phrases and vocabulary, thereby defining her own position as an Ashkenazic Jew.

It is surprising that Behrens's cyclical novel *Im Wasser tanzen* (1990),
published concurrently with the fall of the Berlin Wall, does not refer
to the reorganization of Europe or German unity. Instead, it revisits
the German-Jewish problematic, implying that no political or social
solution is in sight. The motif of the crossing of borders and futile attempts at overcoming otherness are played out by the estrangement of
two siblings who lead separate lives in Germany and the United States,
respectively. The only possible synthesis is portrayed on an elemental

level, water being the leitmotif. Each chapter of *Im Wasser tanzen* is preceded by observations about water, unifying the world and all bodies with all elements and with one another. On this basic level, Behrens suggests, rather than in the political or cultural arena, there exists an interconnectedness entwining human beings, cultures, and events, past and present (26).

From this all-encompassing, cosmic perspective, reminiscent of views expressed by Kolmar and Hutmacher, the separated siblings, symbolizing German and Jewish history, are united as participants in a universal scheme. Moreover, the water imagery signifies the merging of the narrator's memories with her present, as she visualizes her Gentile's father's journey to America, his transition into a new language after having left her and her Jewish mother. Recounting her family history alongside major political events, Behrens interconnects the private and public spheres, and from the global, almost Buddhist, perspective of her novel, she uncovers brutality and fascist behavior within the family and in world events, patterns that impacted on her own life as well as on the existence of people in the last remote frontiers of the United States. *Im Wasser tanzen* dissolves specific historical contexts and events and interprets them as integral parts of the human character and the laws of nature.

Behrens's self-reflective anthology *Salomo und die anderen* (1993), with the programmatic subtitle "Jewish Stories," forms a mosaic, each one of its texts reflecting different aspects of the Nazi legacy and the Holocaust after German unification. Like the seven lights of the menorah, the seven stories are intended to provide illumination about facts such as the role of German industries in the Gulf War in the story "Juliette" (1993, 19–42). It is ironic that Behrens, despite her German-centered perspective, subtitles her postunification work "Jewish Stories," whereas Ruth Klüger, to whom Germany is peripheral at best, calls her autobiography *weiter leben* (1992), "a German book." Both designations reflect each author's position: contrary to Klüger, Behrens places the Holocaust and its aftermath into the context of Jewish history.[18] She regards her mother's and her shame as a "Jewish" dilemma until she is old enough to contextualize her fate in the context of German history ("Alles normal," 1993, 1). Klüger, on the other hand, treats the genocide as a chapter of German history, ascribing the responsibility for her and her family's suffering to Germany and the Germans.

In the first story of *Salomo,* the narrator separates herself from her
German contemporaries. Through the classic ploy of an encounter between an old teacher and his former student, a conversation between
the German man and the Jewish woman is initiated, revealing fundamentally different viewpoints. Too young to have been aware of the
danger facing her mother and herself during the Nazi era, the narrator
has assimilated her mother's impulse to escape and hide (7). Now that
years have past, she still suffers from feelings of inferiority. They are,
however, distinct from those of her former teacher, who has lost his self-
confidence because his "master race" was shattered. Allusions to other
discussions with Germans confirm the impression of difference: when
it comes to the past, the Germans are pedantic "like accountants" (8) in
their attempt to reduce the number of Holocaust victims or in denying
the Holocaust altogether, whereas their victims, traumatized for life, are
unable to compartmentalize their past in such a way.

Behrens's vignettes expose the reality behind the obliging facades of
German people. One of her stories involves a party at the villa of a
former Nazi criminal, who lives under a false identity (11); another stay
describes the unannounced visit of a German woman looking up the
narrator's mother because she had never seen a concentration camp prisoner—an experience that, ironically, the narrator and her mother had
been spared because they survived in hiding (12). There are instances
of blatant anti-Semitism. Couched in commonly used pseudorational
terms, these statements are held up to scrutiny. Typically, those affected
by the Holocaust wish to discuss the past, but the former perpetrators
and their collaborators, who continue to defend the Nazis, wish to lay
history to rest (14). The more that members of both groups open up,
the less chance there is for a reconciliation—they age but do not change.
In addition, Behrens depicts the difference in mentality between young
Germans and Israelis in "Salomo und die anderen," a text without direct
reference to the Holocaust. In the seemingly lighthearted encounter of
men and women of both nationalities, profound cultural differences are
revealed, which upon closer contact lead to grave misunderstandings in
spite of the initial good will.

"Alles normal" brings these undercurrents to light, demonstrating
that the Holocaust discourse is the discourse of the victims. The feeling
of defeat calls to mind the same conclusion as the one suggested in Peter
Weiss's drama *Die Ermittlung* (The Investigation) (1963). Representing

the point of view of a Jewish woman, Behrens's narrator articulates her feelings toward a German man: "He was stronger than I was. As far as he is concerned, the past is laid to rest. He looked as if he slept soundly. They all sleep soundly. They have nothing to fear" (17). From Behrens's perspective, German unification is ultimately of little consequence: all it does is confirm the prevailing attitudes and strengthen the former perpetrators' point of view. Now that Germany is on the road to becoming a major power, it demands international recognition and respect. As a result, the survivors and their children become further marginalized, a situation that forces them to find a position apart from the German context.

In "Juliette," Behrens explores the life of a woman as the paradigm of the predicament created by the long-term effects of the Holocaust. Juliette, indolent, bored, and frustrated, antagonizes the narrator, who nonetheless cannot help but feel connected to her as if to an alter ego. Approximately the same age as the narrator, Juliette represents a fate that might have been the narrator's had circumstances been slightly different. Juliette has neither a family nor a community; she has lived in different cultures and speaks several languages. Deprived of a sense of self and lacking in feminine appeal, Juliette is marginalized as a woman, and her life at a convent—nuns saved her from deportation—does not allow her to establish a Jewish identity, even in Israel, although she desperately clings to both. The narrator's memory of Juliette is prompted by the Gulf War; she imagines Juliette and other Israelis carrying gas masks.

Juliette's difficulties evince that the legacy of the Holocaust and the Second World War has not been overcome, not even in the Jewish State, "the big melting pot," as it is called in "Salomo und die anderen" (46). Like Dischereit, Behrens quotes the popular verses of "Humpty Dumpty" to illustrate her protagonist's dilemma. Behrens, not unlike Beckermann and Neumann, considers Israel a site of crippling conflicts, hence her decision to remain in Germany as the lesser of two evils, even if there is no healing, no safety, for the survivors of the Nazi terror.

"Today I ask myself, how a person does it, simply continuing to hope, whether it is stupid or courageous, not to let one's dream be taken away" (34), comments the narrator, as much on Juliette's as on her own behalf. The open-endedness of the story, toying with a happy ending for Juliette and her lover, an immigrant from Romania, is undercut by the notion that the fairy-tale ending of marriage and family implies a new generation of soldiers and the perpetuation of war. In view of that, imagining Juliette at the convent does not seem the worst possibility.

Weighing life in Israel against life in Germany, occasioned by German unification and the Gulf War, Behrens's stories suggest that neither place has a viable alternative to offer to a Jewish woman feminist. Her criticism of patriarchy uncovers the problematic aspects of European, American, and Israeli culture for women, and through her antimilitarism she indicts Germany and Israel to a similar degree. Skeptical toward Israel as well as to her native Germany, she opts for the latter. The closer that Behrens approaches the present, the more murky become the boundaries between right and wrong, which are more clear-cut in her interpretation of the past. In the last story of the cycle, the young generation of Israeli men are portrayed as no less belligerent than the men of all war-waging nations. The realization that as cultural contacts increase and Western patriarchal values become universalized, there is no mainstream offering alternatives to violence and global competition leaves for Behrens, who is not given to satire, the narrative position of a critic and observer.

Conclusion

To be able to define a coherent development in the literature of German-speaking Jewish women writers would be surprising, indeed, in view of the shifting paradigms regarding identities, roles, and positions, German, Jewish, male, and female. The interplay of the concepts of nationhood and social class with more general considerations pertaining to individual and group psychology, and the changing definitions of the human being, race, nation, gender, and character from the eighteenth to the end of the twentieth century further complicate matters as they rule out straightforward patterns of interaction and communication. In addition, the landscape of the political entities where the German language is spoken has changed radically in the course of the last three hundred years, from the dissolution of the multination state of the Roman Empire of the German Nation to the recent unification of East and West Germany, and the separate developments in Austria, except for the period of the annexation by Nazi Germany from 1938 to 1945. The role of Jews has likewise changed, from the position of sometimes tolerated, sometimes persecuted, foreigners to that of citizens and, during the Nazi era, outcasts, doomed to be killed, until the official rehabilitation of the survivors after World War II. The foundation of Israel has added yet another dimension to Jewish identity, providing simultaneously a sense of minimal security derived from the awareness that there is a state open to all Jews and the feeling of being remiss in their duty, if not guilty, for those who did not heed the call to Aliyah.

Jewish women writers have expressed their experiences in literary works reflecting their unique positions within this history. In conjunction with the shifting political and social paradigms, they cast and recast their domain, the motherland, *schamaim,* as a Yiddish, Ashkenazic, Austrian, German, cosmopolitan, or radically private space. The woman-orientedness of this sphere is the reason why despite their different styles, concepts of reality, points of view, and concerns, there are certain aspects in their works that make for an affinity among the majority of them. The interconnectedness between them may remain unnoticed in studies limited to a certain epoch and among authors specializing in particular genres or members of literary movements, but it becomes apparent in a historical survey such as this one. Links between authors as different as the Jewish salonnières and twentieth-century autobiographers, for example, arise from an admittedly general communality of experience regarding gender and ethnic discrimination or persecution, and the physical and psychological effects these phenomena have on women. Further affinities are engendered by the necessity of adopting a position with respect to these external constraints and of designing strategies to cope with them. More important still is the fact that with a few exceptions these experiences can be traced back to a common culture, that of Ashkenazic Jewry and the Yiddish language.

Although these issues take on a different form in each text, and the strategies of addressing them differ from one author to the next, partly because not all Jewish women faced the same difficulties and pressures or to the same extent, their situation was nevertheless distinct from that of women not exposed to anti-Semitism, but also from that of Jewish men. Almost without exception, the writers examined in this study interpreted their lives in the larger context of Jewish traditional historiography highlighting persecution, oppression, and the hope for deliverance (A. Reiter 1995, 76). At the same time, as speakers of German and writers of German texts or, more loosely, as participants in German culture, they were affiliated with the fate of Germany, Austria, or German culture. Even if this relationship was one of negativity and rejection, it distinguished them from other diaspora Jews and, after 1945, from the Jews in Israel, causing an additional quality of estrangement and a new sense of pariah existence, even among Jews. This consciousness was closely related to being a Jew living in Germany or Austria. Some authors even derive from their language and citizenship the sense of disrepute shared by the perpetrators and their children, the non-Jewish Germans, and, to a lesser degree, Austrians, while others continually negotiate German and Jewish identity, claiming neither one.

The theme of persecution pervades German-Jewish literature: it already looms large in the first chapter of Glikl Hamil's autobiography, and it is present in the opening episode of one of the earliest novels in the German language that emphasizes German-Jewish history, Heinrich Heine's *Rabbi of Bacharach* (1956). It would be virtually impossible to identify a text by a German- or Austrian-Jewish author that does not address oppression and religious or ethnic strife in one form or another. The threat of extermination is coupled with the awareness of vulnerability, expressed in a variety of ways: directly, by defining the situation of the Jews within German society as Other, by challenging Jewish and women's marginality either by criticizing and satirizing the German mainstream or by claiming to be part of it; indirectly, by hiding the traces of Jewishness, and in women's texts of the female experience, in the literary work. Simone de Beauvoir's observation that anti-Semitism is not a Jewish but a Gentile problem applies to the same extent as her characterization of the woman problem as "a man's problem" (1957, 128).

Yet, the externally imposed social stigma nonetheless affects and deforms the individuals concerned. With reversed positions, the category of the Other, according to de Beauvoir as "primordial as consciousness itself" (xvi), also structures the perceptions of Jewish women; to them, non-Jews and men represent the Other, the deviation from their norm. The ambiguity that de Beauvoir ascribes to the feeling of women toward their bodies, men, and nature is doubly true for Jewish women in a Gentile environment. Recognizing that the world around them is dominated by men and non-Jews, Jewish women's literature tends to approach reality with detachment and the awareness of being neither in control nor responsible for social processes (618–19, 598).

The examination of specific texts in a chronological order reveals several phases in the development of Jewish women's writing in Germany and Austria. Characteristic of the preemancipation era, in the Yiddish-speaking world of Glikl Hamil, is the acceptance of gender as well as religious and cultural identity, including the subordination under the laws and conventions pertaining to a woman's status. Limiting as they were, these rules provide women with a predictable structure, which they learn to manipulate, and with demarcation lines within which some of them prospered. Although assigned a specific place in a society segregated by gender, women of that era considered themselves an integral part of their community.

The following generations of Jewish women writers, adopting and trying to master the German language, experience both their gender and their Jewishness as impediments. By trying to deemphasize their

Jewish characteristics and their indebtedness to the Jewish legacy and by embracing Gentile culture through conversion and intermarriage, these exceptional women hide their Jewishness, exposing their newly acquired Gentile exterior to their Gentile friends and associates and allowing their Jewish self to come to the fore only in their interaction with relatives and friends, converts or unconverted Jews. Having abandoned their Jewish environment and trying hard to assimilate themselves to Christian culture and the German language, Jewish concerns assume the character of museum pieces in their works. If they address Jewish issues at all, they treat such concerns as relics of the past and cast themselves in the roles of interpreters and guides. Although they avoid relating to Jewish culture as an integral part of their existence, they acknowledge, for the most part, its importance in terms of their background and development. Most of them are aware of the fact that being Jewish or of Jewish background is an important factor in their reception by the German-speaking public. Along with their often complex gender roles, they problematize Jewish identity, the status of women, and social structures, occasionally flaunting the image the Gentile world has made of them, that of the "Beautiful Jewess," femme fatale and exotic creature.

Aware of their continued vulnerability, women intellectuals of Jewish background were in the forefront of the fight for the rights of women, Jews, and the working classes since the middle of the nineteenth century, regardless of whether the struggle for equality was in their own "class interest." Many of them attracted public attention because of their uncompromising stand in the fight for their own rights and for the rights of others, women and Eastern European Jews, and expressed their concerns in lucid, unsentimental texts. The process of aesthetization at the *fin de siècle,* a reaction to the stark literature of naturalism, also influenced the writing of German-Jewish women. Yet their nostalgic, mystical, utopian, and visionary texts are for the most part informed by the radical social and political avant-garde as well. Whereas some of the modernists deprioritize Jewish themes, most of their works include subtexts reflecting the specific marginalization of Jewish women and characters typified as Jewish.

The latent Jewish textual markers were brought distinctly to the fore when National Socialism was gaining momentum, forcing the traditionally oppressed groups—Jews, women, and the working class, who believed themselves to be close to reaching the point of complete integration into German and Austrian society—to reevaluate their situation. On the eve of the Nazi dictatorship, Jewish writers, men and women, undertook a partly nostalgic, partly disillusioned, stocktaking of German-Jewish culture and the processes of emancipation and assimilation that had promised them progress and security. In addition to their disillusionment as German Jews, women writers were overwhelmed by the blatant disregard of women, mothers, and children in Nazi Germany in spite of the prominent role that they were accorded in political propaganda. Disheartened by the forces shaping the cultures to which they had believed they belonged, some set out to explore and reconstruct their Jewish identity, while others held onto and affirmed their status as German Jews and Germans. In either case, they tried to come to terms with the same basic problems of legislated disassimilation and their reduction to the status of nonpersons. For persecuted authors and concentration camp prisoners, writing became a survival strategy, hence the disregard of form among many writers of memoirs and survival accounts. Frequently, however, the literary texts by Jewish women writers, written after the Holocaust or in exile, excel in terms of form and subtlety. Considering the works of women authors such as Ilse Aichinger, Cordelia Edvardson, and Ruth Klüger, and male writers such as Jurek Becker, Edgar Hilsenrath, and Paul Celan, Andrea Reiter's assertion that "the Holocaust did not produce any authors" (1995, 261) must be emphatically dismissed.

From the postwar era to the present time, German-speaking Jewish writers again wrestled with social and political problems as they pertained to their specific position of marginality. Oftentimes they couched their point of view in highly sophisticated literary discourse reflecting the writer's awareness of the complexity of her own reality, overshadowed by the disasters of German-Jewish history, most notably the Holocaust, and conscious of the achievement of forgotten and repressed Jewish literature. The knowledge and appreciation of the international context, already present in the earliest texts by Jewish women writers, had become especially pronounced as a result of the diaspora of German-speaking Jews and is an integral part of the new Jewish consciousness, particularly after German unification and rising German nationalism (F. Stern 1994, 44). The German literature of Jewish women authors developed in conjunction with international literary and cultural movements; hence it is cosmopolitan, although its medium is the

German language. German writing by Jewish women benefited from the larger national and international literary scene, intellectual movements, and the intertextuality with other Jewish writers. In their search for literary models, they repeatedly refer to the works of earlier Jewish women authors, establishing through this intertextuality a "minor" literature within the German "major" literature and culture, with its own literary tradition and canon (Deleuze and Guattari 1986, 16). Moreover, the texts of different authors are often connected through references, open or implied, to the same Jewish core texts by Rahel Levin Varnhagen, Heinrich Heine, Else Lasker-Schüler, Nelly Sachs, Paul Celan, and Jean Améry, to each other's works, and to German classical and Romantic literature and women's literature, the latter often being accompanied by a distancing gesture.

Over time, the definitions of what it meant to be Jewish changed. So did the way in which Jewishness expressed itself in texts; naturally and naively in Glikl, inadvertently in Dorothea Schlegel, and as something to be rediscovered and studied, as a memory to be retrieved, in the works of authors of the early 1900s and 1920s. Since the late eighteenth century, when the desire to belong to the larger social context prompted Jewish women to set out on their quest into the German language and culture up to the present day, Jewish women's literature appears to have come full circle. The move away from being Jewish in the late eighteenth century has ended in the rediscovery and study of Jewish history by intellectuals and scholars such as Margarete Susman and Hannah Arendt in the first third of the twentieth century, and since the mid-1980s, and more intensely so after German unification, a deliberate distancing from German-defined positions is apparent; many writers loosen their ties with the German mainstream. Their desire to redefine themselves as Jewish women is expressed, among other things, by their rejection of the formula German-Jewish. But even with the attempts of constructing a new Jewish women's identity and with a Jewish Minor Culture under way, both of which encompass the breaking up of rigid language patterns and a rebellion against the repression of Jewish otherness in German texts, the German language that the first generations fought so hard to acquire proves to be a lasting connection to German culture, in some cases into the second and third generation of exiles, as is the case with Jeanette Lander, Irene Dische, and Anita Desai. Women's and Jewish history and literature, feminism, German alternative discourses, and the Yiddish language, once shunned as the idiom of the unassimilated Jews, inform and are incorporated into the texts of contemporary Jewish women writers in German-speaking countries. There is a fast-growing body of literature that expresses a Jewish identity based in Germany and Austria, cast in the German language, and entwined with German and Austrian sites, but with an eye on international agendas—cultural, political, ecological—all of them distinctly detached from German specificity.

Since Glikl Hamil, Jewish women authors have established the woman's position in their texts, but unlike Gentile authors, they did not do so by focusing on eroticism and sexuality, as is apparent from a comparison with Simone de Beauvoir's classical treatise, *The Second Sex* (1957), which is strongly informed by Gentile literature. Instead of being insignificant per se, sexuality as a topic is deprioritized as a result of the emphasis on motherhood. Mother and child, configured as the smallest but most essential social unit, are represented as the most intimate Jewish domain in comparison to which the phallocentric concerns in the texts of male writers—circumcision, heterosexuality, and sexual prowess—are made to seem insignificant by being rarely discussed at all. In the majority of texts, mother-daughter relationships and female-female relationships are featured as being more important than those with husbands and lovers. Beginning with Glikl Hamil's universe segregated along gender lines, there is a strong tendency among Jewish women authors to focus on women's concerns, and in the works of numerous authors, such as Ilse Aichinger, Ruth Klüger, and Katja Behrens, all-female environments are emphasized.

Being positioned in a women's sphere, concretely or intellectually, causes Jewish women authors to question the male-dominated Gentile cosmos with a clear recognition of its shortcomings, engendered by the awareness of marginality and the embracing of otherness as the norm. From the perspective of the elusive motherland, all categories are in flux, including gender and humanity itself. Jewish women authors not only cross geographic and political boundaries; they also cross the boundaries between man and animal, conceiving of the animalization of the human being and the humanization of the animal as positive and as a basis for a truly integrated cultural and ecological vision. These seeming transgressions are part of the "nomadic" writing of Jews in Germany, which is particularly pronounced in the works by the women authors, such as Hutmacher, Dischereit, Behrens. The bending of language rules, the creative linguistic expression, and the aggressive satires of Jelinek are part of the larger phenomenon of a Minor Literature or, rather, a Minor Culture.

Resisting the ingrained patterns of the German language, Gentile culture, and patriarchal structures, which devaluate Jewish women as Jews and as women, Jewish and female identity are inseparably intertwined in the texts of most authors. It is undoubtedly the close connection between Jewishness and femininity in Gentile discourse that causes Inge Stephan to argue that as far as modern society is concerned, there is a "secret symmetry between the position of woman in the cultural hierarchy and that of Jewishness" (1994, 72). From the point of view of women authors positioned in or trying to position themselves into the Jewish context, the situation appears yet more complex. Following Stephan's line of reasoning, even other women would cast them into a female role.

Like Glikl Hamil, many later women authors consider themselves as Jews par excellence in spite of the male-dominated cultural context and the patriarchal hierarchy that causes Gentile women to be considered and to consider themselves as deviations from the male norm. The outrage and shame of Jewish girls upon discovering their social inferiority—Klüger's realization, for instance, that she is not qualified to say *Kaddish* and Schwarz-Gardos's feelings of humiliation at being female and Jewish while reading Otto Weininger's *Geschlecht und Charakter*— suggest that prior to their disillusionment, they must have had a sense of security that, as de Beauvoir portrays it, Christian girls lacked all along (Klüger 1992, 23; Schwarz-Gardos 1991, 72–73).

Some authors represent the suffering as originating from their female and their Jewish identity; others construct antiworlds and delineate coping mechanisms; but most of them do both. Paradoxically, the mere act of writing about their anguish, which is engendered by being who they are, as is the case in concentration camp memoirs, constitutes an act of coping, since language and literary genres provide meaning and help the writer to interpret and contextualize her personal situation (A. Reiter 1995, 22). In many cases, negotiating dual or multiple marginalizations leads to complex personality issues, not only to a disturbed sense of self-worth, as is discussed by Inge Stephan in conjunction with Sabina Spielrein, C. G. Jung's Jewish lover, who defines her sources of low self-esteem as femininity and Jewishness. External territorial displacement and even more so, the integration into one's identity of a fate not personally experienced—in the case of contemporary authors, the Holocaust—promote the development of a double identity (Stephan 1994, 64; Adelson 1994b, 329). The self-consciously perceived fragmentation of identity, aggravated by the offensive launched by postmodern critics against the concepts of identity in terms of gender and ethnicity in the postmodern era, further complicates the dilemma of Jewish women writers, as it does that of minority writers or the members of the "post-diaspora community of displaced writers," as Salman Rushdie calls them, in general (Rushdie 1991, 15).

In his essay "On the Necessity and Impossibility of Being a Jew," Jean Améry reveals the ambiguities facing him as an intended Nazi victim, a Holocaust survivor, and a Jew in Gentile society. The issues he raises continue to mold the texts of contemporary Jewish authors, male and female; Améry appears to be one of the critics/philosophers who speak particularly to women authors. In his essay he admits his discomfort at being included in conversations about "us Jews" (1986, 80). He senses the inauthenticity of this inclusion because of his memories of Christmas trees and Alpine valleys, although he was used to being considered Jewish by the outside world; his schoolmates called him a Jew, and his Jewish identity was established once and for all in 1935 by the Nürnberg Laws. Yet, he asserts that "after I had read the Nuremberg Laws I was no more Jewish than a half hour before. . . . But the Jew—and I now was one by decree of law and society—was more firmly promised to death, already in the midst of life" (82–83). Being a Jew meant for Améry to be "a dead man on leave, someone to be murdered, who only by chance was not yet where he properly belonged; and so it has remained, in many variations in various degrees of intensity, until today" (1986, 83). Strongly rejecting the myth of the universal man as well as Jewish self-hate, produced by the desire to be German and the inability to become so (84–85), Améry, like many young Jews today, has misgivings about his position. According to him, anti-Semitism was the foremost factor that made a Jew of him, and he defines his Jewishness as primarily consisting of "solidarity in the face of the threat" that links him with his Jewish contemporaries, "the believers, as well as the non-believers" (94).

In the wake of the events of the mid-1980s and early 1990s, it may well be anti-Semitism that is making Jews once again aware of their status as existential outsiders, to use Hans Mayer's term, causing them to make the conscious decision to define themselves as Jews, thereby becoming intentional outsiders as well (1975, 18). The political and spiritual bankruptcy of the revolutionary movements of the 1960s and early 1970s, including feminism, and the co-optation of alternative Gentile culture into the corporate mainstream of religious and political conservatism prompted Jewish women intellectuals to explore agendas appropriate to their own situation. Among the options available to them were assimilating into larger groups such as the Green movement, returning to or forming Jewish allegiances in religious and political terms, developing a secular Jewish cultural agenda, or remaining unassimilated Jewish-defined individuals exploring whichever avenues they considered relevant. In the 1990s, Jewish women writers express themselves in all of the above-described ways, producing a wide variety of literary and filmic texts, thereby expanding and transforming contemporary Jewish and German literature and culture, as well as their own literary sphere.

Notes

1. Gordon's characterization of *Halakhah* as a legal system that has been historically unjust by making women the objects rather than the subjects of laws, and by preventing them from being lawmakers and judges, applies to German and Austrian secular law as well (1995, 3).

2. Prior to the American Revolution, the 1740 ruling of the English colonies' Parliament admitted Jews to full citizenship after seven years of residence.

3. Juxtaposing Jewish and Gentile women, Silvia Bovenschen's observations in *Die imaginierte Weiblichkeit* (1979, 10) must be kept in mind. Bovenschen dismisses the idea that women had a cultural history of their own, claiming that women's history was a lack of history. She notes that Walter Benjamin observed the silence of women that usually "went unnoticed in the noise of the never-ending compensatory discourse about femininity" (41).

4. Krobb in *Die schöne Jüdin* (1993, 55) perceives Jews as moving away from traditional Jewish life and increasing their contacts with Gentiles at the beginning of the emancipation movement.

5. One example is the philosopher Edith Stein. A convert and a Carmelite nun, she professed her Jewish identity under National Socialism, knowing that her decision would result in her deportation.

6. Glikl Hamil was an ancestor of Heinrich Heine, Fanny Lewald, and Bertha Pappenheim.

7. Krobb (1993, 59–61) writes that Jewish women met with criticism as soon as they came in contact with Berlin's Gentile society in the 1780s. The wealth of the Jewish elite and their conspicuous consumption were interpreted as signs of immorality. Furthermore, Jews were ridiculed because of their accent, their diction, their interest in the arts, and their supposedly contrite manners.

8. Krobb (1993, 56) points out that family background and social and marital status did not guarantee Jewish women the respect enjoyed by both

single and married Christian women. Jewish women had to develop special qualities to gain the approval of Christian society and assume the role of social and cultural mediators.

9. McNay (1993, 18) submits, "This derogation of the female body through comparison with the male body, and the consequent definition of femininity through reference to biological capacities, leads to a series of different strategies of corporeal oppression: the restriction of sexuality within the framework imposed by the opposition of masculinity and femininity, the subjection of women in confinement to medical power, the contemptuousness of menstruation, the construction of female sexuality as 'lack' or frigidity, etc."

10. Sorkin (1987, 131) asserts that High German was an integral part of the educational standard.

1. WRITING THE MOTHERLAND

1. Glikl, the form of the author's name most closely reflecting the Yiddish גליקל, rather than the Germanized "Glückel," is used throughout. Likewise, Glikl's surname, often rendered as "von Hameln," appears here as Hamil to better match the Yiddish.

2. A detailed analysis of the text, its background, and its reception is found in Dorothy Bilik, "The Memoirs of Glikl of Hameln: The Archeology of the Text" (1992: 5–21).

3. The ghetto in Prague was abolished as late as 1852.

4. Morais (1976, 167) writes about the concept of blood purity in Spain and Portugal in *A Short History of Anti-Semitism*. In 1543 Martin Luther rescinded his earlier defense of Jews in "Von den Juden und ihren Lügen" (412–552). Since his 1523 work "Daß Jesus ein geborener Jude sei" (307–36), designed to make converts, he had a change of mind no less dramatic than his earlier defense and later condemnation of the peasants who revolted.

5. Sightings of Jewish refugees were reported in Gdansk and Hamburg in 1547, in Hamburg in 1564 and 1566, in Spain in 1575, in Vienna in 1599, in Lübeck, Cracow, and Moscow in 1601 and 1603, in Paris in 1604, and in Silesia in 1612 (Knecht 1977, 27f., 41; Maccoby 1986, 250).

6. Vienna's first documented Jewish settlement and its destruction date back to the thirteenth century. Vienna's first and second ghettos were destroyed in 1421 and 1670, respectively. The survivors of the latter pogrom were admitted to Brandenburg in 1671, from which Jews had been expelled some time earlier. In 1744, Maria Theresa decreed the expulsion of Jews from Moravia and Bohemia (Pichler 1974, 23).

7. Carlebach describes the traditional women's tasks as taking care of the home, storing goods for sale, providing for the family, employing and supervising servants, and supervising the education of the children (1981, 164–74).

8. Weiss-Rosmarin (1940, 5–6) maintains that to this day conservative marriage deprives women of their basic rights as individuals. See also Adler, "The Jew Who Wasn't There: *Halakhah* and the Jewish Woman" (1983, 12–18). Simone de Beauvoir's more general observations assessing historical conditions apply as well: "The wife, therefore, should not share in the mana of the husband, she should be a stranger to him and hence a stranger to his clan" (1957, 74).

9. Blau (1989, 20–23) points out in *Das altjüdische Zauberwesen* that sorcery was outlawed. Single women, virgins, and widows were suspected of sorcery in Jewish society.

10. Glückel von Hameln, *Denkwürdigkeiten,* trans. Alfred Feilchenfeld (1913). Other editions include *Zikhroynes: The Memoirs of Glueckel of Hamelin,* trans. Marvin Lowenthal (1977); *The Life of Glueckel of Hameln, 1646–1724, Written by Herself,* trans. Beth-Zion Abrahams (1963); *The Adventures of Glückel of Hameln,* ed. Bea Stadtler (1967); and *Denkwürdigkeiten der Glückel von Hameln* (1979).

11. Glikl had family ties with prominent former Viennese, later Berlin, families such as Ries, Mirels, and Veit. She considered Poland and southeastern France important because of their religious communities and Denmark because of the high status enjoyed by Danish Jews.

12. Chayim Hamil, her first husband, died in 1689 in Hamburg; Hirz Levy, her second husband, died in 1712 in Metz. Her children were Zipora, Nathan, Mate (died as a child), Esther, Hanna, Mordechai, Löb (died in 1701), Hendele, Josef, Samuel (died in 1702), Moses, Freudchen, Mirjam. See Glikl's genealogy in *Denkwürdigkeiten* (1979, 327–28).

13. Wittgenstein (1922, 149): "The limits of my language near the limits of my world."

14. Glikl contracted her second marriage at the age of fifty-four in 1699. Hirz filed for bankruptcy, undermining her aspiration for a secure old age. Glikl coped with these hardships with a stoicism based on her unshakable faith. Aware of the risks of arranged marriages, she did not indicate any regret over her second marriage.

15. For information about the Wertheimer family, see Wistrich (1989, 9–10).

16. Zewi's Messianic movement reached its climax in 1665–67. He was recognized as the Messiah and Savior, first in Jerusalem and then in other communities. His movement expanded across Europe to Amsterdam

and Hamburg, where the Portuguese Jews in particular became involved in it. Having led his followers on a path of disobedience in order to force the coming of the Messiah (he married a prostitute), Zewi was captured by Moslems and converted to Islam. Jakob Wassermann's novel *Die Juden von Zirndorf* ([1897] 1918) discusses Zewi and his followers.

17. "Thus the preferential treatment accorded to the Jewish nation through the present amendment is due to the following: Our aim is to make them more useful and of greater service to the state." Iggers (1992, 48–52) contains the text of the Moravian Edict of Toleration in its entirety.

18. After the arrival of the Viennese refugees in 1671, the Jewish community in Berlin began to prosper. As Weissberg (1987, 206) points out, the Prussian Elector was concerned about the decay of Berlin-Kölln after the Thirty Years' War and invited Jews and Protestants from Austria and Bohemia and Hugenots from France to immigrate.

19. Spiel 1962, 71; Weissberg 1987, 208. Fanny von Arnstein's father-in-law wore a beard and traditional clothes; Markus Levin, Rahel Levin Varnhagen's father, is clean-shaven and wears a fashionable suit. The portrait of Henriette Herz shows a Hebe figure with a full head of hair. Paucker (1993, 44) notes that the visual representation of Jewish women is a mixture of the stereotypical image created by Jewish and non-Jewish painters of Jewish women according to their own desires (or those of their family), and that counter to general perception, Jewish women approximate with few exceptions the ideal of femininity created by the society in which they live.

20. In her letters of 1803, Herz discusses Börne's courtship and her dodging. Such directness on her part is, however, rare (1984, 372ff.).

21. The tone of this description is reminiscent of the heroic-idyllic central episode in Heinrich von Kleist's novella *The Earthquake in Chili* (Herz 1984, 193).

22. Susman (1929, 46f.) discusses Friedrich Schlegel's involvement with Dorothea Veit and Caroline Schlegel, later Schelling. Weissberg (1987, 220–22) and Behrens (1981, 331–33) also discuss these and other interpersonal relationships. About the changing reception of Dorothea Schlegel's work, see Schmitz (1991, 91–131).

23. Dorothea Schlegel, *Florentin: Roman, Fragmente, Varianten,* ed. Liliane Weissberg (1986). See also Dorothea M. Schlegel, *Florentin: A Novel,* trans. Edwina Lawler and Ruth Richardson (1989).

24. Veit was baptized a Protestant. In 1808 she and Friedrich Schlegel converted to Catholicism. Except for some attempts at poetry, Friederike-Dorothea Schlegel's creativity ceased when her husband established him-

self in Vienna. On Schlegel's work as an author in the context of German Romanticism, see Deibel (1905). Schlegel's novella *Camilla* and other works will not be discussed here.

25. In opposition to Gutzkow's verdict, Behrens (1981b, 437–38) maintains that unlike Rahel Varnhagen, Dorothea Schlegel has more than one literary voice.

26. "'Your fatherland does not hold you?' the count asked.—'Where is my fatherland?' retorted the other one in a tone of bitter melancholy and ironically went on: 'As far as I can remember, I have been an orphan and an alien on earth. Therefore I intend to call that country fatherland where I shall be called father for the first time'" (Schlegel 1986, 16).

27. Dorothea Veit's letter to Schleiermacher (Weissberg 1987, 235).

28. Gerhardt (1983, 12) raises this issue by exploring the tradition and history of Veit's non-Jewish contemporaries. According to her, Friedrich Schlegel also constructed his utopias from literary sources, whereas Novalis imagined his version of the Christian Middle Ages, and Kleist dreamed up a fictitious Prussia. In contrast to Veit, however, they derive the components of their literary universe from their native tradition.

29. Hahn and Schuller address the problems facing the editors of Rahel's texts in "Kann man einen Nachlass edieren?" (1993, 235–41).

30. Weissberg (1992, 53–70) discusses Rahel's letters in the context of emancipation.

31. Laschke (1988, 2) considers the "dialogue character" a characteristic trait of the letters of Jewish women.

32. Tewarson (1993, 145–59) argues that Rahel's travels also constitute a crossing of boundaries in more than a physical sense.

33. As a result of Varnhagen's untiring activities, Rahel acquired a cult following. Isselstein (1987, 16–36) exonerates Varnhagen from much of the negative criticism.

34. Arendt (1962, 94–95) explains: "Rahel acquired to the point of mastery the art of representing her own life: the point was not to tell the truth, but to display herself."

35. Varnhagen stressed the significance of this relationship (1979, 492; 30 December 1815). Rahel addressed her sister as "Meine geliebte Rosentochter! Teure Schwester!" The latter form of address corresponds to the Yiddish address צדייטע.

36. Weissberg examines Rahel's and Veit's correspondence (1991, 140–53).

37. For example, Varnhagen (1979, 2: 57), in her letter of 25 March 1795. Schweikert overlooks the chronology of Rahel's quest when he claims

that Rahel "never" experienced the circumstances of her birth other than as a threefold shame of being a Jew, a woman, and unattractive (1983, 29).

38. Barbara Breysach (1989) discusses several other relevant correspondences.

39. In Varnhagen and Wiesel (1978, 118) Marlis Gerhardt notes that Varnhagen edited and censored the correspondence, eliminating what he considered compromising in order to create the impression of a romantic soul friendship.

40. Varnhagen and Wiesel (1978, 106, 111-13). Gerhardt mentions that Rahel had a questionable reputation at the time.

41. Cocalis and Goodman (1982) are correct in noting that while women of the Romantic School "began to assert their rights for more sexual freedom," others, "like Pauline Wiesel who were not intimately associated with the romantic circle, were ostracized, so that even a woman like Rahel Varnhagen was careful about her reputation." They overlook, however, that additional reasons for Wiesel's and Varnhagen's isolation were their Jewishness and the lack of a powerful male protector.

42. Ludwig Robert describes the prurient sadistic interest of the masses — giggling and laughing among children as Jews are brutalized. He notes the absence of the clergy, who, as teachers of the religion of love, ought to assist the persecuted, and he underscores the devastating effects of alcohol abuse among the masses (Varnhagen 1979, 4: 502-3).

2. AT THE CROSSROADS

1. Hermand analyzes Heine's situation in "The Wandering Jew's Rhine Journey: Heine's *Lorelei*" (1994). See also DiMaio 1991.

2. On the impact of the 1848 movement on women and Jews, see Carlebach (1981, 157-59). Lewald's political awareness is obvious in her 1845 novella *Der dritte Stand,* which is discussed by Pazi (1983).

3. Rogols-Siegel (1988, i) points out that Lewald has been compared to George Sand and to George Eliot, who in 1854 became one of Lewald's friends. Lewald was a role model for other women who wanted to write for a living.

4. Rogols-Siegel (1988, 2ff.) informs us that Lewald's paternal grandfather, a banker, had gone bankrupt because of an unjust accusation during the reign of Friedrich Wilhelm II. Her parents had to struggle to obtain permission to get married and stay in Prussia as a result of the Prussian anti-Jewish legislature.

5. When Lewald was twenty-three and still unmarried, her father took her on a trip to Berlin, Leipzig, Weimar, Frankfurt, and Baden-Baden. Hoping that she would find a husband, he introduced her to David

Lewald in Breslau. The trip during which she met Rahel Levin is highlighted in *Meine Lebensgeschichte* ([1866] 1988). Lewald's father, her husband Adolf Stahr, and several male friends and colleagues played a significant role in her development, but Lewald also emphasizes female bonding and mentions some of her aunts and motherly friends, Rahel Levin and the actresses Clara and Berta Stich, as her role models.

6. Rogols-Siegel (1988, 34) discusses the relationship between these first novels and Lewald's biography.

7. On the influence of Lewald's work on Fontane, see Rogols-Siegel (1993).

8. "These women did not know how Jewish they were, through their inherited spirituality they became strong pillars of the feminist movement, which movement brought to the timid, uncertain steps of Jewish women a goal and determination" (Edinger 1968, 80).

9. Pappenheim translated the *Ma'asse Buch* into German as *Allerlei Geschichten* in 1929 and the first volume of the *Frauenbibel*, the *Zennoh Rennoh*, the *Song of Songs*, into German in 1930.

10. Edinger's edition of *Bertha Pappenheim: Freud's Anna O.* first appeared as *Bertha Pappenheim: Leben und Schriften*. Pappenheim died in 1936 in Isenburg by Frankfurt, and her life's work was obliterated by the Nazis (Kaplan 1979, 30-32).

11. Kaplan (1979, 4) speaks of "convergent spheres of German, Jewish, and women's history."

12. Karminski died in the Holocaust (Kratz-Ritter 1993, 205-6).

13. Luxemburg comes to the defense of gentle women, "even if they are good for nothing but adorning the earth like humming-birds and orchids" (1982: 180).

14. This is the dominant theme in most of Pappenheim's work, including *Zur Sittlichkeitsfrage* (1907).

15. Engelstein (1993) reveals that white slavery was a theme of Russian anti-Semitism and that, indeed, numerous brothel madams and a disproportionate number of the prostitutes were Jewish.

16. Pappenheim's "Remarks about a study plan" (Edinger 1968, 91ff.) Kaplan (1979, 187) points out that the *Frauenbund* school at Wolfratshausen was allowed to function until the so-called *Kristallnacht*. Ironically, the integration of women into the Jewish clergy seemed imminent on the eve of the destruction of the Jewish communities. In 1935 Regine Jonas became the first ordained German woman rabbi (Kellenbach 1993, 196).

17. According to Pappenheim, who was outraged by the notion of collective education and promiscuity, American Zionism developed in ways more acceptable to women. While in Palestine, she took exception to

the narrow Zionist debates: "Is there nothing else, nothing wider, nothing bigger in the entire world?" Almost unwillingly she does concede that placing Jewish orphans in Zionist homes might save them from becoming the "victims of Christian missions" (Edinger 1968, 82, 41).

18. Kaplan (1991, 147–50) discusses the discrimination against Russian women students, using the example of Elizabeth Bab to reveal that before the First World War, women students were an oddity in Berlin.

19. See Luxemburg's letter to Gertrud Zlottko in 1913 (1982, 191). See also Wimmer (1990, 33ff.), Ettinger (1986), and Nettl (1989), all of which contain critical biographies.

20. Luxemburg condemned Germany's belated attempts to take colonies in "Brauchen wir Kolonien?" (1972, 642–43), and she criticized the United States and Europe for expanding their markets at the expense of non-European countries.

21. Moderates criticized her rigidity; see, for example, Karl Kautsky's 1891 work *Erfurter Programm.*

22. Trotsky (1970, 222, 225, 364, 457, 487, 528, 582).

23. Her charisma is reflected in the reactions to her death. Despite their differing views, Clara Zetkin praised Luxemburg's revolutionary fight in *Um Rosa Luxemburgs Stellung zur russischen Revolution* (1922).

24. She was in jail for high treason in 1915 and again from 1916 to the end of World War I for participating in demonstrations in Wronke and Breslau. Numerous letters address these experiences.

25. "Entgegnung" (Luxemburg 1972, I, part 2: 256). The German nationalist paper *Deutsche Wacht,* for example, referred to her as *jüdisches Frauenzimmer* (Jewish bitch).

26. Luxemburg had been a friend of the feminist leader Clara Zetkin, the editor of the women's paper *Die Gleichheit.* She was also August Bebel's friend, who in 1879 published the influential feminist text *Die Frau und der Sozialismus.*

27. "Frauenwahlrecht und Klassenkampf" "Die Proletarierin" (Luxemburg, 1972, 3: 163ff., 413f.).

28. "Das eigene Kind" (Luxemburg 1972 I, part 2: 220–23).

29. Cf. Luxemburg (1972 I, part 2: 23ff.) on her views on French Catholicism.

30. Luxemburg frequently turns to literature for inspiration, mentioning, for example, that she overcame the sense of isolation in the prison cell by reciting Mörike poems. Of the nineteenth-century authors, Heinrich von Kleist and Franz Grillparzer were among her favorites, and she had a predilection for two rather conservative authors among her contemporaries:

Gerhart Hauptmann, who later allied himself with National Socialism, and Hans Thoma, a social-critical dramatist (Luxemburg 1980, 82).

31. Carl Stern (1989, 296–97) quotes Louis Fürnberg as explaining Lasker-Schüler's storytelling, which impresses him as fantastic and associative, as "not at all haphazard: much of it is deliberately staged."

32. This notion occurs in works by German and Austrian writers. Clare in *The Last Waltz in Vienna* writes: "Franz Josef himself, no less, looked down benevolently on his people, Jews and non-Jews alike" (1983, 310).

33. Bauschinger (1980, 27) notes that Lasker-Schüler's first marriage was dissolved in 1903, the year she married Herwath Walden.

34. Lasker-Schüler in *Verse und Prosa aus dem Nachlaß* (1961, 3: 104) states: "As long as only one child starves, God will do without any synagogue. I believe that I speak in the name of God, with all due respect. . . . I count the poor donkeys, *so* often overburdened, among the *sins* of the inhabitants of Jerusalem. One ought to talk also to the influential Arab priests." The topic of animal abuse in Israel is one of the major topics in Alice Schwarz-Gardos's *Die Abrechnung* (Schwarz 1962) and Gertrud Seehaus's *Katzengesang und Eselsschrei* (1985).

35. Despite improved economic conditions, some of her letters indicate that she was afraid of dying of starvation (Lasker-Schüler 1986, 23).

36. Heid (1993, 218) points out that in the mid-1920s, Berlin also had extensive German-Jewish and Eastern European Jewish communities, and she describes the interaction between the two groups as tense and at times even openly hostile.

37. On the marginality of military men in German literature, see D. C. G. Lorenz (1995).

3. THE TROUBLED METROPOLIS

1. A comparison between the Dreyfus affair and the Redl affair in Austria properly characterizes the difference between the situation in France and in Franz Josef's empire. The Austrian colonel Alfred Redl, a homosexual officer of obscure Galician, possibly partly Jewish, lineage, was framed for a high treason that members of the highest nobility had committed. Redl was forced to commit suicide, and in the notoriously anti-Semitic Austrian capital, the affair could be successfully hushed up (D. C. G. Lorenz 1994c).

2. Marie-Thérèse Kerschbaumer devoted a chapter of her acclaimed work on feminine resistence, *Der weibliche Name des Widerstands* (1980), to Alma Johanna König. Before that time Oskar Jan Tauschinski had been virtually the only one to write about her.

NOTES TO PAGES 84-88

3. Wimmer (1990, 237–308) discusses Hannah Arendt's 1929 dissertation, "Der Liebesbegriff bei Augustin: Versuch einer philosophischen Interpretation."

4. *Der Gläserne Garten* (1989, 335). Goll was buried at the Père Lachaise next to Yvan Goll, who had died in 1950 (Jäschke 1977, 192).

5. For information about Kolmar's life, see Woltmann (1995) and Eichmann-Leutenegger (1993). Kolmar held a position as governess with a well-to-do Hamburg family in 1927.

6. Eichmann-Leutenegger (1993, 173) shows the death certificate for Gertrud Kolmar, made in Berlin-Wilmersdorf on 21 August 1951. The date of her death is established as 2 March 1943. Eichmann-Leutenegger (172) indicates that Kolmar was apprehended on 27 February 1943 at her place of work. Her last letter to her sister Hilde Wenzel was written on 21 February.

7. Eichmann-Leutenegger (1993, 10) writes that Kolmar's paternal ancestors were rural people and her maternal family was urbanized.

8. Ludwig Chodziesner defended Count Eulenburg, a close friend of Emperor William, who was charged with homosexuality (Eichmann-Leutenegger 1993, 10). The abdication of Wilhelm II in 1918 marked the collapse of the world of Ludwig and Elise Chodziesner (17).

9. Hilde Benjamin-Lange was the wife of Dr. Georg Benjamin, Walter Benjamin's brother. She joined the KPD in 1927 and instigated show trials against former Nazis in the years 1953–67. She preserved Kolmar's manuscripts (Eichmann-Leutenegger 1993, 166).

10. Claire Goll's 1918 work "Die Pflicht der Frauen" condemned the military as a self-serving male bastion, and her 1917 work "Die Mission der deutschen Frau" (1989, 13, 18) called for a women's rebellion to save their children and improve their own lot. Also in the collection is "Die Frauen und das Reichsjugendwehrgesetz" (11–37), a text with a specifically pacifist-activist message to women.

11. Claire Goll, "Das verwüstete Frankreich" (1989, 24–28) and "Ein Schrei aus Belgien" (28–34). Yvan Goll had nothing but praise for Claire Studer in his *Requiem: Für die Gefallenen von Europa* (1917), and she reciprocated with a "Portrait of the Poet Yvan Goll" (1917, 702).

12. Goll's *Der Neger Jupiter raubt Europa* (1987) was first published with the subtitle *Liebeskampf zwischen zwei Welten* (Battle of Love between Two Worlds).

13. Hermand (1986, 73) describes graphically the racist image of Africans in German expressionism.

14. It seems unlikely that, contrary to Joachim Schultz in "Das Afrika- und

'Neger'-Bild in den Werken von Claire und Ivan Goll" (1990), the portrait of Africans and Africa in *Der Neger Jupiter* (1987) and *Ein Mensch ertrinkt* (1988) represent Claire Goll's actual views.

15. This is contrary to Monika Shafi's reading of Kolmar's novellas as emphasizing female creativity and the woman as artist (1991, 690).

16. Lotte Paepcke (1972, 49) observed the same reaction among socialists in Nazi-Germany. "You have to understand, we cannot burden ourselves with Jews. It would be dangerous for the cause," an SPD comrade said to her father after the Nazi takeover in 1933.

17. *Die Gelbe Straße* resembles the city novels of other Jewish novelists such as Alfred Döblin's *Berlin Alexanderplatz,* Israel Joshua Singer's *The Family Carnovsky,* and Isaac B. Singer's prose works about life in the Warsaw Jewish quarter. Cf. also Beckermann (1984), who in a photo documentary recaptures the atmosphere of this district, which was severely damaged by bombs during World War II.

18. This view of the masses coincides with Elias Canetti's portrayal of mass phenomena in *Masse und Macht* (1981).

4. BEYOND HUMANISM

1. Häusler in "Vom 'Antisemitismus des Wortes' zum 'Antisemitismus der Tat'" (1993, 44) mentions the anti-Semitic propaganda of the Austrian Social Democratic Party, in particular the 1923 brochure *Der Judenschwindel,* which operated with slogans such as "Judaified anti-Semites" or "the Swastika and rich Jews belong together."

2. Herrmann's circle was modeled after Stefan George's association of poets.

3. Herf questioned Adorno's assumption that the Enlightenment itself had become counterproductive, contending that the principles of the Enlightenment had never been taken to their full consequence.

4. *Susanna* was newly published by the Jüdischer Verlag at the Suhrkamp publishing company in 1994. Earlier it had been available in the anthology *Das leere Haus: Prosa jüdischer Dichter* (1959, 293–338).

5. Some of the personae in Kolmar's poetry express psychological states; others, characterized as members of marginalized groups, are "surrogate Jews" in Nancy Lauckner's terminology, such as "Die Fahrende" (Kolmar 1938, 9), "Die Drude" (11), "Die Landstreicherin" (18), "Die Lumpensammlerin" (131).

6. In her letter of 15 May 1940, Kolmar mentions that she was the center of some of the events organized by the Jewish *Kulturbund* (1970, 24).

7. On the attitude of German Jews, see Werner T. Angress in "The German Jews, 1933–1939" (1980).

8. Contrary to the more common view that Kolmar lost her life because of her devotion to her father, Amy Colin describes the poet as one of the Just who sacrificed herself for the sake of her fellow sufferers or wished to perish because she believed this to be God's will (1994, 219).

9. Alice Miller (1980) examines the pedagogical principles applied still today. Intended to prevent rebellious behavior, they enforce discipline supposedly in the child's best interest.

10. Elias Canetti, a contemporary of Kolmar's, addresses the same concern in his publications. In *Die gerettete Zunge: Geschichte einer Jugend* (1984, 11), for example, he makes the global assertion that death is the enemy of mankind.

11. E. Canetti (1965, 436–58), originally published in 1935. Veza Canetti suggests a similar relationship in section two of the first chapter of *Die Gelbe Straße*. In the Prater, Mr. Vlk passes a showcase with a gorilla carrying a woman. "He overlooked the naked woman and despised the gorilla as if he were alive" (1990, 20).

12. In her cursory discussion of *Susanna,* Woltmann does not comment on the protagonist's explicit identification with her dog (1995, 230–40). Citing the poem "Die Kröte" (The Toad), she remarks: "Animals symbolize the poetic I" (165). The same goes for Richard H. Lawson's attempt to come to terms with Canetti's animal themes in *Understanding Elias Canetti* (1991, 91).

13. A. C. Bhaktivedanta and Swami Prabhupada interpret: "Animal killing is very prominent among demoniac people. Such people are considered the enemies of the world because ultimately they invent or create something that will bring destruction to all" (1981, 280). Also in Buddhism, any occupation involving the killing of animals is considered inappropriate.

14. The term *Staubgesicht* (face of dust) calls to mind the term *Kalkgesicht* (face of chalk) in Else Lasker-Schüler's drama *Ich und Ich* (1980, 252), where it is used by the character Goebbels to insult Faust. While Lasker-Schüler emphasizes the dehumanizing meaning of the term, Kolmar takes it literally and imbues it with a life and vitality all its own.

15. Hermann Hesse referred to Sachs (who loved dance, poetry, and puppeteering) as the "sad child." Sachs's private education and the reasons for it call to mind Fanny Lewald and Else Lasker-Schüler.

16. As early as 1951, Heinz Dieckmann of the *Saarländischer Rundfunk* ranked Sachs next to Else Lasker-Schüler (Sachs 1984, 145).

17. Although on 8 August 1942 Kolmar criticizes her father's newly discov-

ered interest in the religious establishment, she does not criticize spirituality, as shown by her letter of 2 February 1943, in which she mentions that she keeps *Oneg Schabbath* (an hour to honor Sabbath proposed by Chaim Nachman Bialik) by reading Martin Buber and writing (1970, 165, 201–2).

18. Ingeborg Nordmann writes that Susman wanted to remind her readers that the Jewish people had come close to achieving a community without state, and she quotes from Susman's unpublished manuscript, "Entwurf einer Geistesgeschichte und Soziologie der deutschen Juden seit der Emanzipation," expressing Susman's fear that Zionism may lead to a new nationalism in direct opposition to the spirit of Judaism (Nordmann, 101–2).

19. Helene Adolf (1986, 114) details the significance of Buber for her contemporaries, including Nelly Sachs. "She was forced into a Jewish identity, and she discovered in the Old Testament and in Martin Buber the confirmation of her own experience of suffering," comment editors Ruth Dinesen and Helmut Müssener (Sachs 1984, 8).

20. In a letter to Berendson of 23 May 1946, Sachs states that too much tragedy entered her "entirely overwhelming material, the mystery of the eternal," which to express she consulted Buber and *Sohar* (Sachs 1984, 57).

21. Sachs did consider the existence of Israel as the state where persecuted Jews would find refuge, a dire necessity; however, Zionist militancy was foreign to her.

5. GERMAN AND JEW

1. Richarz (1986, 14) summarizes a statement made by Robert Welsch in 1946: "We cannot assume that there are Jews who feel drawn to Germany. It smells here of corpses—of gas chambers and of torture cells."

2. Among the works by historical witnesses documenting the end of the "symbiosis" between German Jews and Gentiles are Arnold Zweig's *Bilanz der deutschen Judenheit* (1934) and Lion Feuchtwanger's *Die Geschwister Oppenheim* (1933).

3. Starke (1975, 47–48) mentions the contest during which Ilse Weber, a lyric poet who was soon thereafter deported to Auschwitz, was likewise honored for her work.

4. Roslyn Abt Schindler (1994) discusses this problem by analyzing the situation of Hilde Burger.

5. Peter Edel writes about the futility of his and his fiancée's conversion, which caused them humiliation but did not "rehabilitate" them, in *Wenn es ans Leben geht* (1979, 225). Ilse Blumenthal-Weiss reveals the spiritual

dilemma of converts and the intolerance with which Jews treated them in "Im Auftrag des Reichskommissars" (1957). See the discussion of Blumenthal-Weiss's memor in Dagmar Lorenz (1992b, 92). In one episode in *Die größere Hoffnung* (1974), Ilse Aichinger shows Jewish children hoping to save a non-Jewish child from drowning in order to rehabilitate themselves (Lorenz 1992b, 164).

6. Arno Herzig (1993, 10) indicates that in big cities such as Hamburg approximately one-third of the marriages entered by Jewish individuals were interfaith marriages.

7. Ilse Aichinger shared the interests of Ernst Schnabel (1958) in Anne Frank's life and background.

8. Sigrid Weigel (1987, 33) argues that in Aichinger's texts reality collides with visionary and mystical elements (11), and she observes that Aichinger's texts emulate certain aspects of the dream.

9. Using a similar technique, Hermlin recalls the uprising in the Warsaw Ghetto in *Die Zeit der Gemeinsamkeit* (1980b).

10. The Auschwitz survivors Nina Weilovà and Kitty Hart emphasize that their youthful boldness contributed substantially to their survival. While their mothers, who were deported with them, possessed the circumspection and organizational skills of adults, the older women lacked their daughters' bravery (Hart 1982, 1979; Weilovà n.d.).

11. The poems "Ortsanfang" and "Ortsende" (1978) and the story "Zweifel an Balkonen" (1974b).

12. As reflected in the poem "Mittlerer Wahlspruch" (1978) or the radio play "Gare Maritime" (1974).

13. This view is similar to that of Walter Benjamin, who considered genocide as an integral part of his culture and pointed out that historians traditionally have sided with the victor (1974, 696).

14. See also "Neuer Bund" (1978).

15. Cordelia Edvardson, *Gebranntes Kind sucht das Feuer* (1990, 9–12). The Hebrew translation is entitled *Yaldah she-nikhvetah nimshekhet le-esh*.

16. Edvardson believes that the destruction of Israel is within the realm of possibility, and she is convinced that such a tragedy would mean the end of the Jewish nation — hence her statement that a Messiah is needed only when there is no hope left for the world (Koelbl 1989, 51–52).

17. Langgässer's mother had an illegitimate son before marrying a Jewish architect. As a twenty-nine-year-old teacher, Langgässer gave birth to her daughter Cordelia, whose father was a married Jewish man, the father of three children. In her autobiography, Edvardson thematizes the matriarchal structure of her family, her dependency on her mother, and the

conflicts between her mother and her grandmother, as well as the legacy of illegitimacy, in much the same way as Katja Behrens in *Die dreizehnte Fee* (1983) and *Im Wasser tanzen* (1990). In several works, notably *Das unauslöschliche Siegel* (1946) and *Märkische Argonautenfahrt* (1950) Langgässer represents Jewish individuals and Judaism in spiritual terms inferior to the Christian characters and Catholicism.

18. Claire Goll's *Der gestohlene Himmel* was first published in French under the title *Education barbare* (1941–42).

19. "The mother's caresses were vehement, passionate, and greedy" (1990, 30). "But then one of the girls [in the schoolyard] said something about her mother and called her a paint-box" (40).

20. Langgässer lived with Hoffmann in Berlin and performed forced labor. In 1948, she moved to Reinzabern, where she died in 1950. She was not informed about her daughter's liberation until 1947.

21. Langgässer, to create goodwill for herself and her daughter, accepted an invitation to a ball at an SS officer's house and took Edvardson with her. Edvardson muses: "Was it that . . . she wanted to present this child with her precocious charm in order to plead for mercy? 'Just look at her, gentlemen (and help yourselves?).' "

22. Venske (1987a, 38, 53) comments on the feminine configuration of the political and private aspects in Domin's novel with reference to the Talmudic statement: "The wife is the husband's home country. Is the husband the wife's home country?"

23. Koonz (1987, 407) maintains that close attachments and familylike relationships among women enabled the weakest of the weak to survive.

24. The same nursery rhyme, "Maikäfer flieg," occurs in Helma Sanders-Brahms's film *Deutschland, bleiche Mutter,* sung by the female protagonist after having been rendered homeless by an Allied bombing raid.

25. Frederiksen (1989, 95–97) points out that between 1945 and 1955 Elisabeth Langgässer was considered the most significant German woman poet. Subsequently, her work was almost forgotten. Frederiksen concedes that there is a certain opposition to the male order, expressed in women's topics and a feminine sensitivity.

26. She compares herself and her son to small boats and her partner to the safe "mothership" (116).

27. During the trials at Nürnberg and thereafter, the terms *war crimes* and *war criminals* were in reference to all crimes committed at the time of World War II, including mass extermination and genocide.

28. Susannah Heschel, "Configurations of Patriarchy, Judaism, and Nazism in German Feminist Thought" (Rudavsky 1995, 135–54), discusses new

Christian anti-Semitic tendencies in Germany, mentioning as "the first antisemitic best-seller since 1945" Franz Alt's *Jesus: Der erste neue Mann* (142).

6. THE DIASPORA IN THE DIASPORA

1. Screenplay by William A. Drake.
2. Until its destruction after the Nazi occupation, Vicki Baum and many other exile authors, including Anna Seghers, Alfred Döblin, Lion Feucht-wanger, Erika Mann, and Ludwig Marcuse, published with the German-language publishing house Querido of Amsterdam. Later, editions of her works were published in English, such as *Shanghai* (1939), *Marion Alive* (1942), and *Hotel Berlin* (1944).
3. Arendt's views on mass psychology were influenced by the Austrian Jewish novelist and theorist Hermann Broch, who died in 1951. Arendt had reviewed Broch's works and took charge of his posthumous works (Wimmer 1990, 264).
4. One passenger, for example, reacts to Libussa's recollections by saying: "We have often heard such propaganda stories. We do not believe and we do not like them" (1984, 49).
5. Joseph Roth's *Die Kapuzinergruft* (1938) is a prime example.
6. The attachment is obvious from her diary, *Rückkehr nach Wien: Tage-buch, 1946* (1968), titles such as *Verliebt in Döbling* (In Love with Döbling) (1965), and her study of Vienna from the time of Emperor Franz Josef until the Nazi takeover, *Glanz und Untergang: Wien, 1866–1938* (1987), translated as *Vienna's Golden Autumn, 1866–1938*. Spiel and de Mendel-sohn's marriage ended in divorce, and in 1971 she married the author Hans Flesch Edler von Brunningen.
7. See, for example, "Warum ich Wien verlasse" (1982).
8. Spiel goes beyond Deborah Hertz, who recognizes the significance of the friendships and relationships that Jewish women had with Jewish and Christian women, providing the Jews with psychological role models and the Christians with intellectual ones (Hertz 1978, 106).
9. Spiel, *Die hellen und die finsteren Zeiten: Erinnerungen, 1911–1914* (1989). *Lisas Zimmer* was first published as *The Darkened Room* (1961).
10. The term *alltäglicher Faschismus* (everyday fascism) was coined during the 1968 student movement. Cf. Kienast et al. 1981 and Mecklenburg 1977. Ingeborg Bachmann, who also uses the term *fascism* to describe a "private" phenomenon, has her protagonist in *Der Fall Franza* (1981, 71) comment on a statement of her brother's: "You say 'fascism,' that is funny, I have never heard it as a term for a private mode of behavior."

344

11. Although this term is an icon of the Reagan-Bush era, it can be applied to Spiel's typology. The concept *moral majority* corresponds roughly to the personality profile of the authoritarian, ethnocentric personality as developed by Adorno et al. (1950).

12. Alice Schwarz-Gardos's pseudonyms include Alice Gardos, Alisha Ghachor, and Elishewa Jaron. Her third marriage was to Eli Gardos, the director of the music conservatory of Chedera, who died in 1980.

13. Schwarz-Gardos discusses the restitution agreement of the West German government in 1952, the protests against one of the first German films shown in Israel, *Sissy*, and the controversy about the arrival of the first German passenger ship in Haifa in 1959 (Schwarz-Gardos 1991, 183f.).

14. In her narrative "Beschreibung eines Krieges aus dem Hinterland," Schwarz-Gardos blends her memories of 1939 and her escape from Prague with the wartime memories of 1948, 1956, and 1967 (Schwarz-Gardos 1984, 179–232).

15. In her autobiographical sketch "Nachwort in eigener Sache," Schwarz-Gardos compares the fate of her generation to that of Rahel Varnhagen, noting that both were the target of virulent anti-Semitic and misogynist nationalism (1991, 137).

16. She represented, for example, the Berliner *Tagesspiegel* in Israel and received the *Bundesverdienstkreuz 1. Klasse* from the Federal Republic of Germany.

17. Pazi mentions that the *Verein deutschsprachiger Schriftsteller in Israel,* founded in 1975, consisted of sixty-eight members, most of them older people (1989, 15).

18. Arendt's report on the Eichmann trial, *Eichmann in Jerusalem* (1964), was satirized by Robert Neumann in *Der Tatbestand oder der gute Glaube der Deutschen* (1965).

19. Schwarz-Gardos crosses species lines in other works as well, as in "Beschreibung eines Krieges aus dem Hinterland," which entwines her memories of the 1967 war with caring for a motherless kitten whom she refuses to have euthanized (1991, 228–29). The Nazi poet Bernward Vesper, in keeping with popular views, stated in his autobiography, "Cats are unpredictable and untrainable creatures of inferior origin in the orient—they are a semitic race" (Weinberger 1992, 43). As an interesting contrast, in Art Spiegelmann's comic strip *Maus: A Survivor's Tale,* the Germans are portrayed as cats and the Jews as mice.

20. Kaplan (1984, 196) elaborates in opposition to the editorial collective of *Ästhetik und Kommunikation* 51 (1983) that Jews were less than 1 percent

of the German population and that they were a heterogeneous population without a particular ideological consensus.

21. Nelly Sachs's poem "Auf daß die Verfolgten nicht Verfolger werden"
(1961, 77).

22. In Freytag's *Soll und Haben* and Raabe's *Der Hungerpastor,* the Jewish
protagonists and their culture are characterized as deeply flawed. This
pattern is modified in Wassermann's biography, *Mein Weg als Deutscher
und Jude* (1921), which exposes the impasse the author faces as a result of
anti-Semitism. In Hilsenrath's *Der Nazi und der Friseur* (1977), the model
is reversed entirely. The Jewish character possesses the physical and mental attributes that the "Aryans" claim as their own, and the Gentile Max
Schultz resembles the Jewish stereotype of Nazi propaganda.

7. JEWISH WOMEN AUTHORS AND THE LEFT

1. This notion is also expressed in Jurek Becker's novel *Bronsteins Kinder*
(1986), based on the author's experience of growing up as the son of Jewish Holocaust survivors in the GDR.

2. Hermlin, "Die Zeit der Gemeinsamkeit" (1947) in *Lebensfrist* (1980b),
and "Hier liegen die Gesetzgeber" (1949) in *Äußerungen: 1944–1982*
(1983), two narratives thematizing the Warsaw Ghetto and the Jewish
experience as distinct from the fate of communists and other survivors.

3. Hans Mayer, underscoring Seghers's particular brand of integrity, states:
"Whoever wants to judge Anna Seghers has to accept or condemn her in
her entirety. The later President of the Writers' Association, who allowed
much to happen, and who oftentimes tried to prevent the worst in her
discreet, very private manner, did not act differently than she had in her
early beginnings in the late twenties" (1991, 202).

4. *Anna Seghers: Eine Biographie in Bildern* reveals how autobiographical
Der Ausflug der toten Mädchen actually is: not only the author's name
but also that of other characters, namely her teacher Johanna Sichel, a
convert to Judaism, remained unchanged (Wagner, Emmerich, and Radvanyi 1994, 23).

5. Claudia Koonz, *Mothers in the Fatherland* (1987), argues this point.

6. The name of Segher's mother, Hedwig Reiling, appeared on the same
deportation list as that of her teacher Johanna Sichel (Wagner, Emmerich, and Radvanyi 1994, 31–34).

7. A brief stay in Santo Domingo on her way to Mexico, a critical reading of Heinrich von Kleist's novella *Die Verlobung in St. Domingo,* historical sources on slavery, and the interaction between Caucasians, black

slaves, and mestizos in the Carribean colonies are the source material for Segher's three narratives.

8. This reading differs from that of Kappeler, who maintains that the imagery "undermines the thrust of the final passage," which "strives for a universal and conciliatory vision of human fate through an erasure of racial difference" (1994, 71).

9. "The presence of Jews in this country was of great importance for the Germans' moral 'rehabilitation'—the existence of a Jewish community within the Federal Republic of Germany fulfilled the purpose of lending credibility to the new state on an international scale. Nationwide a reidentification of Germans with Germany was taking place. In order to accommodate the Germans' desire for *Normalität*—'normalcy'—the continued presence of Jews in Germany was necessary" (Diner 1988, 226).

10. Guy Stern notes, "Honigmann's prose fiction itself, however, defies an easy categorization. . . . Both novels . . . are autobiographical" (1994, 330–32).

11. For example, see Babu's reaction upon seeing a newspaper picture of a child in the Warsaw ghetto about to be shot by a German soldier. She is unable to share her fear, shame, and compassion with her Gentile friend "because I wanted to spare her or because looking at the picture together would have made us so helpless that it would have separated us" (1986, 21).

12. Georg Honigmann was secretly called an "Itzig" (Jew-Boy) by his housekeeper (Honigmann 1991, 92).

13. Guy Stern points out, "Without pathos she tells of the Communist suppression of Jewish activities; some of the rituals must be conducted clandestinely, and the community leader is ultimately exiled to Siberia" (1994, 331).

14. Guy Stern observes that Alfried was the director of the East Berlin theater where Honigmann worked; in other words, he was part of the system that exploited her (1994, 341).

8. BETWEEN EDEN AND UTOPIA

1. Adelson (1994a, 309) argues that *identity* and *home*, rather than being neutral terms, are no less politicized than their past.

2. See Norbert Mecklenburg 1993; Stefan Kaszinski 1987; Martin Pollak 1984; Verena Dohrn 1991. Galicia, with its large Jewish population, had been a significant site of Jewish civilization and spirituality in Eastern Europe. Like the Bukovina, with its capital city Czernowitz, it was formerly a part of the Austro-Hungarian Empire.

3. Jeanette Lander is the author of scholarly studies, such as *William Butler Yeats: Die Bildersprache seiner Lyrik* (1967) and *Ezra Pound* (1971b). In addition to literary and scholarly works, she also produced television films.

4. Adelson (1993, 87–129) provides an insightful interpretation of this work.

5. Gilman in *Jews in Today's German Culture* differentiates between the *Galut*, the "voluntary dispersion of the Jews" and the diaspora, the "involuntary exile of the Jews" (1995, 6).

6. Lander indicates the discrepancy between appearance and being, surface structure and deep structure. "After all, who is what he seems?" she comments (1976, 17).

7. The series was aired in 1978–79. Johanna Moosdorf expressed her gratification about the fact that the television series cracked the "whitewashed facade of the Fatherland." Cf. her poems "9. November 1978," and "Holocaust" (1979, 72f.).

8. For example, Richard Beer-Hoffmann's "Schlaflied für Mirjam" (1968, 341); Gertrud Kolmar's "Die Jüdin," and "Ewiger Jude" (Chodziesner 1938, 36f., 99f., 101f.); Else Lasker-Schüler's 1905 work "Mein Volk"; Ilse Aichinger's "Marianne" (1978, 10).

9. Broder observed that the children of Nazi parents, no matter how strongly they articulate their antifascist sentiments in general, not only refrain from criticizing their parents but exonerate them. In "Diese Scheißbilder trage ich mit mir rum," Broder exposes this tendency (1987, 166f.).

10. This is already the case in Friedrich Wolf's drama *Professor Mamlock* (1963), which was written in 1933, and applies to postwar novels as well, such as Jan Koplowitz, *"Bohemia"—Mein Schicksal* (1979), and Peter Edel, *Schwester der Nacht* (1979).

11. Elias Canetti believes that there are only two factions in the case of war, a peaceful one and a warlike one (1981, 48).

12. These attitudes transpire in the interviews with Beckermann's parents as well as in the voice-over in *Die papierene Brücke*. In *Unzugehörig* (1989, 65), Beckermann states that the Austrian chancellor Julius Figl welcomed Jews if they would live "as Austrians, not as Jews."

13. Posner (1991) examines the mind-set of numerous children of former Nazis, providing valuable insights into the problem addressed by Beckermann, Fleischmann, and others.

14. Even the Jewish chancellor Bruno Kreisky had difficulty saying the word *Jude*, Jew. In his speech in honor of Erich Fried at the University of Vienna, 29 April 1986, he referred to Judaism as "the religion of my

fathers," the "background" that he and Fried shared, and as the "religious community which is a community of fate." Beckermann is unsure whether to define herself as "a Jewish Viennese, a Viennese Jew, or a Jew in Vienna."

15. *Nach Jerusalem* was first shown on 23 February 1991 at the International Forum of Young Films, Delphi-Filmpalast, Berlin, and was screened in Austria 11 April 1991 at the Künstlerhaus-Kino Wien and thereafter at the VOTIV KINO Wien.

16. Adelson (1993, 97), with reference to Santner, aptly terms the modifier *post-Holocaust* an allusion "to a racially overwritten history." The modifiers *postmodern* and *postwar* as applied by both critics apply to Beckermann's work as well.

17. As defined by Deleuze and Guattari (1986, 17) and elaborated by Zipes (1994, 22): "By deterritorialization of language they mean the impossibility of a minority such as the Jews to write in the language of the masses, because they are cut off from them. Excluded from the majority, the minority invents an artificial or deterritorialized language for unusual and minor uses."

18. Löffler suggests that Mitgutsch's novel was influenced by the work of the Swiss psychoanalyst Alice Miller, a child-abuse expert. In 1994 *In fremden Städten* was performed as a drama at the Vienna women's theater, *Theater in der Drachengasse.*

9. ENCOUNTERS AND CONFRONTATIONS

1. In her interview with Hoffmeister (1987, 109, 111), Jelinek states that literary satire is an oddity in post-Holocaust Austria and Germany "because the Jews are no longer alive," and she emphasizes the affinity of her approach to Kraus's and Canetti's method of literary dissection.

2. In her interview with Alexandra Reinunghaus (1988), Jelinek maintains, regarding her novel *Lust,* that she is interested in the issue of lust only in its social and political context. In her interview with Riki Winter (1991, 9), she states that she left the Communist Party.

3. Berka (1993, 136) mentions in her interview with Jelinek Marlen Haushofer's early feminist novel *Die Wand* (1968), which is strongly influenced by Simone de Beauvoir's feminist study *The Second Sex* (1957). Jelinek is familiar with Haushofer's book and mentions it approvingly.

4. This distance between Jews and non-Jews is not remedied by an apparent preoccupation with the topics of Nazism and the Holocaust. Andreas Huyssen comments on the situation in the 1980s and 1990s: "Despite the growth of Holocaust revisionism in recent years, the problem for Holo-

caust memory in the 1980s and 1990s is not forgetting, but rather the ubiquitousness, even the excess of Holocaust imagery in our culture," including "the fascination with fascism in film and fiction" (1985, 255).

5. Among the Gentile authors who continued to use Jewish stereotypes were Günter Grass in *Die Blechtrommel* (1959), Luise Rinser in *Der schwarze Esel* (1974), and Gerhard Zwerenz in *Die Erde ist unbewohnbar wie der Mond* (1973). Rainer-Werner Faßbinder's *Der Müll, die Stadt und der Tod* (1981), a play about real estate speculators and criminals based on Zwerenz's anti-Semitic novel, initiated a public controversy that brought long-repressed anti-Jewish resentments out into the open and led to the Historians' Debate.

6. Seelich published poetry, short stories, and radio plays while a student in Prague. Her poetry anthology, *Akdar Ajdan Leporello,* written in 1969, was prepared for publication but did not appear in print. It is scheduled for publication in Prague in the near future.

7. *Kieselsteine* received mixed reviews; cf. Streibel (1984) and Christoph (1984). Seelich's children's films, liked by young and adult audiences, have received international awards, such as *Jonathana* at the International Festival for Children's Film in Chicago and at Bratislava.

8. Among Seelich's works not discussed here are the screenplays *Ein Spielfilm für 2 Berge, 3 Schauspieler und einen Feuersalamander* (1983), *Nett* (1984), *Mein Name ist Egon* (1988), *Who Is Who in Mistelbach* (1989), the four-part television series *Mein Zuhause, dein Zuhause* (1989), and *Lisa und die Säbelzahntiger* (1995).

9. Kubes-Hofmann (1991) observes that the opening of the borders inspired Seelich to greater freedom of expression. Peter Wallner (1992) emphasizes the film's Praguer Jewish atmosphere.

10. Among them are Jana Cerna's 1990 work *Clarissa a jine texty* and the 1991 work *Co cist z torby spisovtely Jihomoravskeho kraje 1990.* Cerna's book on Jesenska, *Adresat Milena Jesenska* (1969), was widely received, translated, and republished by Concordia in Prague in 1991. Translations include *Vie de Milena: De Prague à Vienne* (in 1988), *Kafka's Milena* (in 1988), and *Milena Jesenska* (in 1986). Egon Bondy's rich productions since 1990 include *3x Egon Bondy* (in 1990), *Lesbicky sen* (in 1993), *Bez pameti zilo by se lepe* (in 1990), *Cesta ceskem nasich otcu* (in 1992), *Indicka filosofie* (in 1992), *Orwelliada* (in 1990), and many other titles. Seelich states in her unpublished lecture manuscript "Film, Staat und Gesellschaft in Ost- und Westeuropa und ich" (n.d., 7-8): "It turned out, unfortunately, that the film scripts written in Prague during the last twenty years and prevented from being realized, have become obsolete for the most part, and there is no need to produce them now."

11. In *Unzugehörig* (1989, 17f.), without mentioning Seelich by name, Ruth Beckermann criticizes the polarity Jewish woman–German man in *Kieselsteine*, pointing out that the Austrians were anything but innocent bystanders.

12. Unlike with Deborah Lefkowitz's *Intervals of Silence* (1989), which remains within the bounds of polite discourse, most critics felt uncomfortable about *Kieselsteine*. Tramontana (1984) calls it an "uninforming film" and, oddly enough, perceives Hannah's desire for revenge as "masochism." Distl (1984), on the other hand, describes the work as "responsible," praising the outstanding performance of the actors.

13. Seelich contextualizes her children's films in terms of the Bohemian literary tradition. "The phenomenon 'child' has traditionally been considered of great value in Czech culture and society. . . . Most of the important Czech writers wrote for children. Children's literature was not considered inferior since children are not considered inferior human beings. The fact that this is not the case in other countries, including Austria, played a significant role in the culture shock I experienced in the West" (D. C. G. Lorenz forthcoming).

14. For example, several stories in Irene Dische's *The Jewess* (1992) first appeared in German in *Fromme Lügen* (1989).

15. Since the original text was written in English, quotes will follow the text in Irene Dische, *Pious Secrets* (1991).

16. Remmler maintains that Dische undoes the memory work accomplished by Esther Dischereit and Barbara Honigmann. "As a constructed Jewish writer in Germany, she herself seems to reconstruct negative relations between Jews and Germans that mirror anti-Semitic stereotypes, instead of addressing and protesting against them" (1994, 203).

17. Diner (1990, 255–56) coined the term *Deckerinnerung* to characterize a "new historical assiduity that brings one closer to the events of 1933–1945, yet at the same time leaves out the source for one's own ease."

18. According to Gilman's (1988) observations on Hilsenrath and Becker, Charles Allen's "hidden," and at the same time apparent, linguistic identity is German.

19. Huyssen (1995, 1–37) examines the paradox of the frequent attempts at historical stocktaking and the equally frequently raised issue of cultural amnesia.

10. TOWARD A NEW JEWISH WOMEN'S LITERATURE

1. Remmler defines this kind of literature in which identity is established through memory and genealogy as a process that locates "the many-

layered bodies of identity that reject a nostalgic return to an origin or to unity" (1994, 189).

2. Venske (1987b, 191–219) discusses Johanna Moosdorf, a contemporary of Weil's, who constructs in her texts troubled female-female relationships similar to those portrayed by Weil. Venske mentions the strong taboo against the representation of lesbian relationships in Germany during the middle to late 1970s.

3. "Once again, back to Antigone my great sister, so unlike me . . . My beloved. Without whom it would have been so much harder for me to tolerate the world," she writes in *Generationen* (1983, 209).

4. Another example of these transgressions is a scene at a gay bar where the narrator enjoys the company of women, but dances with a man. Similarly, in Seelich's *Kieselsteine* a spontaneous affinity arises between the Jewish woman protagonist and a gay man.

5. Gilman (1995, 36) points out that "the brochure contained an essay by Beate Bongartz, the women's rights representative of the Green Party in North Rhine–Westphalia, who labeled Jews (defined as male) as child rapists since (according to her) they advocate the sexual violation of three-year-old girls."

6. Neumann does not escape a tendency that Weigel criticizes in "Frau und 'Weiblichkeit': Theoretische Überlegungen zur feministischen Literaturkritik" as a "new myth" of femininity. Asserting that femininity is not identical with the character of women or with women, Weigel points out that everything a man claims for himself—such as individuality, intellect, rationality—was defined as unfeminine (1984, 103–4). Brigitte Wartmann (1983, 114) points out that male critics, including Marcuse, have traditionally associated utopian hopes with the concept of femininity.

7. Susan Cernyak-Spatz (1985, 3) observes the use of stereotypes in the literature of the 1940s and 1950s. By portraying the victims as noble, the ss personnel as diabolic, and average Germans as ignorant, such literature made it possible to disassociate from the events under discussion altogether.

8. The guard's inner monologue is indicative of the male view of the women, which correspond to a certain extent to the anti-Semitic view of Jews as incapable of fighting and physically unfit: "Broads, nothing but stubborn, silly broads, I'll show them, mother, I'll show them, broads, broads' asses, fat broads' asses . . . don't look at me like that, you female geese, this is ridiculous, a women's revolt, a revolt of geese" (1991, 96).

9. Adelson points out that Germans appear merely as marginal figures in Klüger's memoirs (1994b, 96).

10. Berel Lang (1988, 2) asks: "Is the enormity of the Holocaust at all capable of literary representation? And what would be the justification for attempting such representation even if it were possible? In his much-quoted statement condemning the 'barbarism' of writing poetry after Auschwitz, Theodor Adorno suggests a larger boundary question for *any* writing that takes the Holocaust as its subject: Placed in the balance with the artifice that inevitably enters the work of even the most scrupulous author, what warrant—moral or theoretical or aesthetic—is there for writing about the Holocaust at all?" See also Lawrence Langer (1988, 26).

11. Klüger exercises what James E. Young (1988, 24) calls "the right to invoke the empirical bond that has indeed existed between a writer and events in his narrative," "the right to invoke the experiences as one's own."

12. Douglas Hauer (1993, 2ff.) argues convincingly that Arendt uses the biography of Rahel Levin Varnhagen to reflect on her own identity, that of a German-Jewish woman and exile writer.

13. In *Der Brautpreis* (1988) Grete Weil engages in a similar undertaking, reinterpreting segments of the Torah from a feminist point of view.

14. As Hans Thalberg put it in the title of his memoirs, *Von der Kunst, Österreicher zu sein* (1984). See D. C. G. Lorenz (1992b, 139).

15. Remmler notes that "by entwining memory and female Jewish identity, texts by Dischereit and Honigmann give voice to the silenced victims of the Shoah without speaking for the dead or displacing them into metaphorical tropes" (1994, 204).

16. "I like neither the rich, bad, real estate rich Jews, nor the ones who consider other people's water their own and merrily plant trees on the houses of other nations as if it could not be otherwise and were ordained this way," the narrator states (10).

17. Walter Benjamin maintained that brutality and imperialist aggression were the foundations of Western culture, which was misrepresented by historians who traditionally identified with the victors (1974, 696).

18. So does Frank Stern (1994, 56): "I would like to stress that Auschwitz—from this point of view—is not a metaphor but a German place, and as such it is not of merely passing interest to German history."

Bibliography

Adelson, Leslie A. 1994a. "Nichts wie zuhause: Jeanette Lander und Ronnith Neumann auf der utopischen Suche nach jüdischer Identität im westdeutschen Kontext." In *Jüdische Kultur und Weiblichkeit in der Moderne,* ed. Inge Stephan, Sabine Schilling, and Sigrid Weigel. Cologne: Böhlau.

———. 1994b. "Ränderberichtigung: Ruth Klüger und Botho Strauß." In *Zwischen Traum und Trauma—Die Nation: Transatlantische Perspektiven zur Geschichte eines Problems,* ed. Claudia Mayer-Iswandy. Tübingen: Stauffenburg Verlag.

———. 1993. *Making Bodies, Making History.* Lincoln: University of Nebraska Press.

Adler, Rachel. 1983. "The Jew Who Wasn't There: Halakhah and the Jewish Woman." In *On Being a Jewish Feminist: A Reader,* ed. Susannah Heschel. New York: Schocken.

Adolf, Helene, ed. 1986. *Die Familie Höchst.* Bad Soden: Woywood.

Adorno, Theodor W., Else Frenkel-Brunswick, Daniel Levinson, and Newitt Sanford, eds. 1950. *The Authoritarian Personality.* New York: Harper.

Aichinger, Ilse. 1987. *Kleist, Moos, Fasane.* Frankfurt am Main: Fischer.

———. 1978. *Verschenkter Rat.* Frankfurt am Main: Fischer.

———. 1974a. *Die größere Hoffnung.* Frankfurt am Main: Fischer.

———. 1974b. *Schlechte Wörter.* Frankfurt am Main: Fischer.

———. 1967. "Aufruf zum Mißtrauen." In *Aufforderung zum Mißtrauen: Literatur, bildende Kunst, Musik in Österreich seit 1945,* ed. Otto Breicha and Gerhard Fritsch. Salzburg: Residenz.

———. 1965. *Eliza, Eliza.* Frankfurt am Main: Fischer.

———. 1957. *Zu keiner Stunde.* Frankfurt am Main: Fischer.

———. 1954a. "Plätze und Straßen." *Jahresring* 3:19–24.

———. 1954b. "Spiegelgeschichte." In *Wo ich wohne,* 9–18. Frankfurt am Main: Fischer.

———. 1953. *Der Gefesselte.* Frankfurt am Main: Fischer.

———. 1952. *Rede unter dem Galgen.* Vienna: Jungbrunnen.

———. 1948. *Die größere Hoffnung.* Vienna: Bermann-Fischer.

———. 1946. "Aufruf zum Mißtrauen." *Plan* 7 (July): 588.

Améry, Jean. 1986. "On the Necessity and Impossibility of Being a Jew." In *Germans and Jews since the Holocaust: The Changing Situation in West Germany,* ed. Anson Rabinbach and Jack Zipes. New York: Holmes & Meier.

———. 1982. "Der ehrbare Antisemitismus." In *Weiterleben: Essays.* Stuttgart: Clett-Cotta.

———. 1974. *Lefeu oder der Abbruch.* Stuttgart: Klett.

———. 1964. *Wir Eichmannssöhne: Offener Brief an Klaus Eichmann.* Munich: Beck.

Anders, Günter. 1964. *Wir Eichmannssöhne: Offener Brief an Klaus Eichmann.* Munich: Beck.

Angress, Ruth K[lüger]. 1986. "Lanzmann's Shoah and Its Audience," *Simon Wiesenthal Center Annual* 3:250–51. New York: Kraus International.

Angress, Werner T. 1980. "The German Jews, 1933–1939." In *The Holocaust: Ideology, Bureaucracy, and Genocide; The San José Papers,* ed. Henry Friedlander and Sybil Milton. New York: Kraus International.

Arendt, Hannah. 1978. *The Jew as Pariah: Jewish Identity and Politics in the Modern Age.* New York: Grove Press.

———. 1964. *Eichmann in Jerusalem.* Munich: Piper.

———. 1962. *Rahel Varnhagen: Lebensgeschichte einer deutschen Jüdin aus der Romantik.* Munich: Piper.

Arnim, Bettina von. 1959. "Die Klosterbeere." In *Werke und Briefe,* vol. 3, ed. Gustav Konrad. Frechen: Bartmann-Verlag.

Ashley, Kathleen, Leigh Gilmore, and Gerald Peters, eds. 1994. *Autobiography and Postmodernism.* Amherst: University of Massachussetts Press.

Atwood, Margaret. 1986. *The Handmaid's Tale.* New York: Fawcett Crest.

Bachmann, Ingeborg. 1981. *Der Fall Franza.* Munich: Deutsche Taschenbuch Verlag.

Bächtold-Stäubli, Hanns. 1935–36. *Handwörterbuch des deutschen Aberglaubens.* Berlin: Walter de Gruyter.

Baioni, Guiliano. 1994. *Kafka—Literatur und Judentum,* trans. Gertrud Billen and Josef Billen. Stuttgart: Metzler.

Balzer, Bernd. 1965. "Wirklichkeit als Aufgabe." In *Eine jüdische Mutter,* ed. Gertrud Kolmar. Munich: Kösel.

Bänsch, Dieter. 1970. *Else Lasker-Schüler: Zur Kritik eines etablierten Bildes.* Stuttgart: Metzler.

Baum, Vicki. 1984. *Schicksalsflug.* Munich: Heyne.

———. 1944. *Hotel Berlin.* Garden City NY: Doubleday, Doran.

———. 1942. *Marion Alive.* Garden City NY: Doubleday, Doran.

———. 1939. *Shanghai*. Trans. Basil Creighton. New York: Doubleday, Doran.

———. 1937. *Liebe und Tod auf Bali*. Amsterdam: Querido.

———. 1929. *Menschen im Hotel: Ein Kolportageroman mit Hintergründen*. Berlin: Ullstein.

———. 1928. *Stud. Chem. Helene Willfür*. Berlin: Ullstein.

Bauschinger, Sigrid. 1985. "'Ich bin ein Jude. Gott sei Dank': Else Lasker-Schüler." In *Im Zeichen Hiobs: Jüdische Schriftsteller und deutsche Literatur im 20. Jahrhundert*, ed. Grimm Bayerdörfer. Königstein: Athenäum.

———. 1980. *Else Lasker-Schüler: Ihr Werk und ihre Zeit*. Heidelberg: Lothar Stiehm.

Beauvoir, Simone de. 1957. *The Second Sex*. Trans. H. M. Parshley. New York: Knopf.

Becker, Jurek. 1986. *Bronsteins Kinder*. Frankfurt am Main: Suhrkamp.

Beckermann, Ruth. 1994a. "The Glory of Austrian Resistance and the Forgotten Jews." In *Insiders and Outsiders: Jewish and Gentile Culture in Germany and Austria*, ed. Dagmar C. G. Lorenz and Gabriele Weinberger. Detroit: Wayne State University Press.

———. 1994b. "Jean Améry and Austria." In *Insiders and Outsiders: Jewish and Gentile Culture in Germany and Austria*, ed. Dagmar C. G. Lorenz and Gabriele Weinberger. Detroit: Wayne State University Press.

———. 1991. "Nach Jerusalem: Ein Film von Ruth Beckermann." Brochure. Vienna: INFO filmladen 13, no. 121.

———, director. 1990. *Nach Jerusalem*. Vienna: filmladen.

———. 1989. *Unzugehörig: Österreicher und Juden nach 1945*. Vienna: Löcker.

———. 1984. *Die Mazzesinsel: Juden in der Wiener Leopoldstadt*. Vienna: Löcker.

Beckermann, Ruth, and Josef Aichholzer, directors. 1983. *Wien Retour*. Vienna: filmladen.

———. 1986. *Die papierene Brücke*. Vienna: filmladen.

Beer-Hofmann, Richard. 1968. "Schlaflied für Mirjam." In *Welch Wort in die Kälte gerufen*. Berlin: Verlag der Nation.

Behrend, Rahel. 1945. *Verfemt und verfolgt*. Zürich: Büchergilde Gutenberg.

Behrend-Rosenfeld, Else R. 1964. *Ich stand nicht allein: Erlebnisse einer Jüdin in Deutschland, 1933–45*. Frankfurt am Main: Europöische Verlagsanstalt.

Behrens, Katja. 1993. *Salomo und die anderen: Jüdische Geschichten*. Frankfurt am Main: Fischer.

———. 1990. *Im Wasser tanzen: Ein Erzählzyklus*. Darmstadt: Luchterhand.

———. 1987. *Von einem Ort zum andern: Erzählungen*. Pfaffenweiler: Pfaffenweiler Presse.

―――. 1983. *Die dreizehnte Fee*. Düsseldorf: Claassen.

―――, ed. 1982. *Das Insel-Buch vom Lob der Frau*. Frankfurt am Main: Insel.

―――. 1981a. *Jonas: Erzählungen*. Pfaffenweil: Pfaffenweiler Presse.

―――, ed. 1981b. *Frauenbriefe der Romantik*. Frankfurt am Main: Insel.

―――. 1978. *Die weiße Frau*. Frankfurt am Main: Suhrkamp.

Ben Chorin, Schalom. 1989. "Die Königin der Lyrik, der schwarze Schwan Israels: Erinnerungen an Else Lasker-Schüler." *Der Literat* 31:339–40.

Benjamin, Walter. 1974. "Über den Begriff der Geschichte." In *Gesammelte Schriften*, vols. 1 and 2, ed. Rolf Tiedemann and Hermann Schwepphäuser. Frankfurt am Main: Suhrkamp.

Benn, Gottfried. 1968. *Gesammelte Werke*. Ed. Dieter Wellershoff. Vol. 4. Wiesbaden: Limes.

Bering, Dietz. 1987. *Der Name als Stigma: Antisemitismus im deutschen Alltag, 1812–1933*. Stuttgart: Klett-Cotta.

Berka, Sigrid. 1993. "Ein Gespräch mit Elfriede Jelinek." *Modern Austrian Literature* 26 (no. 2): 127–55.

Bettauer, Hugo. 1988. *Die Stadt ohne Juden: Ein Roman von Übermorgen*. Frankfurt am Main: Ullstein.

Bettelheim, Bruno. 1979. "The Ignored Lesson of Anne Frank." In *Surviving*. New York: Knopf.

Bhaktivedanta, A. C., and Swami Prabhupada. 1981. *The Bhagavad-Gita As It Is*. Los Angeles: Bhaktivedanta Book Trust.

Bilik, Dorothy. 1992. "The Memoirs of Glikl of Hameln: The Archeology of the Text." *Yiddish* 8:5–21.

―――. 1989. *Jewish Women and Yiddish Literature: Gluckel of Hameln*. Oxford: Oxford University Press.

Birnbaum, Nathan. 1916. *Was sind Ostjuden?* Vienna: R. Löwit.

Blau, Ludwig. 1989. *Das altjüdische Zauberwesen*. Budapest: Gregg International.

Blumenthal, Bernhard. 1983. "Claire Goll's Prose." *Monatshefte* 75 no. 4:358–68.

Blumenthal-Weiss, Ilse. 1957. "Im Auftrag des Reichskommissars." Manuscript. Leo Baeck Institute Archives, New York.

Blümlinger, Christa. 1991. "Interview mit Ruth Beckermann, 'Nach Jerusalem: Ein Film von Ruth Beckermann.'" Vienna: INFO filmladen 13/121.

Bodemann, Y. Michal. 1994. "A Reemergence of German Jewry?" In *Reemerging Jewish Culture in Germany: Life and Literature since 1989*, ed. Sander L. Gilman and Karen Remmler. New York: New York University Press.

Bovenschen, Silvia. 1979. *Die imaginierte Weiblichkeit: Exemplarische Unter-*

suchungen zu kulturgeschichtlichen und literarischen Präsentationsformen des Weiblichen. Frankfurt am Main: Suhrkamp.

Brandes, Ute. 1992. *Anna Seghers.* Berlin: Colloquium.

Brandt, Marion. 1994. "Das Bild des Opfers im Werk von Gertrud Kolmar." In *Jüdische Kultur und Weiblichkeit in der Moderne,* ed. Inge Stephan, Sabine Schilling, and Sigrid Weigel. Cologne: Böhlau.

Brecht, Bertold. 1967. *Furcht und Elend des Dritten Reiches.* In *Gesammelte Werke,* vol. 3, part 3. Frankfurt am Main: Suhrkamp.

Breysach, Barbara. 1989. *Die Persönlichkeit ist uns nur geliehen: Zu den Briefwechseln Rahel Levin Varnhagens.* Würzburg: Königshausen & Neumann.

Broder, Henryk. 1987. "Diese Scheißbilder trage ich mit mir rum: Henryk Broder über die Reaktionen auf Niklas Franks 'Mein Vater, der Nazi-Mörder.'" *Der Spiegel,* week 28, no. 41 (July): 166–67.

Broszat, Martin, Hans-Adolf Jacobsen, and Helmut Krausnick. 1982. *Anatomie des ss-Staates.* Munich: Deutsche Taschenbuch Verlag.

Buber, Martin. 1927. *Die Chassidischen Bücher.* Berlin: Schocken.

Canetti, Elias. 1993. *Aufzeichnungen, 1942–1985.* Munich: Hanser.

———. 1990. "Veza." In Veza Canetti, *Die Gelbe Straße,* ed. Elias Canetti. Munich: Hanser.

———. 1985. *Das Augenspiel: Lebensgeschichte, 1931–1937.* Munich: Hanser.

———. 1984. *Die gerettete Zunge: Geschichte einer Jugend.* Frankfurt am Main: Fischer.

———. 1981. *Masse und Macht.* Frankfurt am Main: Fischer. Original edition, Düsseldorf: Claasen, 1960.

———. 1980. *Die Fackel im Ohr: Lebensgeschichte, 1921–1931.* Munich: Hanser.

———. 1965. *Die Blendung.* Frankfurt am Main: Fischer. Original edition, Vienna: Herbert Reichner, 1935.

Canetti, Veza. 1992. "Geduld bringt Rosen." In *Geduld bringt Rosen,* 7–44. Munich: Hanser.

———. 1991. *Der Oger.* Munich: Hanser.

———. 1990. *Die gelbe Straße.* Ed. Elias Canetti. Munich: Hanser.

Carlebach, Julius. 1981. "Family Structure and the Position of Jewish Women." In *German-Jewish History,* ed. Werner E. Mosse, Arnold Paucker, and Reinhard Rürup. Tübingen: Mohr.

Carmely, Klara Pomeranz. 1981. *Das Identitätsproblem jüdischer Autoren im deutschen Sprachraum: Von der Jahrhundertwende bis zu Hitler.* Königstein: Scriptor.

Carnny-Francis, Anne. 1990. *Feminist Fiction.* Cambridge: Polity Press.

Celan, Paul. 1952. *Mohn und Gedächtnis.* Stuttgart: Deutsche Taschenbuch Verlag.

Cerna, Jana. 1969. *Adresat Milena Jesenska*. Prague: Club Mlada Poesie.

Cernyak-Spatz, Susan. 1985. *German Holocaust Literature*. New York: Peter Lang.

Cheney, Jim. 1989. "Postmodern Environmental Ethics: Ethics as Bioregional Narrative." *Environmental Ethics* 11:117–34.

Chodziesner, Gertrud [Kolmar]. 1938. *Die Frau und die Tiere*. Berlin: Jüdischer Buchverlag Löwe.

Christoph, Horst. 1984. Review of *Kieselsteine*, by Nadja Seelich. *Profil* (23 January): 58.

Clare, George. 1983. *The Last Waltz in Vienna*. New York: Holt, Rinehart & Winston.

Cocalis, Susan L., and Kay Goodman. 1982. "The Eternal Feminine Is Leading Us On." In *Beyond the Eternal Feminine*, ed. Susan L. Cocalis and Kay Goodman. Stuttgart: Akademischer Verlag Hans-Dieter Heinz.

Colin, Amy. 1994. "Macht, Opfer, Selbstzerstörung: Jüdisches Frauenschicksal in Gertrud Kolmars *Nacht: Brücken über dem Abgrund*." In *Bridging the Abyss: Reflections on Jewish Suffering, Anti-Semitism, and Exile*, ed. Amy Colin and Elisabeth Strenger, 199–225. Munich: Wilhelm Fink Verlag.

Cooper, Gabriele von Natzmer. 1993. "Das süßere Obst der Erkenntnis: Gnosis und Widerstand in Kolmars apokalyptischem 'Lied der Schlange.'" *Seminar* 29, no. 2: 138–51.

Dawidowicz, Lucy S. 1981. *The Holocaust and the Historians*. Cambridge: Harvard University Press.

Deibel, Franz. 1905. *Dorothea Schlegel als Schriftstellerin in Zusammenhang mit der romantischen Schule*. Berlin: Mayer & Müller.

Deleuze, Gilles, and Félix Guattari. 1986. *Kafka: Toward a Minor Literature*. Trans. Dana Polan. Minneapolis: University of Minnesota Press.

Desai, Anita. 1989. *Baumgartner's Bombay*. New York: Alfred A. Knopf.

Deutschkron, Inge. 1979. *Ich trug den gelben Stern*. Cologne: Verlag Wissenschaft und Politik.

Dick, Jutta. 1993a. "Pappenheim, Bertha." In *Jüdische Frauen im 19. und 20. Jahrhundert: Lexikon zu Leben und Werk*, ed. Jutta Dick and Marina Sassenberg. Reinbeck: Rowohlt.

———. 1993b. "Spiel, Hilde." In *Jüdische Frauen im 19. und 20. Jahrhundert: Lexikon zu Leben und Werk*, ed. Jutta Dick and Marina Sassenberg. Reinbeck: Rowohlt.

Dick, Jutta, and Barbara Hahn, eds. 1993. *Von einer Welt in die andere: Jüdinnen im 19. und 20. Jahrhundert*. Vienna: Brandstätter.

DiMaio, Irene Stocksieker. 1991. "Jewish Emancipation and Integration:

Fanny Lewald's Narrative Strategies." In *Literaturgeschichtliche Beispiele veränderter Wirkungshorizonte*. Amsterdam: Rodopi.

Diner, Dan. 1990. "Negative Symbiosis." In *Reworking the Past: Hitler, the Holocaust, and the Historians' Debate*, ed. Peter Baldwin. Boston: Beacon Press.

———. 1988. "Negative Symbiose: Deutsche und Juden nach Auschwitz." *Babylon: Beiträge zur jüdischen Gegenwart* 1:9–20.

———. 1986. "Fragments of an Uncompleted Journey on Jewish Socialization and Political Identity in West Germany." In *Germans and Jews since the Holocaust: The Changing Situation in West Germany*, ed. Anson Rabinbach and Jack Zipes. New York: Holmes & Meier.

Dinesen, Ruth. 1994. "Spätfolgen der Verfolgung." In *Nelly Sachs: Neue Interpretationen*, ed. Michael Kessler and Jürgen Wertheimer. Tübingen: Stauffenburg.

Dische, Irene. 1992. *The Jewess: Stories from Berlin and New York*. London: Bloomsbury.

———. 1991. *Pious Secrets*. New York: Viking.

———. 1989. *Fromme Lügen: Sieben Erzählungen aus dem Amerikanischen*, trans. Otto Bayer and Monika Elwenspoek. Frankfurt am Main: Eichborn.

Dischereit, Esther. 1992. *Merryn*. Frankfurt am Main: Suhrkamp.

———. 1988. *Joëmis Tisch*. Frankfurt am Main: Suhrkamp.

Distl, Gottfried. 1984. "Kieselsteine." *ÖH-Express* 2:43.

Döblin, Alfred. 1935. *Flucht und Sammlung des Judenvolkes*. Amsterdam: Querido.

Dohm, Christian von. 1973. *Über die bürgerliche Verbesserung der Juden*. Hildesheim: Olms.

Dohrn, Verena. 1991. *Reise nach Galizien: Grenzlandschaften des alten Europa*. Frankfurt am Main: Suhrkamp.

Domin, Hilde. 1968. *Das zweite Paradies: Roman in Segmenten*. Munich: Piper.

Edel, Peter. 1979. *Wenn es ans Leben geht*. Frankfurt am Main: Röderberg.

———. 1947. *Schwester der Nacht*. Vienna: Erwin Müller.

Edinger, Dora, ed. 1968. *Bertha Pappenheim: Freud's Anna O*. Highland Park IL: Congregation Soleil.

———, ed. 1963. *Bertha Pappenheim: Leben und Schriften*. Frankfurt am Main: Ner-Tamid.

Edvardson, Cordelia. 1991. *Jerusalems leende*. Stockholm: Bromberg.

———. 1990. *Gebranntes Kind sucht das Feuer*. Munich: Deutsche Taschenbuch Verlag.

———. 1989. *Die Welt zusammenfügen*. Munich: Hanser.

————. 1988. *Viska det till vinden.* Stockholm: Bromberg.

————. 1984. *Bränt barn söker sig till elden.* Stockholm: Bromberg.

————. 1976. *Om jag glommer dig . . . : En invandrares dagbok fran Israel.* Stockholm: Forum.

————. 1967. *Till kvinna fodd.* Stockholm: Raben & Sjogren.

————. 1958. *Sa kom jag till Kartago.* Stockholm: Tidens Forlag.

Eich, Günter. 1979. "Der Schriftsteller vor der Realität." *Über Günter Eich,* 19–20. Frankfurt am Main: Suhrkamp.

Eichmann-Leutenegger, Beatrice. 1993. *Gertrud Kolmar: Leben und Werk in Texten und Bildern.* Frankfurt am Main: Jüdischer Verlag bei Suhrkamp.

Eifler, Margret. 1989. "Postmoderne Feminisierung." In *Frauen-Fragen in der Deutschsprachigen Literatur seit 1945.* Amsterdam: Rodopi.

Engelstein, Laura. 1993. "Die Auslöschung der jüdischen Frau: Antisemitische Klischees von Mädchenhandel und Ritualmord im Rußland der Jahrhundertwende." In *Von einer Welt in die andere: Jüdinnen im 19. und 20. Jahrhundert,* ed. Jutta Dick and Barbara Hahn. Vienna: Brandstätter.

Ettinger, Elzbieta. 1986. *Rosa Luxemburg: A Life.* Boston: Beacon.

Faßbinder, Rainer Werner. 1981. *Der Müll, die Stadt und der Tod.* Frankfurt am Main: Fischer.

Feilchenfeldt, Konrad. 1983. "Rahel Varnhagens Ruhm und Nachruhm." In *Gesammelte Werke,* vol. 10, ed. Konrad Feilchenfeldt, Uwe Schweikert, and Rahel E. Steiner. Munich: Matthes & Seitz.

Feldmann, Else. 1993a. *Der Leib der Mutter.* Ed. Adolf Opel and Marino Valdéz. Vienna: Wiener Frauenverlag.

————. 1993b. *Löwenzahn: Eine Kindheit.* Vienna: Verlag für Gesellschaftskritik.

Fénelon, Fania. 1981. *Das Mädchenorchester von Auschwitz.* Munich: Deutsche Taschenbuch Verlag.

Feuchtwanger, Lion. 1965. *Jud Süß.* Hamburg: Rowohlt.

————. 1933. *Die Geschwister Oppenheim.* Amsterdam: Querido.

Fischer, Michael M. J. 1994. "Autobiographical Voices (1, 2, 3) and Mosaic Memory: Experimental Sondages in the (Post)modern World." In *Autobiography and Postmodernism,* ed. Kathleen Ashley, Leigh Gilmore, and Gerald Peters. Amherst: University of Massachussetts Press.

Flechtheim, Ossip, ed. 1975. *Rosa Luxemburg: Politische Schriften.* Frankfurt am Main: Athenäum.

————. 1985. *Rosa Luxemburg.* Hamburg: Junius.

Fleischmann, Lea. 1994. "Identity Problems of Postwar Generation Jews in Germany: A Historical Perspective." In *Insiders and Outsiders: Jewish and*

Gentile Culture in Germany and Austria, ed. Dagmar C. G. Lorenz and Gabriele Weinberger. Detroit: Wayne State University Press.

———. 1991. *Gas: Tagebuch einer Bedrohung; Israel während des Golfkrieges.* Göttingen: Steidl.

———. 1985. *Nichts ist so wie es uns scheint: Vierzig Jahre war Isaak und andere Erzählungen.* Hamburg: Rasch & Röhrig.

———. 1982. *Ich bin Israelin: Erfahrungen in einem orientalischen Land.* Hamburg: Rasch & Röhrig.

———. 1980. *Dies ist nicht mein Land: Eine Jüdin verläßt die Bundesrepublik.* Hamburg: Hoffmann & Campe.

Fleißer, Marieluise. 1972. *Fegefeuer in Ingolstadt* and *Pioniere in Ingolstadt.* In *Gesammelte Werke,* vol. 1, ed. Günther Rühle. Frankfurt am Main: Suhrkamp.

Frankenthal, Käthe. 1981. *Der dreifache Fluch: Jüdin, Intellektuelle, Sozialistin; Lebenserinnerungen.* Frankfurt am Main: Campus.

Frauengruppe Faschismusforschung. 1981. *Mutterkreuz und Arbeitsbuch: Zur Geschichte der Frauen in der Weimarer Republik und im Nationalsozialismus.* Frankfurt am Main: Fischer.

Frederiksen, Elke. 1989. "Literarische (Gegen-)Entwürfe von Frauen nach 1945: Berührungen und Veränderungen." In *Frauen-Fragen in der Deutschsprachigen Literatur seit 1945,* ed. Mona Knapp and Gerd Labroisse. Amsterdam: Rodopi.

———. 1982. "'Emanzipation der Frauen zu Arbeit und Erwerb': German Women Authors in the Nineteenth Century: Where are They?" In *Beyond the Eternal Feminine,* ed. Susan L. Cocalis and Kay Goodman. Stuttgart: Akademischer Verlag Hans-Dieter Heinz.

Freund, Elisabeth. N.d. "Zwangsarbeit für Hitler: Berlin 1941." Manuscript, Leo Baeck Institute Archives, New York.

Fried, Erich. 1975. *Fast alles Mögliche.* Berlin: Wagenbach.

Fritsch-Vivie, Garbiele. 1994. "Der biographische Aspekt in den szenischen Dichtungen der Nelly Sachs." In *Nelly Sachs: Neue Interpretationen,* ed. Michael Kessler and Jürgen Wertheimer. Tübingen: Stauffenburg.

Gauß, Karl-Markus. 1992. "Heimkehr in die Fremde." *Literatur und Kritik* 256, no. 6: 89–91.

Gelber, Mark. 1994. "Nelly Sachs und das Land Israel: Die mystisch-poetischen Funktionen der geographisch-räumlichen Assoziationen." In *Nelly Sachs: Neue Interpretationen,* ed. Michael Kessler and Jürgen Wertheimer. Tübingen: Stauffenburg.

Gerhards, Margret. 1986. "Traditionelles Frauenbild." *Unsere Zeit,* 3, no. 10: 3.

Gerhardt, Marlis, ed. 1983. *Rahel Varnhagen: Jeder Wunsch wird Frivolität genannt; Briefe und Tagebücher.* Darmstadt: Luchterhand.

Gerstl, Elfriede. 1982. *Wiener Mischung: Texte aus vielen Jahren.* Rev. ed. Linz: Edition neue texte.

Gilman, Sander L. 1995. *Jews in Today's German Culture.* Bloomington: Indiana University Press.

———. 1994. "Chicken Soup, or the Penalties for Sounding Too Jewish." In *Insiders and Outsiders: Jewish and Gentile Culture in Germany and Austria,* ed. Dagmar C. G. Lorenz and Gabriele Weinberger. Detroit: Wayne State University Press.

———. 1988. "Jüdische Literaten und deutsche Literatur: Antisemitismus und die verborgene Sprache der Juden am Beispiel von Jurek Becker und Edgar Hilsenrath." *Zeitschrift für deutsche Philologie* 107, no. 2: 269–94.

———. 1986. *Jewish Self-Hatred: Anti-Semitism and the Hidden Language of the Jews.* Baltimore: Johns Hopkins University Press.

Gilman, Sander L., and Karen Remmler, eds. 1994. *Reemerging Jewish Culture in Germany: Life and Literature since 1989.* New York: New York University Press.

Glikl von Hameln; Glückel von Hameln. *See* Hameln; Hamil.

Göbel, Helmut. 1990. "Nachwort." In Veza Canetti, *Die gelbe Straße,* ed. Elias Canetti. Munich: Hanser.

Goll, Claire. 1990. *Der gestohlene Himmel,* ed. Barbara Glauert-Hesse. Frankfurt am Main: Ullstein.

———. 1989. *Der gläserne Garten: Prosa.* Ed. Barbara Glauert-Hesse. Berlin: Argon.

———. 1988. *Ein Mensch ertrinkt.* Berlin: Argon.

———. 1987. *Der Neger Jupiter raubt Europa.* Berlin: Argon.

———. 1977. *Jedes Opfer tötet seinen Mörder.* Berlin: Edition der 2.

———. 1941–42. *Éducation barbare.* Paris: Editions de la Maison Francaise.

———. 1917. *See* Studer.

Goll, Ivan. 1917. *Requiem: Für die Gefallenen von Europa.* Zürich: Rascher.

Gordon, Leonard D. 1995. "Toward a Gender-Inclusive Account of Halakhah." In *Gender and Judaism: The Transformation of Tradition,* ed. Tamar M. Rudavsky. New York: New York University Press.

Grass, Günter. 1959. *Die Blechtrommel.* Berlin: Luchterhand.

Grossmann, Atina. 1986. "Questions of Jewish Identity." In *Germans and Jews since the Holocaust,* ed. Anson Rabinbach and Jack Zipes. New York: Holmes & Meier.

———. 1981. "Sisterhood under Siege: Feminism and Anti-Semitism in Germany, 1904–1938." In *When Biology Became Destiny: Women in Weimar and Nazi Germany,* ed. Renate Bridenthal, Atina Grossmann, and Marion Kaplan. New York: Monthly Review Press.

Grunfeld, Frederic V. 1981. *Vienna.* New York: Newsweek.

Hahn, Barbara. 1993. "Varnhagen, Rahel Friederike Antonie." In *Jüdische Frauen im 19. und 20. Jahrhundert: Lexikon zu Leben und Werk,* ed. Jutta Dick and Marina Sassenberg. Reinbeck: Rowohlt.

———, ed. 1990. *"Im Schlaf bin ich wacher": Die Träume der Rahel Levin Varnhagen.* Frankfurt am Main: Luchterhand.

Hamelin, Glueckel of. 1977. *Zikhroynes: The Memoirs of Glueckel of Hamelin.* Trans. Marvin Lowenthal. New York: Schocken.

Hameln, Glikl von. 1994. *Die Memoiren der Glückel von Hameln: Aus dem Jüdisch-Deutschen von Bertha Pappenheim,* ed. Viola Roggenkamp. Weinheim: Beltz/Athenäum.

Hameln, Glückel of. 1967. *The Adventures of Glückel of Hameln.* Ed. Bea Stadtler. New York: United Synagogue Commission on Jewish Education.

Hameln, Glückel von. 1979. *Denkwürdigkeiten der Glückel von Hameln.* Darmstadt: Verlag Darmstädter Blätter.

———. 1913. *Denkwürdigkeiten.* Trans. Alfred Feilchenfeld. Berlin: Jüdischer Verlag.

Hameln, Glueckel of. 1963. *The Life of Glueckel of Hameln, 1646–1724, Written by Herself.* Trans. Beth-Zion Abrahams. New York: Yoseloff.

Hamil, Glikl. 1967. *Memoirs and Studies on the Jewish Literature,* trans. into modern Yiddish by Yoysef Bernfeld. Buenos Aires: Ateneo Literaraio En El Instituto Cientifico Judio.

Hart, Kitty. 1982. *Return to Auschwitz: The Remarkable Story of a Girl who Survived the Holocaust.* New York: Atheneum.

———. 1979. "Kitty: Return to Auschwitz." Directed by Peter Morley. Yorkshire Television.

Hauer, Douglas. 1993. Resistance and Survival and Jewish Identity in Germany. Honors thesis, Ohio State University, Columbus OH.

Hausdorf, Anna. 1990. "Claire Goll und ihr Roman 'Der Neger Jupiter raubt Europa.'" *Neophilologus* 74, no. 2: 265–78.

Haushofer, Marlen. 1968. *Die Wand.* Hamburg: Claassen.

Häusler, Wolfgang. 1993. "Vom 'Antisemitismus des Wortes' zum 'Antisemitismus der Tat.'" In *Conditio Judaica,* vol. 3, ed. Hans Otto Horch and Horst Denkler. Tübingen: Max Niemeyer.

Hecht, Ingeborg. 1984. *Als unsichtbare Mauern wuchsen.* Hamburg: Hoffmann und Campe.

Hegel, Georg Friedrich Wilhelm. 1955. "Die Vernunft in der Geschichte."

In *Sämtliche Werke: Neue Kritische Ausgabe*, vol. 18 A, ed. Johannes Hoffmeister. Hamburg: Felix Meiner.

Heid, Ludger. 1993. "Die Frau im Kaftan: Ruth Klinger und das jüdisch-literarische Kabarett 'Kaftan.'" In *Von einer Welt in die andere: Jüdinnen im 19. und 20. Jahrhundert*, ed. Jutta Dick and Barbara Hahn. Vienna: Brandstätter.

Heine, Heinrich. 1979. "Die romantische Schule." *Sämtliche Werke*. Vol. 8, ed. Manfred Windfuhr. Hamburg: Hoffmann & Campe.

————. 1956. "Der Rabbi von Bacharach." *Werke*. Vol. 2. Cologne: Kiepenheuer & Witsch.

Heinemann, Marlene. 1986. *Gender and Destiny: Women Writers and the Holocaust*. New York: Greenwood.

Henisch, Peter. 1988. *Steins Paranoia*. Salzburg: Residenz.

Herf, Jeffrey. 1984. *Reactionary Modernism: Technology, Culture, and Politics in Weimar and the Third Reich*. Cambridge: Cambridge University Press.

Hermand, Jost. 1994. "The Wandering Jew's Rhine Journey: Heine's Lorelei." In *Insiders and Outsiders: Jewish and Gentile Culture in Germany and Austria*, ed. Dagmar C. G. Lorenz and Gabriele Weinberger. Detroit: Wayne State University Press.

————. 1986. "Artificial Activism: German Expressionism and Blacks." In *Blacks and German Culture*, ed. Reinhold Grimm and Jost Hermand. Madison: University of Wisconsin Press.

Hermlin, Stephan. 1983. "Hier liegen die Gesetzgeber." In *Äußerungen, 1944–1982*. Berlin: Aufbau.

————. 1980a. *Aufsätze; Reportagen; Reden; Interviews*, ed. Ulla Hahn. Munich: Hanser.

————. 1980b. *Lebensfrist: Gesammelte Erzählungen*. Berlin: Wagenbach.

Hermsdorf, Klaus. 1982. "Deutsch-jüdische Schriftsteller? Anmerkungen zu einer Literaturdebatte des Exils." *Zeitschrift für Germanistik* 3, no. 3: 278.

Hertz, Deborah. 1978. "Salonières and Literary Women in Late Eighteenth-Century Berlin." *New German Critique* 14:97–108.

Herz, Henriette. 1984. *Henriette Herz in Erinnerungen, Briefen und Zeugnissen*, ed. Rainer Schmitz. Frankfurt am Main: Insel.

Herzfelde, Wieland, ed. 1932. *Dreißig Erzähler des neuen Deutschland: Junge deutsche Prosa*. Berlin: Malik.

Herzig, Arno. 1993. "Zur Geschichte des politischen Antisemitismus in Deutschland, 1918–1933." In *Conditio Judaica*, vol. 3, ed. Hans Otto Horch and Horst Denkler. Tübingen: Niemeyer.

Hessing, Jakob. 1985. *Else Lasker-Schüler: Biographie einer deutsch-jüdischen Dichterin*. Karlsruhe: von Loeper.

Heuer, Renate, ed. 1988. *Bibliographica Judaica: Verzeichnis jüdischer Autoren deutscher Sprache.* Frankfurt am Main: Campus.

Heyen, Franz Joseph. 1967. *Nationalsozialismus im Alltag.* Boppard: Harald Bold.

Heym, Stefan. 1983. *Ahasver.* Frankfurt am Main: Fischer.

Hilberg, Raul, and Alfons Söllner. 1988. "Das Schweigen zum Sprechen bringen." *Zivilisationsbruch: Denken nach Auschwitz,* ed. Dan Diner. Frankfurt am Main: Fischer.

Hilsenrath, Edgar. 1977. *Der Nazi und der Friseur.* Cologne: Literarischer Verlag Braun.

Hoess, Rudolf. 1961. *Commandant of Auschwitz,* trans. Constantine Fitzgibbon. London: Pan Books.

Hoffmeister, Donna. 1987. "Access Routes into Postmodernism: Interviews with Innerhofer, Jelinek, Rosei, and Wolfgruber." *Modern Austrian Literature* 20, no. 2: 97–130.

Honigmann, Barbara. 1992. "Selbstporträt als Jüdin." In *Catalogue of the Exhibit Barbara Honigmann: Bilder, April 28–June 6, 1992.* Munich: Michael Hasenclever Galerie.

———. 1991. *Eine Liebe aus Nichts.* Berlin: Rowohlt.

———. 1986. *Roman von einem Kinde.* Darmstadt: Luchterhand.

Horch, Hans Otto, and Horst Denkler. 1993. "Vorwort." In *Conditio Judaica: Judentum, Antisemitismus und deutschsprachige Literatur vom Ersten Weltkrieg bis 1933/1938.* Tübingen: Max Niemeyer.

Hutmacher, Rahel. 1986. *Wildleute.* Darmstadt: Luchterhand.

———. 1983. *Tochter.* Darmstadt: Luchterhand.

———. 1982. *Dona.* Darmstadt: Luchterhand.

———. 1980. *Wettergarten.* Darmstadt: Luchterhand.

Huyssen, Andreas. 1995. *Twilight Memories: Marking Time in a Culture of Amnesia.* New York: Routledge.

Iggers, Wilma Abeles, ed. 1992. *The Jews of Bohemia and Moravia: A Historical Reader.* Detroit: Wayne State University Press.

Isselstein, Ursula. 1993. *Der Text aus meinem beleidigten Herzen: Studien zu Rahel Levin Varnhagen.* Turin: Tirrenia.

———. 1987. "Karl August Varnhagens editorische Tätigkeit nach Dokumenten seines Archivs." In *Rahel Levin Varnhagen: Die Wiederentdeckung einer Schriftstellerin,* ed. Barbara Hahn and Ursula Isselstein. Göttingen: Vandenhoeck & Ruprecht.

———. 1983. "Rahel Levins Einbrüche in die eingerichtete Welt." In *Von einer Welt in die andere: Jüdinnen im 19. und 20. Jahrhundert,* ed. Jutta Dick and Barbara Hahn. Vienna: Brandstätter.

Jäschke, Bärbel. 1977. "Nachwort." In Claire Goll, *Jedes Opfer tötet seinen Mörder.* Berlin: Edition der 2.

Jelinek, Elfriede. 1985. *Die Ausgesperrten.* Reinbeck: Rowohlt.

————. 1983. *Die Klavierspielerin.* Reinbeck: Rowohlt.

————. 1975. *Die Liebhaberinnen.* Reinbeck: Rowohlt.

Jensen, Ellen M. 1984. *Streifzüge durch das Leben von Anna O./Bertha Pappenheim: Ein Fall für die Psychiatrie—ein Leben für die Philanthropie.* Frankfurt am Main: Deutsche Taschenbuch Verlag.

Jones, Calvin N. 1994. *The Literary Reputation of Else Lasker-Schüler.* Columbia SC: Camden House.

Kahn, Lisa. 1994. "Österreichische Emigrantinnen schreiben in den USA." In *Bridging the Abyss: Reflections on Jewish Suffering, Anti-Semitism, and Exile,* ed. Amy Colin and Elisabeth Strenger. Munich: Wilhelm Fink Verlag.

Kaplan, Marion. 1994a. "Schwesterlichkeit auf dem Prüfstand: Feminismus und Antisemitismus in Deutschland, 1904–1938." In *Bridging the Abyss: Reflections on Jewish Suffering, Anti-Semitism, and Exile.* Munich: Wilhelm Fink Verlag.

————. 1994b. "What Is 'Religion' among Jews in Contemporary Germany?" In *Reemerging Jewish Culture in Germany: Life and Literature since 1989,* ed. Sander L. Gilman and Karen Remmler. New York: New York University Press.

————. 1991. *The Making of the Jewish Middle Class: Women, Family and Identity in Imperial Germany.* Oxford: Oxford University Press.

————. 1984. "To Tolerate Is to Insult." *New German Critique* 31:195–200.

————. 1981. "Family Structure and the Position of Jewish Women: A Comment." In *Revolution and Evolution: 1848 in German-Jewish History,* ed. Werner E. Mosse, Arnold Paucker, and Reinhard Rürup. Tübingen: Mohr.

————. 1979. *The Jewish Feminist Movement in Germany.* Westport CT: Greenwood Press.

————. 1978. "Women's Strategies in the Jewish Community in Germany." *New German Critique* 14:109–18.

Kappeler, Sima. 1994. "Historical Visions: Anna Seghers on the Revolution in Haiti." In *Insiders and Outsiders: Jewish and Gentile Culture in Germany and Austria,* ed. Dagmar C. G. Lorenz and Gabriele Weinberger. Detroit: Wayne State University Press.

Kaszinski, Stefan. 1987. *Galizien: Eine literarische Heimat.* Poznan: Wyd. Nauk. Universy Letu.

Katz, Jacob. 1980a. *From Prejudice to Destruction: Anti-Semitism, 1700–1933.* Cambridge: Harvard University Press.

———. 1980b. *Out of the Ghetto: Social Background of Jewish Emancipation, 1770–1870.* Cambridge: Harvard University Press.

Kecht, Marie-Regina. 1992a. "Auflehnung gegen die Ordnung von Sprache und Vernunft: Die weibliche Wirklichkeitsgestaltung bei Waltraug Anna Mitgutsch." In *Women in German Yearbook* 8. Lincoln: University of Nebraska Press.

———. 1992b. "Gespräch mit Waltraud Anna Mitgutsch." In *Women in German Yearbook* 8. Lincoln: University of Nebraska Press.

Kellenbach, Katharina von. 1993. "Jonas, Regina." In *Jüdische Frauen im 19. und 20. Jahrhundert: Lexikon zu Leben und Werk,* ed. Jutta Dick and Marina Sassenberg. Reinbeck: Rowohlt.

Kerschbaumer, Marie-Thérèse. 1980. *Der weibliche Name des Widerstands: Sieben Berichte.* Olten: Walter.

Keun, Irmgard. 1990. *Ferdinand, der Mann mit dem freundlichen Herzen.* Munich: Deutsche Taschenbuch Verlag.

———. 1989. *Das kunstseidene Mädchen.* Munich: Deutsche Taschenbuch Verlag.

Khittl, Klaus. 1982. "Warum ich Wien verlasse." *Wochenpresse* 51:39–40.

Kienast, Anni, et al. 1981. *Der alltägliche Faschismus.* Berlin: Dietz.

Klüger, Ruth. 1994. "Gibt es ein 'Judenproblem' in der deutschen Nachkriegsliteratur?" In *Katastrophen.* Göttingen: Wallstein.

———. 1992. *weiter leben.* Göttingen: Wallstein.

Knecht, Edgar. 1977. *Le mythe du juif errant: Essai de mythologie litteraire et de sociologie religieuse.* Grenoble: Presses Universitaires de Grenoble.

Koelbl, Herlinde. 1989. "Cordelia Edvardson." *Jüdische Porträts.* Frankfurt am Main: Fischer.

Kolmar, Gertrud. 1994. *Susanna.* Ed. Thomas Sparr. Frankfurt am Main: Jüdischer Verlag.

———. 1970. *Briefe an die Schwester Hilde (1938–1943).* Ed. Johanna Zeitler. Munich: Kösel.

———. 1965. *Eine jüdische Mutter.* Munich: Kösel.

———. 1960. *Das lyrische Werk.* Munich: Kösel.

———. 1959. "Susanna." *Das leere Haus: Prosa jüdischer Dichter.* Ed. Karl Otten. Stuttgart: Cotta.

———. 1938. *See* Chodziesner.

Koonz, Claudia. 1987. *Mothers in the Fatherland.* New York: St. Martin's Press.

Koplowitz, Jan. 1979. *"Bohemia"—Mein Schicksal.* Halle: Mitteldeutscher Verlag.

Kratz-Ritter, Bettina. 1993. "Karminski, Hannah." In *Jüdische Frauen im 19. und 20. Jahrhundert: Lexikon zu Leben und Werk,* ed. Jutta Dick and Marina Sassenberg. Reinbeck: Rowohlt.

Kristeva, Julia. 1990. *Fremde sind wir uns selbst.* Trans. Xenia Rajewsky. Frankfurt am Main: Suhrkamp.

Krobb, Florian. 1993. *Die schöne Jüdin: Jüdische Frauengestalten in der deutschsprachigen Erzählliterature vom 17. Jahrhundert bis zum Ersten Weltkrieg.* Tübingen: Max Niemeyer Verlag.

Krumbholz, Martin. 1994. "Holle, Jahrmarkt, Garten Eden: Zum dramatischen Werk der Else Lasker-Schüler." *Zeitschrift für Literatur* 122:42–54.

Kubes-Hofmann, Ursula. 1991. "Die Macht der Poesie." *Stimme der Frau* 2:17.

Kurz, Horst. 1992. "Die Transzendierung des Menschen im 'bio-adapter': Oswald Wieners "Die Verbesserung von Mitteleuropa, Roman." Ph.D. diss., Ohio State University.

Lander, Jeanette. 1993. *Jahrhundert der Herren.* Berlin: Aufbau Verlag.

———. 1980. *Ich, allein.* Munich: Autoren Edition.

———. 1976. *Die Töchter.* Frankfurt am Main: Insel.

———. 1972. *Auf dem Boden der Fremde.* Frankfurt am Main: Insel.

———. 1971a. *Ein Sommer in der Woche der Itke K.* Frankfurt am Main: Suhrkamp.

———. 1971b. *Ezra Pound.* New York: Frederick Ungar.

———. 1967. *William Butler Yeats: Die Bildersprache seiner Lyrik.* Stuttgart: Kohlhammer.

Lang, Berel, ed. 1988. *Writing and the Holocaust.* New York: Holmes & Meier.

Langer, Lawrence. 1988. "Interpreting Survivor Testimony." In *Writing and the Holocaust,* ed. Berel Lang. New York: Holmes & Meier.

———. 1975. *The Holocaust and Literary Imagination.* New Haven: Yale University Press.

Langgässer, Elisabeth. 1950. *Märkische Argonautenfahrt.* Hamburg: Claassen.

———. 1946. *Das unauslöschliche Siegel.* Hamburg: Claassen.

Lappin, Elena, ed. 1994. *Jewish Voices, German Words: Growing Up Jewish in Postwar Germany and Austria.* North Haven CT: Catbird Press.

Laschke, Jutta. 1988. *Wir sind eigentlich, wie wir sein möchten, und nicht so wie wir sind: Zum dialogischen Charakter von Frauenbriefen Anfang des 19. Jahrhunderts gezeigt an den Briefen von Rahel Varnhagen und Fanny Mendelsohn.* Frankfurt am Main: Peter Lang.

Lasker-Schüler, Else. 1986. "Was soll ich hier?" In *Exilbriefe an Salman Schocken,* ed. Sigrid Bauschinger and Helmut Hermann. Heidelberg: Lambert Schneider.

————. 1980. *Ich und ich: Eine theatralische Komödie.* Munich: Kösel.

————. 1969a. *Lieber gestreifter Tiger.* Vol. 1 of *Briefe von Else Lasker-Schüler.* Ed. Margarete Kupper. Munich: Kösel.

————. 1969b. *Wo ist unser buntes Theben?* Vol. 2 of *Briefe von Else Lasker-Schüler.* Ed. Margarete Kupper. Munich: Kösel.

————. 1962. *Prosa und Schauspiele.* Vol. 2 of *Gesammelte Werke.* Ed. Friedhelm Kemp. Munich: Kösel.

————. 1961. *Gesammelte Werke.* Vol. 3. Ed. Werner Kraft. Munich: Kösel.

————. 1959. *Gedichte, 1902–1943.* Vol. 1 of *Gesammelte Werke.* Ed. Friedhelm Kemp. Munich: Kösel.

Lauckner, Nancy. 1974. "The Surrogate Jew in the Postwar German Novel." *Monatshefte* 66 no. 2: 132–43.

Lawson, Richard H. 1991. *Understanding Elias Canetti.* Columbia: University of South Carolina Press.

Lefkowitz, Deborah, director. 1989. *Intervals of Silence: Being Jewish in Germany.* Cambridge MA: Lefkowitz Films.

Lessing, Gotthold Ephraim. 1967. *Die Juden.* In *Werke,* ed. Kurt Wölfel. Frankfurt am Main: Insel.

Lessing, Theodor. 1930. *Der jüdische Selbsthaß.* Berlin: Jüdischer Verlag.

Lévy-Hass, Hanna. 1979. *Vielleicht war das alles erst der Anfang.* Berlin: Rotbuch.

Lewald, Fanny. [1866] 1988. *Meine Lebensgeschichte.* 2 vols. Frankfurt am Main: Helmer.

————. 1850. *Erinnerungen aus dem Jahre 1848.* Braunschweig: Vieweg & Sohn.

Lewis, Hanna B. 1994. "Fanny Lewald and Judaism: The Writer, the Woman, the Prussian, the Jew." In *The Germanic Mosaic: Cultural and Linguistic Diversity in Society,* ed. Carol A. Blackshire-Belay. Westport CT: Greenwood.

————, ed. 1992. *The Education of Fanny Lewald: An Autobiography.* Albany: State University of New York Press.

————. 1990. "Fanny Lewald and the Revolution of 1848." In *Festschrift für Herbert Lehnert zum 65. Geburtstag.* Tübingen: Niemeyer.

Lind, Jakov. 1964. *Eine Seele aus Holz.* Munich: Knaur.

Liptzin, Solomon. 1944. *Germany's Stepchildren.* Philadelphia: Jewish Publication Society of America.

Löffler, Sigrid. 1985. "Körperfeindschaft." *Profil* 65, no. 20: 63.

Lorenz, Dagmar C. G. Forthcoming. Interview with Nadja Seelich. In *From the Shadows: Austrian Women Filmmakers,* ed. Margarete Lamb-Feffelberg. Riverside CA: Ariadne Press.

—. 1995. "Der Tod des soldatischen Mannes bei Theodor Fontane und Joseph Roth." In *Nicht allein mit den Worten,* ed. Thomas Müller, Johannes G. Pankau, and Gert Ueding. Stuttgart: Friedrich Frommann.

—. 1994a. "Memory and Criticism: Ruth Klüger's *weiter leben.*" In *Yearbook of Women in German* 9. Lincoln: University of Nebraska Press.

—. 1994b. "Social Darwinism in Edgar Hilsenrath's Ghetto Novel *Nacht.*" In *Insiders and Outsiders: Jewish and Gentile Culture in Germany and Austria,* ed. Dagmar C. G. Lorenz and Gabriele Weinberger. Detroit: Wayne State University Press.

—. 1994c. "Szabo's Colonel Redl and Mephisto." In *Insiders and Outsiders: Jewish and Gentile Culture in Germany and Austria,* ed. Dagmar C. G. Lorenz and Gabriele Weinberger. Detroit: Wayne State University Press.

—. 1992a. "Hilde Spiel: Lisas Zimmer: Frau, Jüdin, Verfolgte." *Modern Austrian Literature* 25, no. 2: 79–96.

—. 1992b. *Verfolgung bis zum Massenmord.* Frankfurt am Main: Peter Lang.

—. 1990. "Hilsenrath's Other Genocide." In *Simon Wiesenthal Center Annual* 7. New York: Allied Books.

—. 1989. "Inside Auschwitz: Four Memoirs." In *Simon Wiesenthal Center Annual* 6. New York: Allied Books.

—. 1981. *Ilse Aichinger.* Königstein: Athenäum.

Lorenz, Konrad. 1963. *Das sogenannte Böse: Zur Naturgeschichte der Aggression.* Vienna: Borotha-Schöler.

Luther, Martin. [1523] 1990. "Daß Jesus ein ge borener Jude sei." In *D. Martin Luthers Werke: Kritische Gesamtausgabe,* vol. 2, 307–35. Weimar: Hermann Böhlaus Nachfolger.

—. [1542–43] 1890. "Von den Juden und ihren Lügen." In *Reformationsschriften,* ed. Johann Georg Walch. Vol. 20 of *Luthers Sämmtliche Schriften.* St. Louis MO: Lutherischer Concordia-Verlag.

—. 1883. *Weimarer Ausgabe.* Vol. 2. Weimar: Hermann Böhlau.

Luxemburg, Rosa. 1984. *Briefe aus dem Gefängnis.* Berlin: Dietz.

—. 1982. *Gesammelte Briefe.* Berlin: Dietz.

—. 1980. *Ein Leben für die Freiheit: Reden, Schriften, Briefe, Ein Lesebuch.* Ed. Frederik Hetmann. Frankfurt am Main: Fischer.

—. 1979. *Comrade and Lover: Rosa Luxemburg's Letters to Leo Jogiches.* Cambridge MA: MIT Press.

—. 1972. *Gesammelte Werke.* 2 vols. Berlin: Dietz.

———. 1971. *Briefe an Leo Jogiches*. Frankfurt am Main: Europäische Verlags-anstalt.

———. 1950. *Briefe an Freunde nach dem von Luise Kautsky fertiggestellten Manuskript*. Ed. Benedikt Kautsky. Hamburg: Europäische Verlagsanstalt.

———. 1898. *Die industrielle Entwickelung Polens*. Leipzig: Duncker & Humbolt.

Maccoby, Hyam. 1986. "The Wandering Jew as Sacred Executioner." In *The Wandering Jew: Essays in the Interpretation of a Christian Legend,* ed. Galit Hasan-Rokem and Alan Dandes. Bloomington: Indiana University Press.

Magris, Claudio. 1985. "Ein Schriftsteller, der aus vielen Personen besteht." In *Hüter der Verwandlung*. Munich: Hanser.

———. 1966. *Der habsburgische Mythos in der österreichischen Literatur*. Salzburg: Otto Müller.

Marcuse, Herbert. 1965. *A Critique of Pure Tolerance*. Boston: Beacon.

Mayer, Hans. 1994. *Der Widerruf: Über Deutsche und Juden*. Frankfurt am Main: Suhrkamp.

———. 1991. *Erinnerung an eine Deutsche Demokratische Republik: Der Turm von Babel*. Frankfurt am Main: Suhrkamp.

———. 1975. *Außenseiter*. Frankfurt am Main: Suhrkamp.

McNay, Lois. 1993. *Foucault and Feminism: Power, Gender and the Self*. Boston: Northeastern University Press.

McVeigh, Joseph. 1988. "Zur sogenannten 'Kulturkrise der 50er Jahre.'" In *Kontinuität und Vergangenheitsbewältigung in der österreichischen Literatur nach 1945*. Vienna: Braumüller.

Mecklenburg, Norbert. 1993. "'Bei den Juden ist es nun einmal so': Interkulturelle Erzählkunst in 'Leib Weihnachtskuchen und sein Kind' von Karl Emil Franzos." *Sprachkunst* 24, no. 2: 203–32.

Mecklenburg, Werner. 1977. "Faschismus und Alltag in deutscher Gegenwartsprosa: Kempowski und andere." In *Gegenwartsliteratur und drittes Reich: Deutsche Autoren in der Auseinandersetzung mit der Vergangenheit*. Stuttgart: Reclam.

Menasse, Robert. 1993. *Das Land ohne Eigenschaften: Essay zur österreichischen Identität*. Vienna: Sonderzahl.

Miller, Alice. 1980. *Am Anfang war die Erziehung*. Frankfurt am Main: Suhrkamp.

Mitgutsch, Anna. 1995. *Abschied von Jerusalem*. Berlin: Rowohlt.

———. 1994. *In fremden Städten*. Munich: Deutsche Taschenbuch Verlag.

———. 1989. *Ausgrenzung*. Darmstadt: Luchterhand.

———. 1986. *Das andere Leben*. Düsseldorf: Claassen.

———. 1985. *Die Züchtigung*. Düsseldorf: Claassen.

Mitscherlich, Alexander. 1965. "Einfühlung in den Angeklagten." *Der Spiegel* 19, no. 5: 78–80.

Moosdorf, Johanna. 1979. *Sieben Jahr, Sieben Tag.* Munich: Limes.

Morais, Vamberto. 1976. *A Short History of Anti-Semitism.* New York: Norton.

Mosse, George L. 1979. *Der nationalsozialistische Alltag: So lebte man unter Hitler.* Königstein: Athenäum.

Nettl, Peter. 1989. *Rosa Luxemburg: A Life.* New York: Schocken.

Neumann, Robert. 1965. *Der Tatbestand oder der gute Glaube der Deutschen.* Munich: Piper.

Neumann, Ronnith. 1991. *Nirs Stadt.* Frankfurt am Main: Fischer.

———. 1985. *Heimkehr in die Fremde.* Göttingen: Bert Schlender.

Nordmann, Ingeborg. 1994. "Wie man sich in der Sprache fremd bewegt." In *Jüdische Kultur und Weiblichkeit in der Moderne,* ed. Inge Stephan, Sabine Schilling, and Sigrid Weigel. Cologne: Böhlau.

Owings, Alison. 1993. *Frauen: German Women Recall the Third Reich.* New Brunswick NJ: Rutgers University Press.

Oxaal, Ivar. 1987. "The Jews of Young Hitler's Vienna." In *Jews, Antisemitism and Culture in Vienna,* ed. Ivar Oxaal, Michael Pollak, and Gerhard Botz. London: Routledge & Kegan Paul.

Paepcke, Lotte. 1979. *Ich wurde vergessen: Berichte einer Jüdin, die das Dritte Reich überlebte.* Freiburg: Herder.

———. 1972. *Ein kleiner Händler der mein Vater war.* Heilbronn: Eugen Salzer.

———. 1952. *Unter einem fremden Stern.* Frankfurt am Main: Verlag der Frankfurter Hefte.

Pappenheim, Bertha. 1954. *Gebete.* Düsseldorf: Verlag Allgemeine Wochenzeitung der Juden in Deutschland.

———. 1930. *Zeenah u-Reenah: Frauenbibel.* Frankfurt am Main: J. Kauffmann.

———. 1929a. *Ma'seh Buch: Allerlei Geschichten.* Frankfurt am Main: J. Kauffmann.

1929b. *Sisyphus-Arbeit.* Vol. 2, *Folge.* Berlin: Berthold Levy.

———. 1924. *Sisyphus-Arbeit: Reisebriefe aus den Jahren 1911 und 1912.* Leipzig: Paul E. Lindner.

———. 1916. *Kämpfe: Sechs Erzählungen.* Frankfurt am Main: Kauffmann.

———. 1913. *Tragische Momente: Drei Lebensbilder.* Frankfurt am Main: Kauffmann.

———. 1907. *Zur Sittlichkeitsfrage.* Hamburg: Verlag des jüdischen Frauenbundes.

———. 1904. *Zur Lage der jüdischen Bevölkerung in Galizien: Reise-Eindrücke und Vorschläge zur Besserung der Verhältnisse.* Frankfurt am Main: Neuer Frankfurter Verlag.

Pass-Freidenreich, Harriet. 1991. *Jewish Politics in Vienna, 1918–1938.* Bloomington: Indiana University Press.

Patsch, Hermann. 1991. "'Als ob Spinoza sich wollte taufen lassen': Biographisches und Rechtsgeschichtliches zur Taufe und Trauung Rahel Levins." *Jahrbuch des Freien Deutschen Hochstifts,* 149–79. Tübingen: Max Niemeyer.

Paucker, Pauline. 1993. "Bildnisse jüdischer Frauen, 1789–1991: Klischee und Wandel." In *Von einer Welt in die andere: Jüdinnen im 19. und 20. Jahrhundert,* ed. Jutta Dick and Barbara Hahn. Vienna: Brandstätter.

Pazi, Margarita. 1994a. "Authors of German Language in Israel." In *Insiders and Outsiders: Jewish and Gentile Culture in Germany and Austria,* ed. Dagmar C. G. Lorenz and Gabriele Weinberger. Detroit: Wayne State University Press.

———. 1994b. "Jüdische Aspekte und Elemente im Werk von Nelly Sachs und ihre Wirkungen." In *Nelly Sachs: Neue Interpretationen,* ed. Michael Kessler and Jürgen Wertheimer. Tübingen: Stauffenburg.

———. 1994c. "'Verkünderin west-östlicher Prägung': Else Lasker-Schüler in Jerusalem." *Zeitschrift für Literatur* 122:65–74.

———. 1989. "Einleitung." In *Auf dem Weg: Eine Anthologie deutschsprachiger Literatur in Israel,* ed. Meir M. Faerber. Gerlingen: Bleicher.

———. 1983. "Fanny Lewald—das Echo der Revolution 1848 in ihren Schriften." In *Juden im Vormärz der Revolution von 1848.* Stuttgart: Burg.

Pichler, Walther. 1974. *Von der Synagoge zur Kirche: Zur Entstehungsgeschichte der Pfarre St. Leopold, Wien II.* Vienna: Wiener Dom-Verlag.

Pollak, Ilse. 1993. "Über Else Feldmann (1884–1942)." *Literatur und Kritik* 28, no. 11:101–7.

Pollak, Martin. 1984. *Nach Galizien: Von Chassiden, Huzulen, Polen und Ruthenen: Eine imaginäre Reise durch die verschwundene Welt Ostgaliziens und der Bukowina.* Vienna: Brandstätter.

Posner, Gerald L. 1991. *Hitler's Children: Sons and Daughters of Leaders of the Third Reich Talk about Themselves and Their Fathers.* New York: Random House.

Rabinovici, Doron. 1994. *Papirnik: Stories.* Frankfurt am Main: Suhrkamp.

Reich, Wilhelm. 1974. *Massenpsychologie des Faschismus.* Frankfurt am Main: Fischer.

Reinunghaus, Alexandra. 1988. "Die Lust der Frauen und die kurze Gewalt der Männer: Gespräch mit Elfriede Jelinek." *Der Standard* (17 November): 9.

Reischer, Alfred A. R. 1990. "Ruth Beckermann und der Jom Jeruschalaim." *Heruth* 34 (June): 6.

Reiter, Andrea. 1995. *"Auf daß sie entsteigen der Dunkelheit": Die literarische Bewältigung der KZ-Erfahrung.* Vienna: Löcker.

Reiter, Gerhard. 1991. "Das Eine und das Einzelne: Zur philosophischen Struktur der Lyrik Rose Ausländers." In *Rose Ausländer: Materialien zu Leben und Werk,* ed. Helmut Braun. Frankfurt am Main: Fischer.

Remmler, Karen. 1994. "En-gendering Bodies of Memory: Tracing the Genealogy of Identity in the Work of Esther Dischereit, Barbara Honigmann, and Irene Dische." In *Reemerging Jewish Culture in Germany: Life and Literature since 1989,* ed. Sander L. Gilman and Karen Remmler. New York: New York University Press.

Richarz, Monika. 1988. "Juden in der Bundesrepublik Deutschland und in der Deutschen Demokratischen Republik." In *Jüdisches Leben in der Bundesrepublik,* ed. Micha Brumlik. Frankfurt am Main: Athenäum.

———. 1986. *Jüdisches Leben in Deutschland seit 1945.* Königstein: Jüdischer Verlag bei Athenäum.

Ringelheim, Joan. 1985. "Women and the Holocaust: A Reconsideration of Research." *Signs* 10, no. 4: 741–61.

Rinser, Luise. 1974. *Der schwarze Esel.* Frankfurt am Main: Fischer.

Roggenkamp, Viola. 1994. "Vorwort." In *Die Memoiren der Glückel von Hameln: Aus dem Jüdisch-Deutschen von Bertha Pappenheim.* Weinheim: Beltz/Athenäum Verlag.

Rogoff, Irit. 1994. "Bräute der Sonne: Geschlechteridentitäten und Impulse aus der Diaspora." In *Jüdische Kultur und Weiblichkeit in der Moderne,* ed. Inge Stephan, Sabine Schilling, and Sigrid Weigel. Cologne: Böhlau.

Rogols-Siegel, Linda. 1993. "Fanny Lewald's Prinz Louis Ferdinand and Theodor Fontane's *Vor dem Sturm.*" *Modern Language Review* 88:363–74.

———. 1988. "The Life and Works of Fanny Lewald: An Introduction." In Fanny Lewald, *Prinz Louis Ferdinand,* trans. Linda Rogols-Siegel. Queenston, Ontario: Edwin Mellen.

Rosenbaum, Max, and Melvin Muroff, eds. 1984. *Anna O.: Fourteen Contemporary Reinterpretations.* London: Free Press.

Roth, Joseph. 1938. *Die Kapuzinergruft.* Bilthoven: De Gemeeinschap.

———. 1927. *Juden auf Wanderschaft.* Berlin: Schmiede.

Rudavsky, Tamar, ed. 1995. *Gender and Judaism: The Transformation of Tradition.* New York: New York University Press.

Rushdie, Salman. 1991. *Imaginary Homelands: Essays and Criticism, 1981–1991.* New York: Penguin.

Sachs, Nelly. 1984. *Die Briefe der Nelly Sachs*. Ed. Ruth Dinesen and Helmut Müssener. Frankfurt am Main: Suhrkamp.

———. 1962. "*Eli:* Ein Mysterienspiel vom Leiden Israels." In *Zeichen im Sand: Die szenischen Dichtungen der Nelly Sachs.* Frankfurt am Main: Suhrkamp.

———. 1961. *Fahrt ins Staublose: Die Gedichte der Nelly Sachs.* Ed. Margaretha Holmquist and Bengt Holmquist. Frankfurt am Main: Suhrkamp.

Santner, Eric L. 1990. *Stranded Objects: Mourning, Memory, and Film in Postwar Germany.* Ithaca: Cornell University Press.

Schindel, Robert. 1992. *Gebürtig.* Frankfurt am Main: Suhrkamp.

Schindler, Roslyn Abt. 1994. "Bezwingt des Herzens Bitterkeit: Hilde Burger's Return from 'Paradise.'" In *Insiders and Outsiders: Jewish and Gentile Culture in Germany and Austria,* ed. Dagmar C. G. Lorenz and Gabriele Weinberger. Detroit: Wayne State University Press.

Schlegel, Dorothea M. 1990. *Camilla.* Trans. Ruth Richardson; ed. Hans Eichner. San Francisco: Edwin Mellen Press.

———. 1989. *Florentin: A Novel.* Trans. Edwina Lawler and Ruth Richardson. San Francisco: Edwin Mellen Press.

———. 1986. *Florentin: Roman, Fragmente, Varianten.* Ed. Liliane Weissberg. Frankfurt am Main: Ullstein.

Schlenstedt, Silvia. 1989. "Suche nach Halt in haltloser Lage. . . ." *Sinn und Form* 41 no. 4: 727–38.

Schmitz, Walter. 1991. "'. . . nur eine Skizze, aber durchaus in einem grossen Stil': Dorothea Schlegel." In *Autoren damals und heute: Literaturgeschichtliche Beispiele veränderter Wirkungshorizonte,* ed. Gerhard P. Knapp. Amsterdam: Rodopi.

Schnabel, Ernst. 1958. *Anne Frank: Spur eines Kindes.* Frankfurt am Main: Fischer.

Schnitzler, Arthur. 1968. *Jugend in Wien.* Frankfurt am Main: Fischer.

Schoeps, Julius H. 1994. "Vom Antijudaismus zum Antisemitismus: Zur Struktur, Funktion und Wirkung eines Vorurteils." In *Bridging the Abyss: Reflections on Jewish Suffering, Anti-Semitism, and Exile,* ed. Amy Colin and Elisabeth Strenger. Munich: Wilhelm Fink Verlag.

Schuller, Marianne. 1993. "Literatur im Übergang: Zur Prosa Else Lasker-Schülers." In *Von einer Welt in die andere: Jüdinnen im 19. und 20. Jahrhundert,* ed. Jutta Dick and Barbara Hahn. Vienna: Brandstätter.

Schultz, Joachim. 1990. "Das Afrika- und 'Neger' -Bild in den Werken von Claire und Ivan Goll." In *Proceedings of the 12th Congress of the International Comparative Literature Association.* Munich: Iudicium.

Schwaiger, Brigitte, and Eva Deutsch. 1982. *Die Galizianerin.* Vienna: Paul Zsolnay.

Schwarz, Alice. 1963. *Versuchung in Nazareth.* Vienna: Hans Deutsch Verlag.

———. 1962. *Die Abrechnung.* Graz: Styria.

Schwarz, Egon. 1994. "Jews in Fin-de-Siècle Vienna." In *Insiders and Outsiders: Jewish and Gentile Culture in Germany and Austria,* ed. Dagmar C. G. Lorenz and Gabriele Weinberger. Detroit: Wayne State University Press.

Schwarz-Gardos, Alice. 1991. *Von Wien nach Tel Aviv: Lebensweg einer Journalistin.* Gerlingen: Bleicher.

———, ed. 1984. *Hügel des Frühlings: Deutschsprachige Autoren Israels erzählen.* Freiburg: Herder.

———. 1983. "Die Einsamkeit der deutschsprachigen Schriftsteller in Israel." In *Heimat ist anderswo,* ed. Alice Schwarz-Gardos. Freiburg: Herder.

———. 1982. *Paradies mit Schönheitsfehlern: So lebt man in Israel.* Freiburg: Herder.

———. 1979. *Frauen in Israel: Die Emanzipation hat viele Gesichter: Ein Bericht in Lebensläufen.* Freiburg: Herder.

Schweighofer, Fritz. 1987. *Das Privattheater der Anna O.: Ein psychologisches Lehrstück; Ein Emanzipationsdrama.* Munich: Ernst Reinhardt.

Schweikert, Uwe. 1983. "'Am jüngsten Tag' habe ich Recht,' Rahel Varnhagen als Briefschreiberin." In Rahel Varnhagen, *Gesammelte Werke,* vol. 10, ed. Konrad Feilchenfeldt, Uwe Schweikert, and Rahel E. Steiner. Munich: Matthes & Seitz.

Seehaus, Gertrud. 1985. *Katzengesang und Eselsschrei.* Zurich: Nagel & Kimche.

Seelich, Nadja. 1992. *Sie saß im Glashaus und warf mit Steinen.* Produced by Nadja Seelich and Bernd Neuburger. Vienna: Extrafilm.

———. 1981. *Kieselsteine.* Directed by Lukas Stepanik. Vienna: Cinéart. Distributed by Hans Peter Hofmann.

———. N.d. Film, Staat und Gesellschaft in Ost- und Westeuropa und ich. Manuscript, Vienna.

Seghers, Anna. 1976. *Die Hochzeit von Haiti.* Frankfurt am Main: Luchterhand.

———. 1979. *Der Ausflug der toten Mädchen: Erzählungen.* Neuwied: Luchterhand.

———. 1962. *Karibische Geschichten.* Berlin: Aufbau.

Seibert, Peter. 1989. "Henriette Herz: Erinnerungen: Zur Rekonstruktion einer frühen Frauenbiographie." *Der Deutschunterricht* no. 41, 2: 37–50.

Seligmann, Rafael. 1994. "What Keeps the Jews in Germany Quiet?" In *Reemerging Jewish Culture in Germany: Life and Literature since 1989,* ed.

Sander L. Gilman and Karen Remmler. New York: New York University Press.

Shafi, Monika. 1995. *Gertrud Kolmar: Eine Einführung in das Werk.* Munich: Judicium Verlag.

———. 1991. "Gertrud Kolmar: 'Niemals die Eine immer die Andere': Zur Künstlerproblematik in Gertrud Kolmars Prosa." In *Autoren damals und heute: Literaturgeschichtliche Beispiele veränderter Wirkungshorizonte,* ed. Gerhard P. Knapp. Amsterdam: Rodopi.

Shahar, Shulamith. 1983. *Die Frau im Mittelalter.* Frankfurt am Main: Fischer.

Sichrovski, Peter. 1985. *Wir wissen nicht was morgen wird, wir wissen wohl was gestern war: Junge Juden in Deutschland und Österreich.* Cologne: Kiepenheuer & Witsch.

Sichrovsky, Heinz. 1979. "Die Ausgesperrten." *Arbeiter Zeitung* (Vienna), 17 November: 8–9.

Sorkin, David. 1987. *The Transformation of German Jewry, 1780–1840.* New York: Oxford University Press.

Spiegelmann, Art. 1986. *Maus: A Survivor's Tale.* New York: Pantheon.

Spiel, Hilde. 1992. *Welche Welt ist meine Welt? Erinnerungen, 1946–1989.* Reinbeck: Rowohlt.

———. 1989. *Die hellen und die finsteren Zeiten: Erinnerungen, 1911–1914.* Reinbeck: Rowohlt.

———. 1987. *Glanz und Untergang: Wien, 1866–1938.* Munich: List.

———. 1986. *Rückkehr nach Wien: Tagebuch, 1946.* Munich: Nymphenburger Verlagsanstalt.

———. 1984. *Lisas Zimmer.* Munich: Deutsche Taschenbuch Verlag.

———. 1982. "Warum ich Wien verlasse." *Wochenpresse* 51:39–41.

———. 1981. "Ich lebe gern in Österreich." In *In meinem Garten schlendernd.* Munich: Nymphenburger Verlagsanstalt.

———. 1965. *Verliebt in Döbling.* Vienna: Verlag für Jugend und Volk.

———. 1962. *Fanny von Arnstein oder die Emanzipation: Ein Frauenleben an der Zeitwende, 1758–1818.* Frankfurt am Main: Fischer.

———. 1961. *The Darkened Room.* London: Methuen.

Spies, Gerty. 1984. *Drei Jahre Theresienstadt.* Munich: Kaiser.

———. 1948. *Theresienstadt: Gedichte.* Munich: Freitag.

———. N.d. "Ein Stück Weges (ein Gedanke und Jahre schmerzvoller Reifung)." Manuscript. Leo Baeck Institute Archives, New York.

Starke, Käthe. 1975. *Der Führer schenkt den Juden eine Stadt.* Berlin: Haude und Spener.

Stephan, Alexander. 1995. *Im Visier des FBI: Deutsche Exilschriftsteller in den Akten amerikanischer Geheimdienste.* Stuttgart: J. B. Metzler.

Stephan, Inge. 1994. "Judentum—Weiblichkeit—Psychoanalyse." In *Jüdische Kultur und Weiblichkeit in der Moderne,* ed. Inge Stephan, Sabine Schilling, and Sigrid Weigel. Cologne: Böhlau.

Stern, Carl. 1989. "Erinnerungen an Else Lasker-Schüler." In *Auf dem Weg: Eine Anthologie deutschsprachiger Literatur in Israel,* ed. Meir M. Faerber. Gerlingen: Bleicher.

Stern, Frank. 1994. "Discourse of Antagonistic Memories." In *Bridging the Abyss: Reflections on Jewish Suffering, Anti-Semitism, and Exile,* ed. Amy Colin and Elisabeth Strenger. Munich: Wilhelm Fink Verlag.

Stern, Guy. 1994. "Barbara Honigmann: A Preliminary Assessment." In *Insiders and Outsiders: Jewish and Gentile Culture in Germany and Austria,* ed. Dagmar C. G. Lorenz and Gabriele Weinberger. Detroit: Wayne State University Press.

Stifter, Adalbert. 1962. *Adalbert Stifters Leben und Werk in Briefen und Dokumenten.* Ed. Kurt Gerhard Fischer. Fischer: Insel.

———. 1908. "Katzensilber." In *Sämmtliche Werke,* vol. 5, no. 1., ed. Franz Egerer and Adolf Raschner. Prague: Calve.

Streibel, Robert. 1984. Untitled review. *Volksstimme* (20 January): 9.

Strobl, Ingrid. 1994. *Das Feld des Vergessens: Jüdischer Widerstand und deutsche "Vergangenheitsbewältigung."* Berlin: Edition ID-Archiv.

Studer, Claire [Goll]. 1917. "Portrait of the Poet Yvan Goll." *Die Aktion* 7, no. 51–52 (29 December): 702.

Susman, Margarete. 1929. *Frauen der Romantik.* Jena: Eugen Diederichs.

Tewarson, Heidi Thoman. 1993. "Rahel Levin Varnhagens Reisen als Überschreitungen." *German Quarterly* 66, no. 2: 145–59.

Thalberg, Hans. 1984. *Von der Kunst, Österreicher zu sein.* Vienna: Böhlau.

Theilhaber, Felix A. 1921. *Der Untergang der deutschen Juden.* Berlin: Jüdischer Verlag.

Theweleit, Klaus. 1988. *Orpheus und Euridike.* Basel: Stroemfeld/Roter Stern.

———. 1980. *Männerphantasien.* Vol. 2, *Zur Psychoanalyse des weißen Terrors.* Hamburg: Rowohlt.

———. 1977. *Männerphantasien.* Frankfurt am Main: Roter Stern.

Torberg, Friedrich. 1981. *Golems Wiederkehr.* Reinbeck: Rowohlt.

Trachtenberg, Joshua. 1943. *The Devil and the Jews: Medieval Conception of the Jew and Its Relation to Modern Antisemitism.* New Haven: Yale Press.

Tramontana, Reinhard. 1984. "Gemischte Gefühle." *Profil* 5: 50–52.

Trotsky, Leon. 1970. *My Life.* New York: Pathfinder.

Varnhagen, Rahel. 1983. *Gesammelte Werke.* 10 vols. Ed. Konrad Feilchen-feldt, Uwe Schweikert, and Rahel E. Steiner. Munich: Matthes & Seitz.

———. 1979. *Briefwechsel.* 4 vols. Ed. Friedhelm Kemp. Munich: Winkler.

Varnhagen, Rahel, and Pauline Wiesel. 1978. *Ein jeder machte seine Frau aus mir wie er sie liebte und verlangte: Ein Briefwechsel.* Ed. Marlis Gerhardt. Darmstadt: Luchterhand.

Varnhagen von Ense, August, ed. 1983. "Rahel: Ein Buch des Andenkens für ihre Freunde." In *Rahel Varnhagen: Gesammelte Werke,* vol. 1, ed. Konrad Feilchenfeldt, Uwe Schweikert, and Rahel E. Steiner. Munich: Matthes & Seitz.

Veigl, Hans, ed. 1992. *Luftmenschen spielen Theater: Jüdisches Karabett in Wien, 1890–1938.* Vienna: Kremayr & Scheriau.

Venske, Regula. 1987a. " 'Flucht zurück als Flucht nach vorn?' Hilde Domin und die 'Rückkehr ins Zweite Paradies.' " In *Frauenliteratur ohne Tradition? Neun Autorinnenporträts,* ed. Inge Stephan, Regula Venske, and Sigrid Weigel. Frankfurt am Main: Fischer.

———. 1987b. "Schriftstellerin gegen das Vergessen: Johanna Moosdorf." In *Frauenliteratur ohne Tradition? Neun Autorinnenporträts,* ed. Inge Stephan, Regula Venske, and Sigrid Weigel. Frankfurt am Main: Fischer.

Wagner, Frank, Ursula Emmerich, and Ruth Radvanyi, eds. 1994. *Anna Seghers: Eine Biographie in Bildern.* Berlin: Aufbau.

Walker, Kizer. 1994. "The Persian Gulf War and the Germans' 'Jewish Questions': Transformations of the Left." In *Reemerging Jewish Culture in Germany: Life and Literature since 1989,* ed. Sander L. Gilman and Karen Remmler. New York: New York University Press.

Wallach-Faller, Marianne. 1985. "Veränderungen im Status der Jüdischen Frau. Ein geschichtlicher Überblick." *Judaica* 41:152–72.

Wallner, Peter. 1992. "Sie saß im Glashaus und warf mit Steinen." *Der Standard* (10 October): 9.

Wartmann, Brigitte. 1983. " 'Es ist von jeher ein Hauch von kosmischer Symbolik über die Frau gelegt': Gesellschaftsvisionen des Bürgertums über das Verhältnis von Frauen und Kunst." In *Feministische Literaturwissenschaft: Dokumentation der Tagung in Hamburg vom Mai 1983,* ed. Inge Stephan and Sigrid Weigel. Berlin: Argument.

Wassermann, Jakob. 1921. *Mein Weg als Deutscher und Jude.* Berlin: S. Fischer.

———. [1897] 1918. *Die Juden von Zirndorf.* Berlin: S. Fischer.

Watt, Helga Schütte. 1993. "Fanny Lewald und die deutsche Misere nach 1848 im Hinblick auf England." *German Life and Letters* 46, no. 3: 220–35.

Weibel, Peter, and Valie Export, eds. 1970. *Wien: Bildkompendium; Wiener Aktionismus und Film.* Frankfurt am Main: Kohlkunst.

Weigel, Sigrid. 1987. "Schreibarbeit und Phantasie: Ilse Aichinger." In *Frauenliteratur ohne Tradition? Neun Autorinnenporträts.* Frankfurt am Main: Fischer.

———. 1984. "Frau und 'Weiblichkeit': Theoretische Überlegungen zur feministischen Literaturkritik." In *Feministische Literaturwissenscaft: Dokumentation der Tagung in Hamburg vom Mai 1983,* ed. Inge Stephan and Sigrid Weigel. Berlin: Argument.

Weil, Grete. 1988. *Der Brautpreis.* Zürich: Nagel & Kimche.

———. 1983. *Generationen.* Zürich: Benziger.

———. 1980. *Meine Schwester Antigone.* Zürich: Benziger.

———. 1968. *Happy, sagte der Onkel.* Wiesbaden: Limes.

———. 1949. *Ans Ende der Welt.* Berlin: Volk und Welt.

Weilovà, Nina. N.d. "71978 Jude: Erinnerungen." Manuscript. Österreichisches Dokumentationsarchiv der Widerstandsbewegung, Vienna.

Weinberger, Gabriele. 1992. *Nazi Germany and Its Aftermath in Women Directors' Autobiographical Films of the Late 1970s: In the Murderers' House.* Lewiston NY: Edwin Mellen Press.

Weininger, Otto. 1906. *Geschlecht und Charakter.* Vienna: Braumüller.

Weinreich, Max. 1993. *Geschichte der jiddischen Sprachforschung.* University of South Florida Studies in the History of Judaism, Ed. Jerold C. Frakes, no. 27. Atlanta: Scholars Press.

Weiss, Peter. 1975. *Die Ästhetik des Widerstands.* Frankfurt am Main: Suhrkamp.

———. 1968. "Meine Ortschaft." *Rapporte.* Frankfurt am Main: Suhrkamp.

———. 1964. *Die Ermittlung.* Frankfurt am Main: Suhrkamp.

Weiss-Rosmarin, Trude. 1973. "Women in the Conservative Synagogues." *Jewish Spectator* 38 (October): 5–6.

———. 1940. *Jewish Women through the Ages.* New York: Posy-Shoulson.

Weissberg, Liliane. 1992. "Turns of Emancipation: On Rahel Varnhagen's Letters." In *In the Shadow of Olympus: German Women Writers around 1800,* ed. Katherine R. Goodman and Edith Waldstein. Albany: State University of New York Press.

———. 1991. "Stepping Out: The Writing of Difference in Rahel Varnhagen's Letters." In *Anti-Semitism in Times of Crisis,* ed. Sander Gilman and Steven T. Katz. New York: New York University Press.

———. 1987. "Nachwort." In Dorothea Schlegel, *Florentin.* Frankfurt am Main: Ullstein.

———, ed. 1986. *Florentin: Roman, Fragmente, Varianten.* Frankfurt am Main: Ullstein.

Welch Wort in die Kälte gerufen. 1968. Berlin: Verlag der Nation.

Wenzel, Hilde. 1960. "Nachwort." In Gertrud Kolmar, *Das lyrische Werk*. Munich: Kösel.

Werres, Peter. 1994. "Identity Problem of Postwar Generation Jews in Germany: A Historical Perspective." In *Insiders and Outsiders: Jewish and Gentile Culture in Germany and Austria*, ed. Dagmar C. G. Lorenz and Gabriele Weinberger. Detroit: Wayne State University Press.

Wiedemann, Conrad. 1986. "Zwei jüdische Autobiographien im Deutschland des 18. Jahrhunderts: Glückel von Hameln und Salomon Maimon." In *Juden in der deutschen Literatur: Ein deutsch-israelisches Symposion*, ed. Stephane Moses and Albrecht Schöne. Frankfurt am Main: Suhrkamp.

Wiesenthal, Simon. 1969. *Die Sonneblume: Von Schuld und Vergebung*. Hamburg: Hoffmann & Campe.

Wimmer, Reiner. 1990. *Vier jüdische Philosophinnen: Rosa Luxemburg, Simone Weil, Edith Stein, Hannah Arendt*. Tübingen: Attempto.

Winter, Riki. 1991. "Gespräch mit Elfriede Jelinek." In *Elfriede Jelinek*, series 2, ed. Kurt Bartsch and Günther Höfler. Wien: Droschl.

Winterfeld, Hans. 1969. "Deutschland, ein Zeitbild, 1926–1945: Leidensweg eines deutschen Juden in den ersten 19 Jahren seines Lebens." Manuscript. Leo Baeck Institute Archives, New York.

Wistrich, Robert S. 1989. *The Jews of Vienna in the Age of Franz Joseph*. Oxford: Oxford University Press.

Wittgenstein, Ludwig. 1922. *Tractatus Logico-Philosophicus*. London: Kegan Paul.

Wolf, Friedrich. 1963. *Professor Mamlock: Ein Schauspiel; Gesammelte Werke in sechzehn Bänden*. Vol. 3. Berlin: Aufbau.

Woltmann, Johanna. 1995. *Gertrud Kolmar—Leben und Werk*. Göttingen: Wallstein Verlag.

Young, James E. 1988. *Writing and Rewriting the Holocaust*. Bloomington: Indiana University Press.

Zetkin, Clara. 1922. *Um Rosa Luxemburgs Stellung zur russischen Revolution*. Hamburg: Verlag der Kommunistischen Internationale.

Zipes, Jack. 1995. "The Contemporary German Fascination for Things Jewish: Toward a Minor Jewish Culture." In *Jews in Today's German Culture*, ed. Sander L. Gilman. Bloomington: Indiana University Press.

———. 1994. "The Negative German-Jewish Symbiosis." In *Insiders and Outsiders: Jewish and Gentile Culture in Germany and Austria*, ed. Dagmar C. G. Lorenz and Gabriele Weinberger. Detroit: Wayne State University Press.

———. 1980. "The Holocaust and the Vicissitudes of Jewish Identity." *New German Critique* 20:155–76.

Zweig, Arnold. 1934. *Bilanz der deutschen Judenheit*. Amsterdam: Querido.

————. 1927. *Caliban oder Politik und Leidenschaft.* Potsdam: Kiepenheuer.

————. 1920. *Das ostjüdische Antlitz.* Berlin: Welt.

Zwerenz, Gerhard. 1973. *Die Erde ist unbewohnbar wie der Mond.* Frankfurt am Main: Fischer.

General Index

Kaddish, 236, 297, 325
Kant, Immanuel, 149
Kaplan, Marion, 49, 50, 52, 73, 304
Kappeler, Sima, 205, 206
Karminski, Hannah, 54
Kecht, Maria-Regina, 63, 244
killing, 123, 129, 137, 155, 232, 233, 254,
  293, 309. *See also* murder
Krausnick, Helmut, 140
Kristallnacht, 73, 79, 117, 120, 147, 192,
  268, 269
Krobb, Florian, 5, 16–19
Kultusgemeinde, 30, 73, 141

Ladino, 7, 15, 216
language, 1–3, 6, 11, 13–16, 19, 20–22,
  25, 26, 36, 39, 53, 56, 69, 73, 84, 104,
  116, 141, 142, 144, 150–52, 155–59, 162,
  165, 182–84, 189, 194, 216, 217, 225,
  228, 231, 232, 237, 239, 243, 246, 250,
  251, 253, 260, 261, 266, 270, 277, 286,
  290, 292, 293, 295, 298, 305, 309, 312,
  314, 316, 323–25; German, 1, 68, 117,
  131, 135, 142, 144, 150, 152, 161, 164,
  165, 182–84, 217, 218, 278, 318–21,
  323–25
Lanzmann, Claude, 293
Lasker, Paul, 70, 78
Laube, Heinrich, 39
Lawrence, D. H., 70
Lenin, Vladimir Ilich, 60
Lessing, Gotthold Ephraim, 19, 35
Lessing, Theodor, 66, 94, 98
letters, 20, 26, 28–30, 32, 33, 54, 62, 63,
  69, 301
liberals and liberalism, 38, 39, 41, 43, 60,
  67, 175, 205
literature, 13, 23, 24, 27, 31, 36; adventure, 112, 173; classical, 24, 74, 120,
  278, 282, 308, 323; colonial, 88, 89;
  German, 2, 18, 23, 100, 101, 319, 322,
  327; romantic, 192. *See also* children's
  literature; minor literature
Lorenz, D. D. G., 25, 97, 142, 144, 168,
  185, 199, 214, 225, 251, 276, 277, 290,
  299

Louis Ferdinand, Prince of Prussia, 33,
  43
love, 23, 24, 34, 41, 45, 79, 84, 92, 115,
  124, 159, 161, 175, 177, 180, 188, 195,
  251, 270, 283, 297, 298, 305; romantic,
  46, 65, 157
Lumpenproletarian, 90, 254
Luther, Martin, 208, 250, 299

magic, 4, 11, 122, 190, 191
Magris, Claudio, 125, 172
marginality, 18, 33, 243, 244, 260, 312,
  320, 322, 324
marginalization, 38, 68, 132, 177, 195,
  224, 227, 252, 258, 285, 300, 316, 321,
  325
marriage, 2, 7, 10, 22, 23, 31, 35, 41–43,
  45, 53, 57, 77, 99, 102, 106, 166, 194,
  195, 224, 229, 234, 316; arranged, 8, 17;
  of convenience, 29, 42, 51, 65
Marx, Karl, 38, 64, 81, 127, 253
Marxism, 50, 51, 61, 141, 200, 215, 253,
  275
masculinity, 82, 92, 86, 88, 141, 188, 277,
  291
mass murder, 133, 159, 182, 251, 254, 283
mass psychosis, 83, 115
matriarchy, 31, 32, 165, 312
Mayer, Hans, 49, 196, 197, 199, 200, 327
memoirs, 1, 5, 7, 11, 12, 20, 21, 42, 65,
  142, 144, 146, 154, 164, 176, 257, 276,
  292, 295, 322
memory and memories, 162, 233, 257,
  261, 266, 267, 269, 278, 280, 286, 289,
  291, 293, 294, 302, 304, 306, 313, 316,
  323, 326
Messiah, 11, 133, 158, 132, 214, 242
Middle Ages, 2, 3, 15, 24, 39
Middle East, 55, 58, 69, 71, 72, 183, 216,
  229, 231. *See also* Arab-Israeli conflict;
  Israel; Palestine
militarism, 40, 60, 70, 141
military, 35, 88, 231, 242
Miller, Henry, 85, 153
minor literature, 38, 199, 277, 323, 325
minor culture, 323, 325

writing (*continued*)
176, 251, 275, 278, 286, 293, 294, 295,
297, 299, 302, 310, 312, 323

xenophobia, 192, 194, 199, 228, 257, 262,
276

Yellow Star, 148, 152, 313

Yiddish, 1, 7, 6, 8, 10, 11, 13–16, 19, 20,
30, 36, 135, 136, 138, 216–19, 237, 257,
266, 294, 295, 304, 313, 318–20, 324

Zionism, 132, 162, 186, 198, 215, 259, 275,
291, 294
Zipes, Jack, 250, 265, 311, 312
zoomorphism, 189, 190, 309

Author-Title Index

In the *Texts and Contexts* series